SB
Shojo Beat

ORESAMA TEACHER

Vol. 26

Story & Art by

Izumi Tsubaki

ORESAMA TEACHER

CHARACTERS AND THE STORY THUS FAR

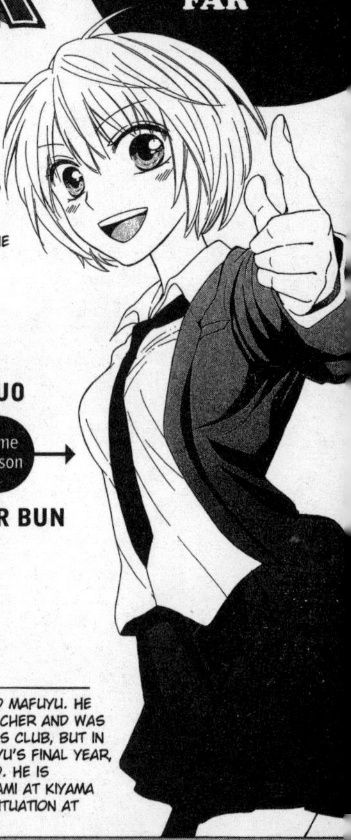

Mafuyu Kurosaki

THE FORMER BANCHO OF SAITAMA EAST HIGH. SHE TRANSFERED TO MIDORIGAOKA ACADEMY AND JOINED THE PUBLIC MORALS CLUB. SHE ALSO PLAYS THE PARTS OF NATSUO AND SUPER BUN. SHE IS CONCERNED BY THE FACT THAT SHE HAS NO FEMALE FRIENDS.

NATSUO

Same Person

SUPER BUN

PUBLIC MORALS CLUB

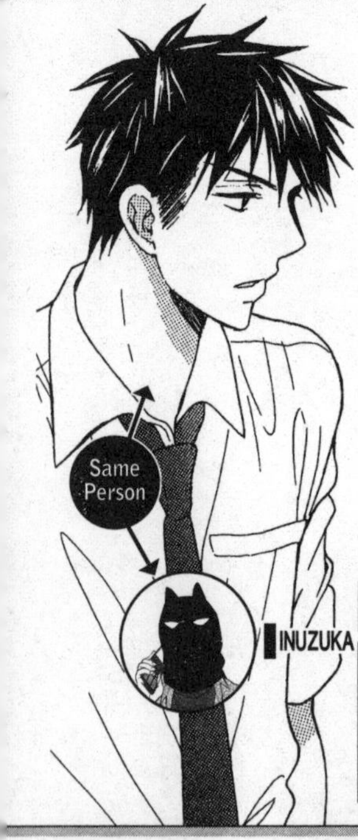

Same Person

INUZUKA

Takaomi Saeki

THE ONE WHO CRUELLY TRAINED MAFUYU. HE WAS MAFUYU'S HOMEROOM TEACHER AND WAS ADVISOR TO THE PUBLIC MORALS CLUB, BUT IN THE FIRST SEMESTER OF MAFUYU'S FINAL YEAR, HE RESIGNED AND DISAPPEARED. HE IS CURRENTLY STAYING WITH NOGAMI AT KIYAMA HIGH AND INVESTIGATING THE SITUATION AT MIDORIGAOKA.

PUBLIC MORALS CLUB

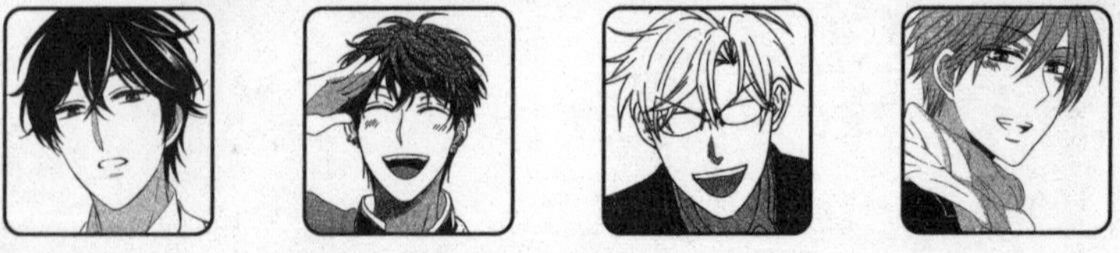

Mr. Maki

A NEW TEACHER. HE REPLACED TAKAOMI AS THE PUBLIC MORALS CLUB ADVISER.

Aki Shibuya

A TALKATIVE AND WOMANIZING UNDERCLASSMAN. HIS NICKNAME IS AKKI. HE'S NOT GOOD AT FIGHTING.

Shinobu Yui

HE WORSHIPS MIYABI, THE FORMER STUDENT COUNCIL PRESIDENT, BUT REJOINED THE PUBLIC MORALS CLUB. HE IS A SELF-PROCLAIMED NINJA.

Hayasaka

MAFUYU'S CLASSMATE. HE APPEARS TO BE A PLAIN AND SIMPLE DELINQUENT, BUT HE'S ACTUALLY QUITE DILIGENT.

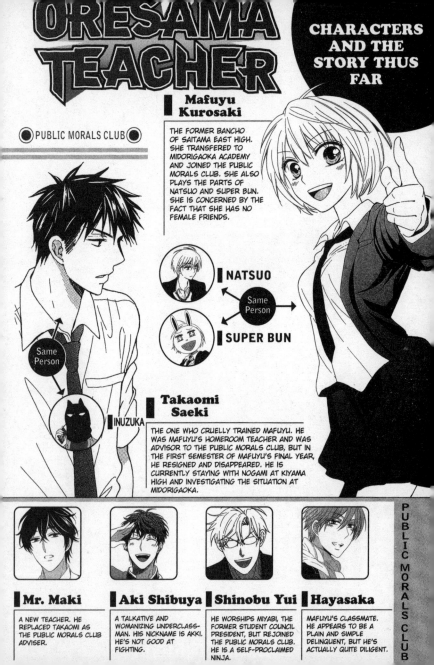

MIDORIGAOKA

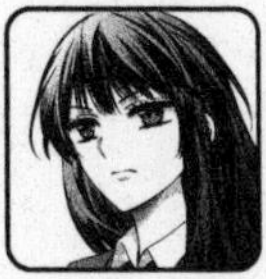

Toko Hanabusa

NEWLY-ENROLLED AT MIDORIGAOKA THIS PAST SPRING. RESERVED, YET A PERSON OF ACTION. INDIFFERENT, BUT CUTTHROAT.

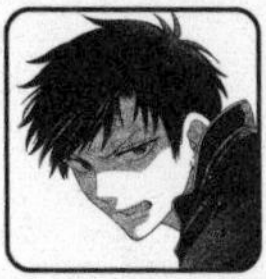

Reito Ayabe

HE LOVES CLEANING. HE GETS STRONGER IN DIRTY PLACES. HE IS A STUDENT COUNCIL OFFICER, BUT HE'S FRIENDS WITH MAFUYU.

EAST HIGH

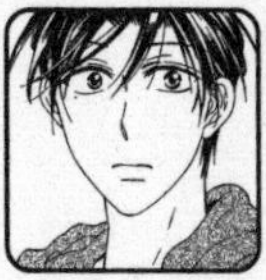

Kohei Kangawa

ONE YEAR YOUNGER THAN MAFUYU. HE IS THE CURRENT BANCHO OF EAST HIGH AND DEEPLY ADMIRES HIS PREDECESSOR, MAFUYU. HE CAN BE CHILDISH.

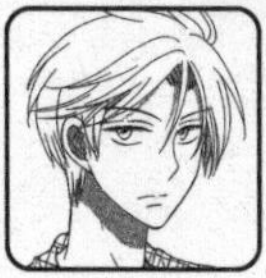

Yuto Maizono

ONE YEAR OLDER THAN MAFUYU AND FORMERLY THE NUMBER TWO AT EAST HIGH. HE CALLS HIMSELF "THE ONE WHO LURES YOU INTO THE WORLD OF MASOCHISM."

WEST HIGH

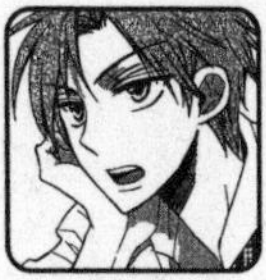

Asahi Sakurada

WEST HIGH'S BANCHO. LIKES CROSSDRESSING. HE KNOWS FRO HAYASAKA AND YUI FROM WHEN WEST HIGH SHARED A SCHOOL TRIP WITH MIDORIGAOKA.

KIYAMA HIGH

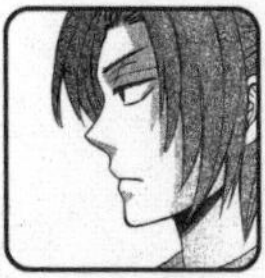

Nogami

THE BANCHO OF KIYAMA HIGH, A RIVAL SCHOOL TO MIDORIGAOKA. HE HAS A PAST WITH KANON NONOGUCHI.

THE GRADUATES

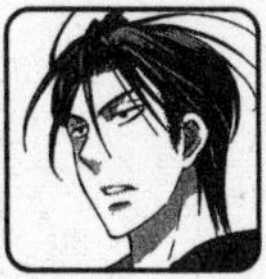

Kyotaro Okegawa

THE FORMER BANCHO OF EAST HIGH. HE IS ATTENDING A LOCAL COLLEGE. HE AND MAFUYU ARE ANONYMOUS PEN PALS.

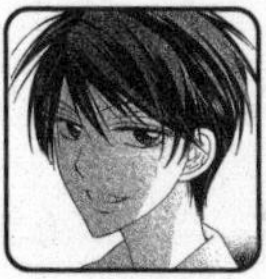

Miyabi Hanabusa

THE SCHOOL DIRECTOR'S SON AND THE FORMER PRESIDENT OF THE STUDENT COUNCIL. HE CAN CHARM OTHERS WITH HIS GAZE. HE IS ATTENDING COLLEGE IN TOKYO.

STORY

★ MAFUYU KUROSAKI WAS A BANCHO FROM EAST HIGH WHO CONTROLLED ALL OF SAITAMA, BUT ONCE SHE TRANSFERRED TO MIDORIGAOKA ACADEMY, SHE COMPLETELY CHANGED AND BECAME A SPIRITED HIGH SCHOOL GIRL...OR AT LEAST SHE WAS SUPPOSED TO. TAKAOMI SAEKI, HER CHILDHOOD FRIEND AND HOMEROOM TEACHER, FORCED HER TO JOIN THE PUBLIC MORALS CLUB AND SHE HAS TO CONTINUE TO LIVE A LIFE THAT IS FAR FROM AVERAGE.

★ THE PUBLIC MORALS CLUB AND THE STUDENT COUNCIL FOUGHT FOR OWNERSHIP OF THE SCHOOL, BUT IN THE END THE PUBLIC MORALS CLUB IS MORE UNITED THAN EVER AND MIYABI HANABUSA GRADUATED KNOWING THAT THE STUDENT COUNCIL MEMBERS HAD OVERCOME THEIR ISSUES.

★ MAFUYU AND HER FRIENDS ARE FINALLY THIRD-YEAR STUDENTS. MIYABI'S YOUNGER SISTER, TOKO, HAS ENROLLED AS A FIRST-YEAR STUDENT. BUT AS SOON AS SHE ENTERS THE PICTURE, TAKAOMI RESIGNS AND DISAPPEARS. MEANWHILE, MAFUYU AND HER FRIENDS INVESTIGATE RUMORS THAT NOGAMI OF KIYAMA HIGH IS KEEPING A "BEAST" AS A PET, BUT YUI DISCOVERS THAT THE BEAST IS ACTUALLY TAKAOMI.

★ MAFUYU AND HER FRIENDS ARE CONCERNED BY THE STRANGE BEHAVIOR OF MR. MAKI, THE NEW TEACHER AT MIDORIGAOKA, AND DURING THEIR INVESTIGATIONS THEY DISCOVER THAT HE WAS A WEST HIGH STUDENT. LATER, MAFUYU DISAPPEARS WHILE GETTING READY FOR THE SCHOOL FESTIVAL WITH MAKI, WITH JUST A TEXT TO SAY SHE'S TAKING SOME TIME OFF BECAUSE OF A COLD!

ORESAMA TEACHER

Volume 26
CONTENTS

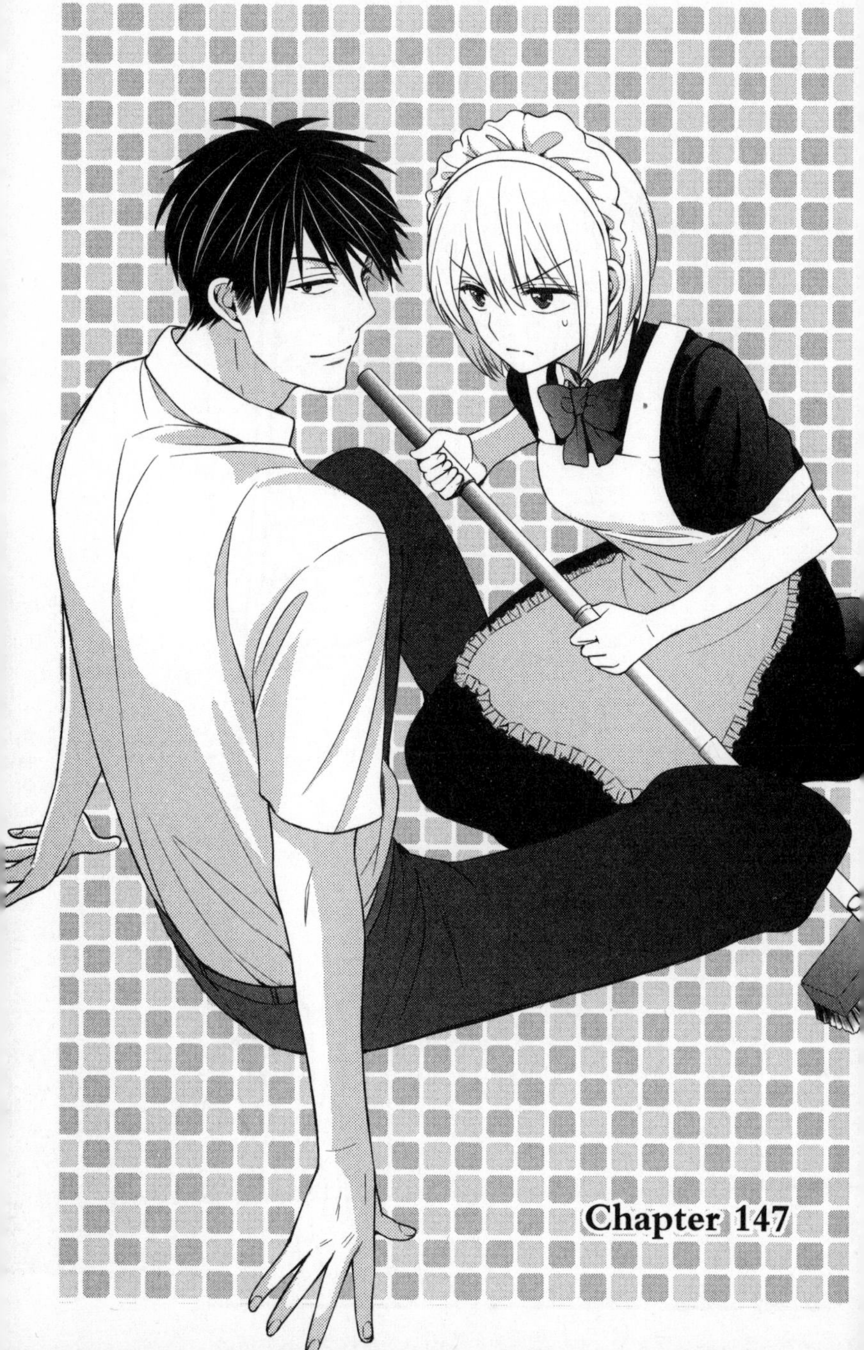

Chapter 147

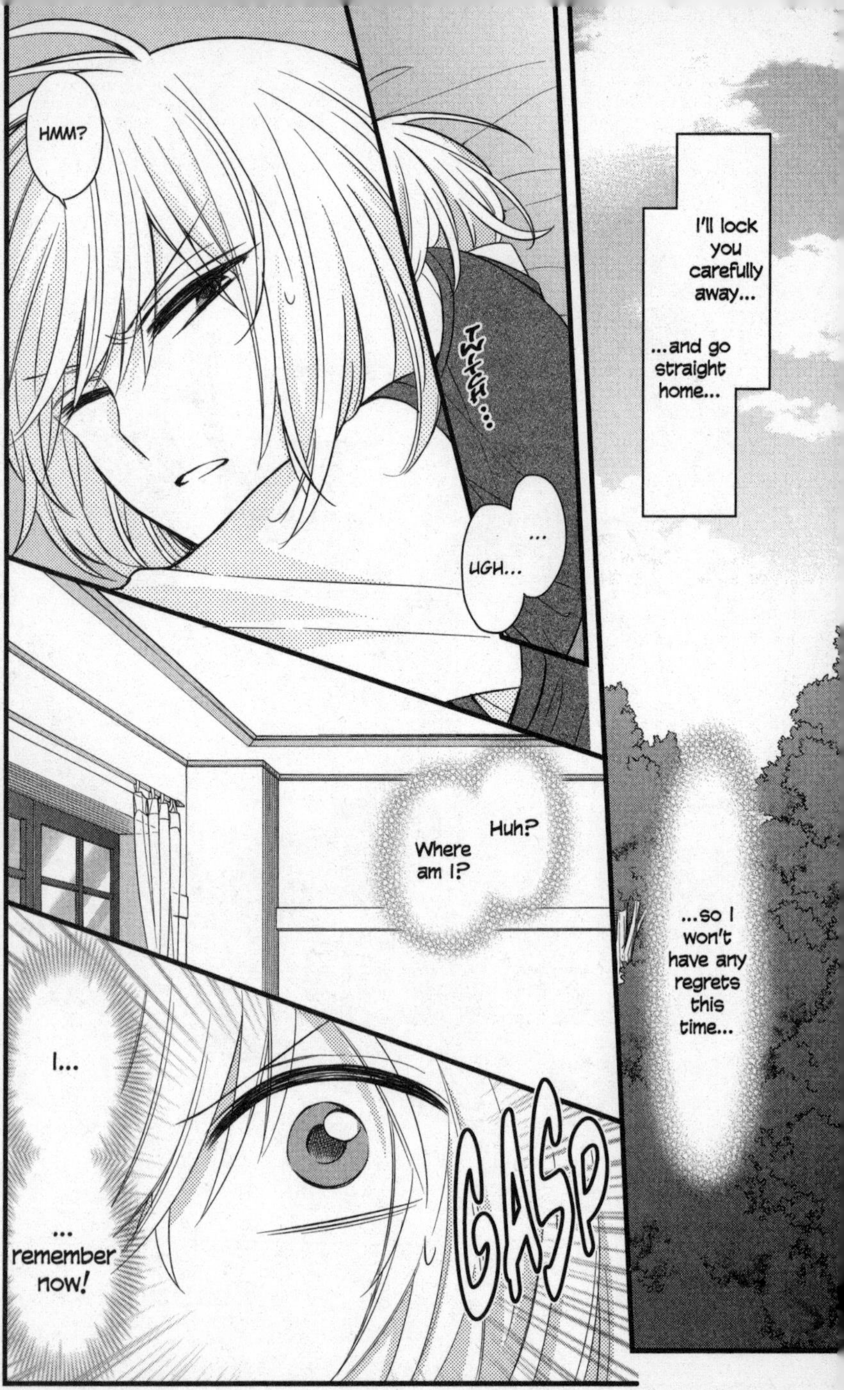

I'll lock you carefully away...
...and go straight home...
...so I won't have any regrets this time...
TWITCH...
...
UGH...
HMM?
Huh?
Where am I?
GASP
I...
...
remember now!

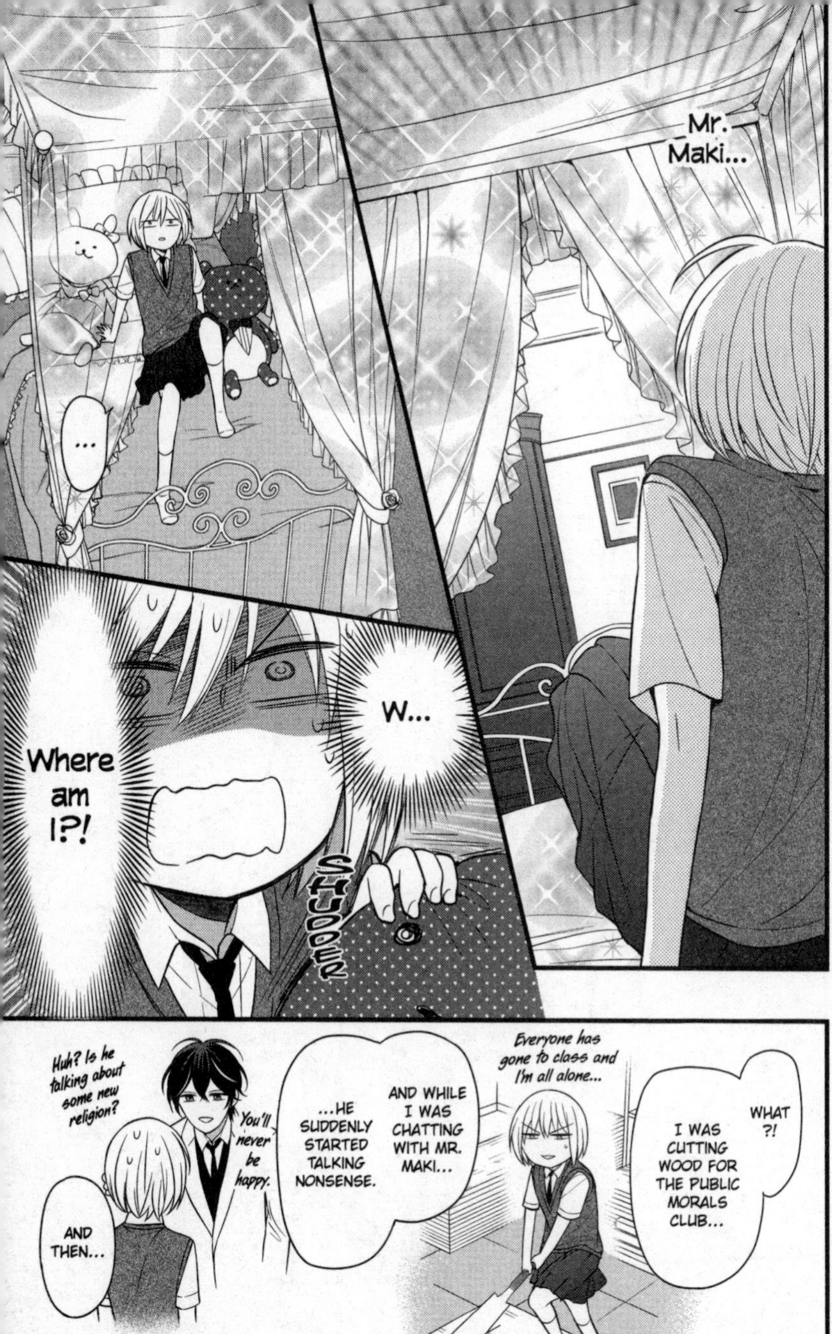
Mr. Maki...
...
W...
Where am I?!
SHUDDER
WHAT?!
I WAS CUTTING WOOD FOR THE PUBLIC MORALS CLUB...
Everyone has gone to class and I'm all alone...
AND WHILE I WAS CHATTING WITH MR. MAKI...
...HE SUDDENLY STARTED TALKING NONSENSE.
You'll never be happy.
Huh? Is he talking about some new religion?
AND THEN...

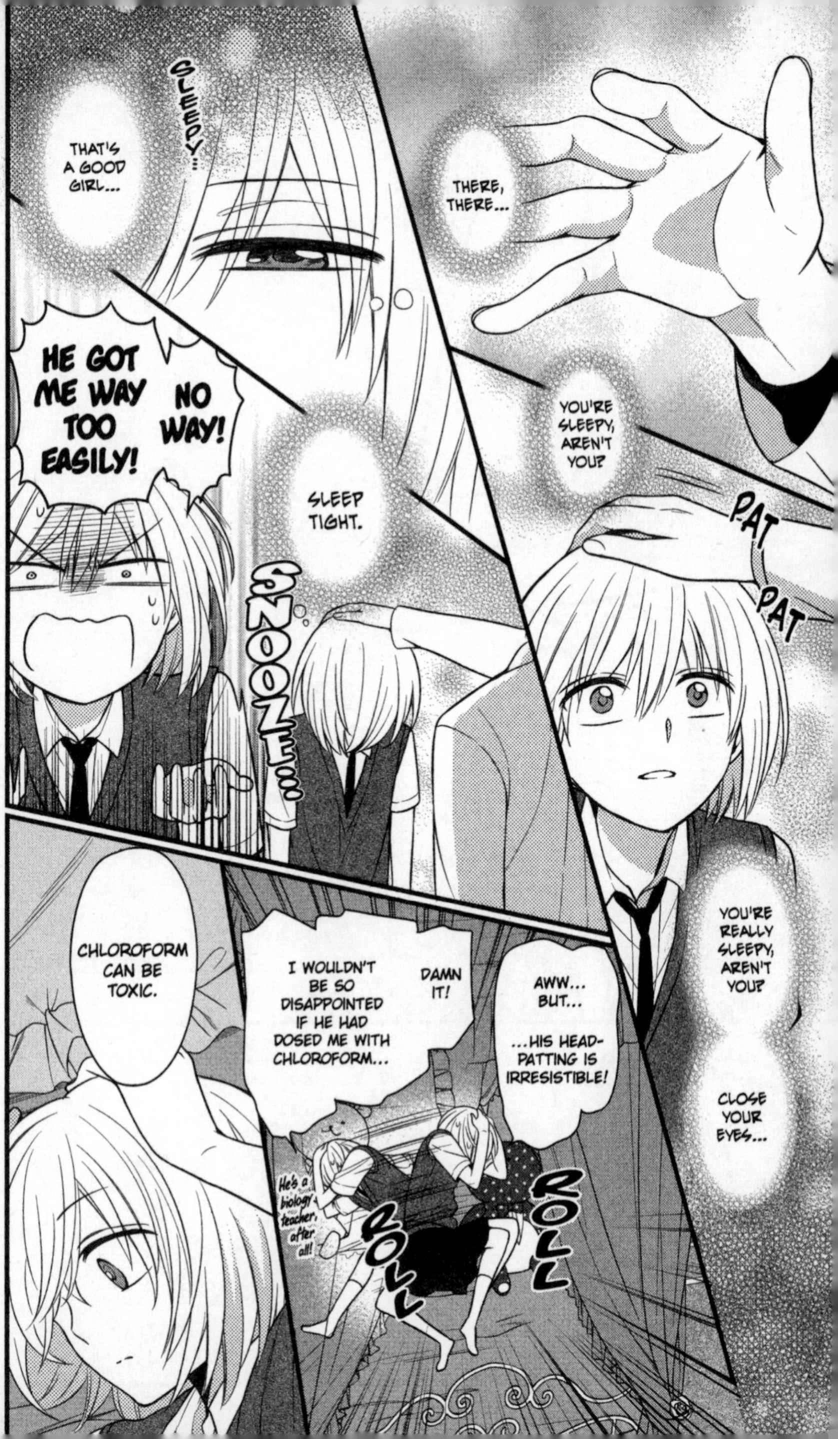
THERE, THERE...
YOU'RE SLEEPY, AREN'T YOU?
PAT
PAT
YOU'RE REALLY SLEEPY, AREN'T YOU?
CLOSE YOUR EYES...
SLEEPY...
THAT'S A GOOD GIRL...
SLEEP TIGHT.
SNOOZE...
NO WAY!
HE GOT ME WAY TOO EASILY!
AWW... BUT...
...HIS HEAD-PATTING IS IRRESISTIBLE!
DAMN IT!
I WOULDN'T BE SO DISAPPOINTED IF HE HAD DOSED ME WITH CHLOROFORM...
ROLL
ROLL
He's a biology teacher, after all!
CHLOROFORM CAN BE TOXIC.

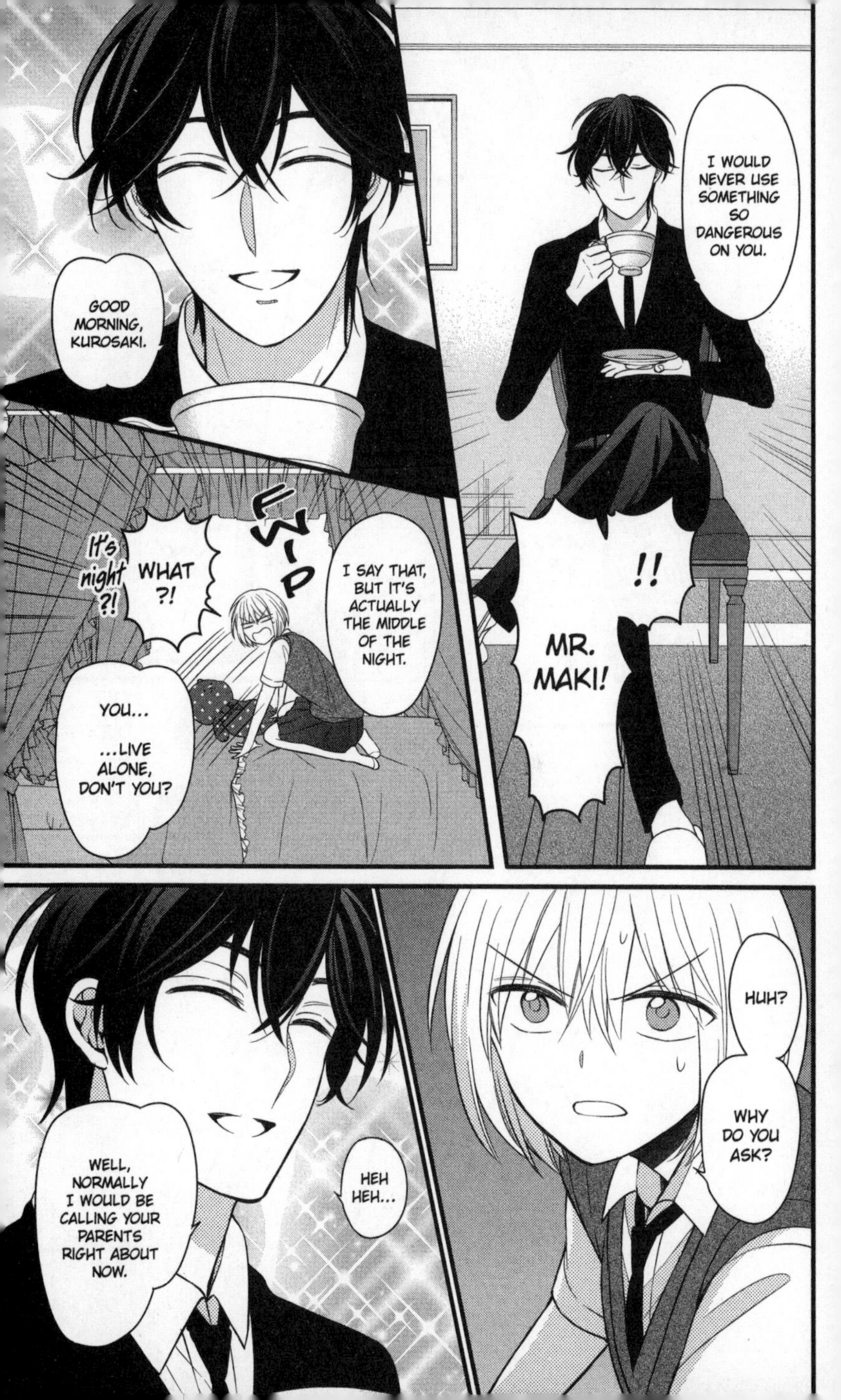
I WOULD NEVER USE SOMETHING SO DANGEROUS ON YOU.
!!
MR. MAKI!
GOOD MORNING, KUROSAKI.
I SAY THAT, BUT IT'S ACTUALLY THE MIDDLE OF THE NIGHT.
FWIP
WHAT ?!
It's night ?!
YOU...
...LIVE ALONE, DON'T YOU?
HUH?
WHY DO YOU ASK?
HEH HEH...
WELL, NORMALLY I WOULD BE CALLING YOUR PARENTS RIGHT ABOUT NOW.

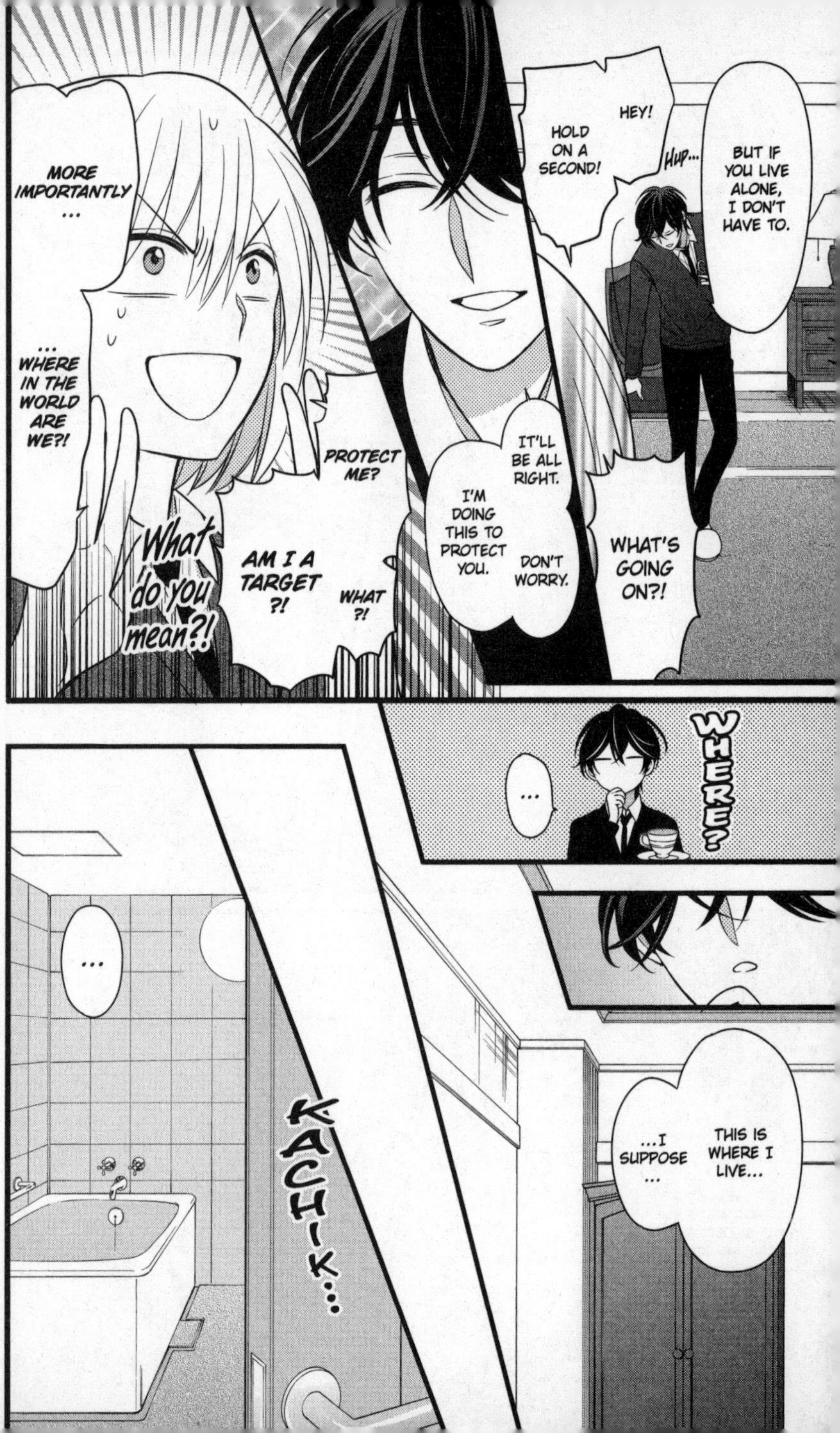
BUT IF YOU LIVE ALONE, I DON'T HAVE TO.
Hup...
HEY!
HOLD ON A SECOND!
WHAT'S GOING ON?!
IT'LL BE ALL RIGHT.
DON'T WORRY.
I'M DOING THIS TO PROTECT YOU.
PROTECT ME?
WHAT ?!
AM I A TARGET ?!
What do you mean?!
MORE IMPORTANTLY ...
... WHERE IN THE WORLD ARE WE?!
WHERE?
...
THIS IS WHERE I LIVE...
...I SUPPOSE ...
KACHIK...
...

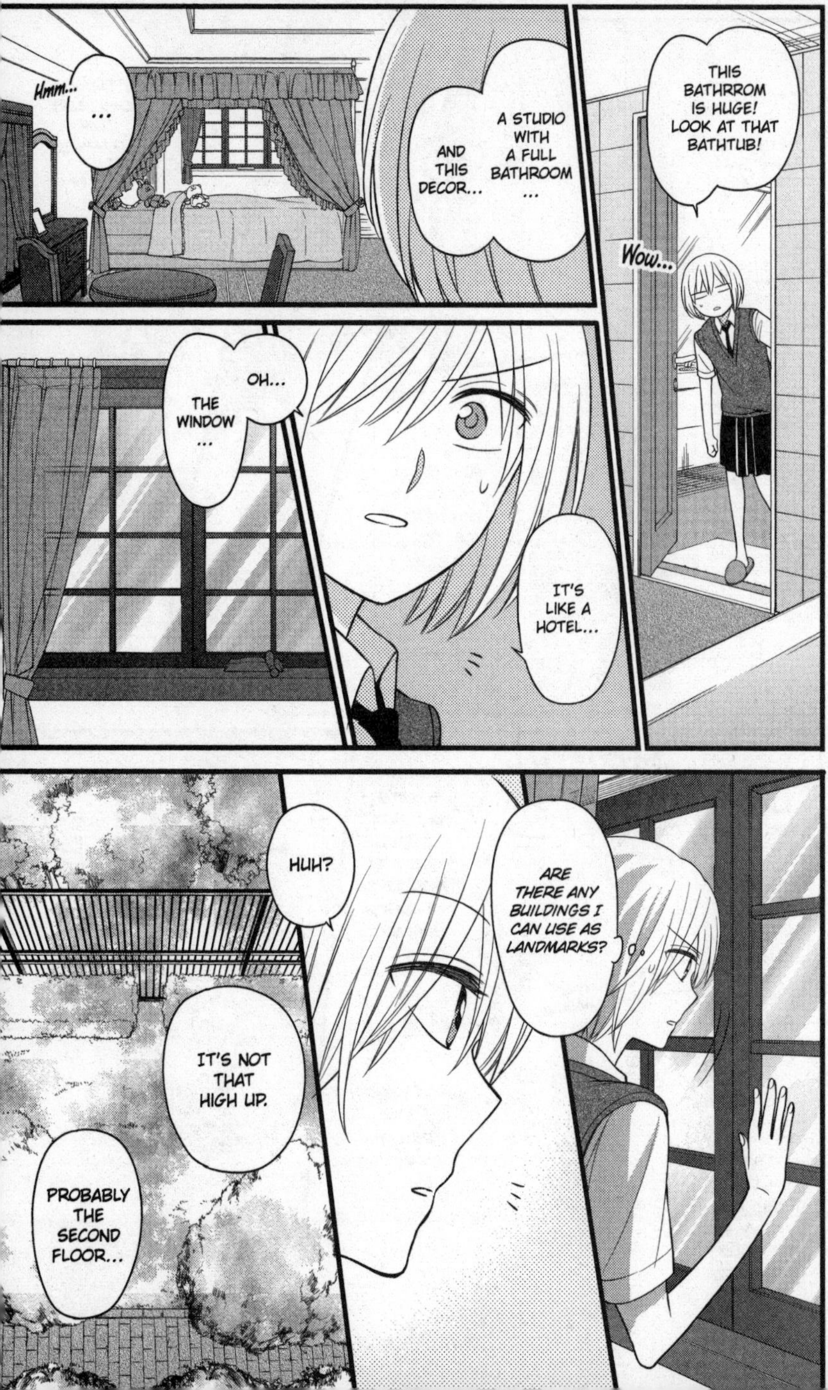
THIS BATHRROM IS HUGE! LOOK AT THAT BATHTUB!
Wow...
A STUDIO WITH A FULL BATHROOM ...
AND THIS DECOR...
Hmm...
...
OH...
THE WINDOW ...
IT'S LIKE A HOTEL...
ARE THERE ANY BUILDINGS I CAN USE AS LANDMARKS?
HUH?
IT'S NOT THAT HIGH UP.
PROBABLY THE SECOND FLOOR...

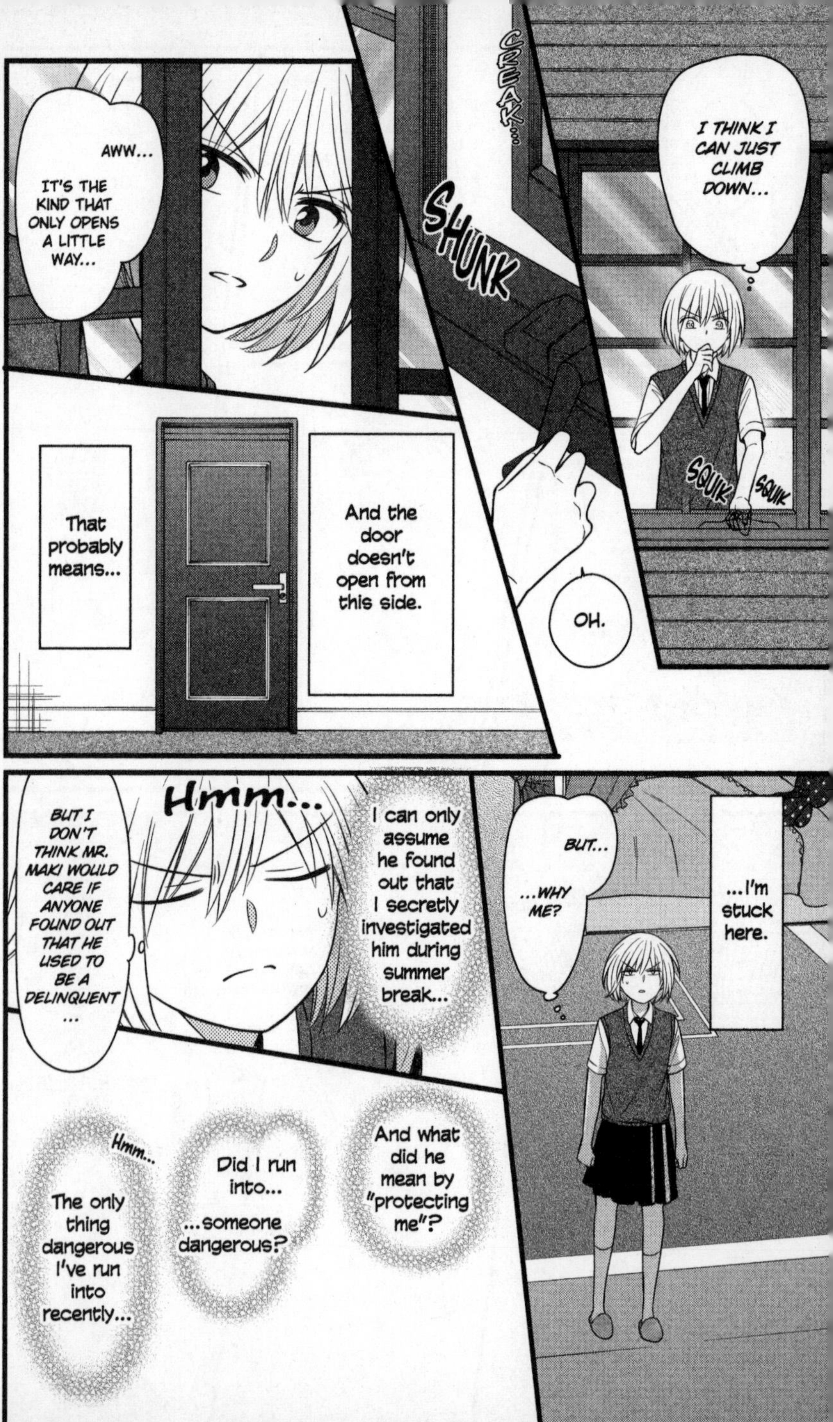
CREAK...
I THINK I CAN JUST CLIMB DOWN...
SQUIK
SQUIK
SHUNK
OH.
AWW...
IT'S THE KIND THAT ONLY OPENS A LITTLE WAY...
And the door doesn't open from this side.
That probably means...
...I'm stuck here.
BUT...
...WHY ME?
Hmm...
I can only assume he found out that I secretly investigated him during summer break...
BUT I DON'T THINK MR. MAKI WOULD CARE IF ANYONE FOUND OUT THAT HE USED TO BE A DELINQUENT...
And what did he mean by "protecting me"?
Did I run into...
...someone dangerous?
Hmm...
The only thing dangerous I've run into recently...

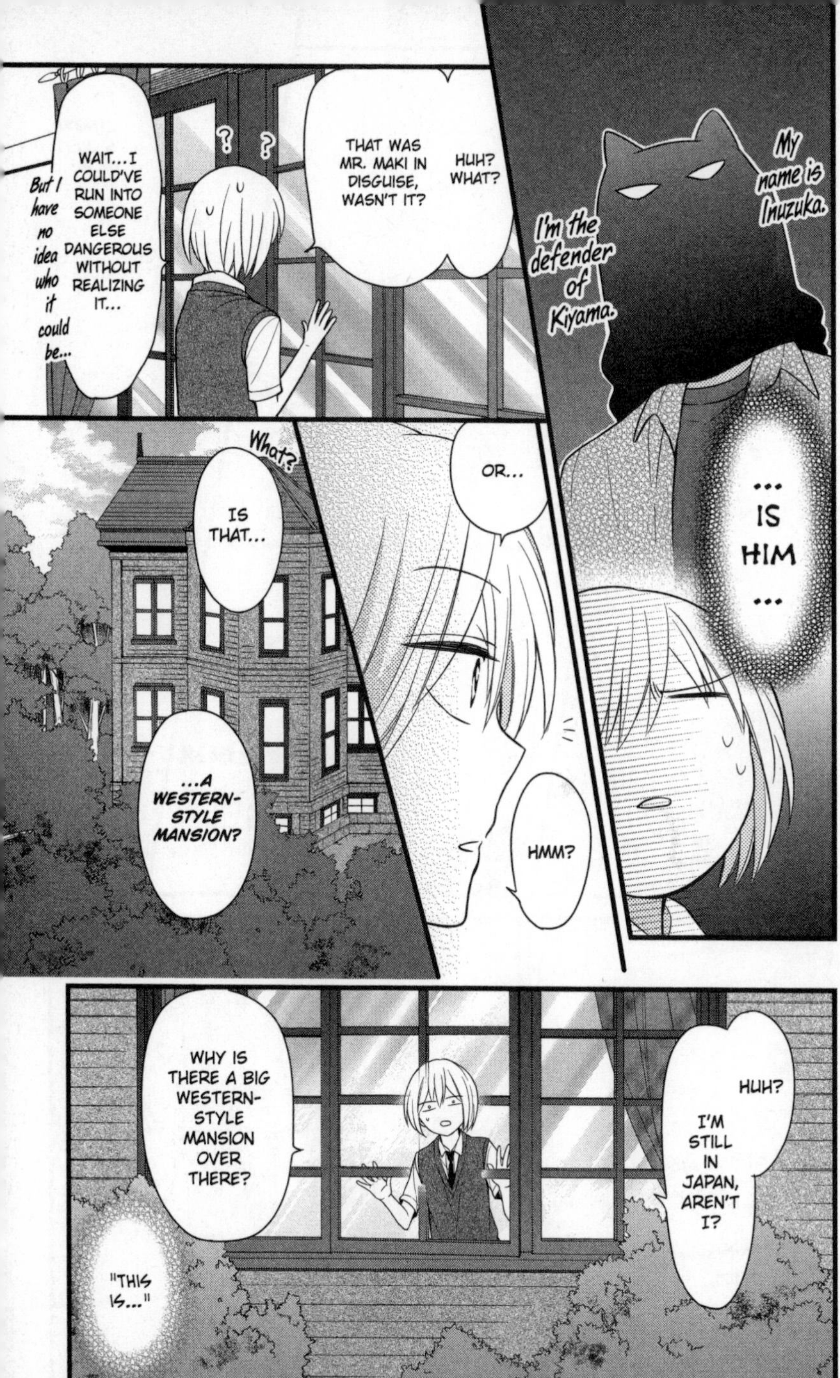
My name is Inuzuka.
I'm the defender of Kiyama.
...IS HIM...
HUH? WHAT?
THAT WAS MR. MAKI IN DISGUISE, WASN'T IT?
??
WAIT...I COULD'VE RUN INTO SOMEONE ELSE DANGEROUS WITHOUT REALIZING IT...
But I have no idea who it could be...
OR...
HMM?
What?
IS THAT...
...A WESTERN-STYLE MANSION?
HUH?
I'M STILL IN JAPAN, AREN'T I?
WHY IS THERE A BIG WESTERN-STYLE MANSION OVER THERE?
"THIS IS..."

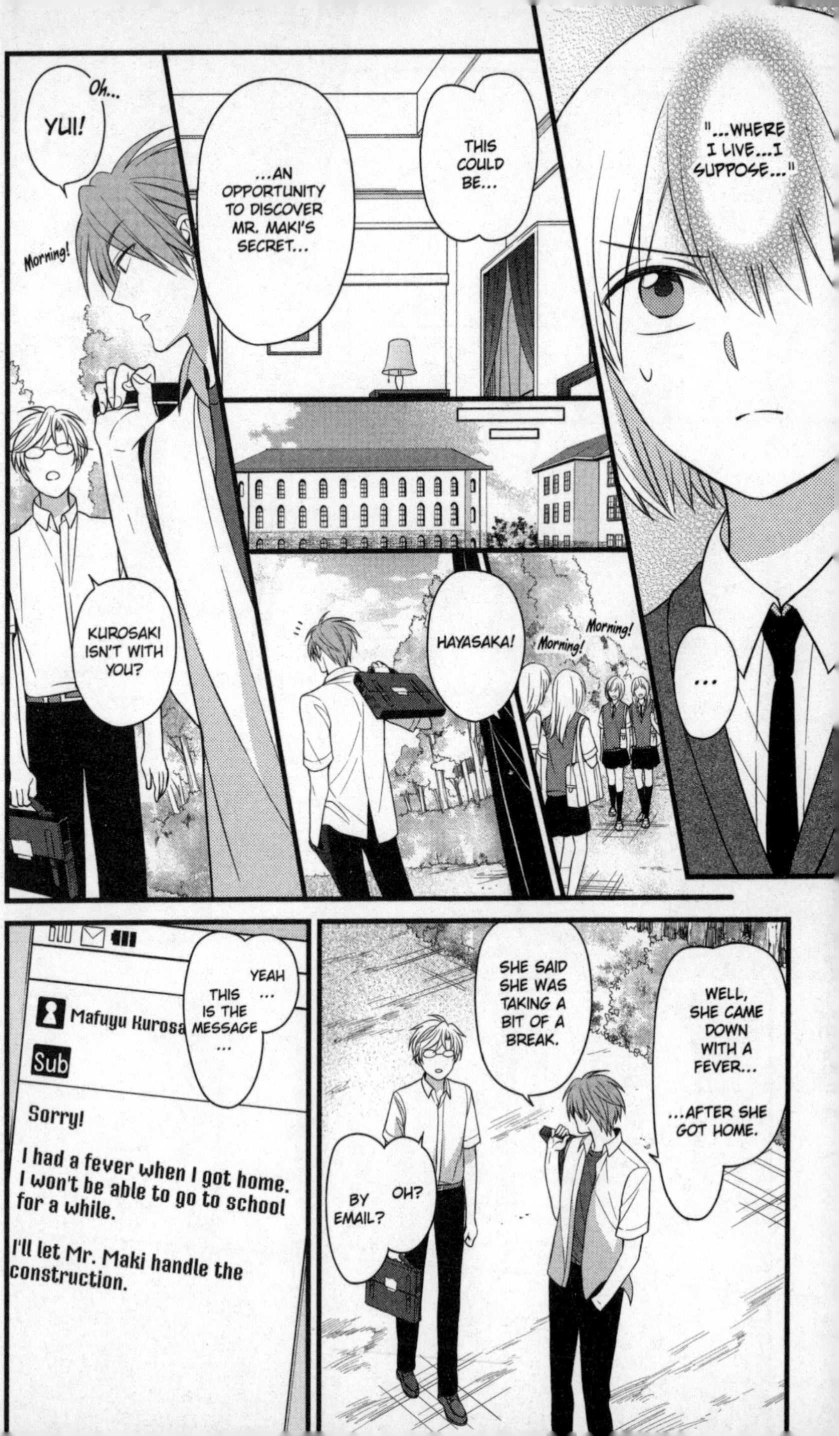
"...WHERE I LIVE...I SUPPOSE..."
...
THIS COULD BE...
...AN OPPORTUNITY TO DISCOVER MR. MAKI'S SECRET...
HAYASAKA!
Morning!
Morning!
Oh... YUI!
Morning!
KUROSAKI ISN'T WITH YOU?
WELL, SHE CAME DOWN WITH A FEVER...
...AFTER SHE GOT HOME.
SHE SAID SHE WAS TAKING A BIT OF A BREAK.
OH?
BY EMAIL?
YEAH...
THIS IS THE MESSAGE...
Mafuyu Kurosa
Sub
Sorry!
I had a fever when I got home. I won't be able to go to school for a while.
I'll let Mr. Maki handle the construction.

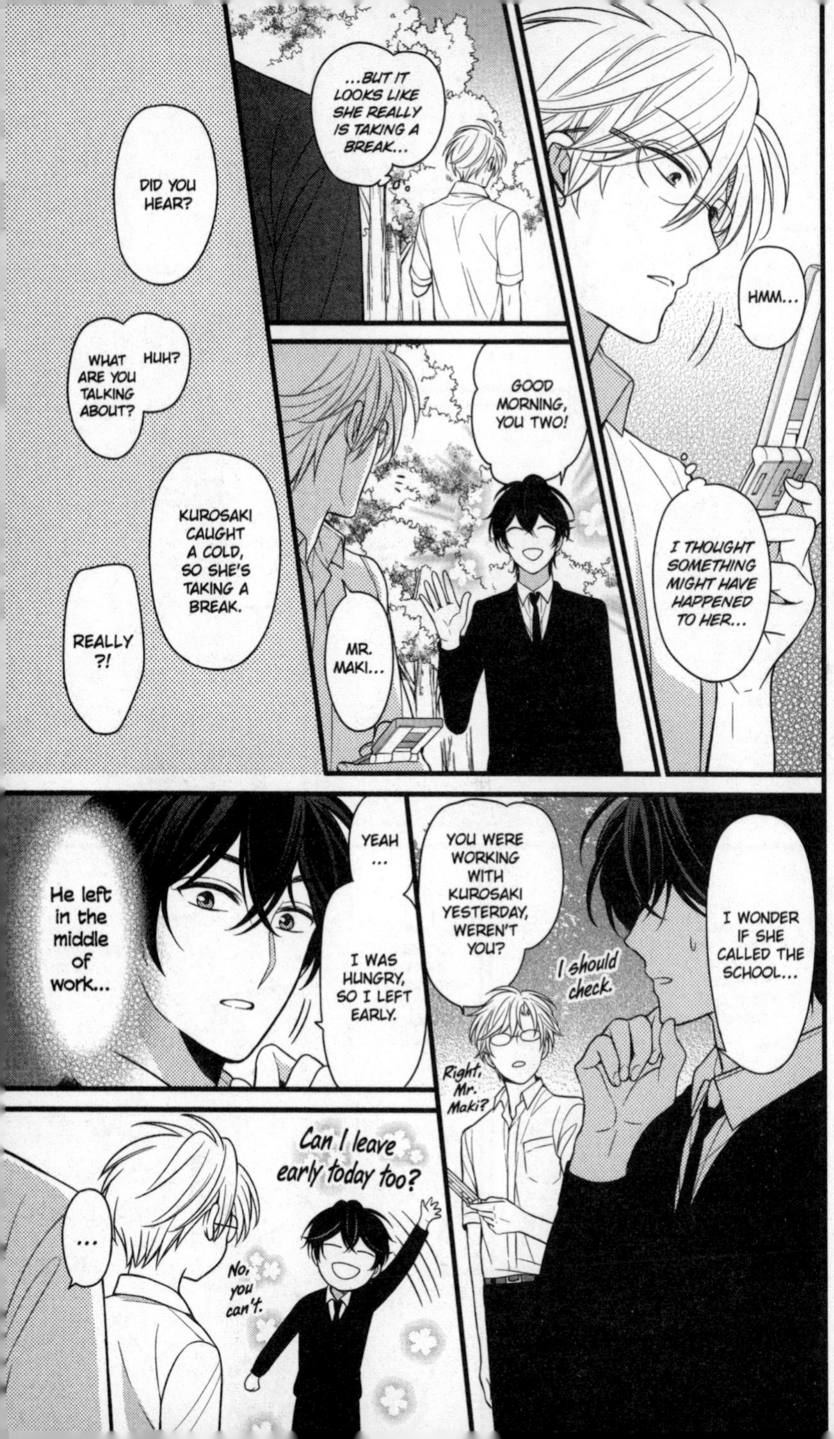
HMM...
I THOUGHT SOMETHING MIGHT HAVE HAPPENED TO HER...
...BUT IT LOOKS LIKE SHE REALLY IS TAKING A BREAK...
GOOD MORNING, YOU TWO!
MR. MAKI...
DID YOU HEAR?
HUH?
WHAT ARE YOU TALKING ABOUT?
KUROSAKI CAUGHT A COLD, SO SHE'S TAKING A BREAK.
REALLY?!
I WONDER IF SHE CALLED THE SCHOOL...
I should check.
YOU WERE WORKING WITH KUROSAKI YESTERDAY, WEREN'T YOU?
Right, Mr. Maki?
YEAH...
I WAS HUNGRY, SO I LEFT EARLY.
He left in the middle of work...
Can I leave early today too?
No, you can't.
...

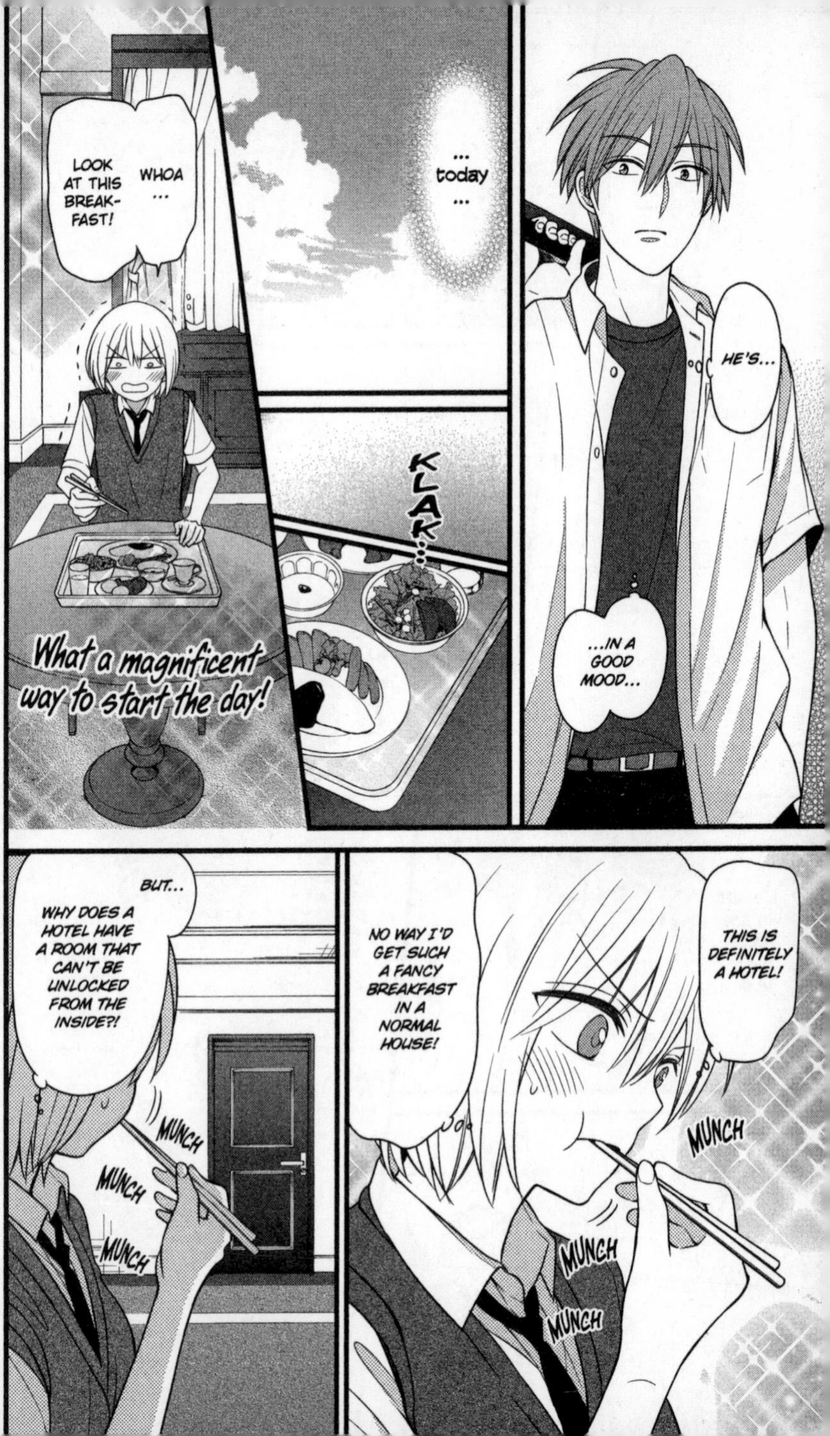
HE'S...
...IN A GOOD MOOD...
... today ...
KLAK...
WHOA ...
LOOK AT THIS BREAK-FAST!
What a magnificent way to start the day!
THIS IS DEFINITELY A HOTEL!
NO WAY I'D GET SUCH A FANCY BREAKFAST IN A NORMAL HOUSE!
MUNCH
MUNCH
MUNCH
BUT...
WHY DOES A HOTEL HAVE A ROOM THAT CAN'T BE UNLOCKED FROM THE INSIDE?!
MUNCH
MUNCH
MUNCH

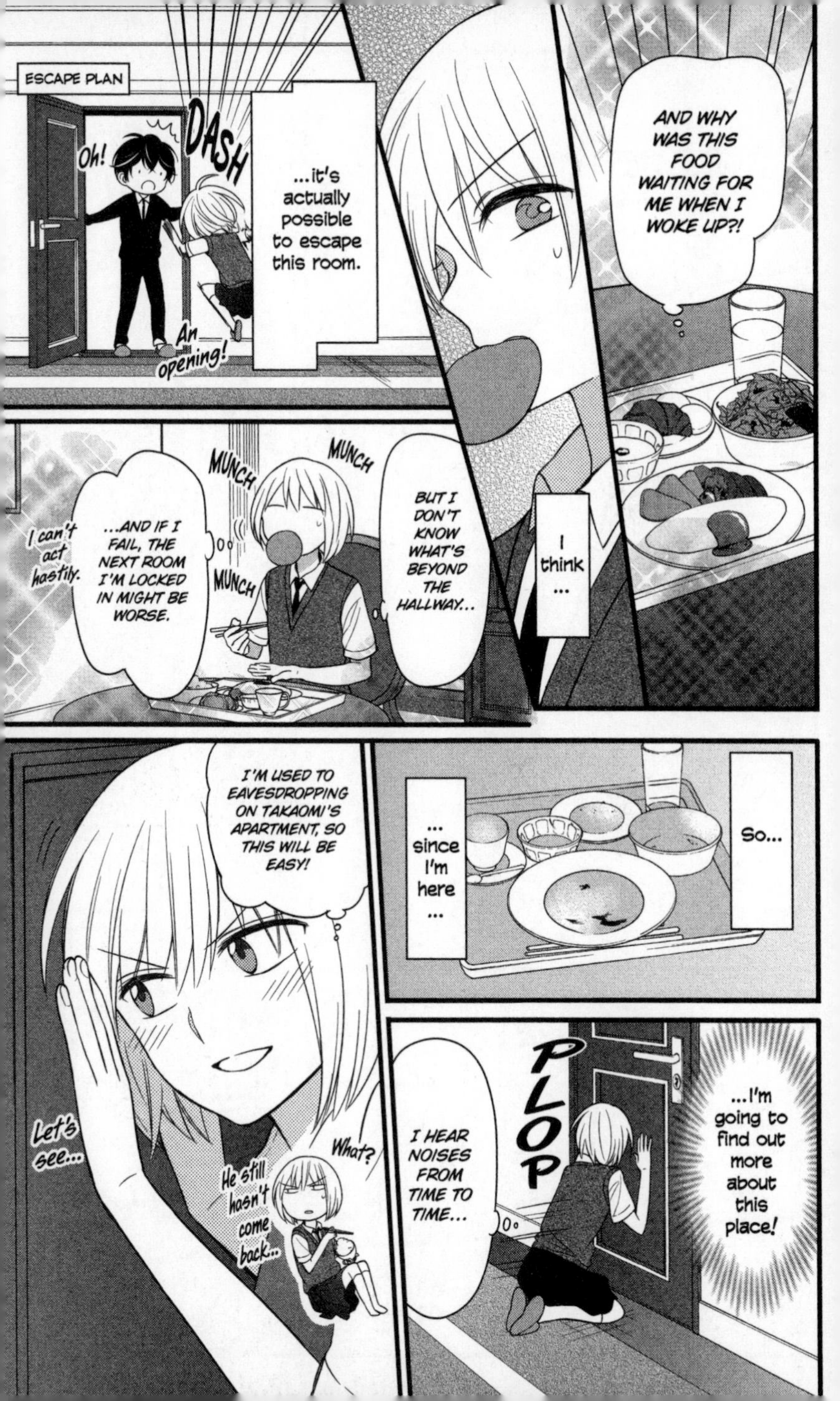
AND WHY WAS THIS FOOD WAITING FOR ME WHEN I WOKE UP?!
I think ...
...it's actually possible to escape this room.
DASH
Oh!
ESCAPE PLAN
An opening!
BUT I DON'T KNOW WHAT'S BEYOND THE HALLWAY...
MUNCH
MUNCH
MUNCH
...AND IF I FAIL, THE NEXT ROOM I'M LOCKED IN MIGHT BE WORSE.
I can't act hastily.
So...
... since I'm here ...
...I'm going to find out more about this place!
PLOP
I HEAR NOISES FROM TIME TO TIME...
I'M USED TO EAVESDROPPING ON TAKAOMI'S APARTMENT, SO THIS WILL BE EASY!
What?
He still hasn't come back...
Let's see...

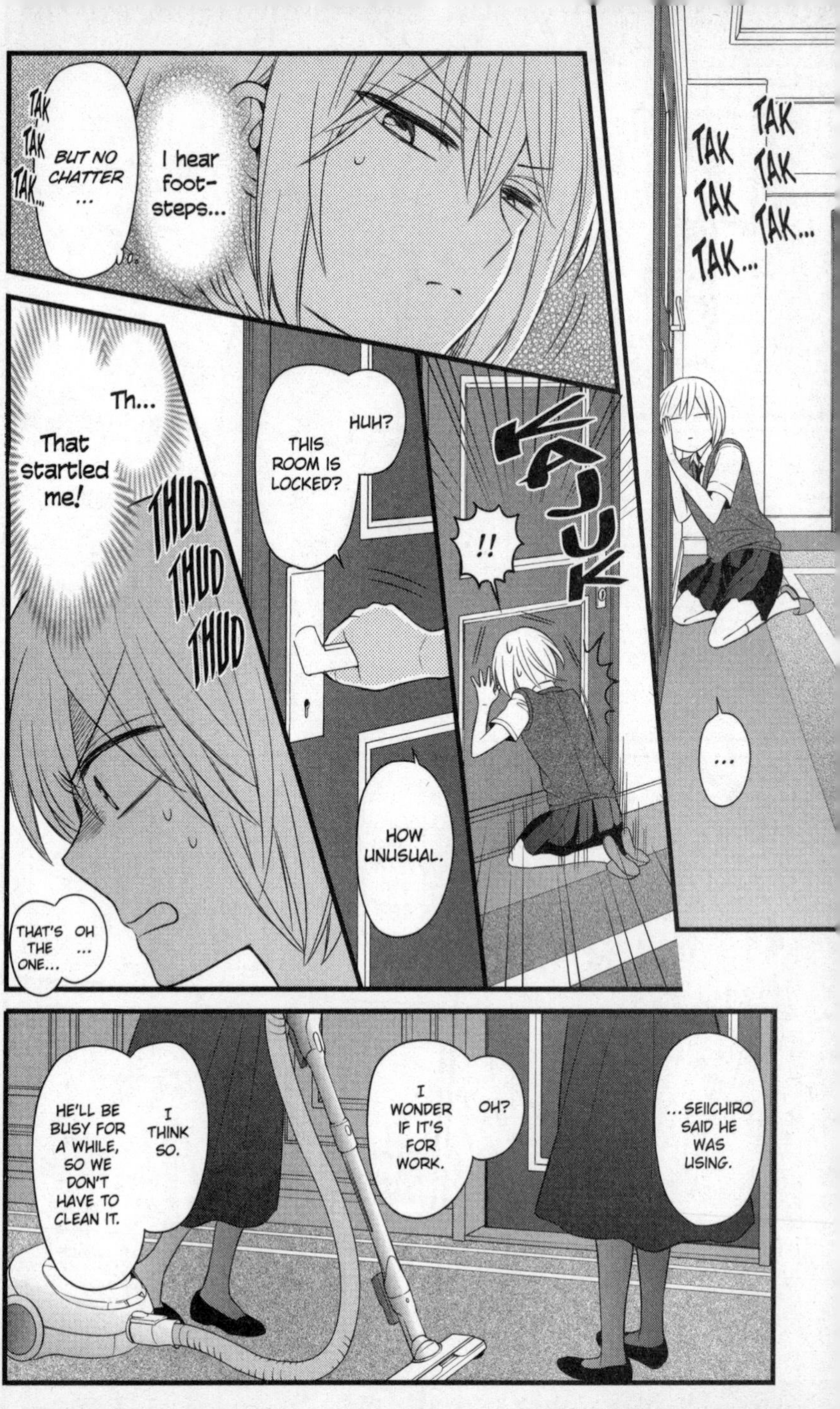
TAK TAK TAK TAK...
TAK TAK TAK...
...
I hear foot-steps...
BUT NO CHATTER ...
TAK TAK TAK...
!!
HUH?
THIS ROOM IS LOCKED?
HOW UNUSUAL.
Th...
That startled me!
THUD THUD THUD
OH ...
THAT'S THE ONE...
...SEIICHIRO SAID HE WAS USING.
OH?
I WONDER IF IT'S FOR WORK.
I THINK SO.
HE'LL BE BUSY FOR A WHILE, SO WE DON'T HAVE TO CLEAN IT.

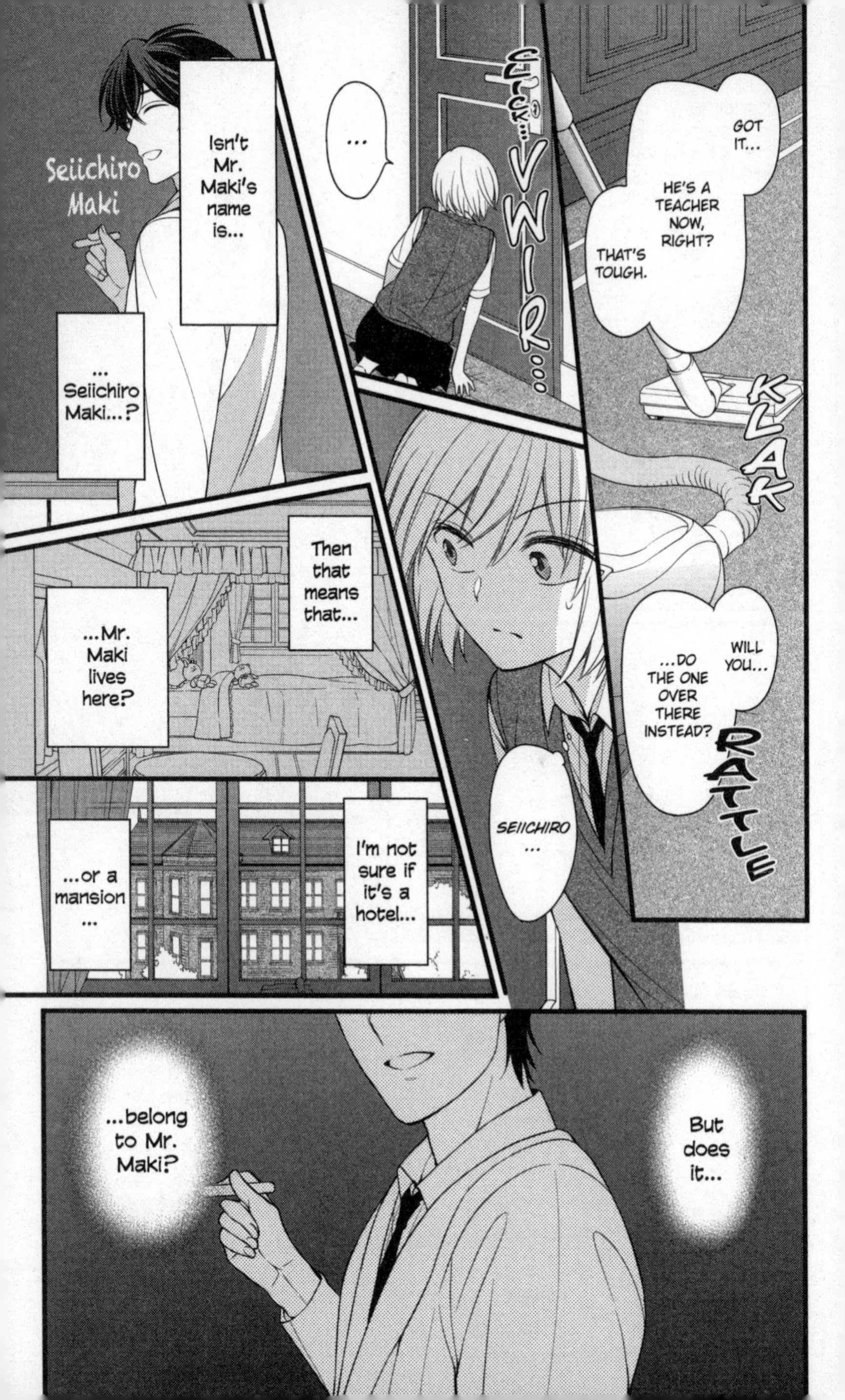
GOT IT...
HE'S A TEACHER NOW, RIGHT?
THAT'S TOUGH.
KLAK
WILL YOU...
...DO THE ONE OVER THERE INSTEAD?
RATTLE
...
CLICK... VWIR...
Isn't Mr. Maki's name is...
Seiichiro Maki
... Seiichiro Maki...?
SEIICHIRO ...
Then that means that...
...Mr. Maki lives here?
I'm not sure if it's a hotel...
...or a mansion ...
But does it...
...belong to Mr. Maki?

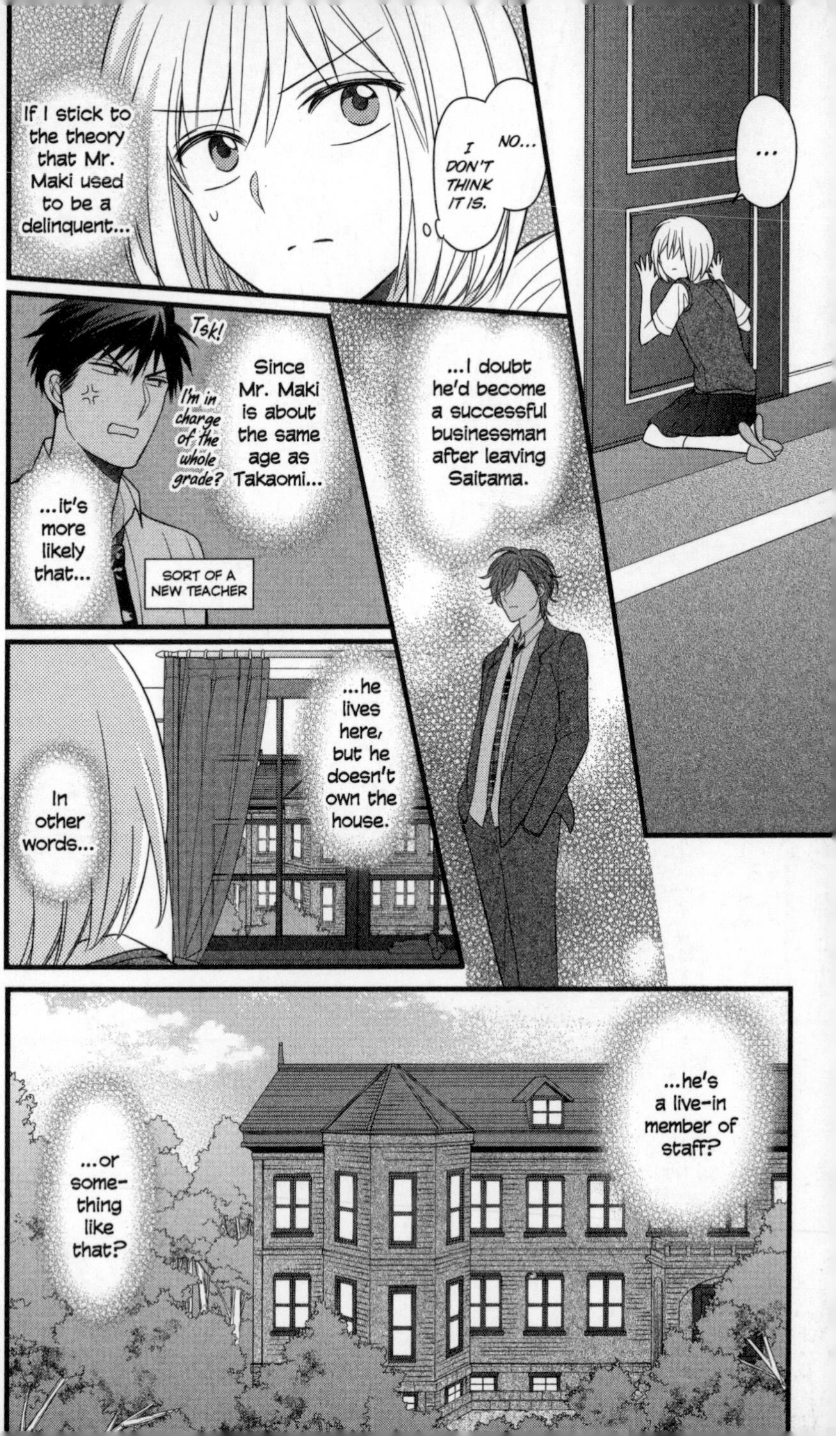
...
NO... I DON'T THINK IT IS.
If I stick to the theory that Mr. Maki used to be a delinquent...
...I doubt he'd become a successful businessman after leaving Saitama.
Tsk!
Since Mr. Maki is about the same age as Takaomi...
I'm in charge of the whole grade?
SORT OF A NEW TEACHER
...it's more likely that...
...he lives here, but he doesn't own the house.
In other words...
...he's a live-in member of staff?
...or something like that?

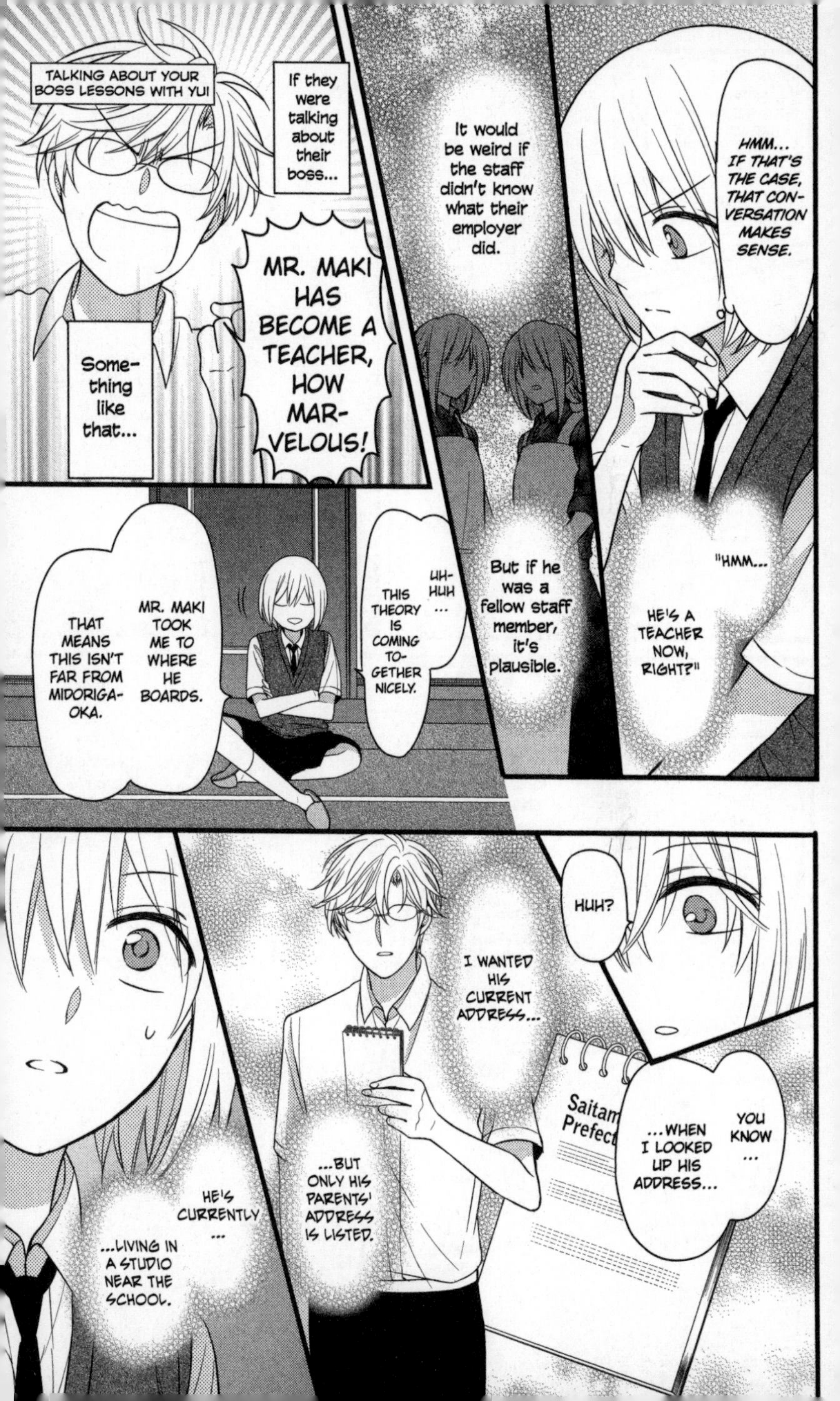
HMM… IF THAT'S THE CASE, THAT CON-VERSATION MAKES SENSE.
"HMM…
HE'S A TEACHER NOW, RIGHT?"
It would be weird if the staff didn't know what their employer did.
But if he was a fellow staff member, it's plausible.
If they were talking about their boss…
TALKING ABOUT YOUR BOSS LESSONS WITH YUI
MR. MAKI HAS BECOME A TEACHER, HOW MAR-VELOUS!
Some-thing like that…
UH-HUH …
THIS THEORY IS COMING TO-GETHER NICELY.
MR. MAKI TOOK ME TO WHERE HE BOARDS.
THAT MEANS THIS ISN'T FAR FROM MIDORIGA-OKA.
HUH?
YOU KNOW …
…WHEN I LOOKED UP HIS ADDRESS…
Saitam
Prefect
I WANTED HIS CURRENT ADDRESS…
…BUT ONLY HIS PARENTS' ADDRESS IS LISTED.
HE'S CURRENTLY …
…LIVING IN A STUDIO NEAR THE SCHOOL.

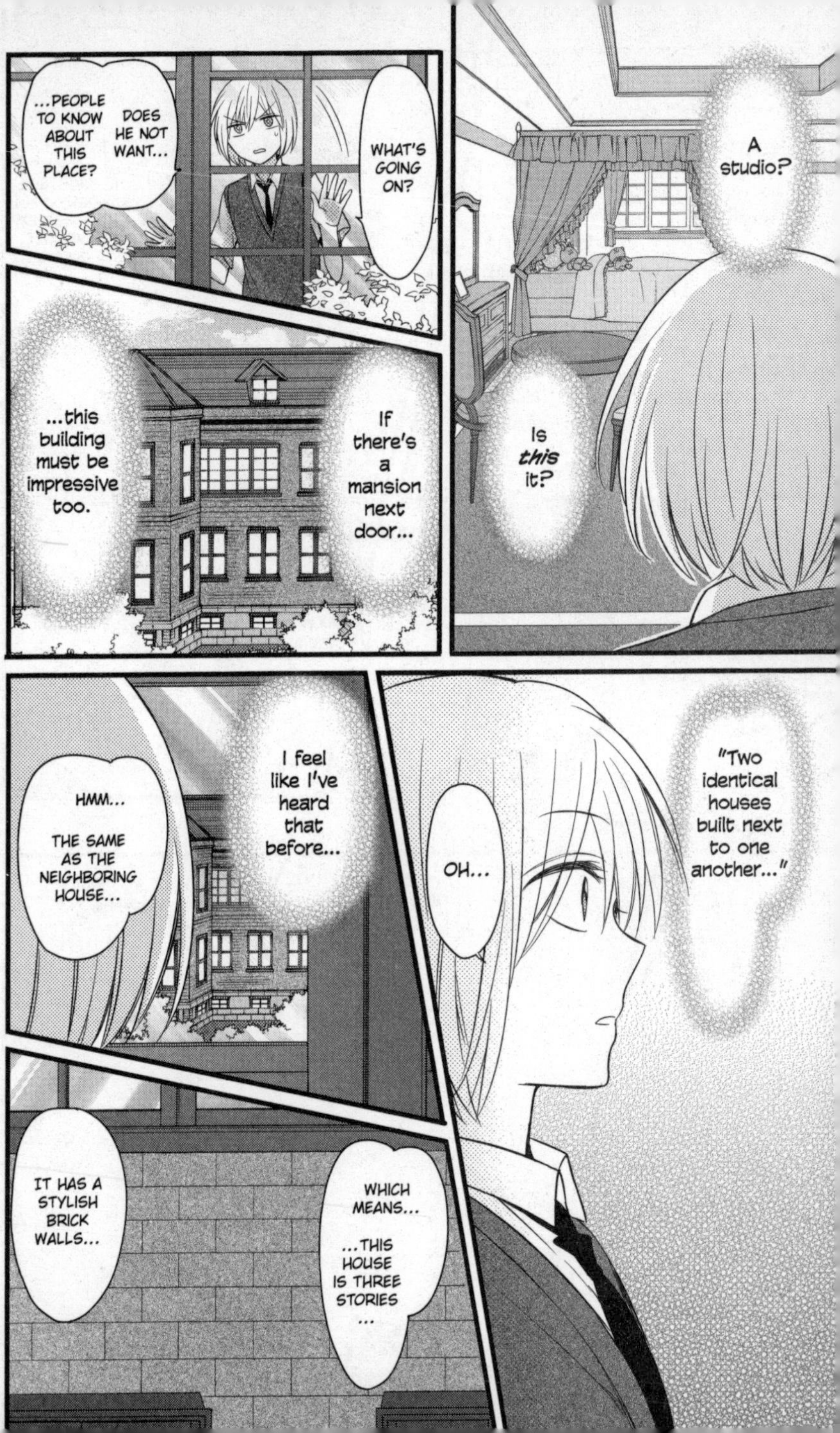
A studio?
Is *this* it?
WHAT'S GOING ON?
DOES HE NOT WANT...
...PEOPLE TO KNOW ABOUT THIS PLACE?
If there's a mansion next door...
...this building must be impressive too.
"Two identical houses built next to one another..."
OH...
I feel like I've heard that before...
HMM...
THE SAME AS THE NEIGHBORING HOUSE...
WHICH MEANS...
...THIS HOUSE IS THREE STORIES ...
IT HAS A STYLISH BRICK WALLS...

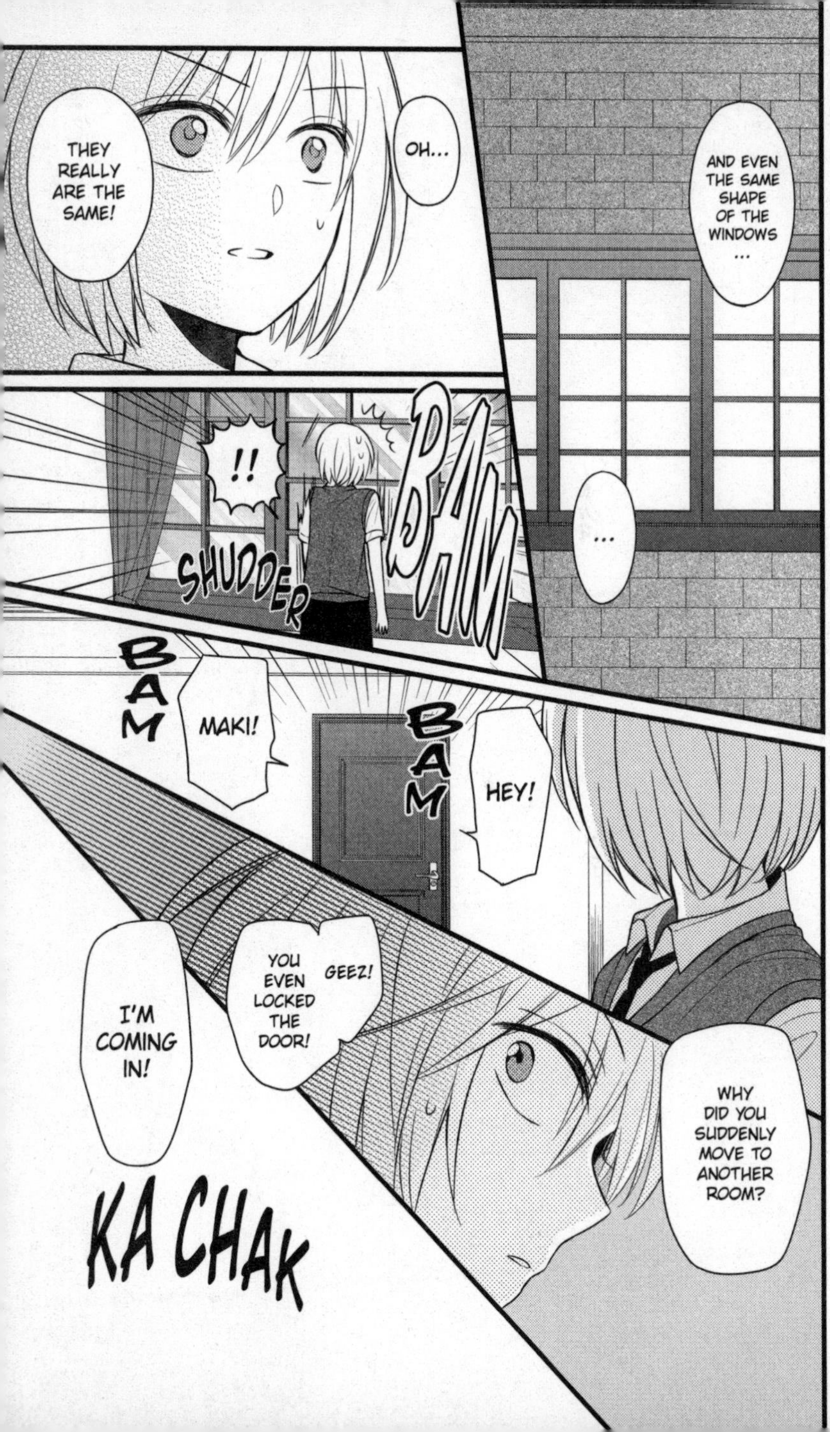

AND EVEN THE SAME SHAPE OF THE WINDOWS ...
...
OH...
THEY REALLY ARE THE SAME!
BAM
!!
SHUDDER
HEY!
BAM BAM
MAKI!
BAM BAM
WHY DID YOU SUDDENLY MOVE TO ANOTHER ROOM?
GEEZ!
YOU EVEN LOCKED THE DOOR!
I'M COMING IN!
KA CHAK

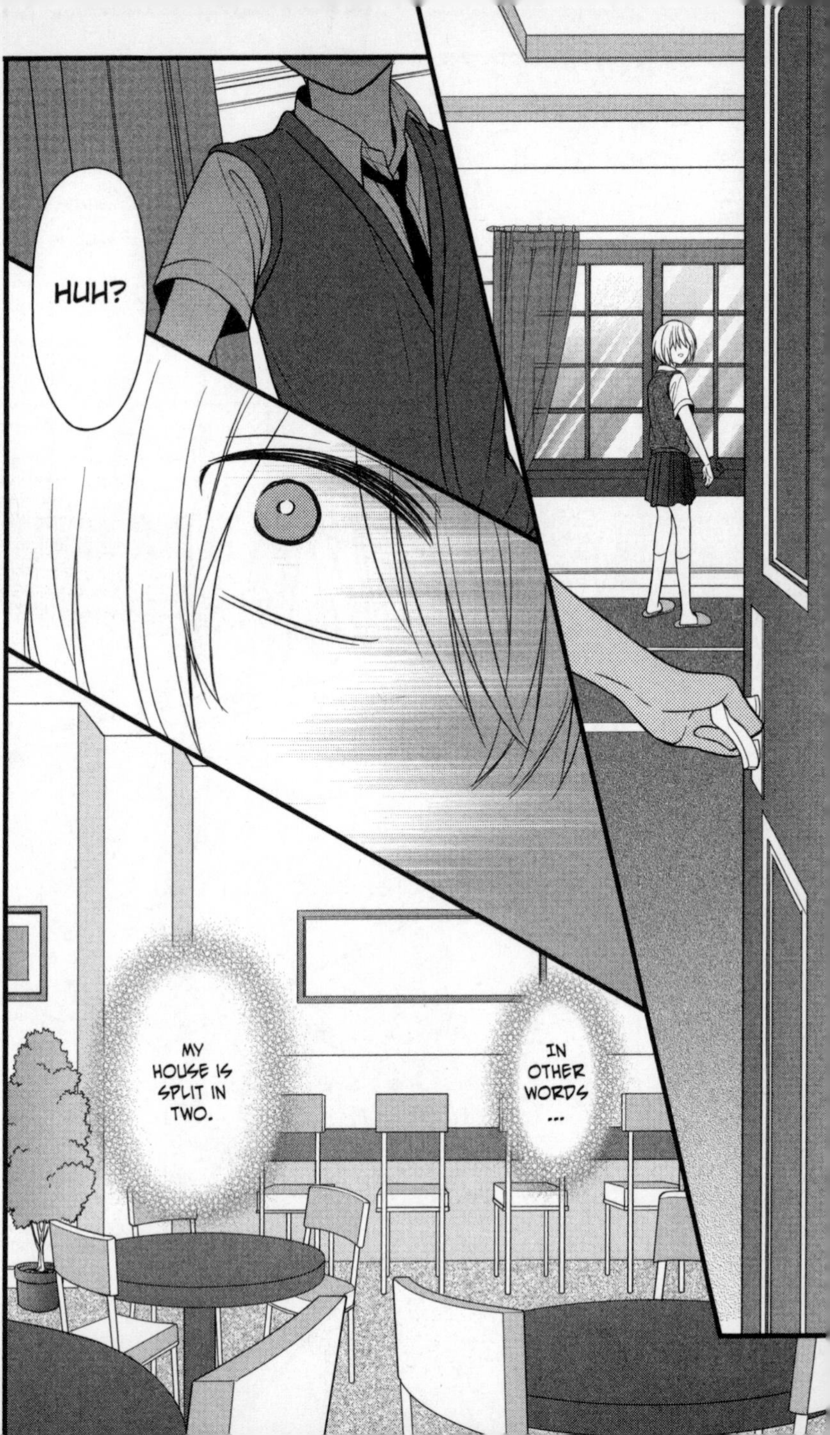
HUH?
IN OTHER WORDS...
MY HOUSE IS SPLIT IN TWO.

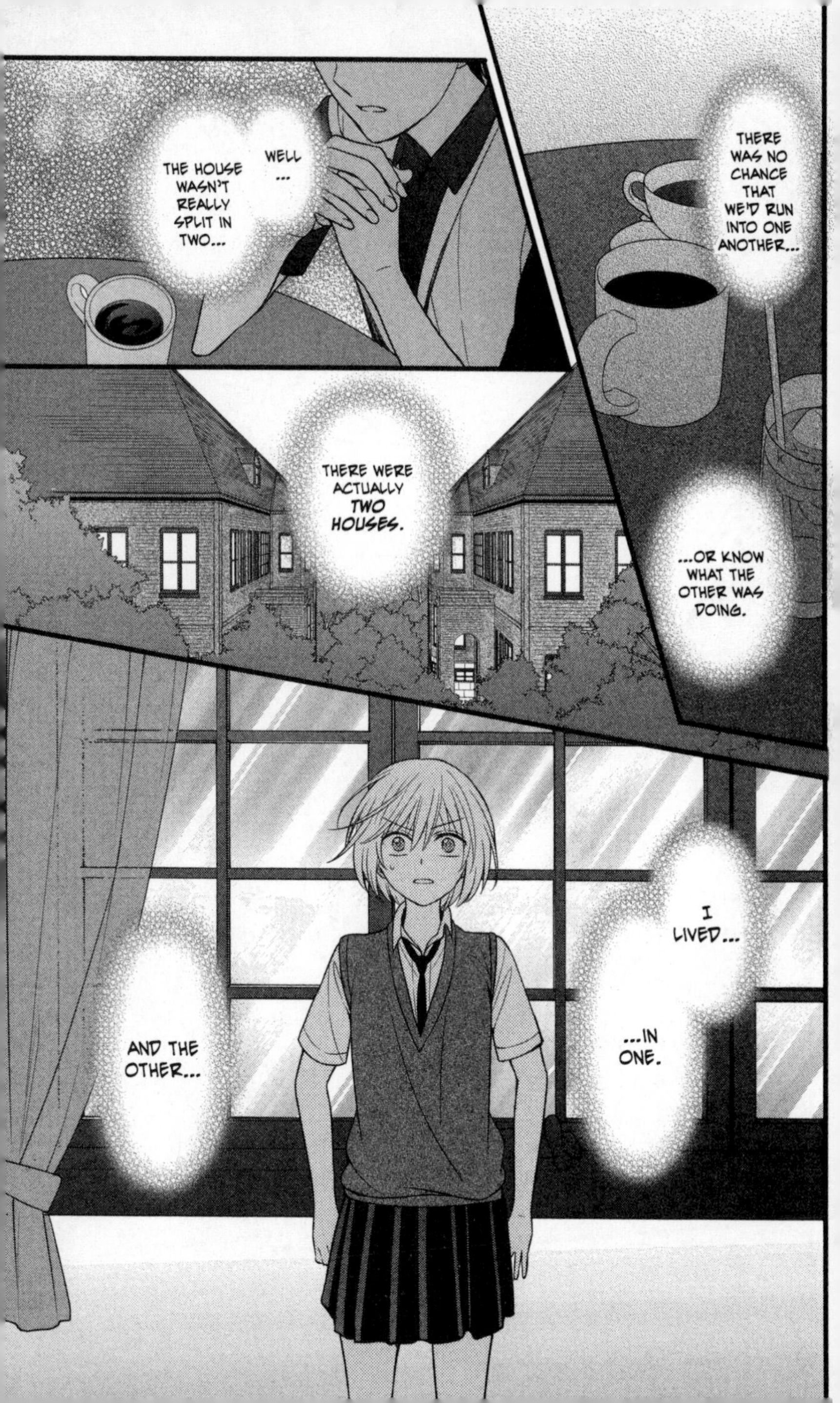
THERE WAS NO CHANCE THAT WE'D RUN INTO ONE ANOTHER...
...OR KNOW WHAT THE OTHER WAS DOING.
WELL...
THE HOUSE WASN'T REALLY SPLIT IN TWO...
THERE WERE ACTUALLY TWO HOUSES.
I LIVED...
...IN ONE.
AND THE OTHER...

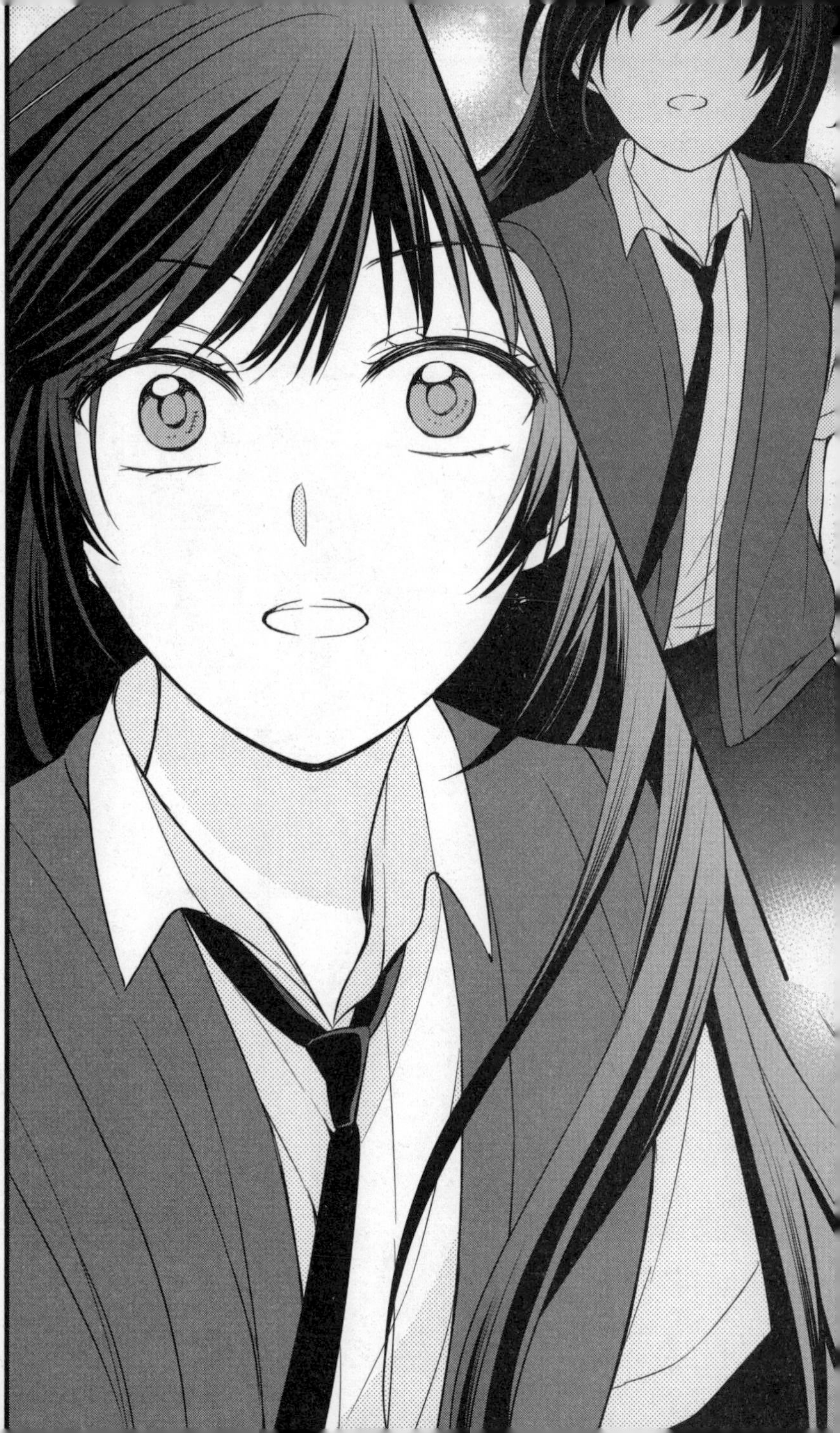

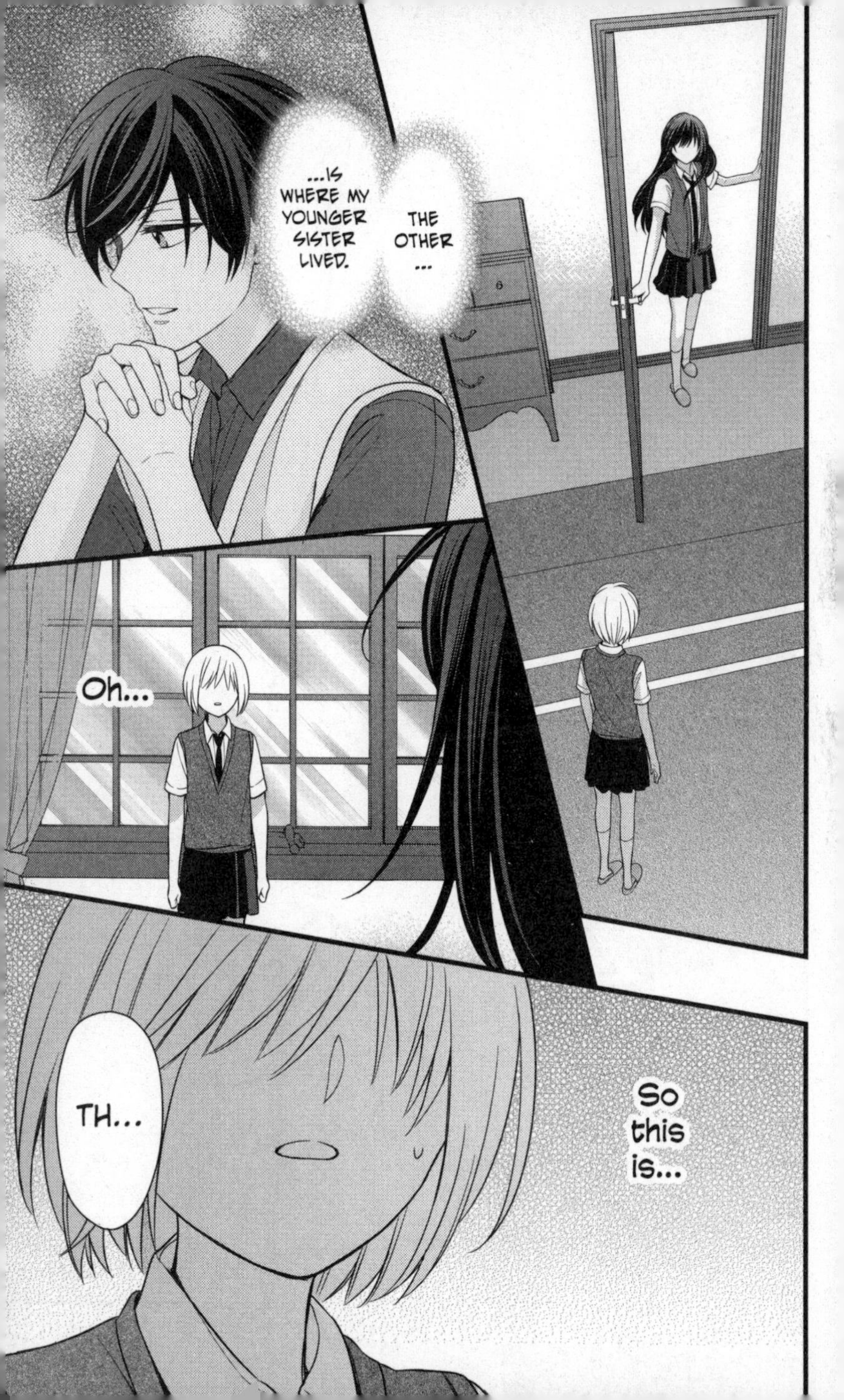
THE OTHER ...
...IS WHERE MY YOUNGER SISTER LIVED.
Oh...
So this is...
TH...

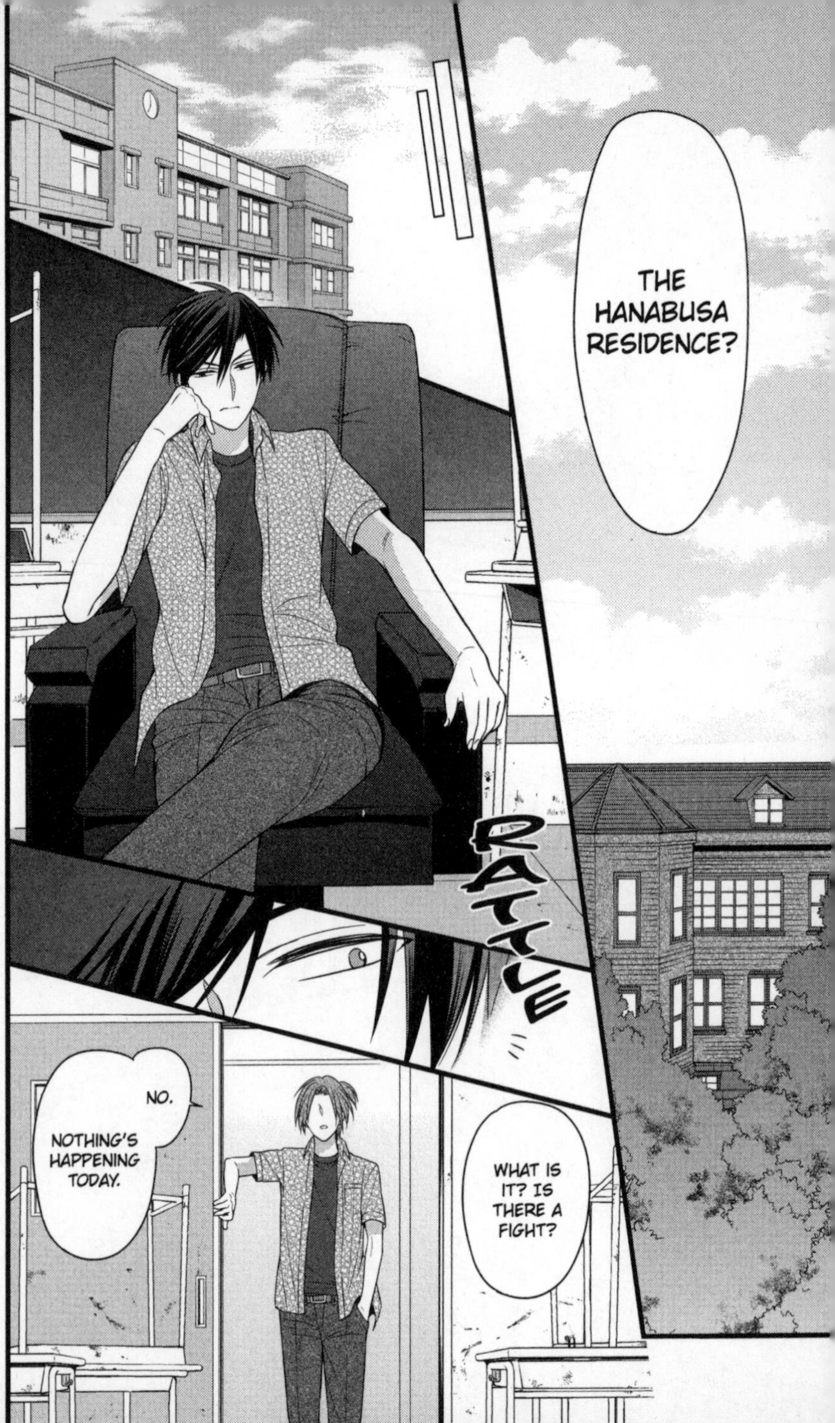

THE HANABUSA RESIDENCE?
RATTLE
WHAT IS IT? IS THERE A FIGHT?
NO.
NOTHING'S HAPPENING TODAY.

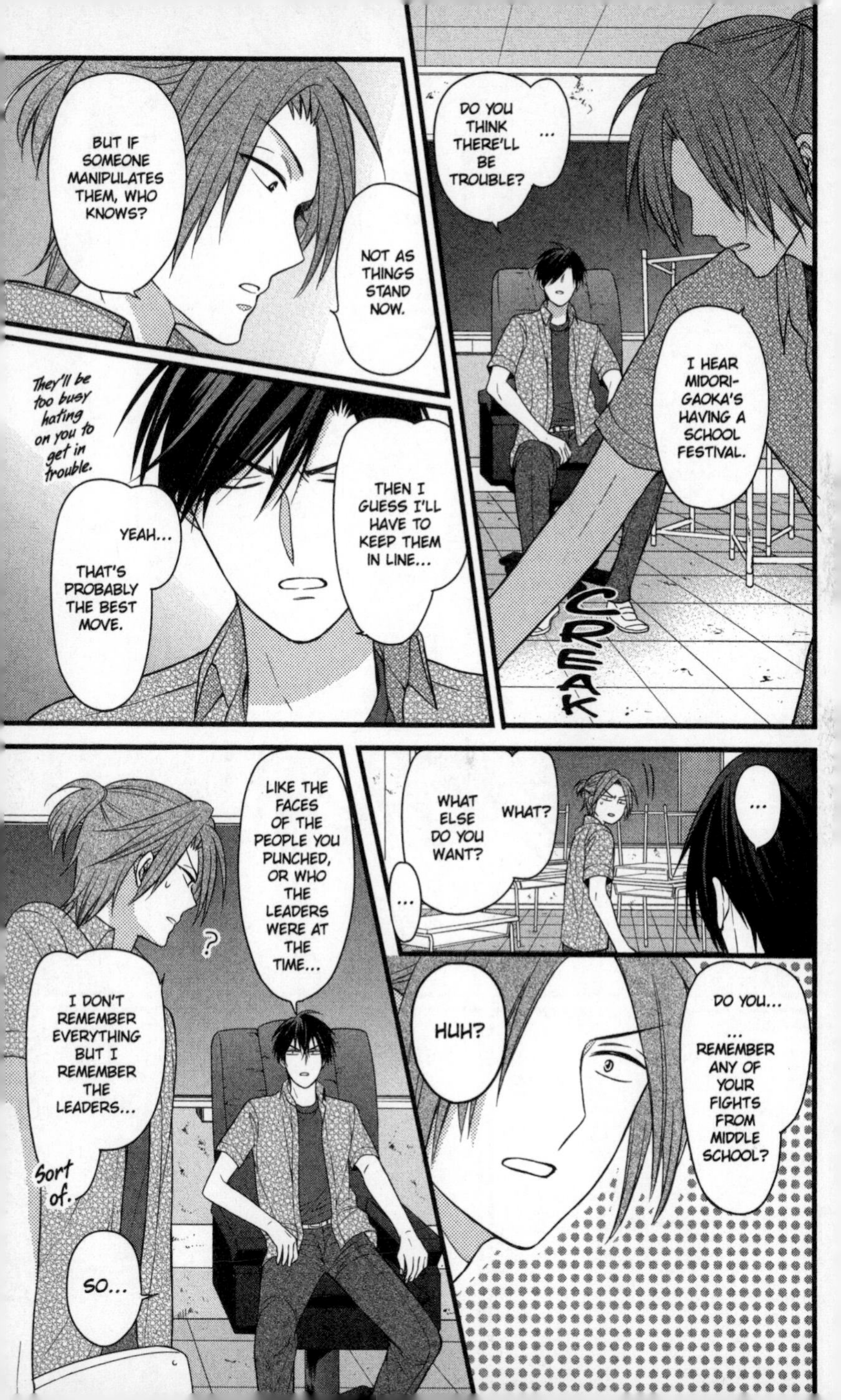

I HEAR MIDORI-GAOKA'S HAVING A SCHOOL FESTIVAL.
...
DO YOU THINK THERE'LL BE TROUBLE?
CREAK
NOT AS THINGS STAND NOW.
BUT IF SOMEONE MANIPULATES THEM, WHO KNOWS?
THEN I GUESS I'LL HAVE TO KEEP THEM IN LINE...
They'll be too busy hating on you to get in trouble.
YEAH...
THAT'S PROBABLY THE BEST MOVE.
...
WHAT?
WHAT ELSE DO YOU WANT?
...
DO YOU...
... REMEMBER ANY OF YOUR FIGHTS FROM MIDDLE SCHOOL?
HUH?
LIKE THE FACES OF THE PEOPLE YOU PUNCHED, OR WHO THE LEADERS WERE AT THE TIME...
?
I DON'T REMEMBER EVERYTHING BUT I REMEMBER THE LEADERS...
Sort of.
SO...

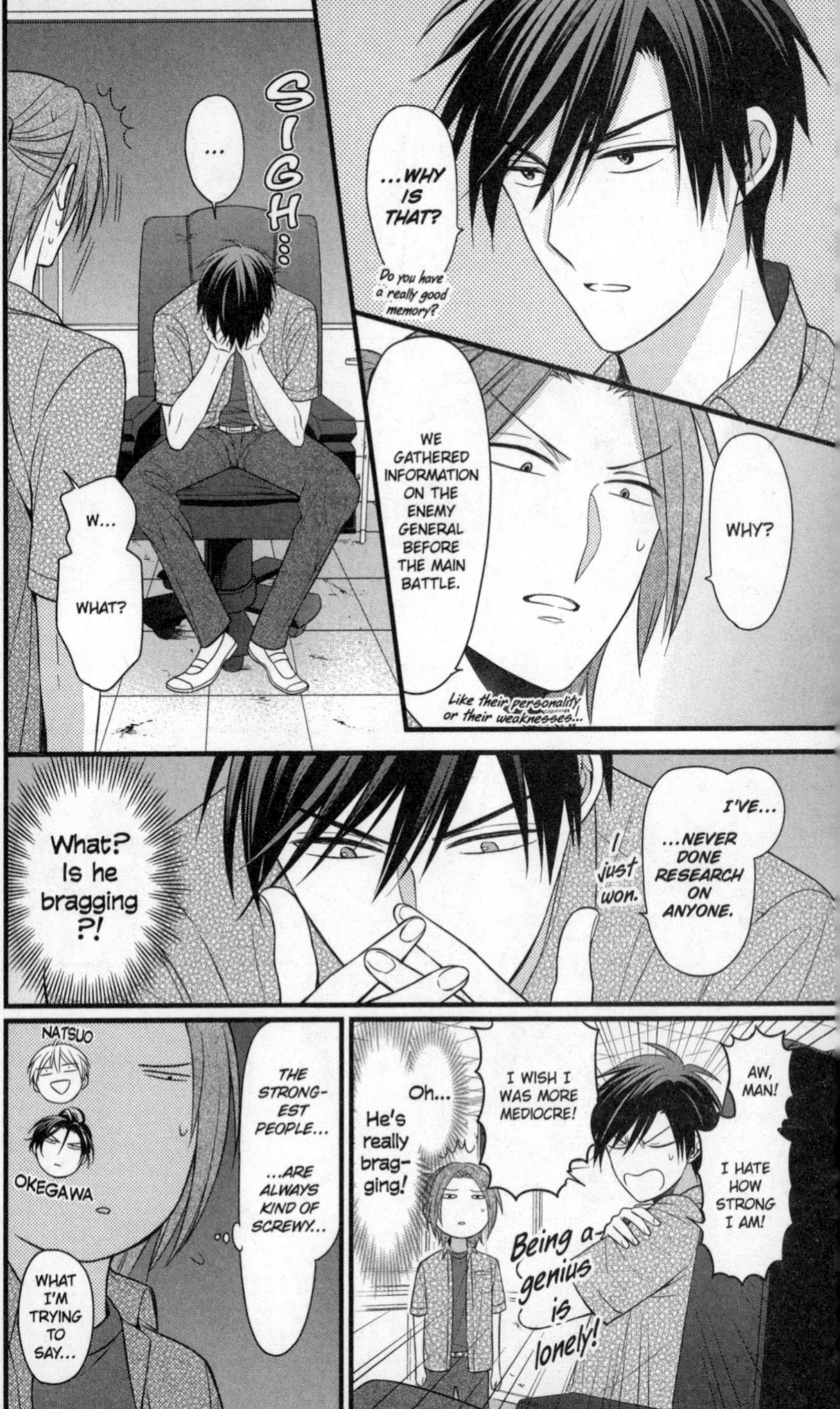
...WHY IS THAT?
Do you have a really good memory?
WHY?
WE GATHERED INFORMATION ON THE ENEMY GENERAL BEFORE THE MAIN BATTLE.
Like their personality or their weaknesses...
SIGH...
...
W...
WHAT?
I'VE...
...NEVER DONE RESEARCH ON ANYONE.
I just won.
What? Is he bragging?!
AW, MAN!
I HATE HOW STRONG I AM!
I WISH I WAS MORE MEDIOCRE!
Being a-genius is lonely!
Oh...
He's really brag-ging!
THE STRONG-EST PEOPLE...
...ARE ALWAYS KIND OF SCREWY...
NATSUO
OKEGAWA
WHAT I'M TRYING TO SAY...

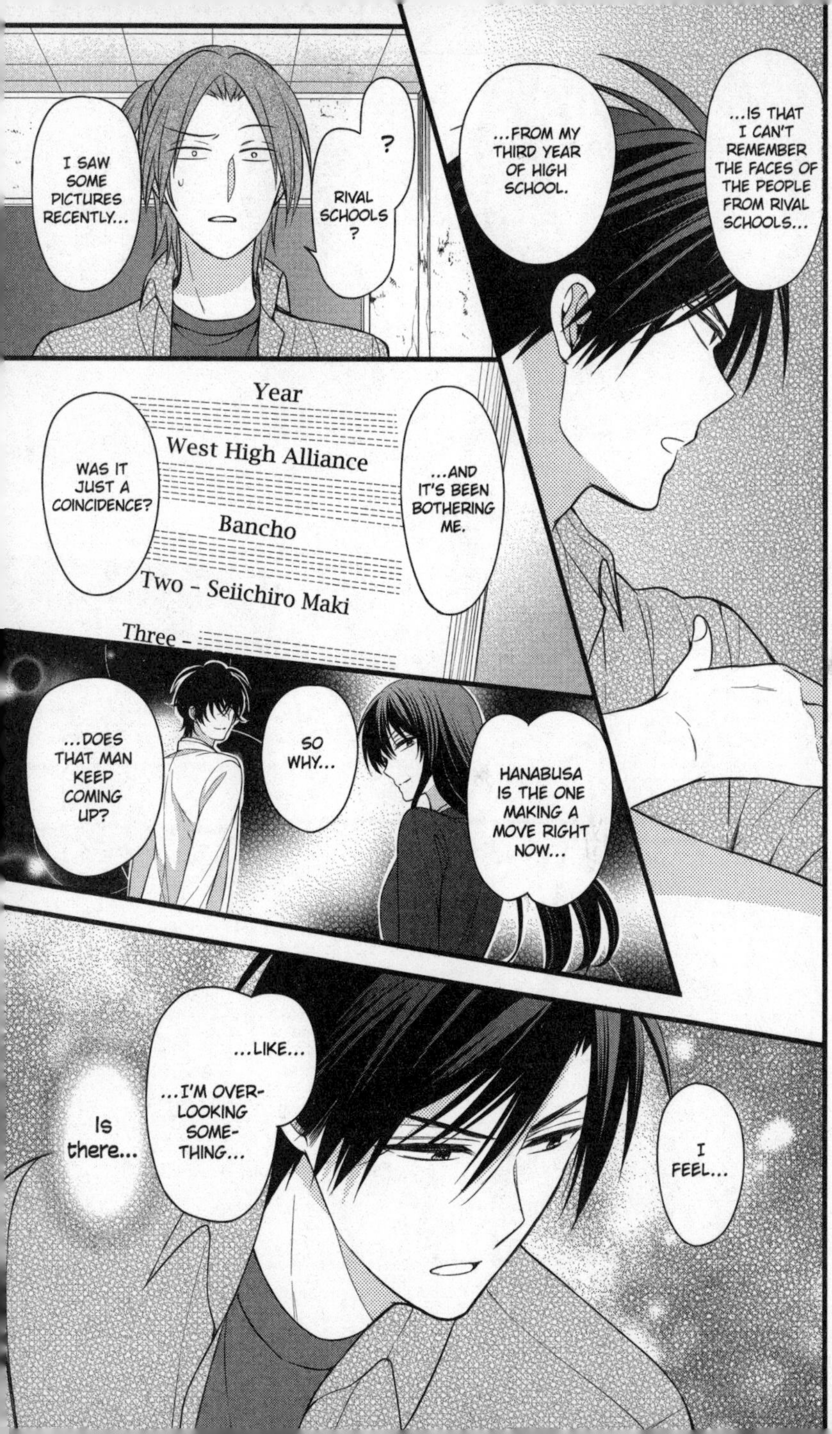
...IS THAT I CAN'T REMEMBER THE FACES OF THE PEOPLE FROM RIVAL SCHOOLS...
...FROM MY THIRD YEAR OF HIGH SCHOOL.
? RIVAL SCHOOLS ?
I SAW SOME PICTURES RECENTLY...
...AND IT'S BEEN BOTHERING ME.
Year
West High Alliance
Bancho
Two - Seiichiro Maki
Three -
WAS IT JUST A COINCIDENCE?
HANABUSA IS THE ONE MAKING A MOVE RIGHT NOW...
SO WHY...
...DOES THAT MAN KEEP COMING UP?
I FEEL...
...LIKE...
...I'M OVER-LOOKING SOME-THING...
Is there...

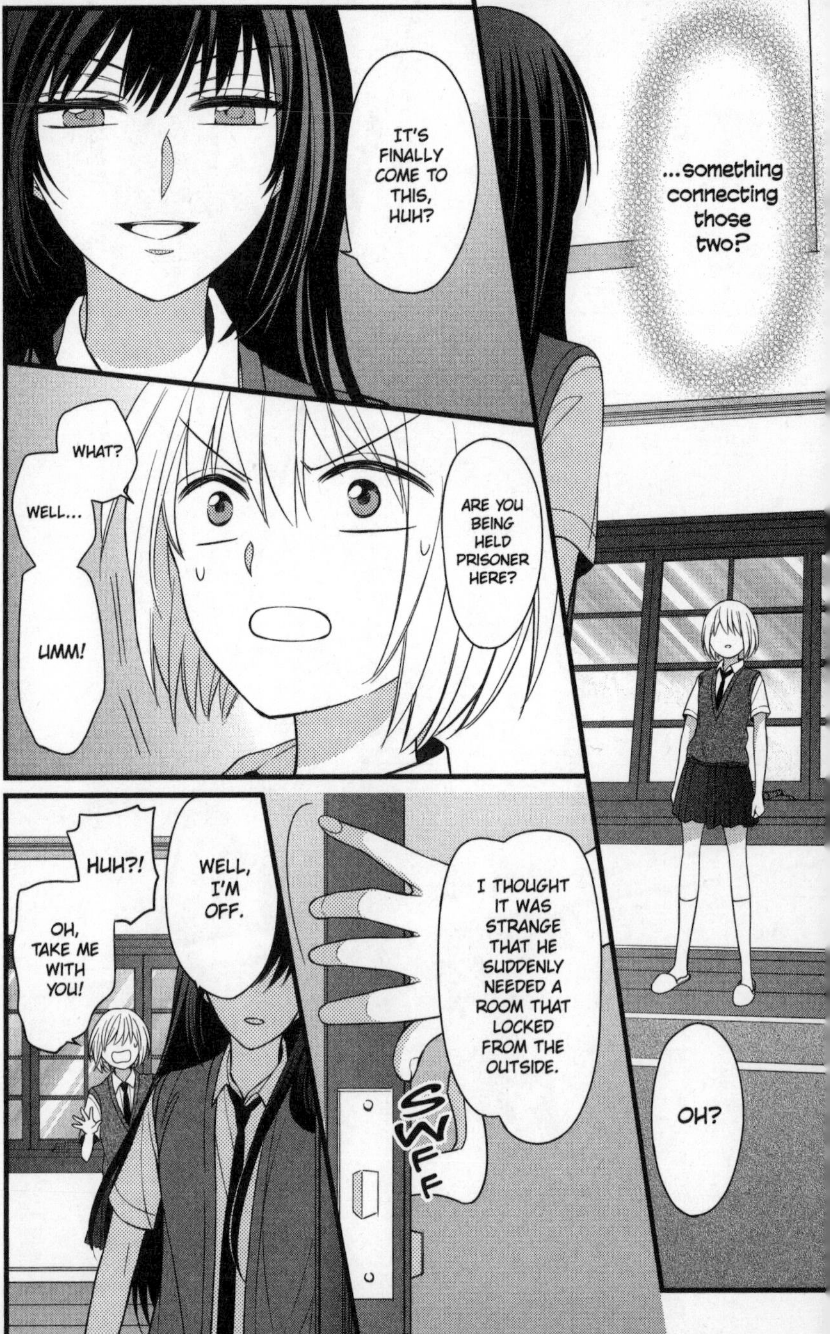
...something connecting those two?
OH?
IT'S FINALLY COME TO THIS, HUH?
ARE YOU BEING HELD PRISONER HERE?
WHAT? WELL... UMM!
I THOUGHT IT WAS STRANGE THAT HE SUDDENLY NEEDED A ROOM THAT LOCKED FROM THE OUTSIDE.
SWFF
WELL, I'M OFF.
HUH?!
OH, TAKE ME WITH YOU!

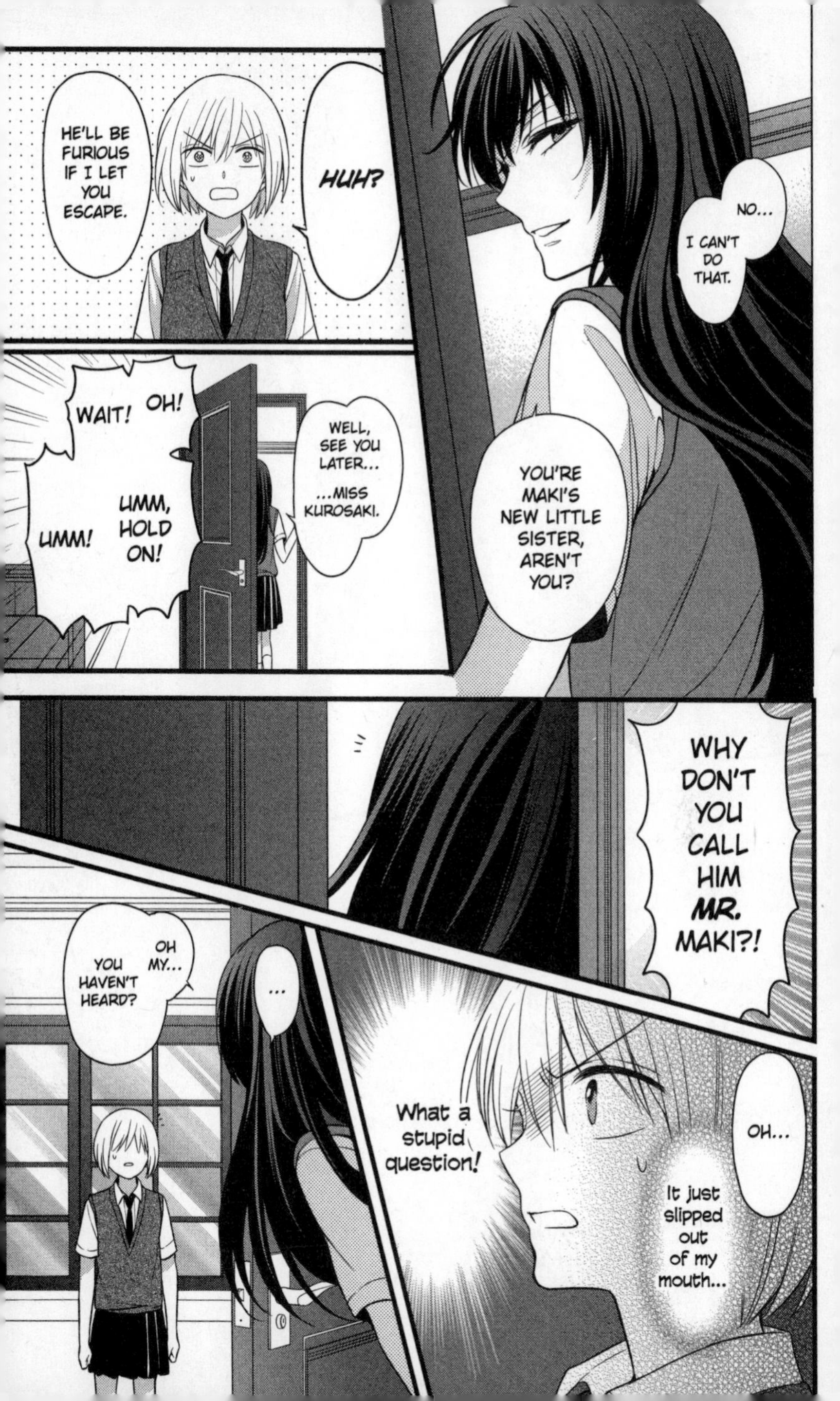

NO...
I CAN'T DO THAT.
YOU'RE MAKI'S NEW LITTLE SISTER, AREN'T YOU?
HUH?
HE'LL BE FURIOUS IF I LET YOU ESCAPE.
WELL, SEE YOU LATER...
...MISS KUROSAKI.
WAIT!
OH!
UMM, HOLD ON!
UMM!
WHY DON'T YOU CALL HIM MR. MAKI?!
...
OH MY...
YOU HAVEN'T HEARD?
OH...
It just slipped out of my mouth...
What a stupid question!

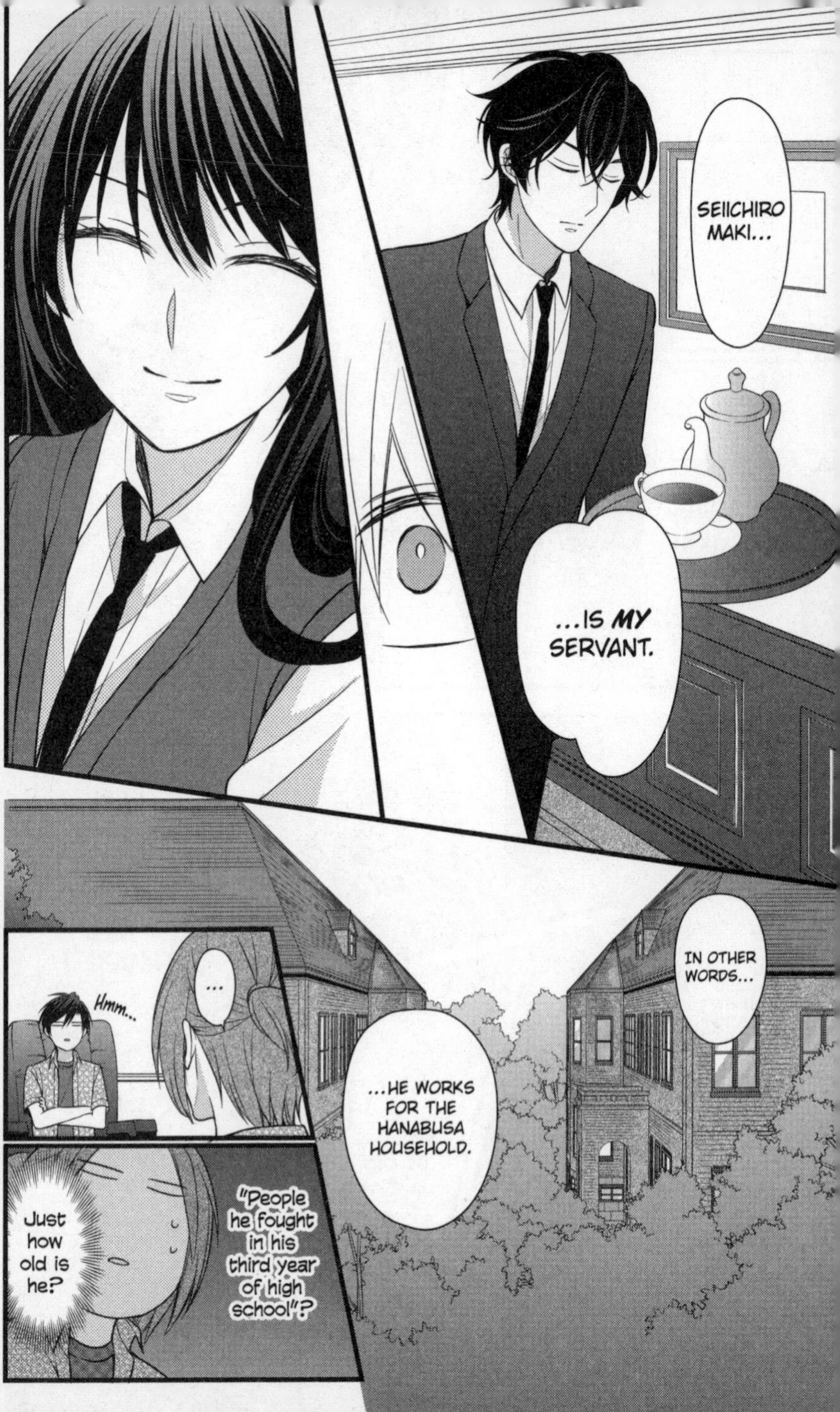
SEIICHIRO MAKI...
...IS MY SERVANT.
IN OTHER WORDS...
...HE WORKS FOR THE HANABUSA HOUSEHOLD.
...
Hmm...
"People he fought in his third year of high school"?
Just how old is he?

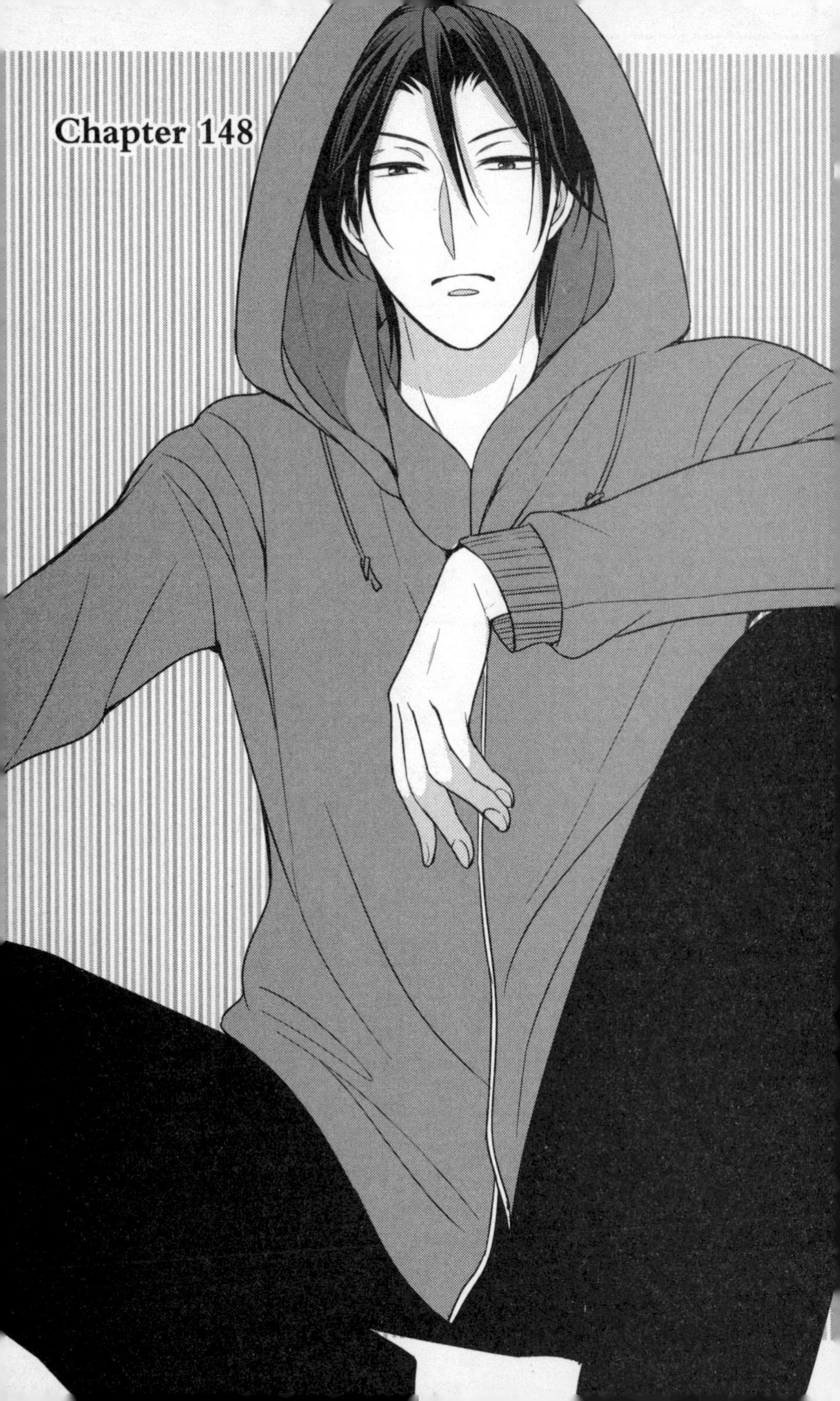
Chapter 148

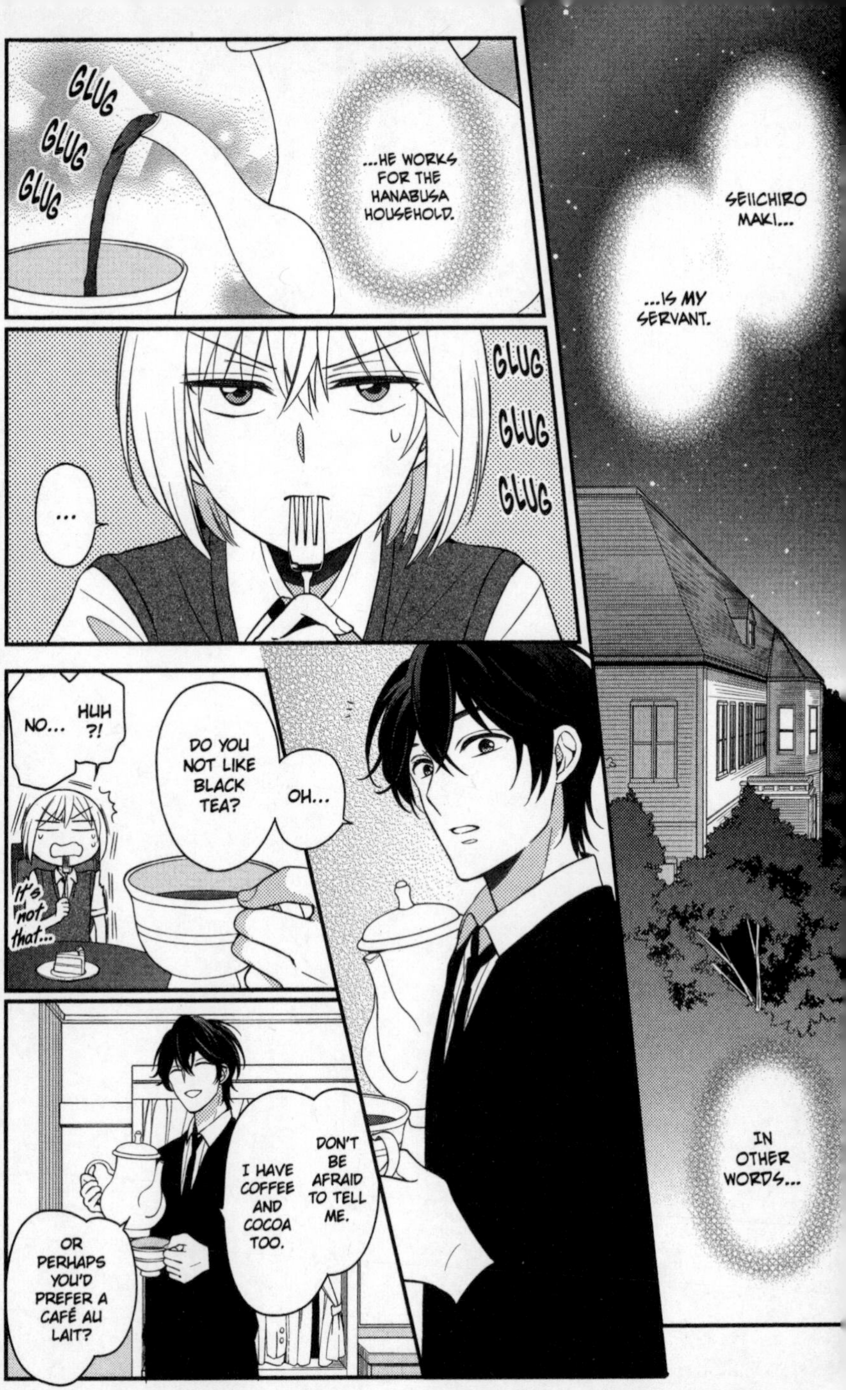
SEIICHIRO MAKI...
...IS MY SERVANT.
IN OTHER WORDS...
...HE WORKS FOR THE HANABUSA HOUSEHOLD.
GLUG GLUG GLUG
GLUG GLUG GLUG
...
OH...
DO YOU NOT LIKE BLACK TEA?
HUH ?!
NO...
It's not that...
DON'T BE AFRAID TO TELL ME.
I HAVE COFFEE AND COCOA TOO.
OR PERHAPS YOU'D PREFER A CAFÉ AU LAIT?

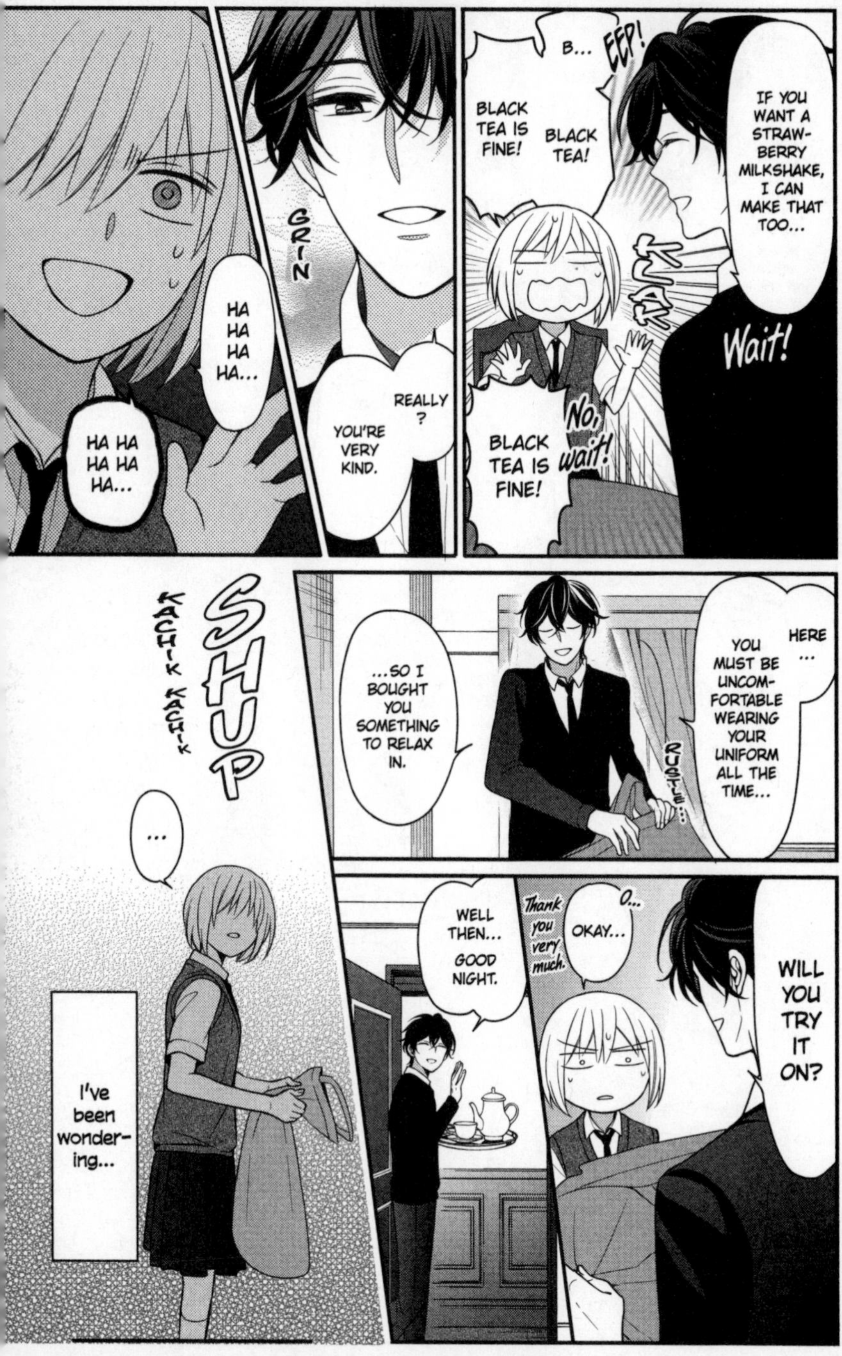
IF YOU WANT A STRAW-BERRY MILKSHAKE, I CAN MAKE THAT TOO...
EEP!
B...
BLACK TEA!
BLACK TEA IS FINE!
Wait!
No, wait!
BLACK TEA IS FINE!
GRIN
REALLY?
YOU'RE VERY KIND.
HA HA HA HA...
HA HA HA HA HA...
HERE...
YOU MUST BE UNCOM-FORTABLE WEARING YOUR UNIFORM ALL THE TIME...
RUSTLE...
...SO I BOUGHT YOU SOMETHING TO RELAX IN.
WILL YOU TRY IT ON?
O... OKAY...
Thank you very much.
WELL THEN... GOOD NIGHT.
SHUP
KACHIK KACHIK
...
I've been wonder-ing...

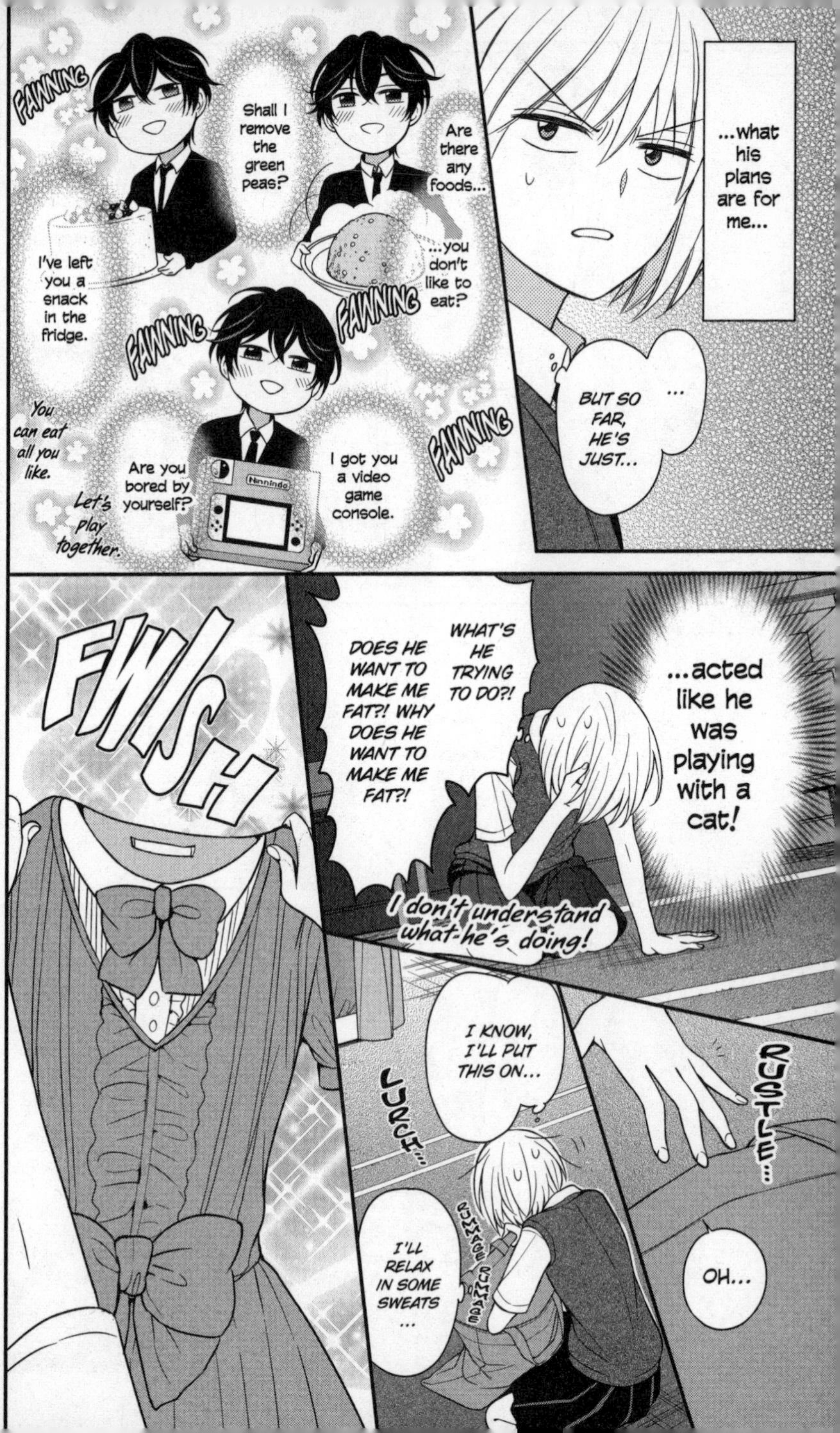

...what his plans are for me...
...
BUT SO FAR, HE'S JUST...
Are there any foods...
...you don't like to eat?
FAWNING
Shall I remove the green peas?
FAWNING
I've left you a snack in the fridge.
FAWNING
FAWNING
I got you a video game console.
Ninindo
Are you bored by yourself?
Let's play together.
You can eat all you like.
...acted like he was playing with a cat!
WHAT'S HE TRYING TO DO?!
DOES HE WANT TO MAKE ME FAT?! WHY DOES HE WANT TO MAKE ME FAT?!
I don't understand what he's doing!
RUSTLE...
OH...
I KNOW, I'LL PUT THIS ON...
LURCH...
RUMMAGE RUMMAGE
I'LL RELAX IN SOME SWEATS...
FWISH

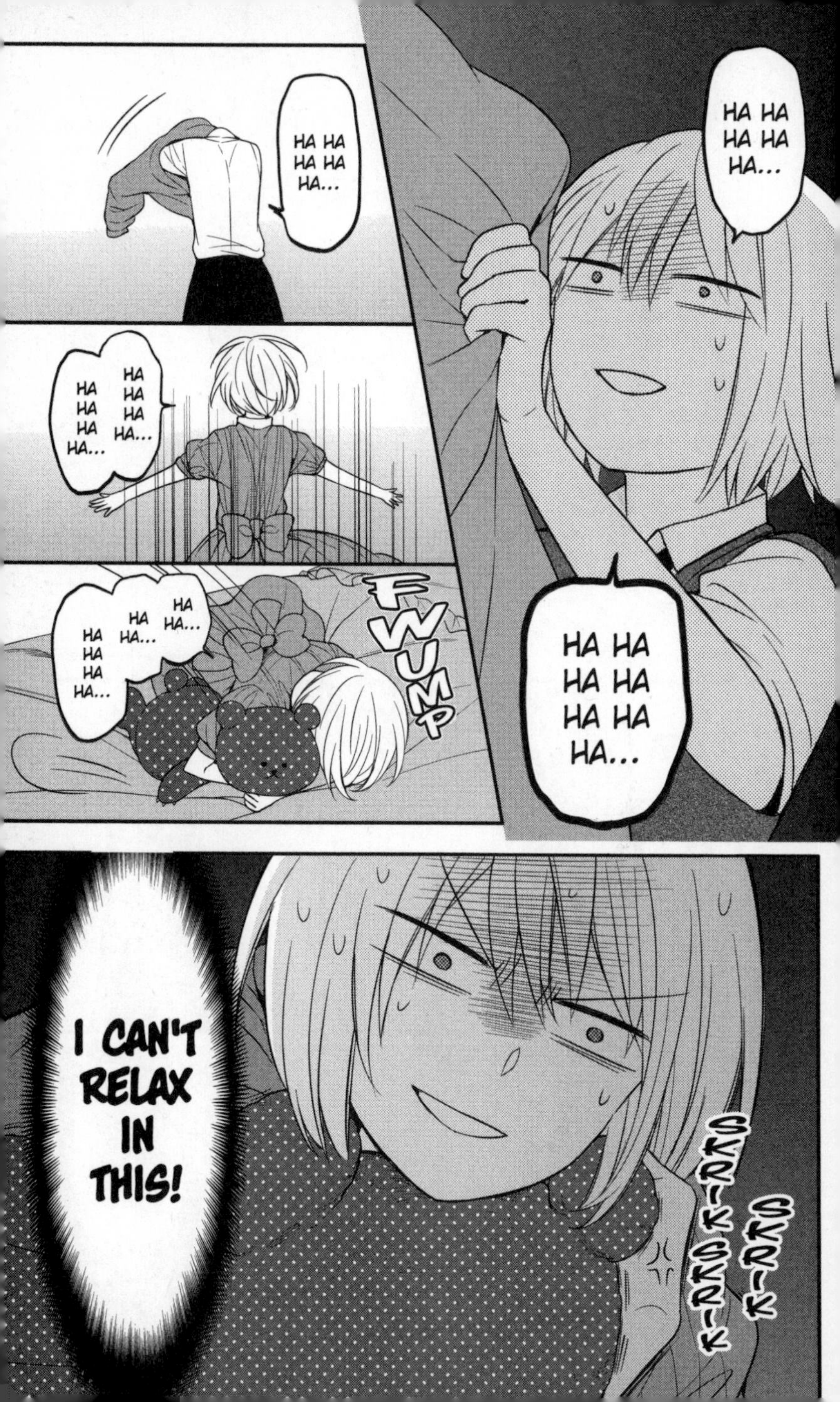
HA HA HA HA HA...
HA HA HA HA HA HA HA...
HA HA HA HA HA...
HA HA HA HA... HA HA HA HA...
HA HA HA HA... HA HA... HA HA...
FWUMP
I CAN'T RELAX IN THIS!
SKRIK SKRIK
SKRIK SKRIK

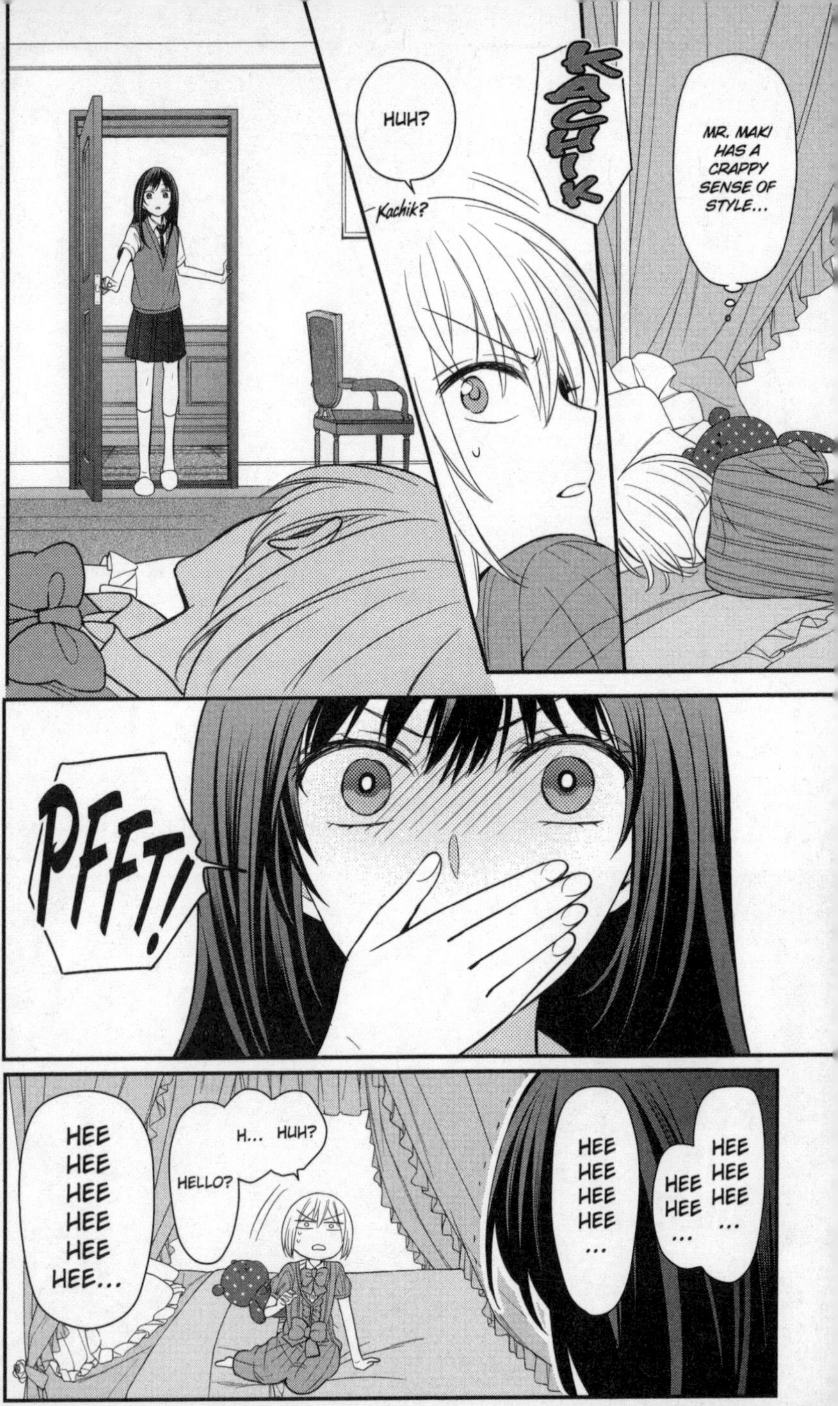
MR. MAKI HAS A CRAPPY SENSE OF STYLE...
KACHIK
HUH?
Kachik?
PFFT!
HEE HEE HEE HEE...
HEE HEE HEE HEE...
HEE HEE HEE HEE HEE HEE...
H... HUH?
HELLO?
HEE HEE HEE HEE HEE HEE...

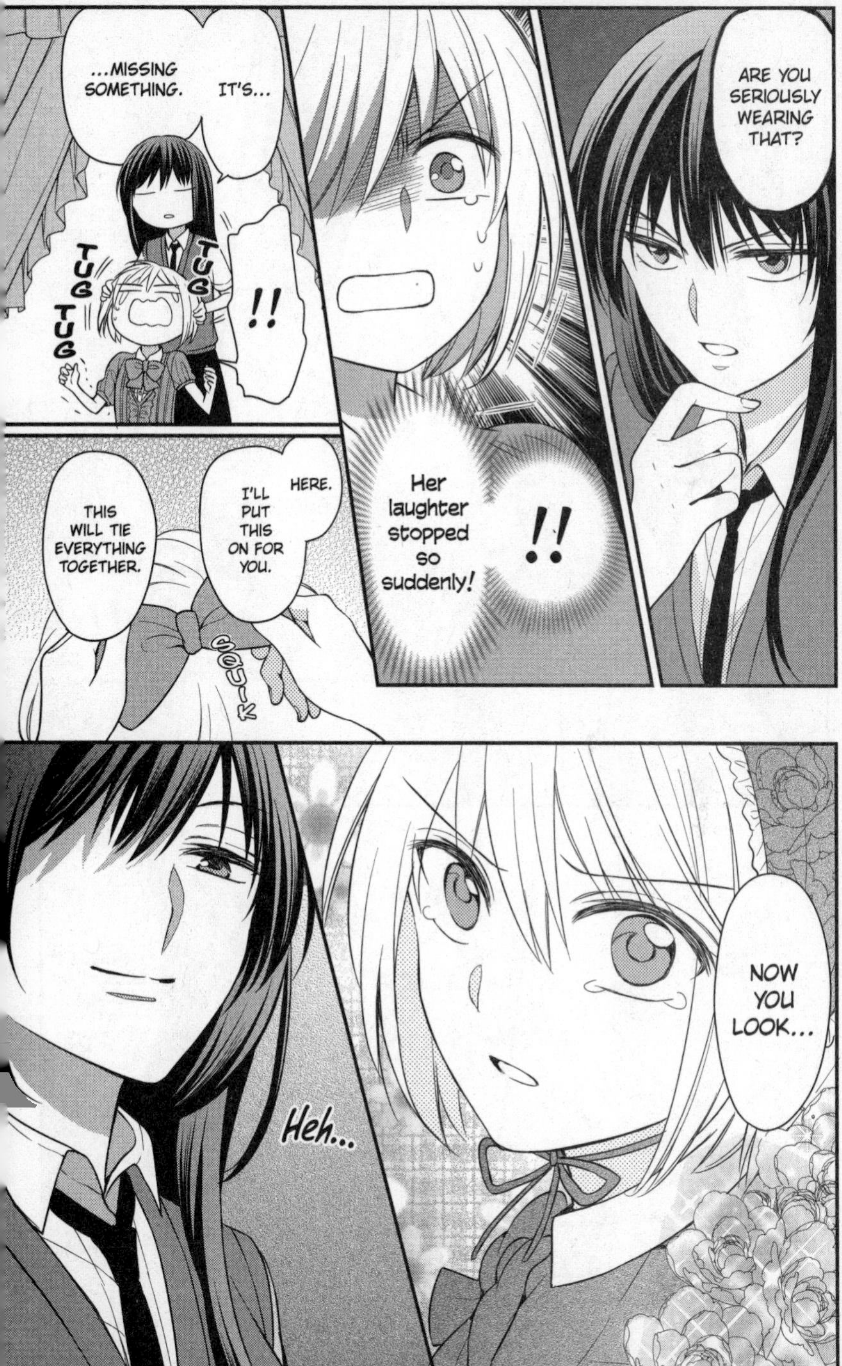
ARE YOU SERIOUSLY WEARING THAT?
Her laughter stopped so suddenly!
!!
IT'S...
...MISSING SOMETHING.
TUG TUG
TUG TUG
!!
HERE.
I'LL PUT THIS ON FOR YOU.
THIS WILL TIE EVERYTHING TOGETHER.
SQUIK
NOW YOU LOOK...
Heh...

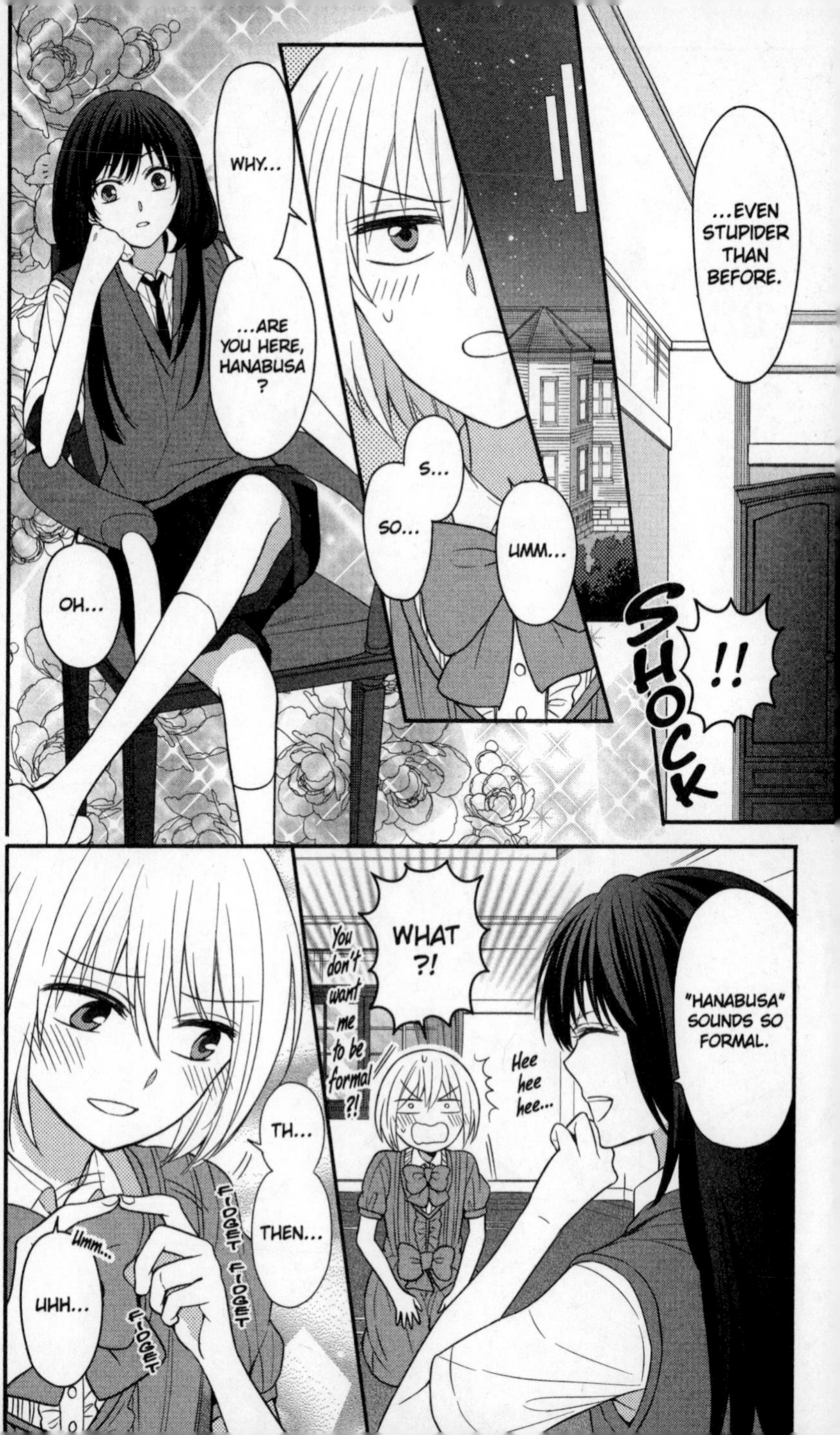
...EVEN STUPIDER THAN BEFORE.
SHOCK
!!
UMM...
S...
SO...
WHY...
...ARE YOU HERE, HANABUSA?
OH...
"HANABUSA" SOUNDS SO FORMAL.
Hee hee hee...
WHAT?!
You don't want me to be formal?!
TH...
THEN...
FIDGET FIDGET
FIDGET
Umm...
UHH...

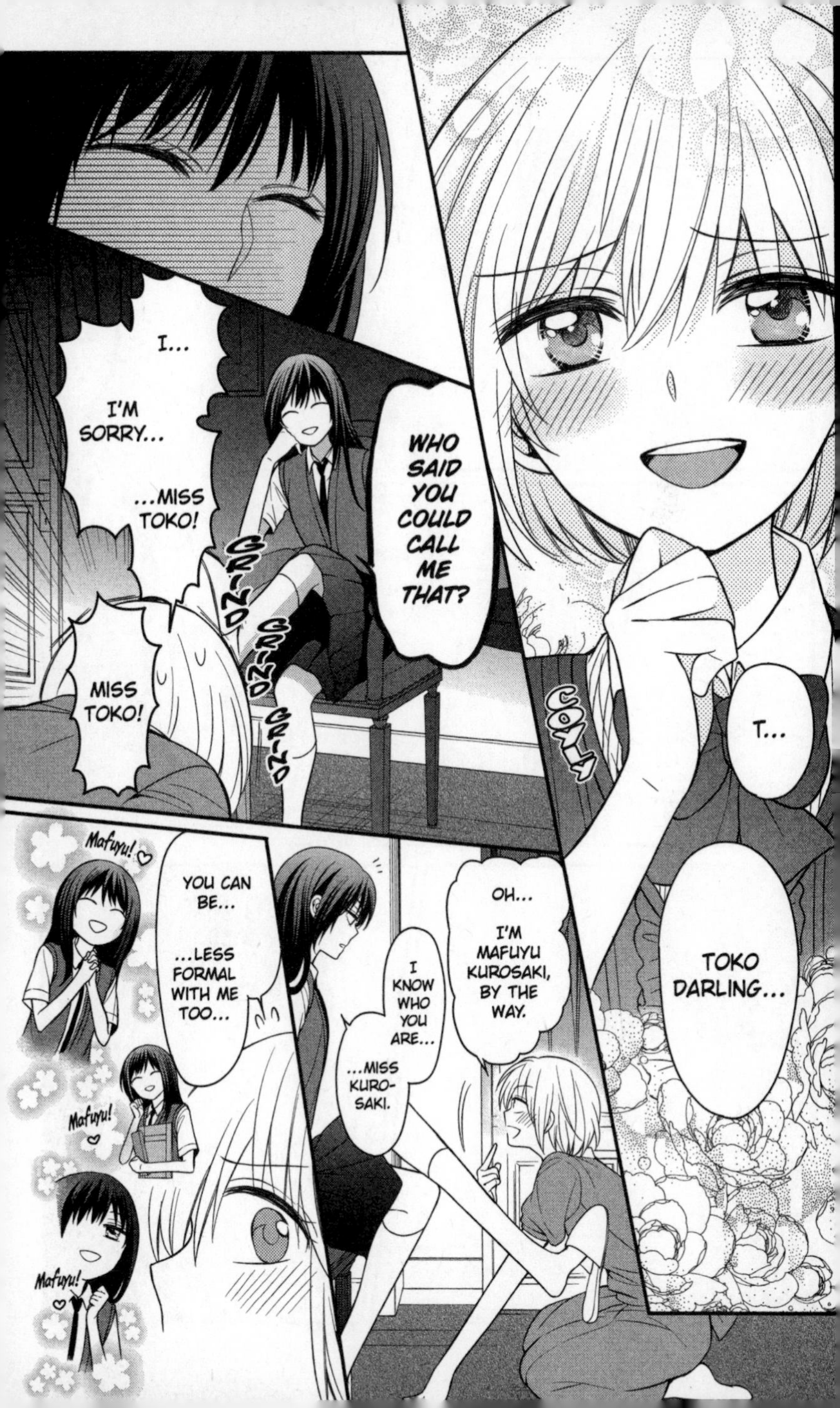
I...
I'M SORRY...
...MISS TOKO!
MISS TOKO!
GRIND GRIND GRIND
WHO SAID YOU COULD CALL ME THAT?
COYLY
T...
TOKO DARLING...
OH...
I'M MAFUYU KUROSAKI, BY THE WAY.
I KNOW WHO YOU ARE...
...MISS KUROSAKI.
YOU CAN BE...
...LESS FORMAL WITH ME TOO...
Mafuyu!
Mafuyu!
Mafuyu!

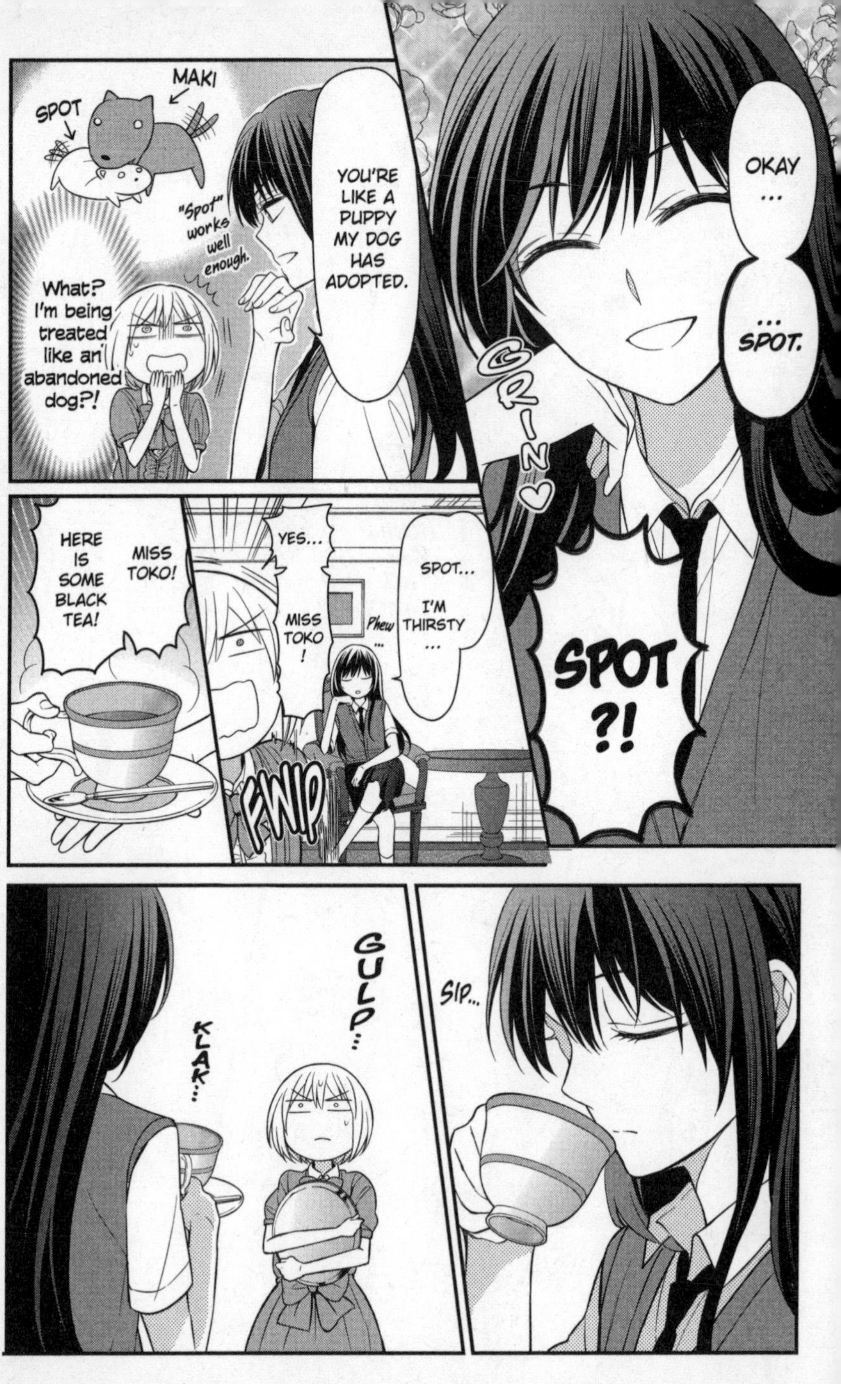
OKAY ...
... SPOT.
GRIN♥
SPOT ?!
YOU'RE LIKE A PUPPY MY DOG HAS ADOPTED.
MAKI
SPOT
"Spot" works well enough.
What? I'm being treated like an abandoned dog?!
SPOT... I'M THIRSTY ...
Phew ...
YES... MISS TOKO!
FWIP
MISS TOKO!
HERE IS SOME BLACK TEA!
SIP...
GULP...
KLAK...

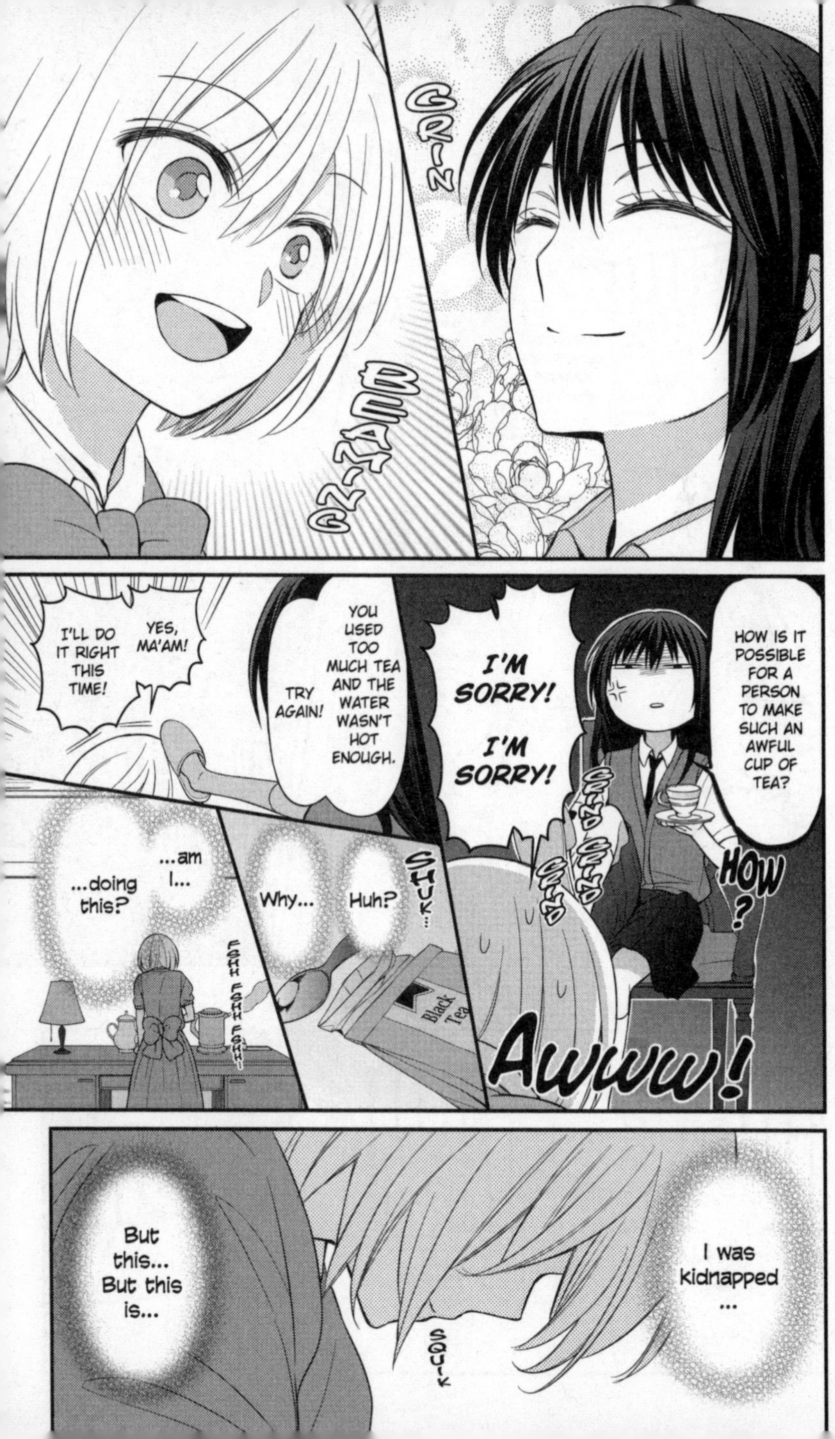
GRIN
BEAMING
HOW IS IT POSSIBLE FOR A PERSON TO MAKE SUCH AN AWFUL CUP OF TEA?
HOW?
GRIND GRIND GRIND
I'M SORRY!
I'M SORRY!
Awwww!
YOU USED TOO MUCH TEA AND THE WATER WASN'T HOT ENOUGH.
TRY AGAIN!
YES, MA'AM!
I'LL DO IT RIGHT THIS TIME!
SHUK...
Huh?
Why...
...am I...
...doing this?
FSHH FSHH FSHH
I was kidnapped ...
SQUIK
But this... But this is...

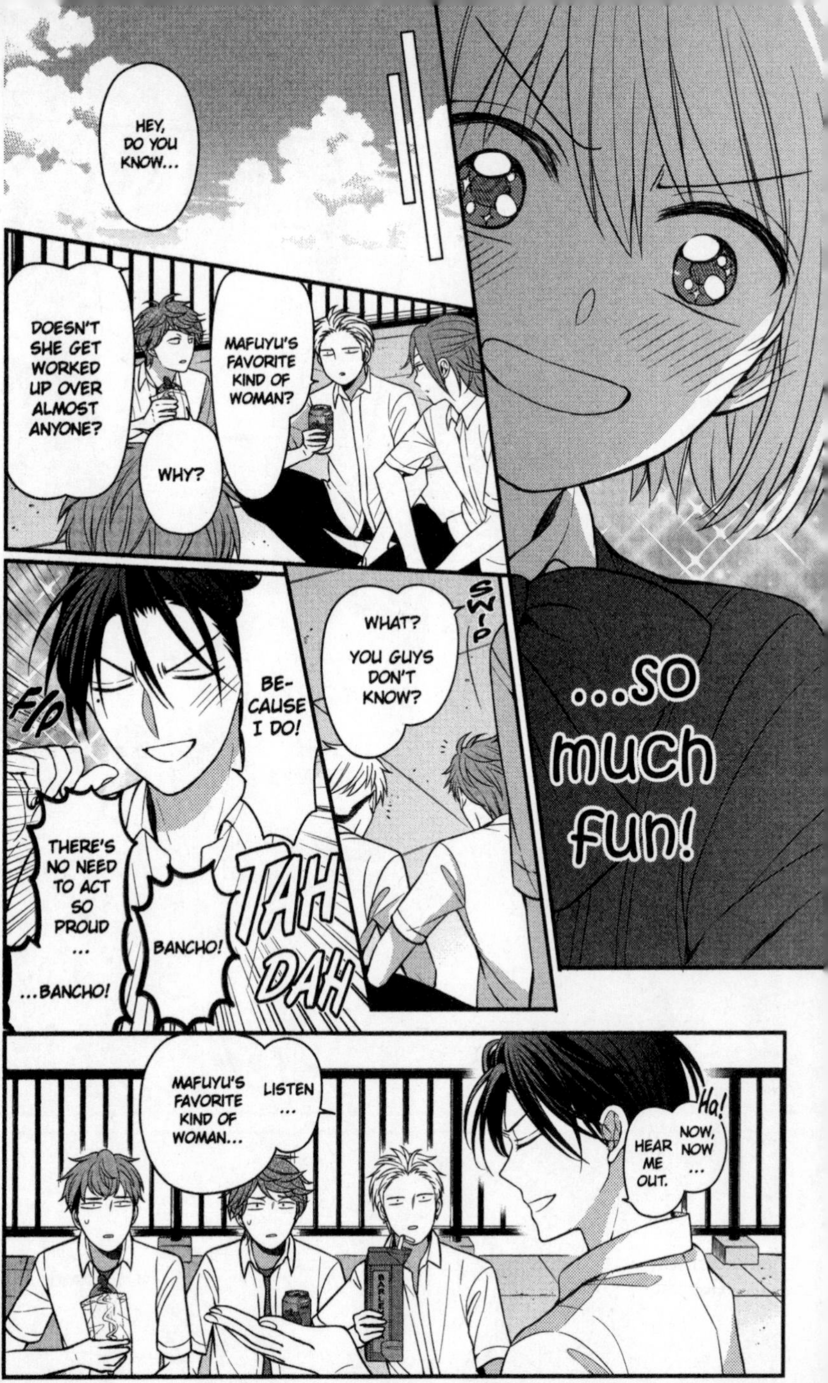
...so much fun!
HEY, DO YOU KNOW...
MAFUYU'S FAVORITE KIND OF WOMAN?
DOESN'T SHE GET WORKED UP OVER ALMOST ANYONE?
WHY?
SWIP
WHAT? YOU GUYS DON'T KNOW?
BE-CAUSE I DO!
FLIP
TAH DAH
BANCHO!
THERE'S NO NEED TO ACT SO PROUD ...
...BANCHO!
Ha!
NOW, NOW ...
HEAR ME OUT.
LISTEN ...
MAFUYU'S FAVORITE KIND OF WOMAN...

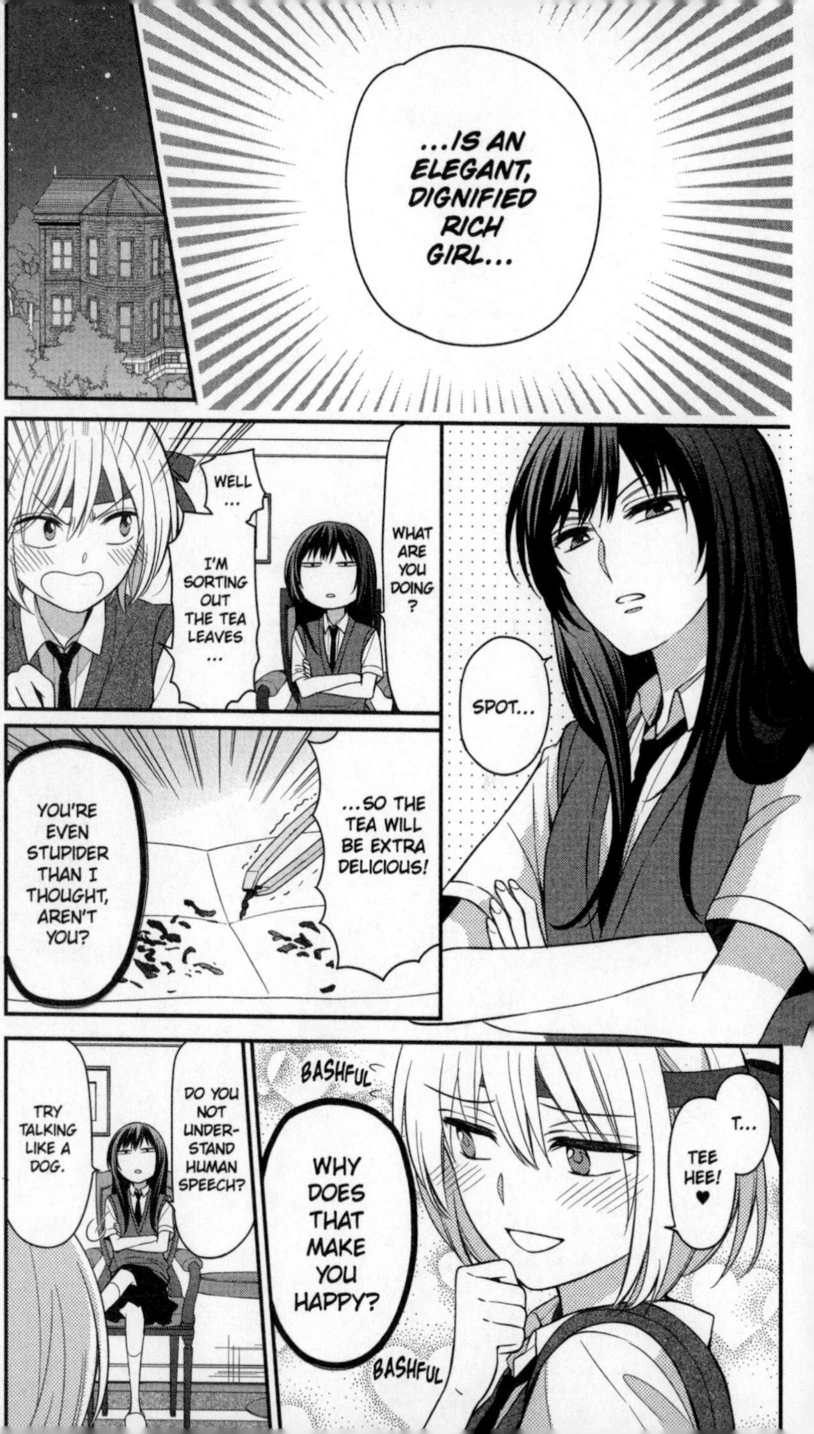
...IS AN ELEGANT, DIGNIFIED RICH GIRL...
SPOT...
WHAT ARE YOU DOING?
WELL...
I'M SORTING OUT THE TEA LEAVES...
...SO THE TEA WILL BE EXTRA DELICIOUS!
YOU'RE EVEN STUPIDER THAN I THOUGHT, AREN'T YOU?
T... TEE HEE! ♥
BASHFUL
WHY DOES THAT MAKE YOU HAPPY?
BASHFUL
DO YOU NOT UNDERSTAND HUMAN SPEECH?
TRY TALKING LIKE A DOG.

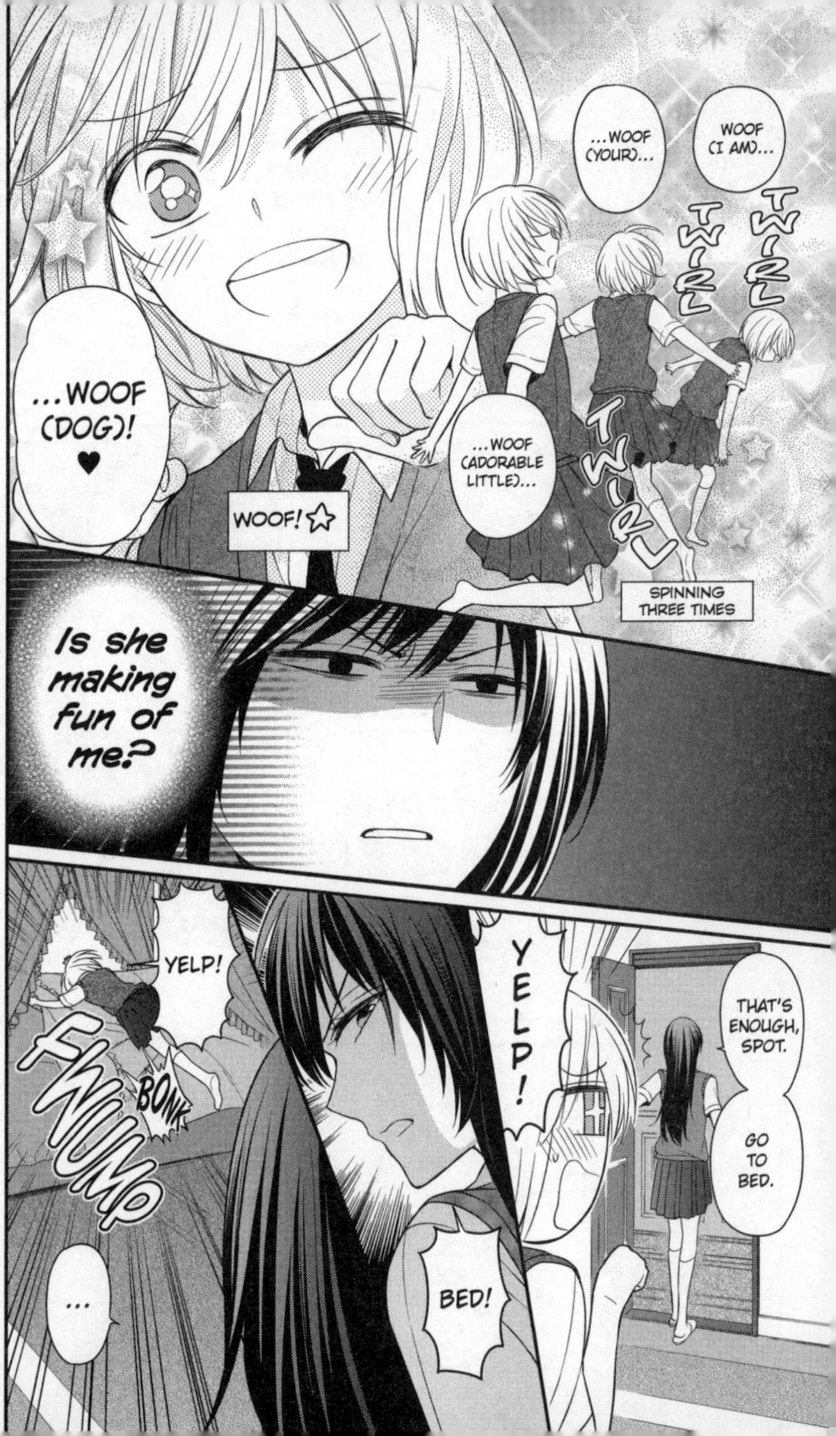
WOOF (I AM)...
...WOOF (YOUR)...
TWIRL
TWIRL
...WOOF (ADORABLE LITTLE)...
TWIRL
SPINNING THREE TIMES
WOOF! ☆
...WOOF (DOG)! ♥
Is she making fun of me?
THAT'S ENOUGH, SPOT.
GO TO BED.
YELP!
BED!
YELP!
BONK
FWUMP
...

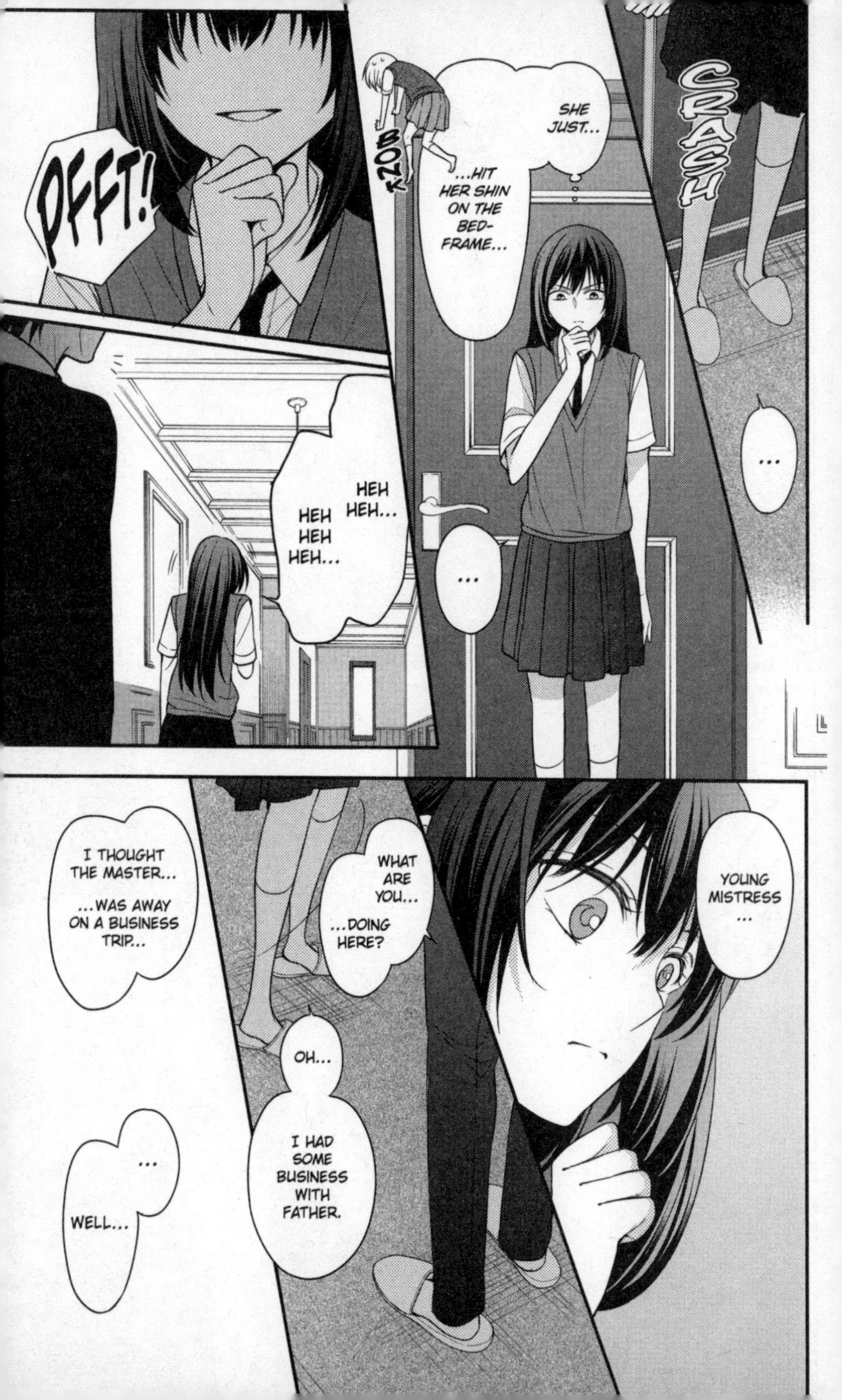
CRASH
...
BONK
SHE JUST...
...HIT HER SHIN ON THE BED-FRAME...
...
PFFT!
HEH HEH...
HEH HEH HEH...
YOUNG MISTRESS...
WHAT ARE YOU...
...DOING HERE?
OH...
I HAD SOME BUSINESS WITH FATHER.
I THOUGHT THE MASTER...
...WAS AWAY ON A BUSINESS TRIP...
...
WELL...

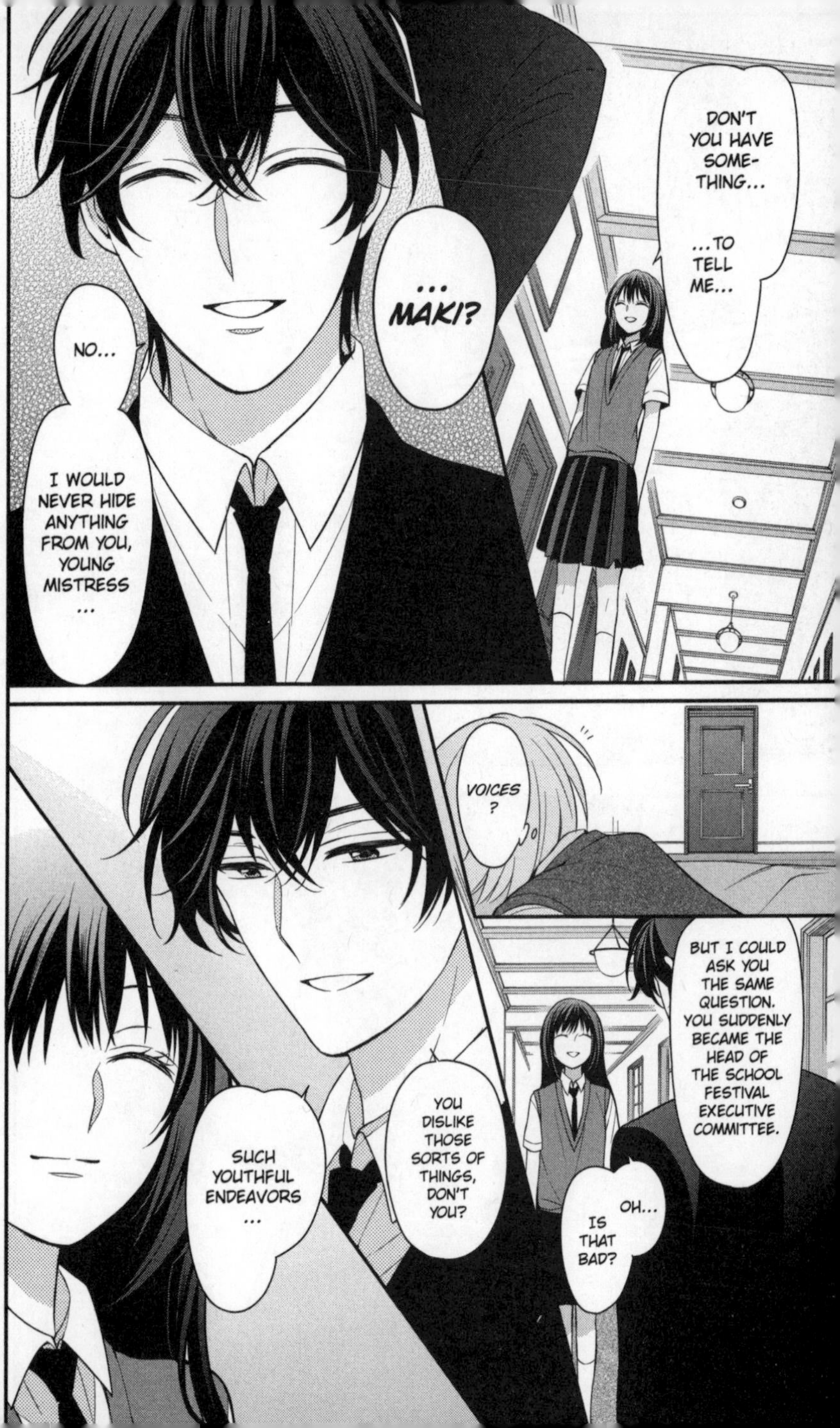
DON'T YOU HAVE SOMETHING...
...TO TELL ME...
...MAKI?
NO...
I WOULD NEVER HIDE ANYTHING FROM YOU, YOUNG MISTRESS...
VOICES?
BUT I COULD ASK YOU THE SAME QUESTION. YOU SUDDENLY BECAME THE HEAD OF THE SCHOOL FESTIVAL EXECUTIVE COMMITTEE.
YOU DISLIKE THOSE SORTS OF THINGS, DON'T YOU?
SUCH YOUTHFUL ENDEAVORS...
OH... IS THAT BAD?

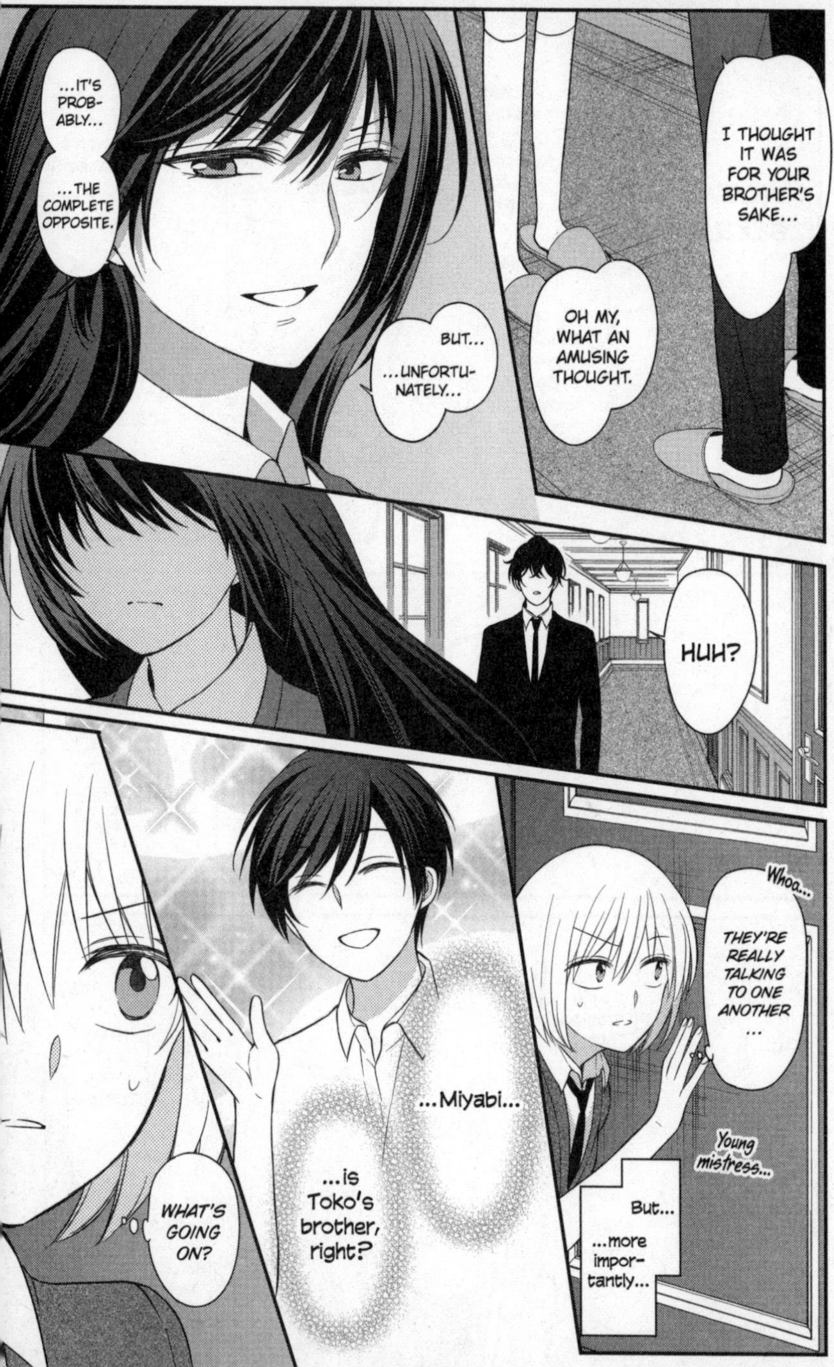
I THOUGHT IT WAS FOR YOUR BROTHER'S SAKE...
OH MY, WHAT AN AMUSING THOUGHT.
BUT... ...UNFORTUNATELY...
...IT'S PROBABLY...
...THE COMPLETE OPPOSITE.
HUH?
Whoa...
THEY'RE REALLY TALKING TO ONE ANOTHER...
Young mistress...
But... ...more importantly...
...Miyabi...
...is Toko's brother, right?
WHAT'S GOING ON?

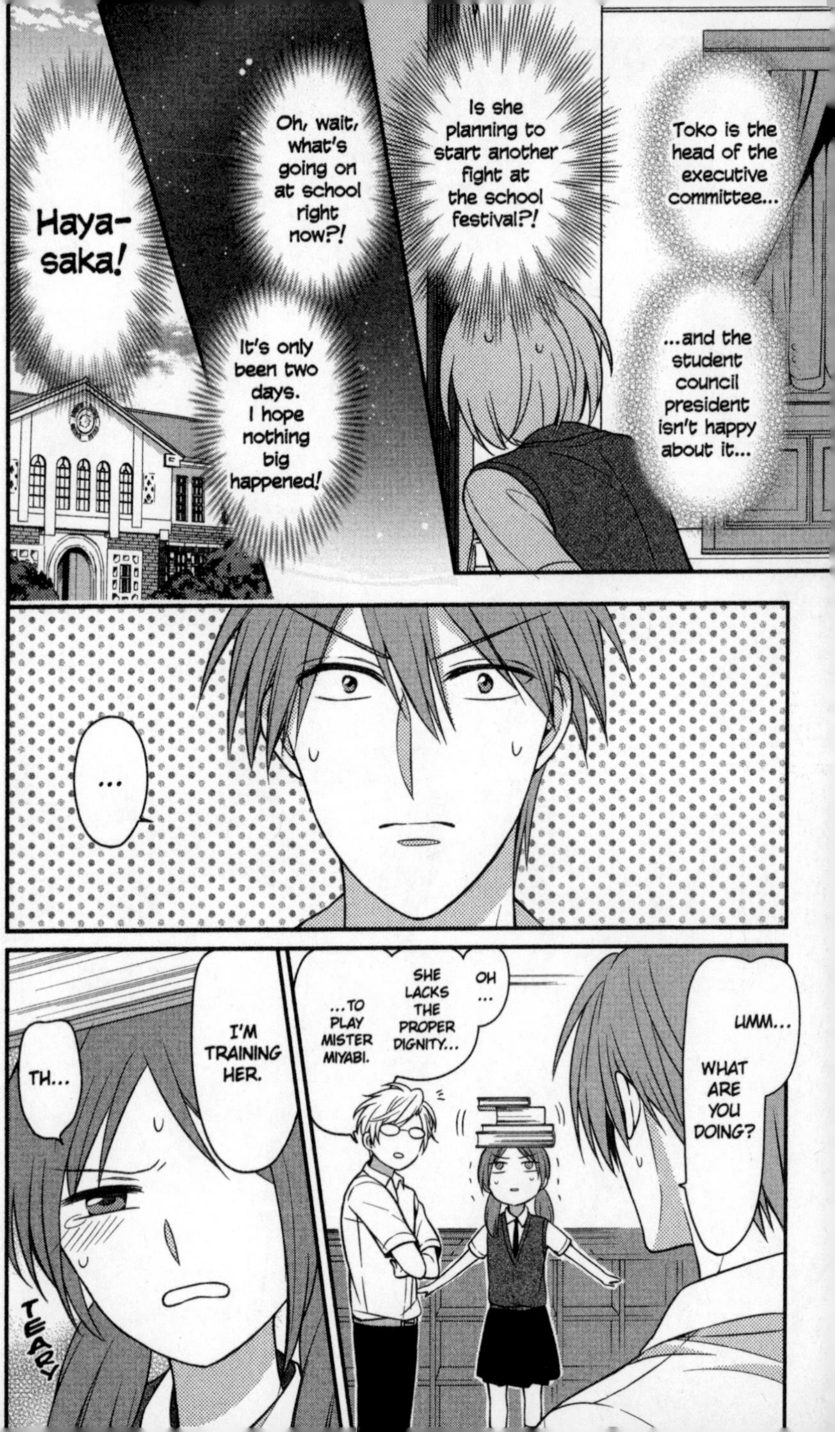
Toko is the head of the executive committee...
...and the student council president isn't happy about it...
Is she planning to start another fight at the school festival?!
Oh, wait, what's going on at school right now?!
Haya-saka!
It's only been two days. I hope nothing big happened!
...
UMM... WHAT ARE YOU DOING?
OH...
SHE LACKS THE PROPER DIGNITY...
...TO PLAY MISTER MIYABI.
I'M TRAINING HER.
TH...
TEARY

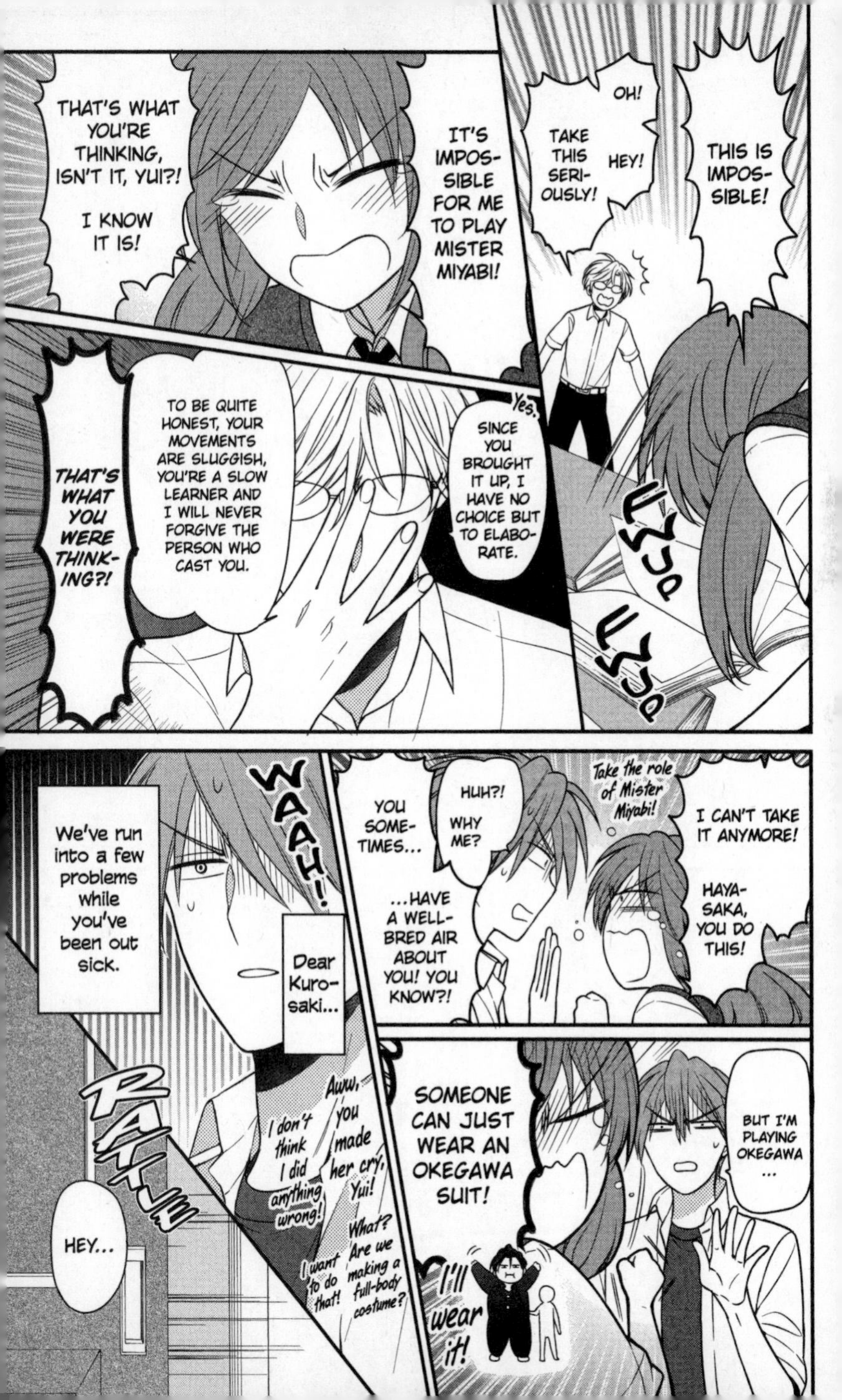
THIS IS IMPOSSIBLE!
OH!
HEY!
TAKE THIS SERIOUSLY!
FWUP
FWUP
IT'S IMPOSSIBLE FOR ME TO PLAY MISTER MIYABI!
THAT'S WHAT YOU'RE THINKING, ISN'T IT, YUI?!
I KNOW IT IS!
Yes.
SINCE YOU BROUGHT IT UP, I HAVE NO CHOICE BUT TO ELABORATE.
TO BE QUITE HONEST, YOUR MOVEMENTS ARE SLUGGISH, YOU'RE A SLOW LEARNER AND I WILL NEVER FORGIVE THE PERSON WHO CAST YOU.
THAT'S WHAT YOU WERE THINKING?!
I CAN'T TAKE IT ANYMORE!
HAYASAKA, YOU DO THIS!
Take the role of Mister Miyabi!
HUH?!
WHY ME?
YOU SOMETIMES...
...HAVE A WELL-BRED AIR ABOUT YOU! YOU KNOW?!
BUT I'M PLAYING OKEGAWA...
SOMEONE CAN JUST WEAR AN OKEGAWA SUIT!
I'll wear it!
What? Are we making a full-body costume?
I want to do that!
Aww, you made her cry, Yui!
I don't think I did anything wrong!
WAAH!
Dear Kurosaki...
We've run into a few problems while you've been out sick.
RATTLE
HEY...

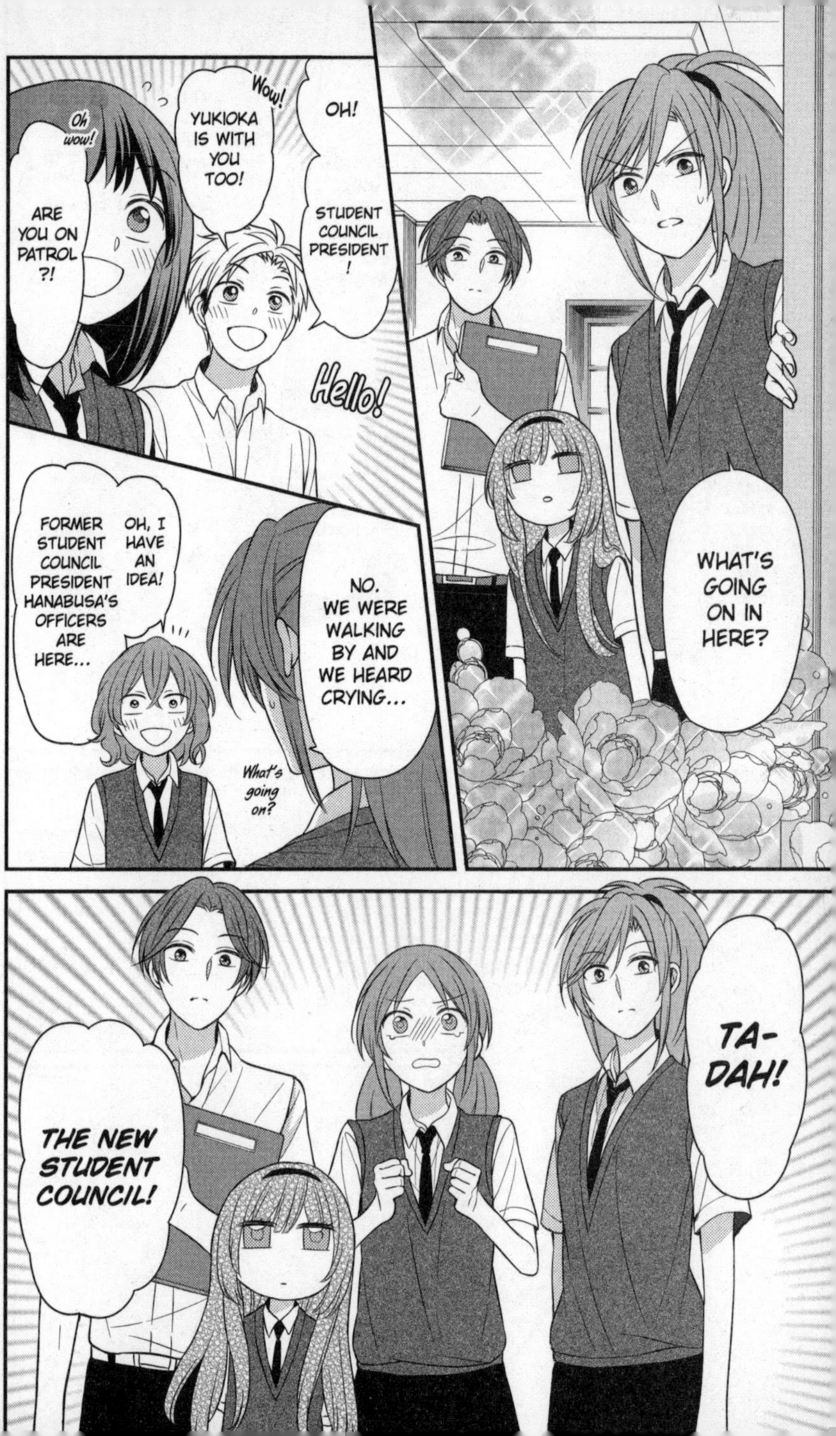
WHAT'S GOING ON IN HERE?
OH!
STUDENT COUNCIL PRESIDENT!
Wow!
YUKIOKA IS WITH YOU TOO!
Oh wow!
ARE YOU ON PATROL?!
Hello!
NO. WE WERE WALKING BY AND WE HEARD CRYING...
OH, I HAVE AN IDEA!
FORMER STUDENT COUNCIL PRESIDENT HANABUSA'S OFFICERS ARE HERE...
What's going on?
TA-DAH!
THE NEW STUDENT COUNCIL!

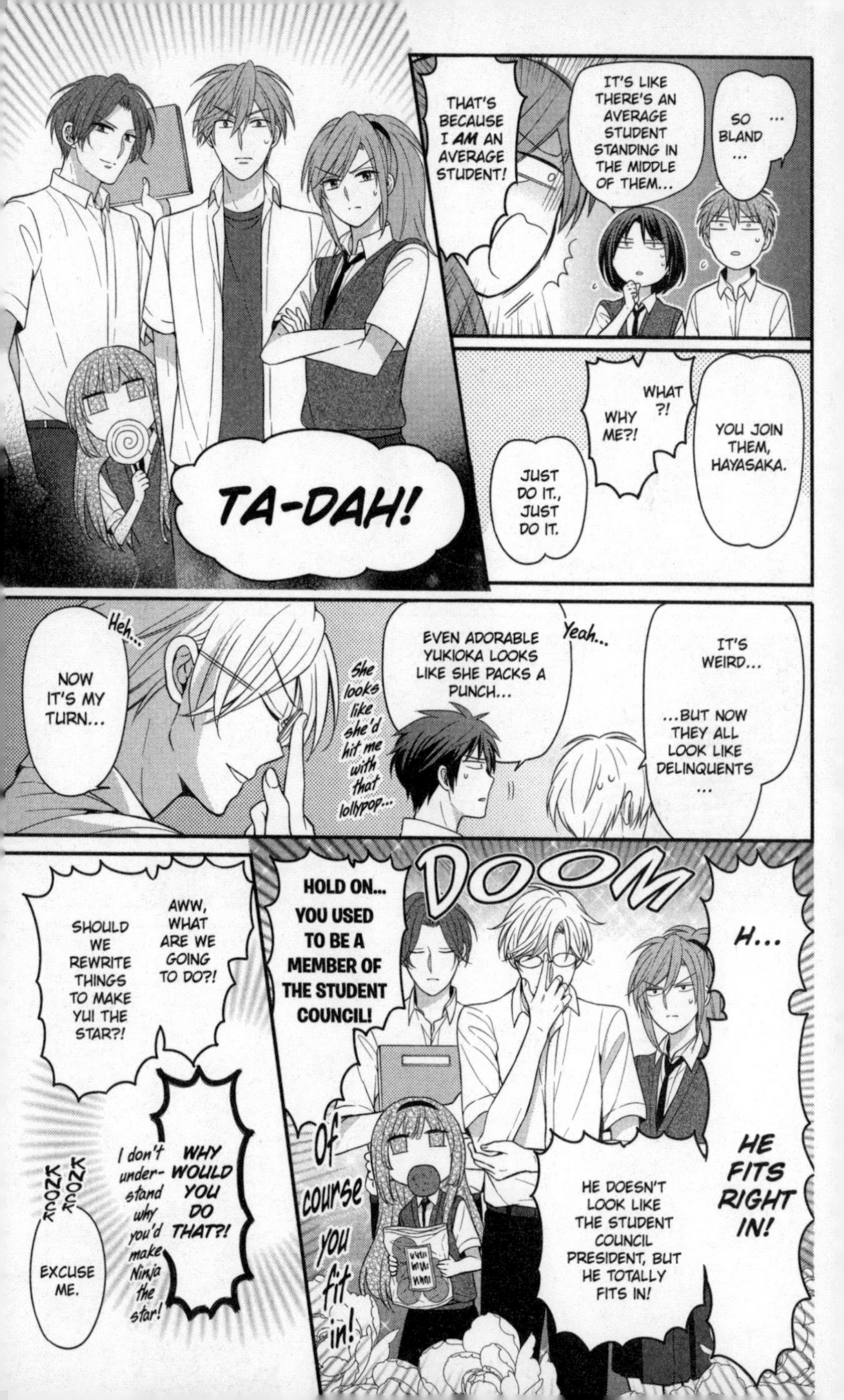
SO BLAND ... ...
IT'S LIKE THERE'S AN AVERAGE STUDENT STANDING IN THE MIDDLE OF THEM...
THAT'S BECAUSE I **AM** AN AVERAGE STUDENT!
YOU JOIN THEM, HAYASAKA.
WHAT ?!
WHY ME?!
JUST DO IT., JUST DO IT.
TA-DAH!
IT'S WEIRD...
...BUT NOW THEY ALL LOOK LIKE DELINQUENTS ...
Yeah...
EVEN ADORABLE YUKIOKA LOOKS LIKE SHE PACKS A PUNCH...
She looks like she'd hit me with that lollypop...
Heh...
NOW IT'S MY TURN...
H...
HE FITS RIGHT IN!
DOOM
HOLD ON... YOU USED TO BE A MEMBER OF THE STUDENT COUNCIL!
HE DOESN'T LOOK LIKE THE STUDENT COUNCIL PRESIDENT, BUT HE TOTALLY FITS IN!
Of course you fit in!
AWW, WHAT ARE WE GOING TO DO?!
SHOULD WE REWRITE THINGS TO MAKE YUI THE STAR?!
WHY WOULD YOU DO THAT?!
I don't under-stand why you'd make Ninja the star!
KNOCK KNOCK
EXCUSE ME.

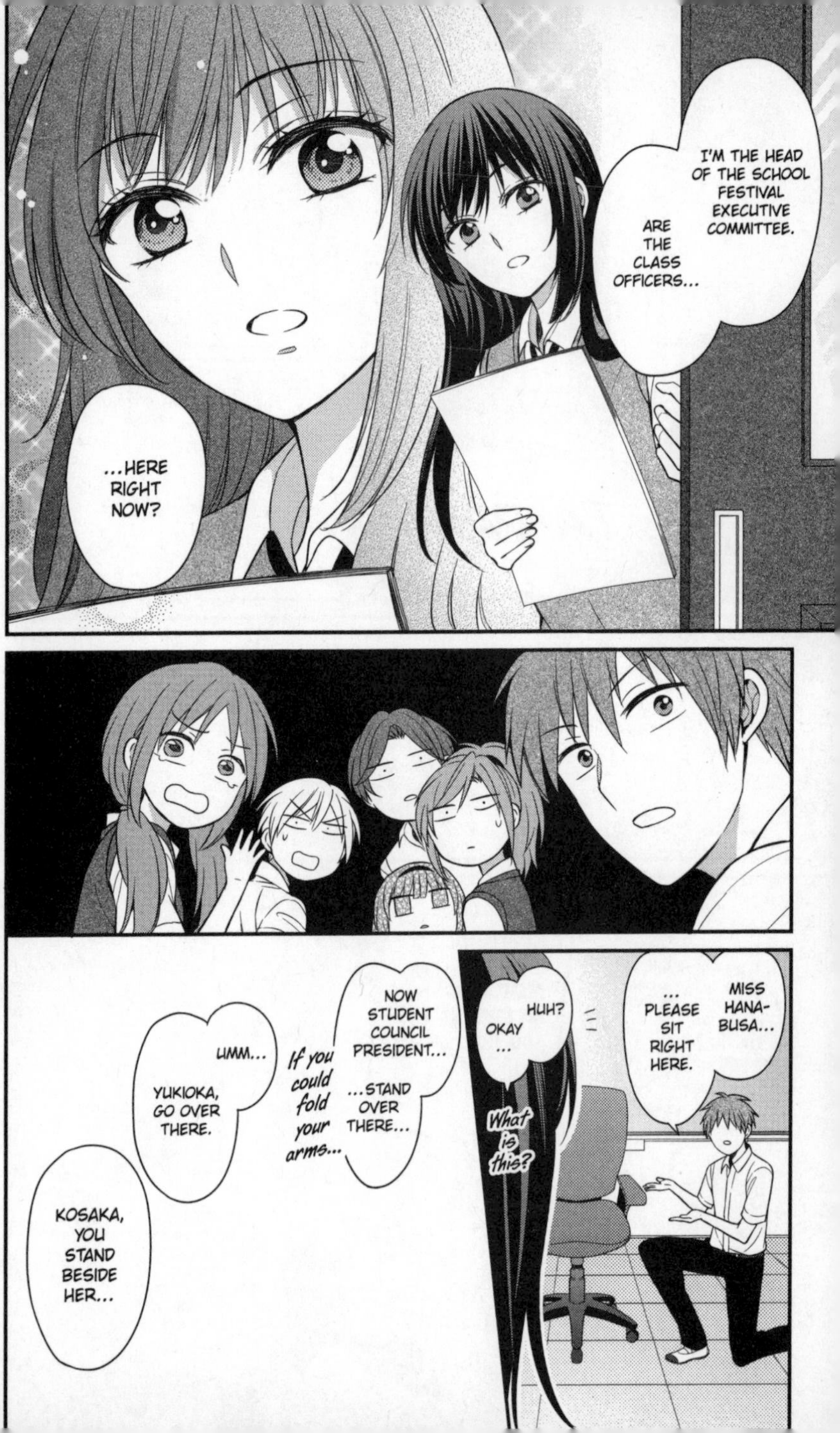
I'M THE HEAD OF THE SCHOOL FESTIVAL EXECUTIVE COMMITTEE.
ARE THE CLASS OFFICERS...
...HERE RIGHT NOW?
MISS HANA-BUSA...
...PLEASE SIT RIGHT HERE.
HUH?
OKAY...
What is this?
NOW STUDENT COUNCIL PRESIDENT...
...STAND OVER THERE...
If you could fold your arms...
UMM...
YUKIOKA, GO OVER THERE.
KOSAKA, YOU STAND BESIDE HER...

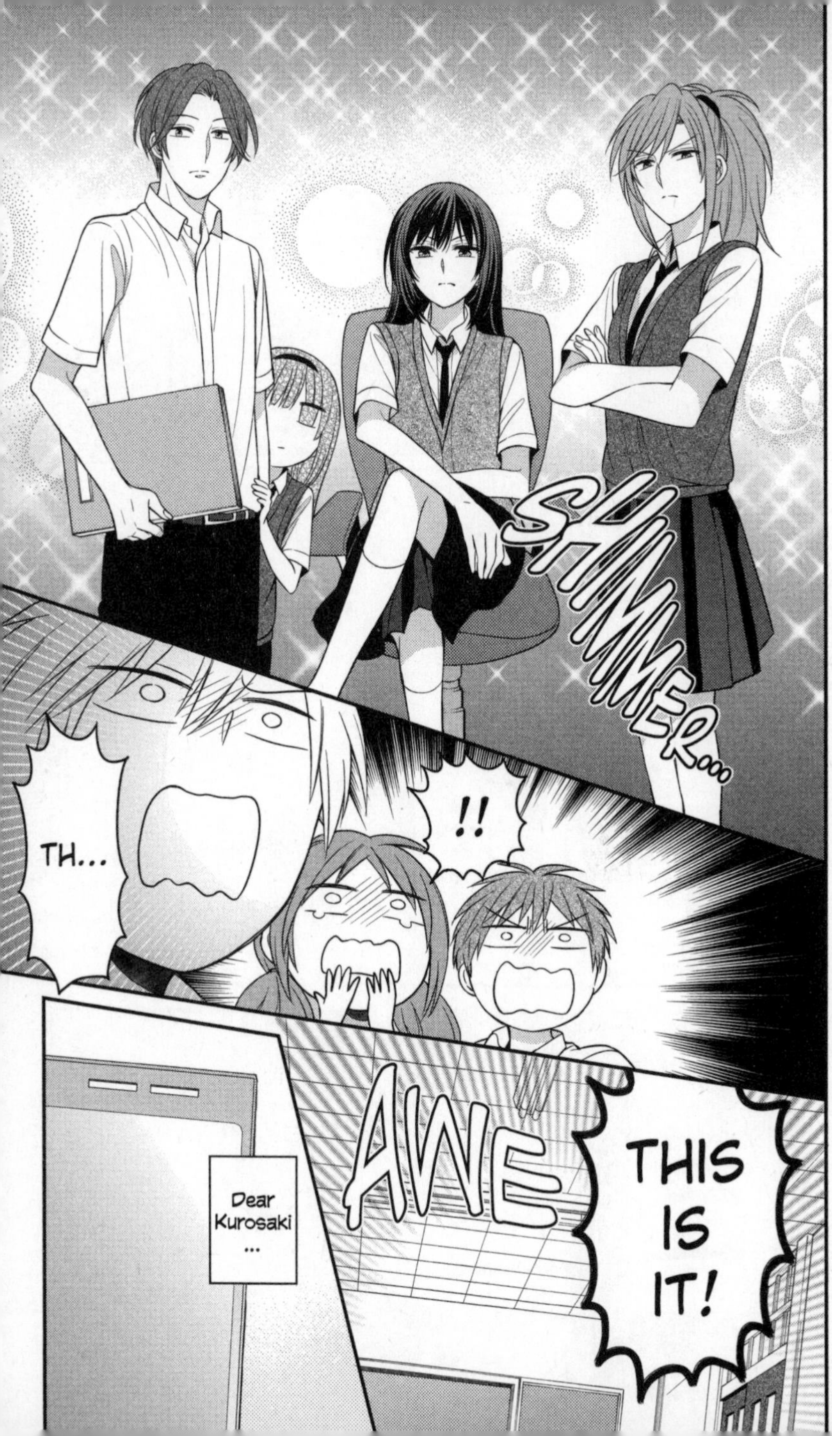
SHIMMER...
!!
TH...
THIS IS IT!
AWE
Dear Kurosaki ...

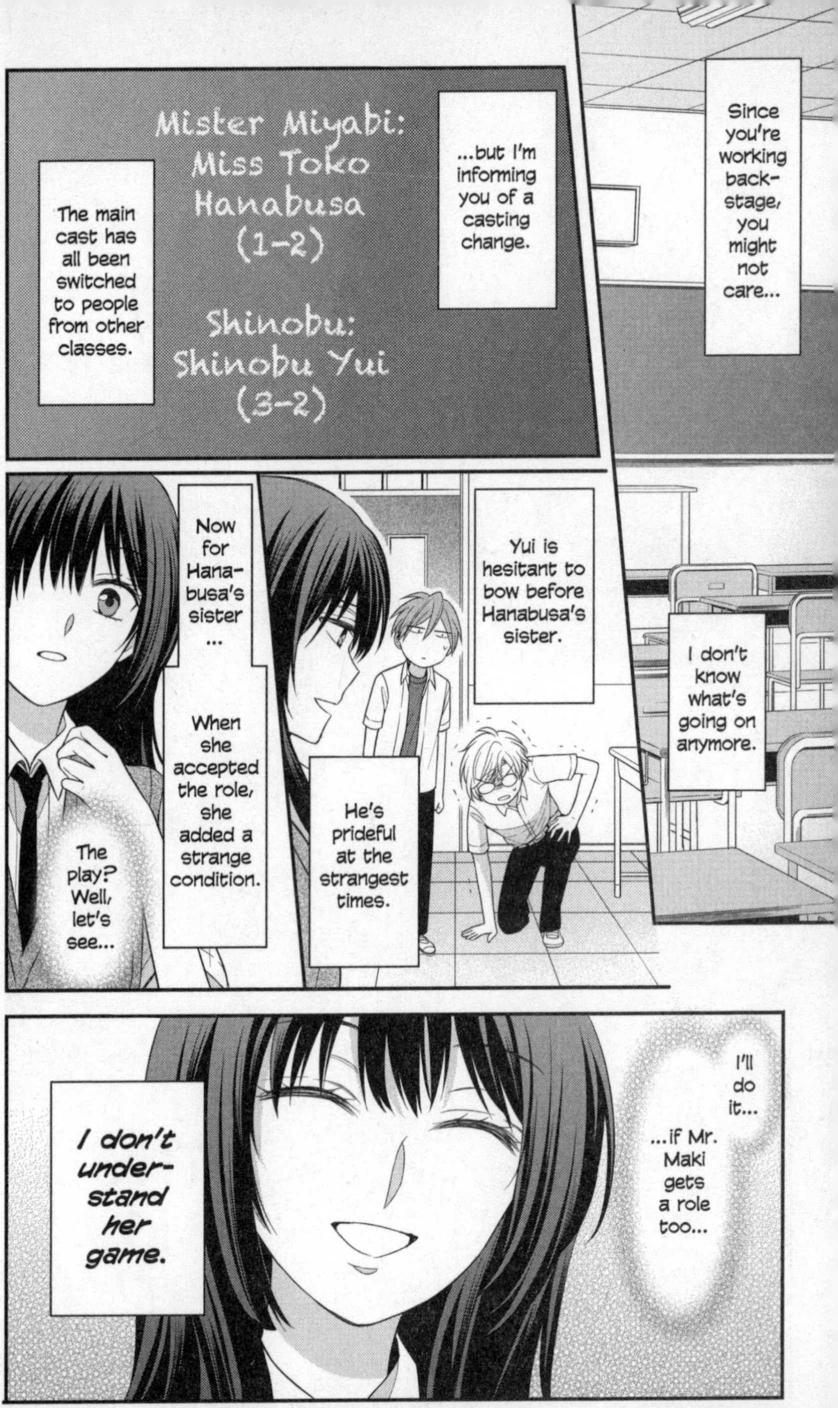
Since you're working back-stage, you might not care...
...but I'm informing you of a casting change.
Mister Miyabi: Miss Toko Hanabusa (1-2)
Shinobu: Shinobu Yui (3-2)
The main cast has all been switched to people from other classes.
Yui is hesitant to bow before Hanabusa's sister.
I don't know what's going on anymore.
He's prideful at the strangest times.
Now for Hana-busa's sister...
When she accepted the role, she added a strange condition.
The play? Well, let's see...
I'll do it...
...if Mr. Maki gets a role too...
I don't under-stand her game.

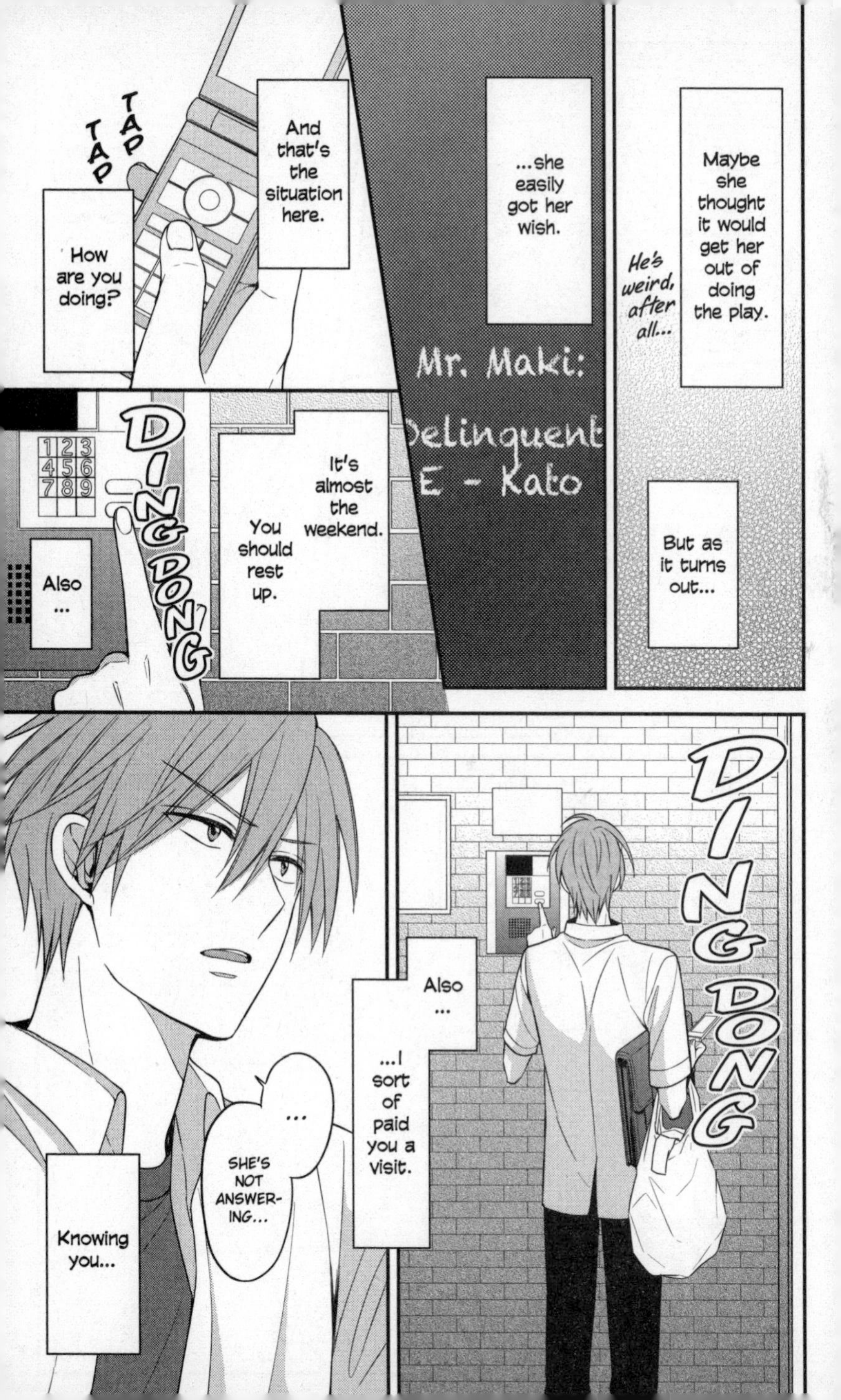
Maybe she thought it would get her out of doing the play.
He's weird, after all...
But as it turns out...
...she easily got her wish.
Mr. Maki: Delinquent E - Kato
And that's the situation here.
TAP TAP
How are you doing?
It's almost the weekend.
You should rest up.
DING DONG
Also ...
DING DONG
Also ...
...I sort of paid you a visit.
...
SHE'S NOT ANSWERING...
Knowing you...

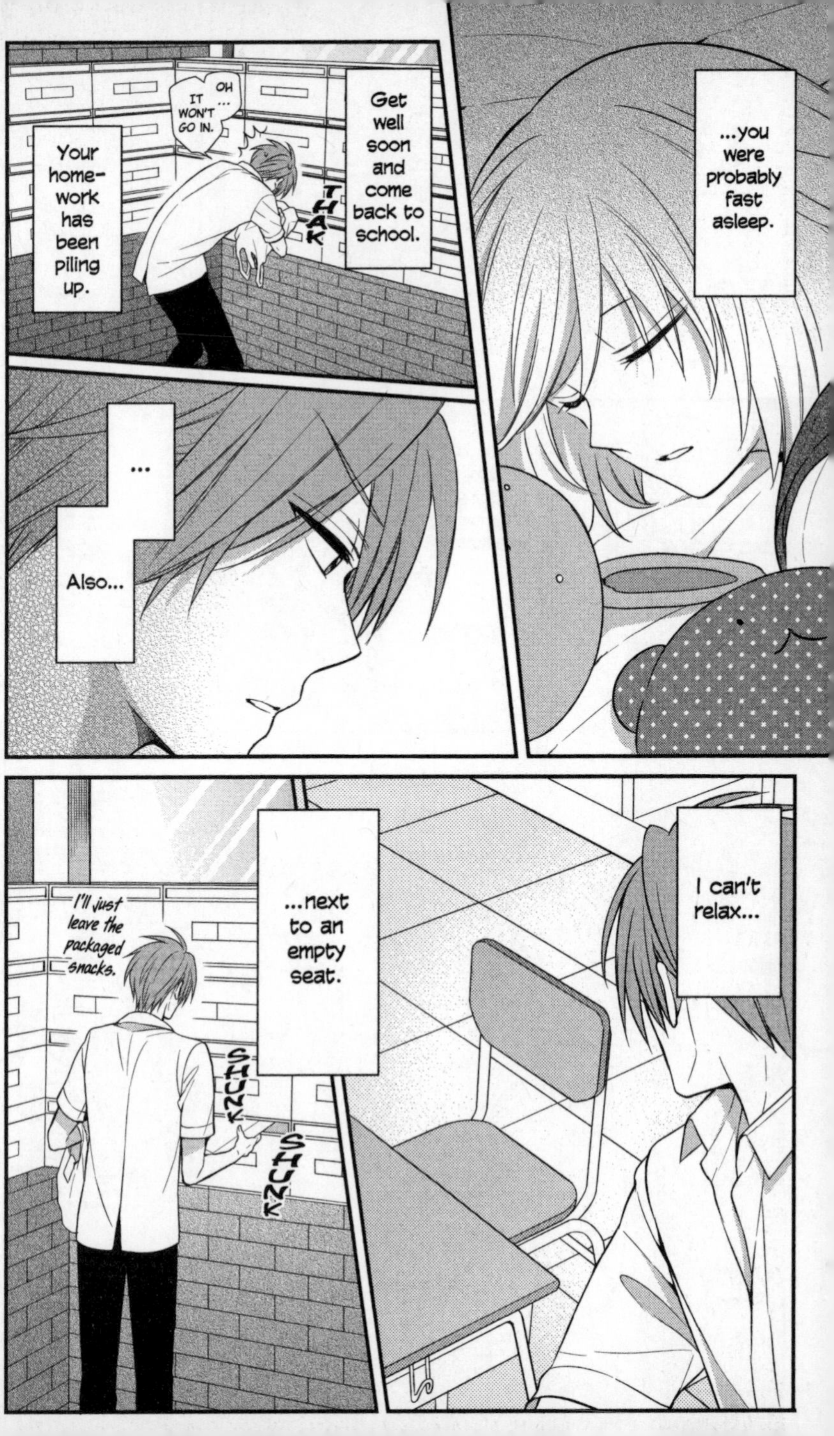
...you were probably fast asleep.
Get well soon and come back to school.
OH... IT WON'T GO IN.
THAK
Your home-work has been piling up.
...
Also...
I can't relax...
...next to an empty seat.
I'll just leave the packaged snacks.
SHUNK
SHUNK

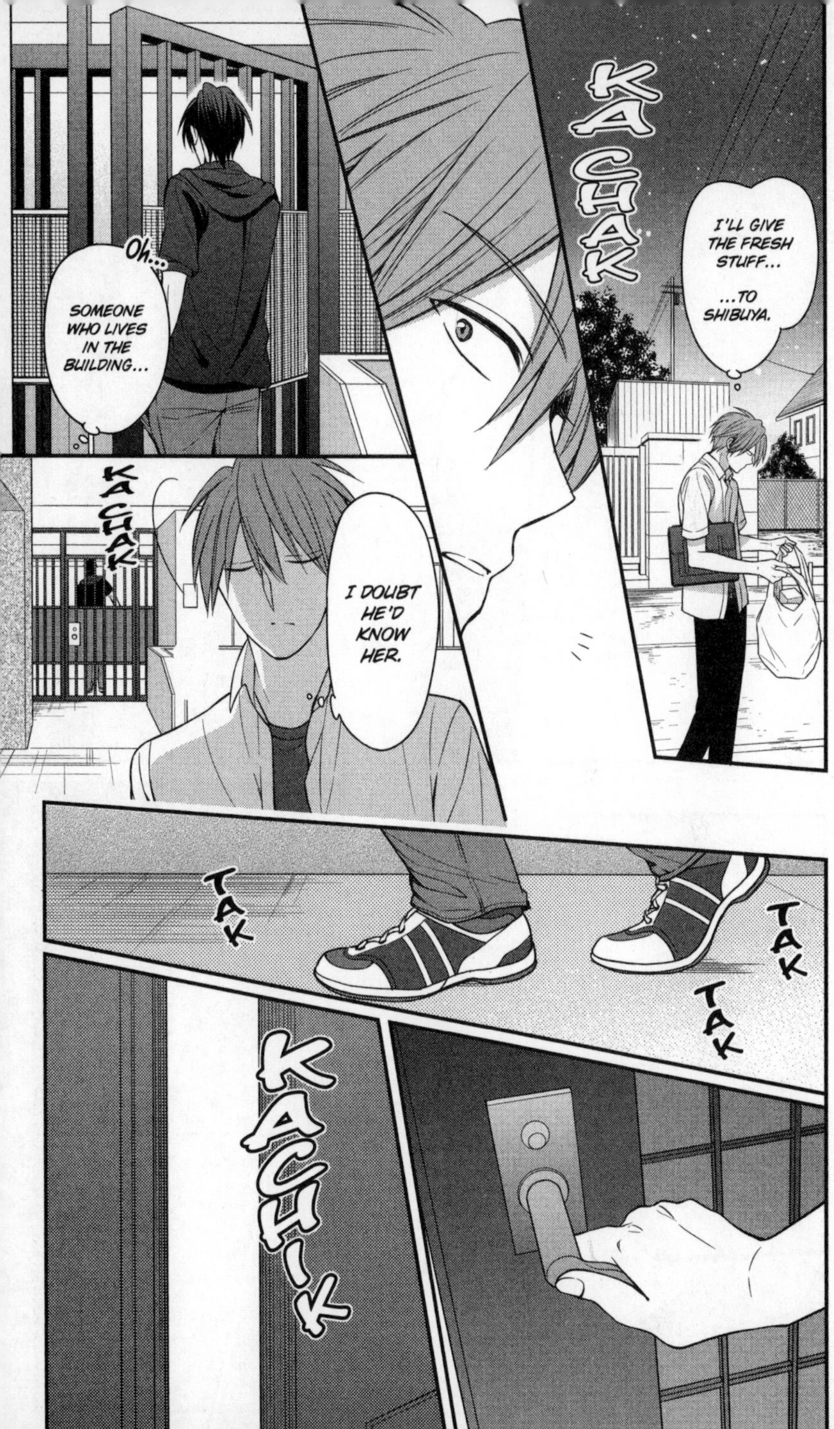
KA CHAK
I'LL GIVE THE FRESH STUFF...
...TO SHIBUYA.
Oh...
SOMEONE WHO LIVES IN THE BUILDING...
KA CHAK
I DOUBT HE'D KNOW HER.
TAK
TAK
TAK
KACHIK

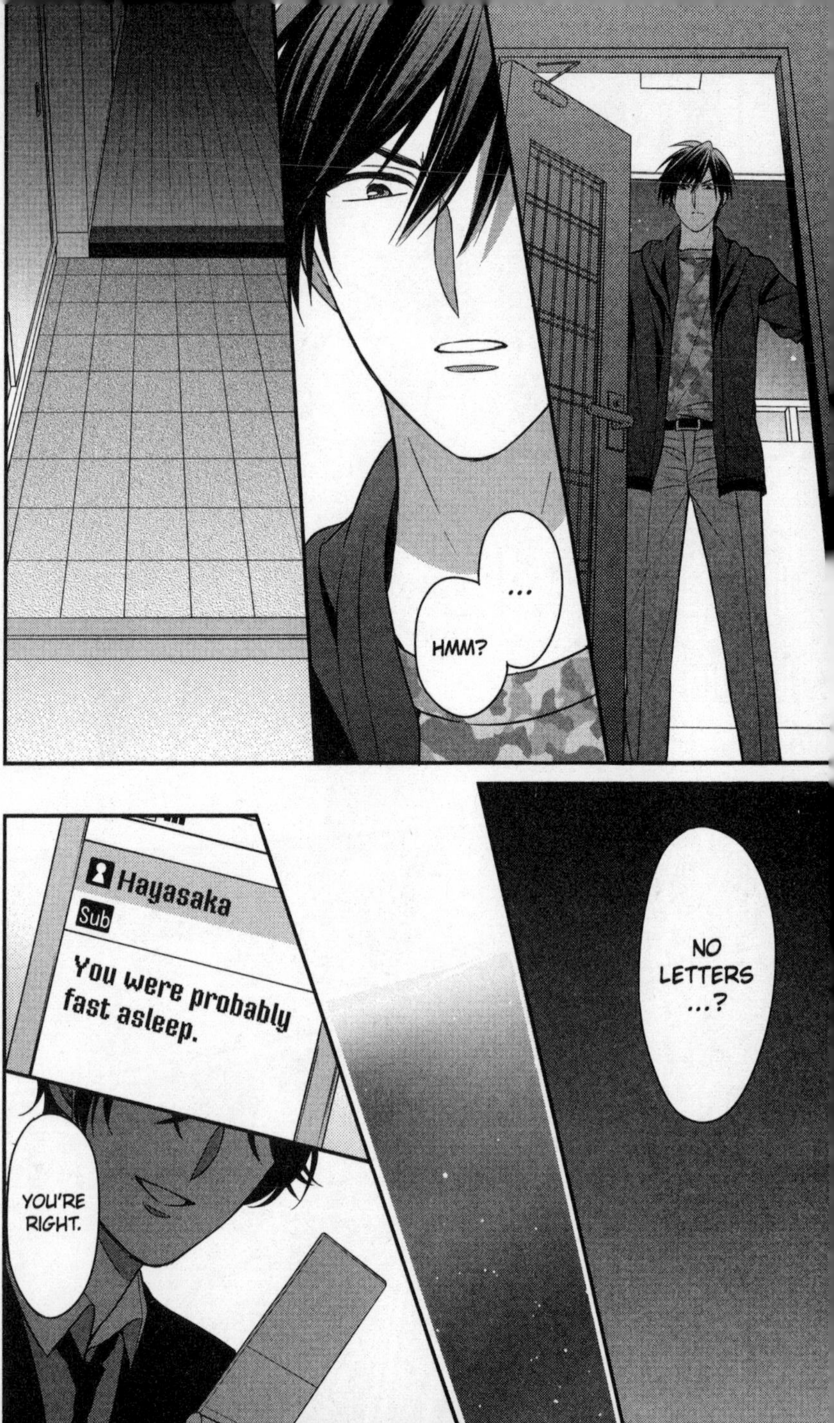
...
HMM?
NO LETTERS ...?
Hayasaka
Sub
You were probably fast asleep.
YOU'RE RIGHT.

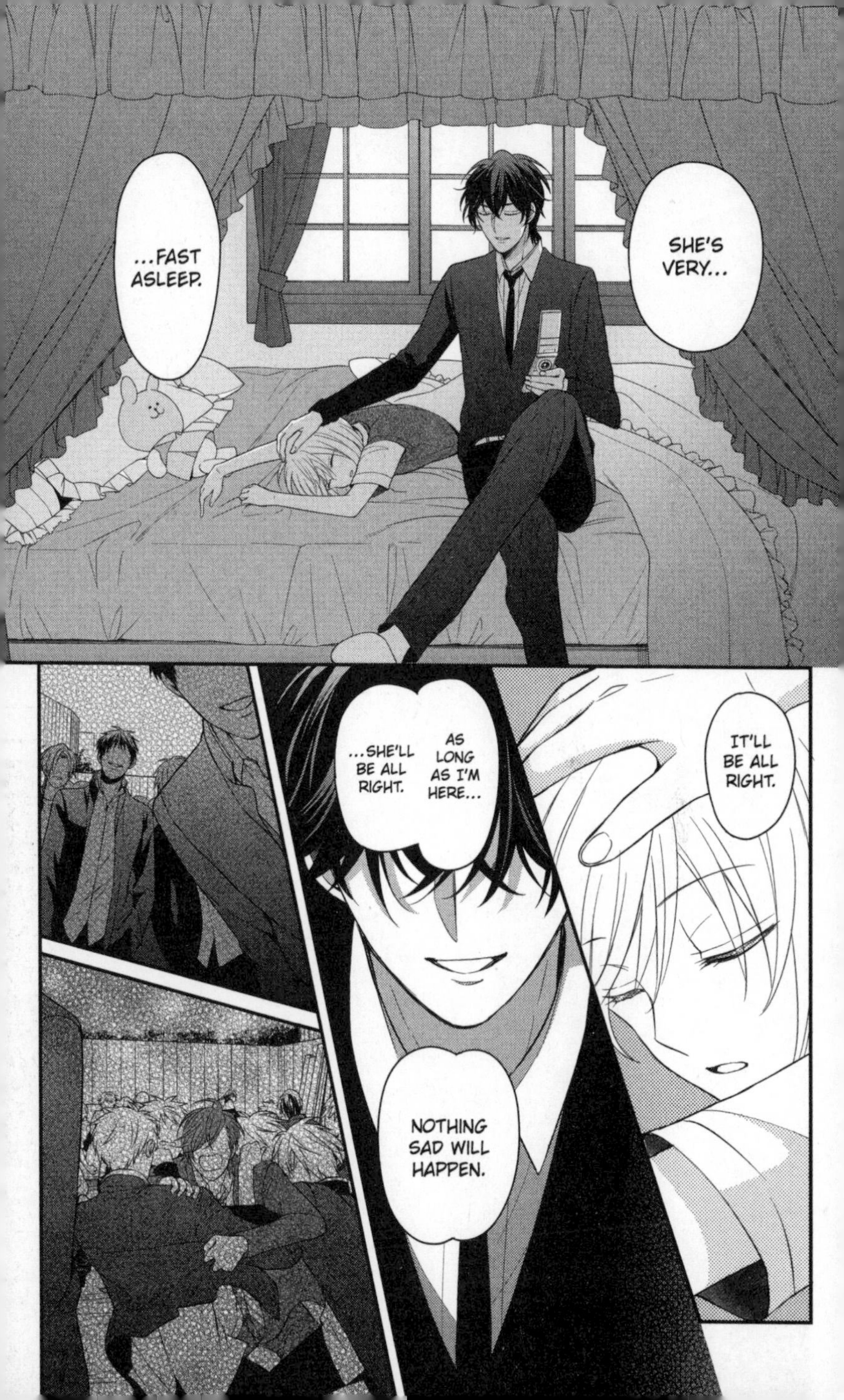
SHE'S VERY...
...FAST ASLEEP.
IT'LL BE ALL RIGHT.
AS LONG AS I'M HERE...
...SHE'LL BE ALL RIGHT.
NOTHING SAD WILL HAPPEN.

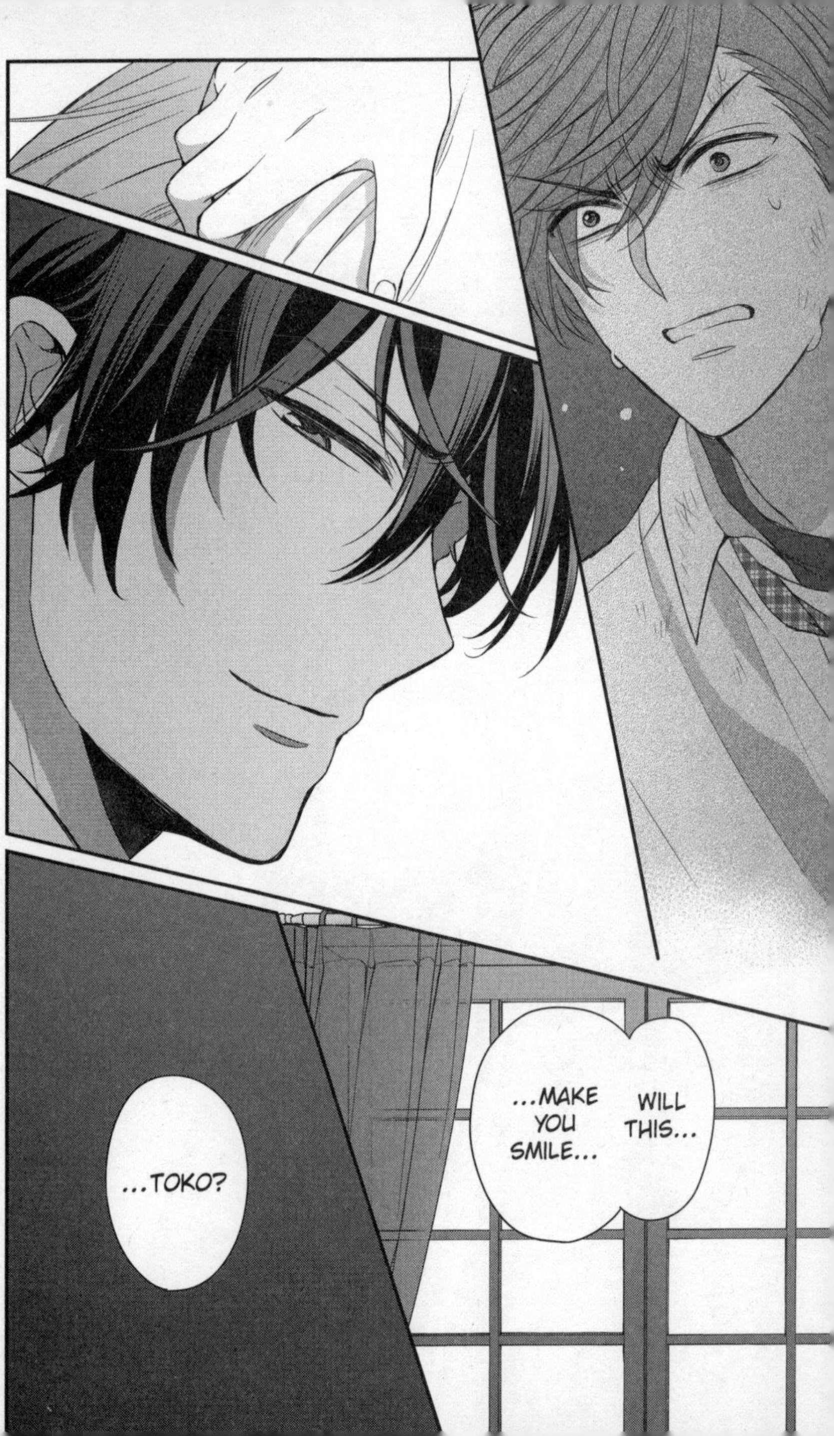
WILL THIS... ...MAKE YOU SMILE...
...TOKO?

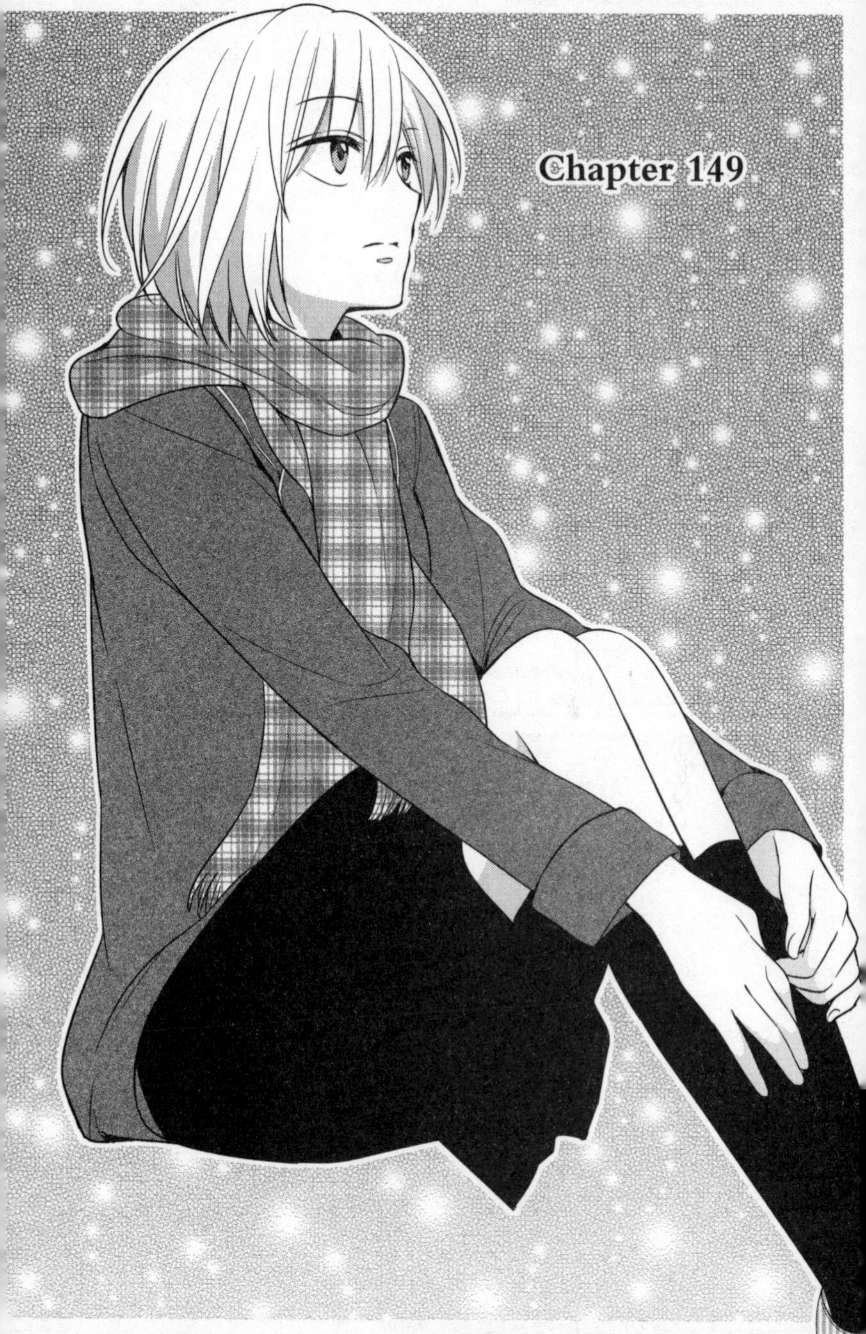
Chapter 149

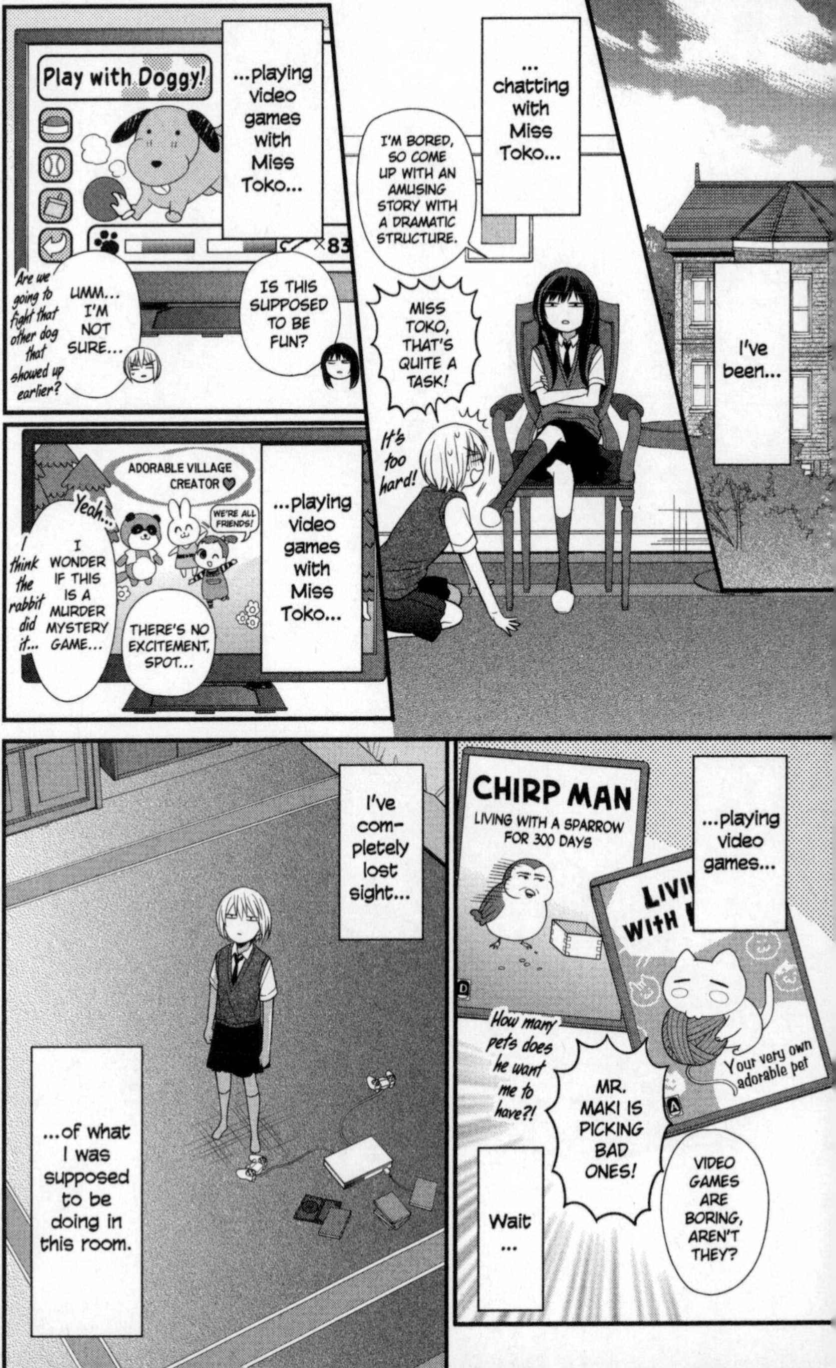
I've been...
...chatting with Miss Toko...
I'M BORED, SO COME UP WITH AN AMUSING STORY WITH A DRAMATIC STRUCTURE.
MISS TOKO, THAT'S QUITE A TASK!
It's too hard!
Play with Doggy!
×83
...playing video games with Miss Toko...
IS THIS SUPPOSED TO BE FUN?
UMM... I'M NOT SURE...
Are we going to fight that other dog that showed up earlier?
...playing video games with Miss Toko...
ADORABLE VILLAGE CREATOR
WE'RE ALL FRIENDS!
THERE'S NO EXCITEMENT, SPOT...
Yeah...
I WONDER IF THIS IS A MURDER MYSTERY GAME...
I think the rabbit did it...
...playing video games...
CHIRP MAN
LIVING WITH A SPARROW FOR 300 DAYS
Your very own adorable pet
VIDEO GAMES ARE BORING, AREN'T THEY?
MR. MAKI IS PICKING BAD ONES!
How many pets does he want me to have?!
Wait...
I've completely lost sight...
...of what I was supposed to be doing in this room.

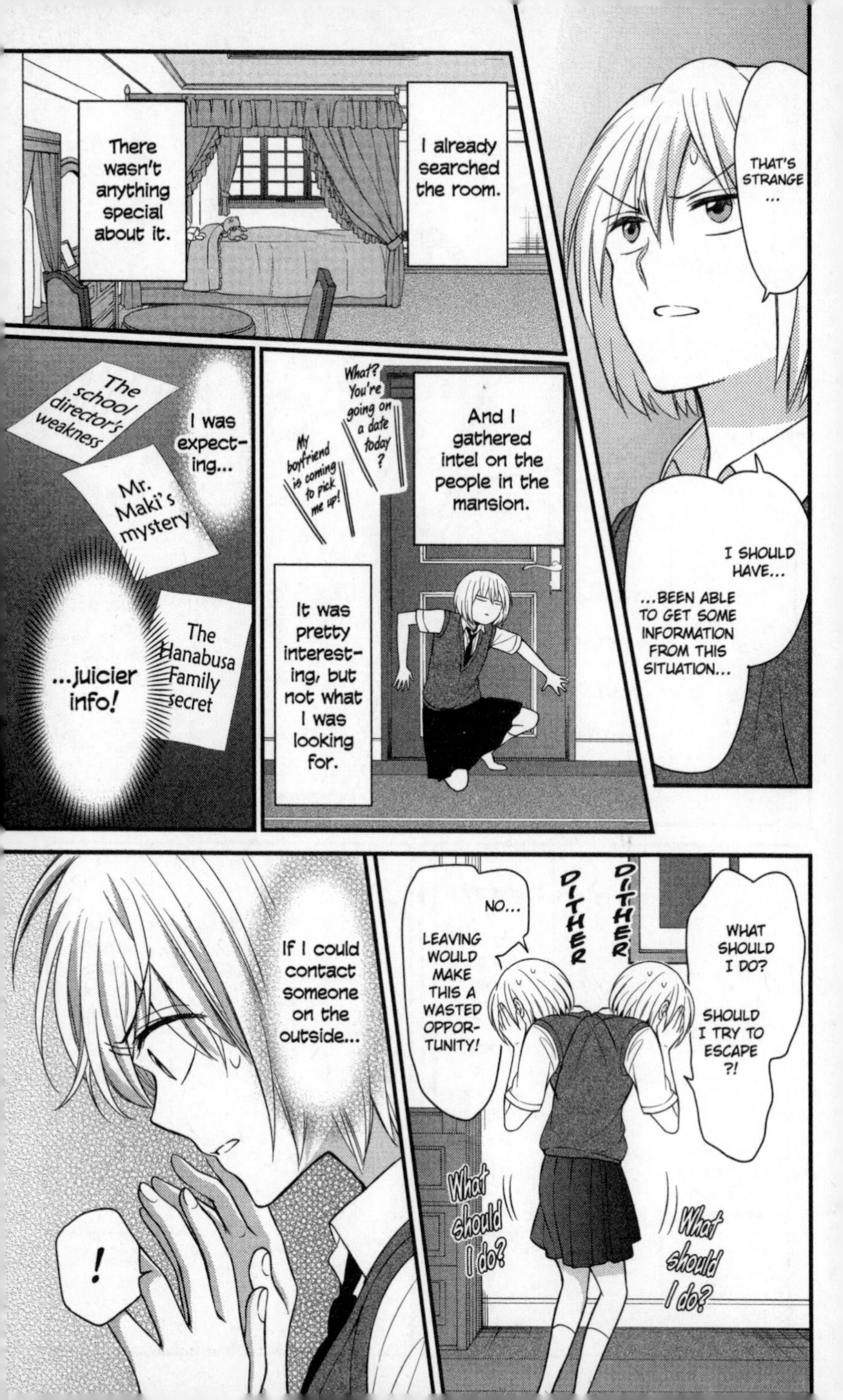

THAT'S STRANGE...
I SHOULD HAVE...
...BEEN ABLE TO GET SOME INFORMATION FROM THIS SITUATION...
I already searched the room.
There wasn't anything special about it.
And I gathered intel on the people in the mansion.
What? You're going on a date today?
My boyfriend is coming to pick me up!
It was pretty interest-ing, but not what I was looking for.
I was expect-ing...
The school director's weakness
Mr. Maki's mystery
The Hanabusa Family secret
...juicier info!
WHAT SHOULD I DO?
SHOULD I TRY TO ESCAPE?!
DITHER
DITHER
NO...
LEAVING WOULD MAKE THIS A WASTED OPPOR-TUNITY!
What should I do?
What should I do?
If I could contact someone on the outside...
!

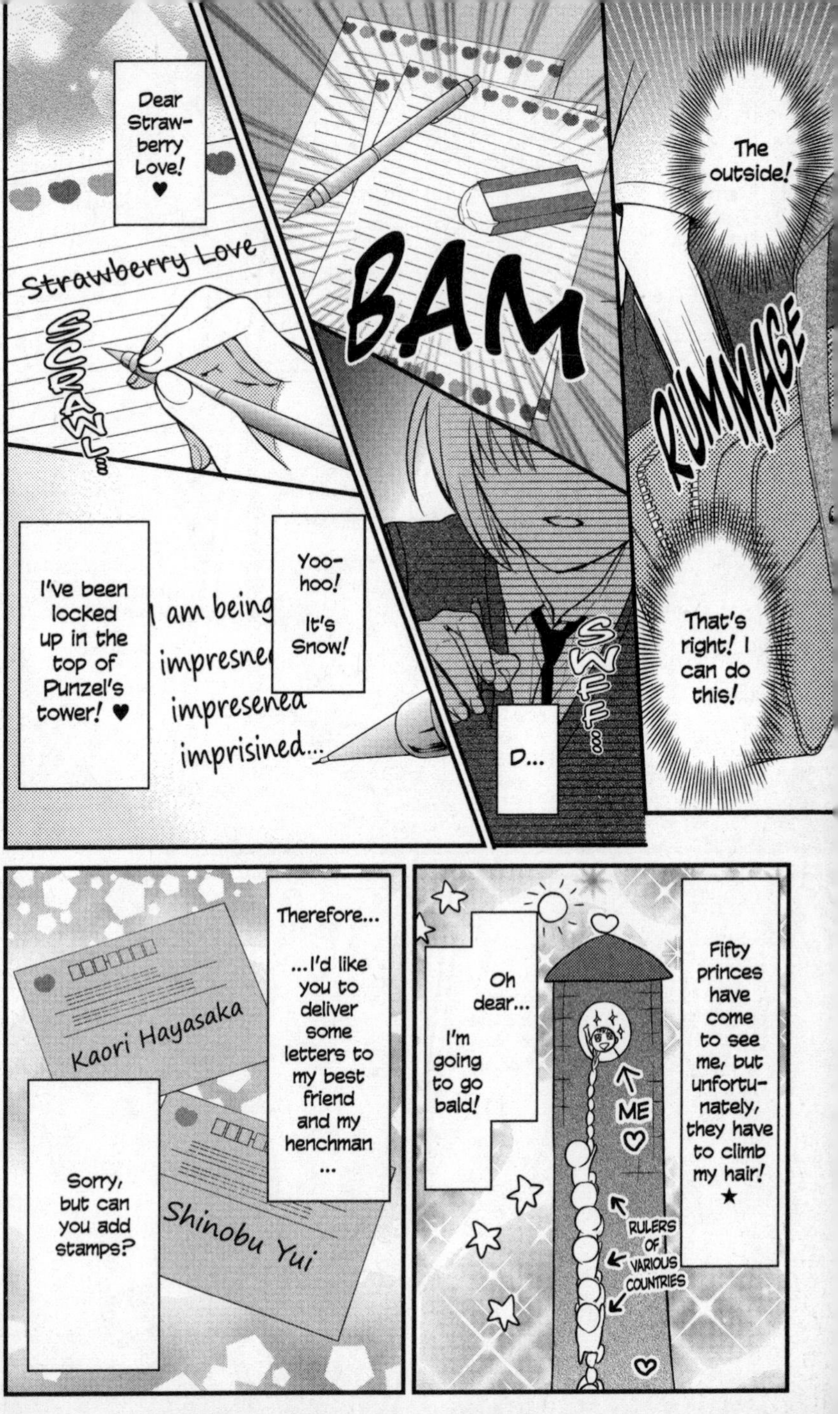
The outside!
RUMMAGE
That's right! I can do this!
BAM
SWFF...
D...
Dear Strawberry Love! ♥
Strawberry Love
SCRAWL
Yoo-hoo! It's Snow!
I've been locked up in the top of Punzel's tower! ♥
I am being impresned impresenea imprisined...
Fifty princes have come to see me, but unfortunately, they have to climb my hair! ★
Oh dear... I'm going to go bald!
ME ♡
RULERS OF VARIOUS COUNTRIES
Therefore... ...I'd like you to deliver some letters to my best friend and my henchman...
Kaori Hayasaka
Shinobu Yui
Sorry, but can you add stamps?

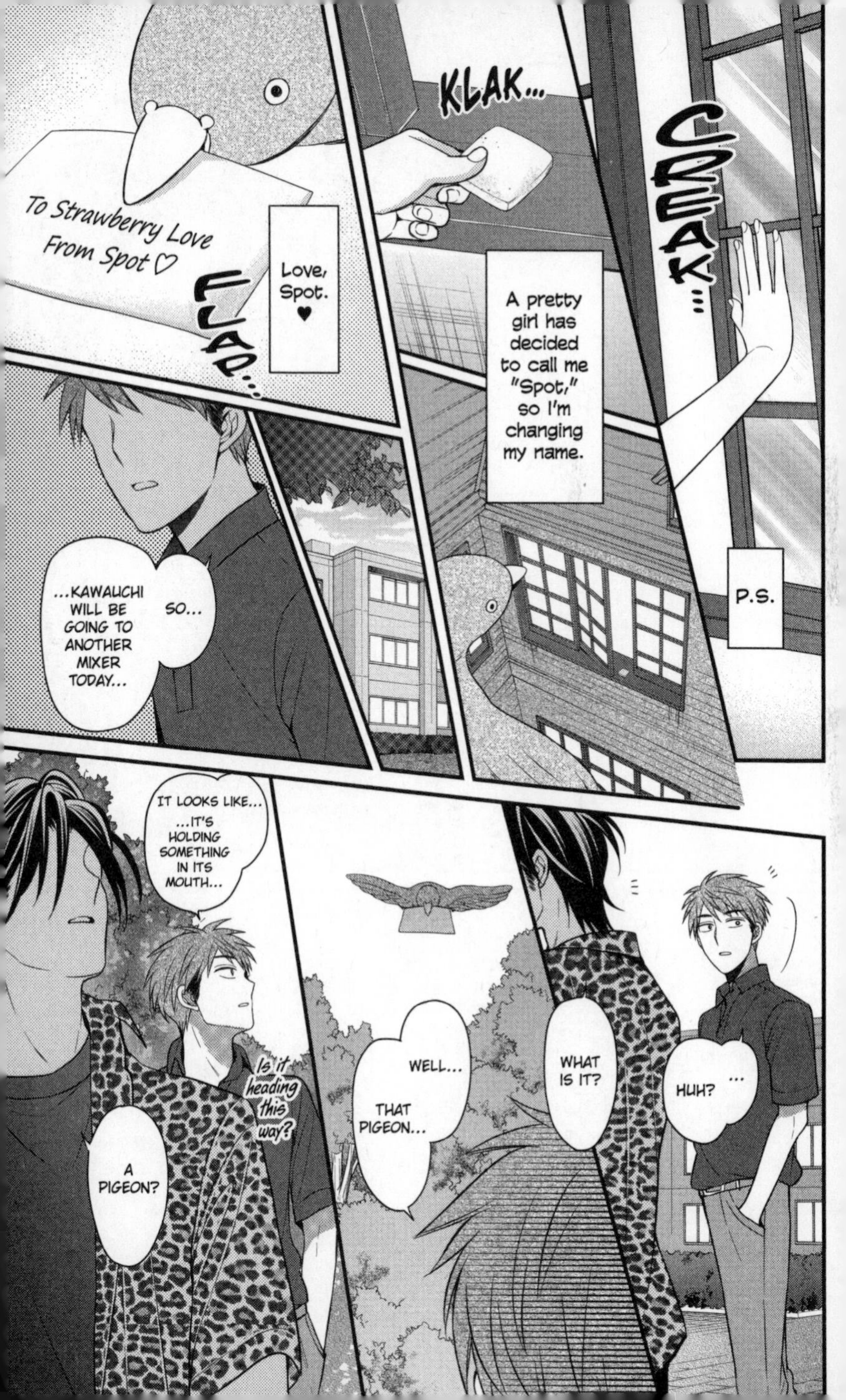
CREAK...
P.S.
KLAK...
A pretty girl has decided to call me "Spot," so I'm changing my name.
To Strawberry Love From Spot ♡
Love, Spot. ♥
FLAP...
SO...
...KAWAUCHI WILL BE GOING TO ANOTHER MIXER TODAY...
...
HUH?
WHAT IS IT?
WELL...
THAT PIGEON...
IT LOOKS LIKE... ...IT'S HOLDING SOMETHING IN ITS MOUTH...
Is it heading this way?
A PIGEON?

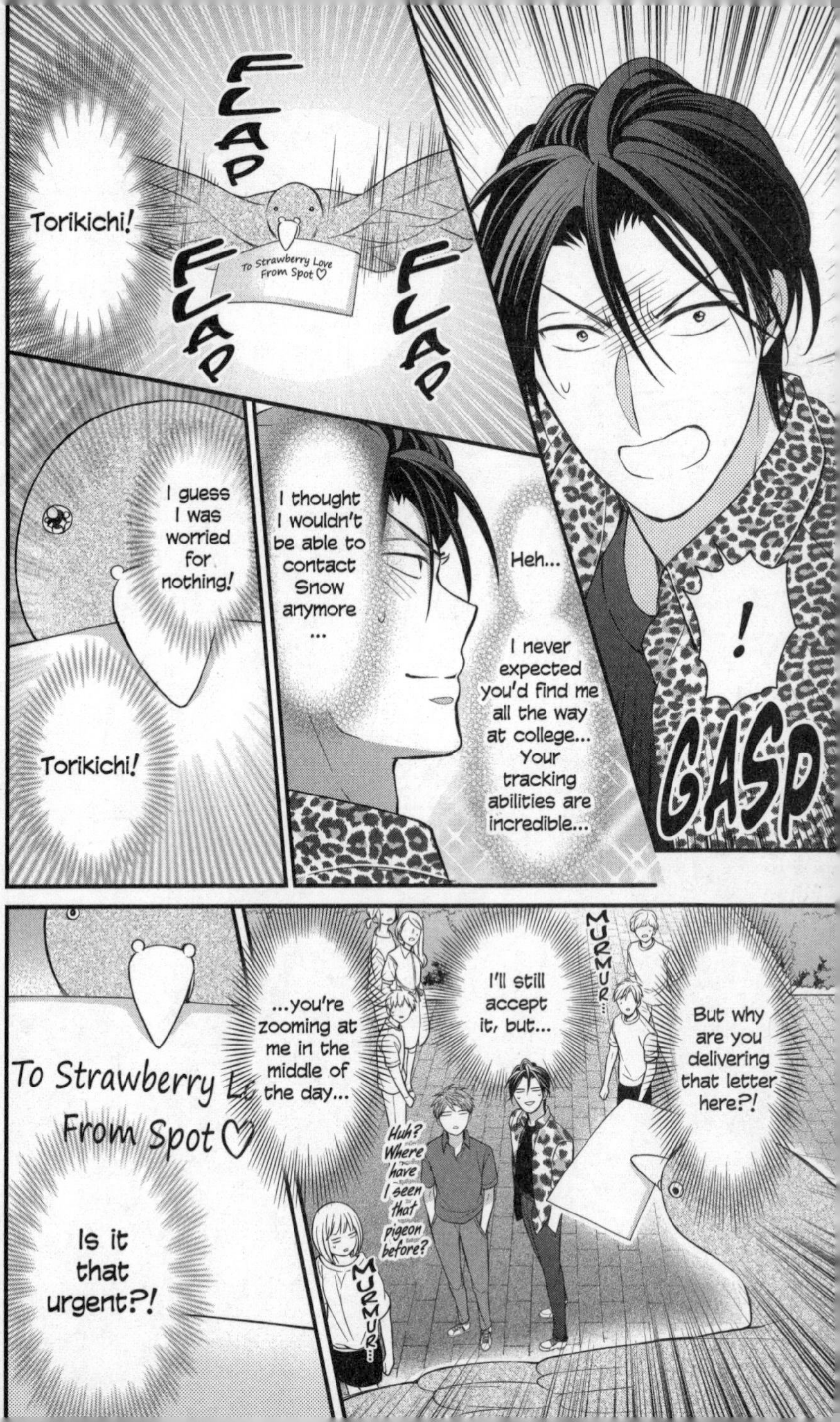
!
GASP
FLAP
FLAP
FLAP
FLAP
Torikichi!
To Strawberry Love From Spot ♡
Heh...
I never expected you'd find me all the way at college... Your tracking abilities are incredible...
I thought I wouldn't be able to contact Snow anymore...
I guess I was worried for nothing!
Torikichi!
MURMUR...
But why are you delivering that letter here?!
I'll still accept it, but...
...you're zooming at me in the middle of the day...
Huh? Where have I seen that pigeon before?
MURMUR...
To Strawberry L
From Spot ♡
Is it that urgent?!

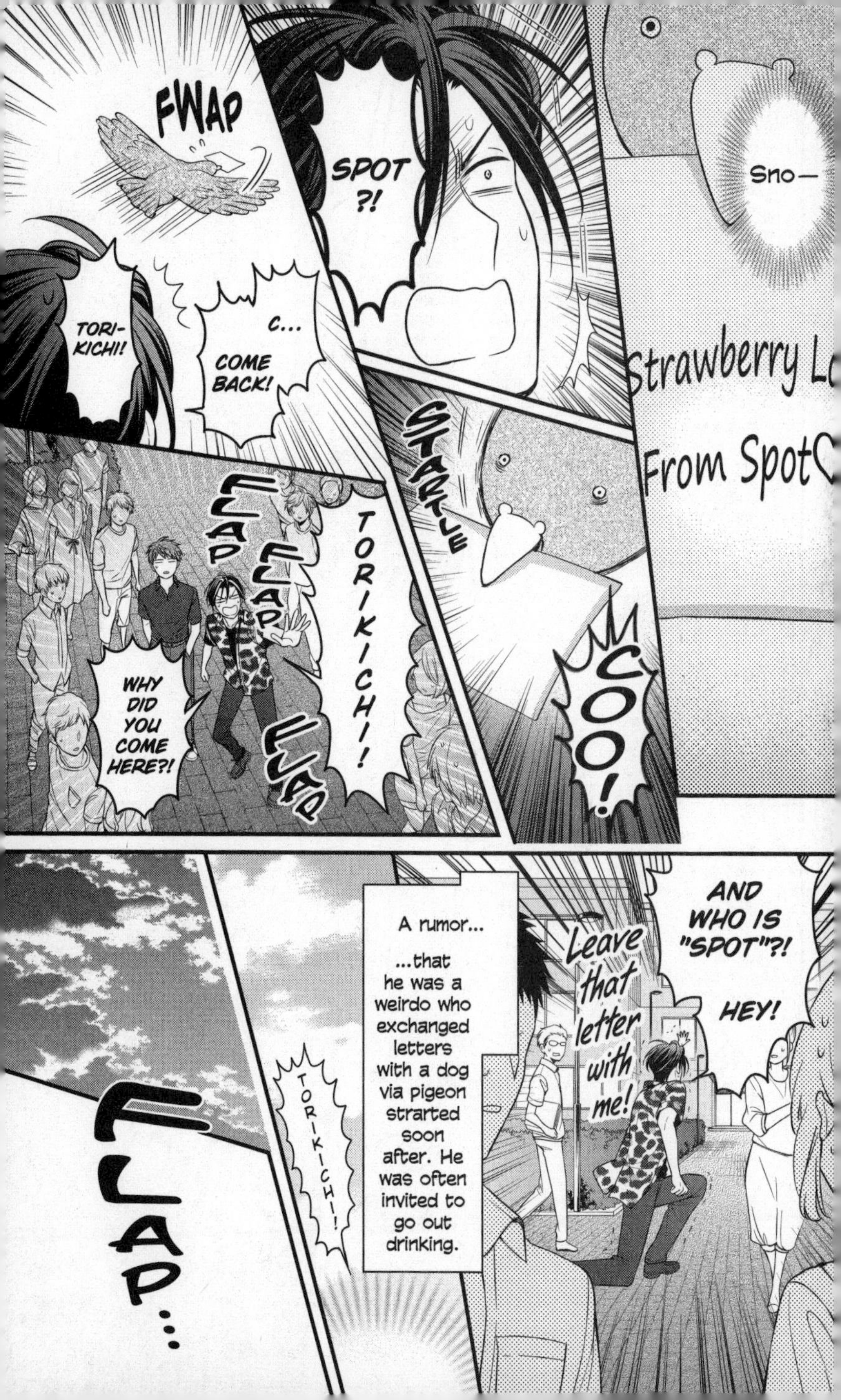
Sno—
Strawberry Lo
From Spot♡
SPOT ?!
STARTLE
COO!
FWAP
C... COME BACK!
TORI-KICHI!
TORIKICHI!!
FLAP
FLAP
WHY DID YOU COME HERE?!
FLAP
AND WHO IS "SPOT"?!
HEY!
Leave that letter with me!
A rumor...
...that he was a weirdo who exchanged letters with a dog via pigeon strarted soon after. He was often invited to go out drinking.
TORIKICHI!
FLAP...

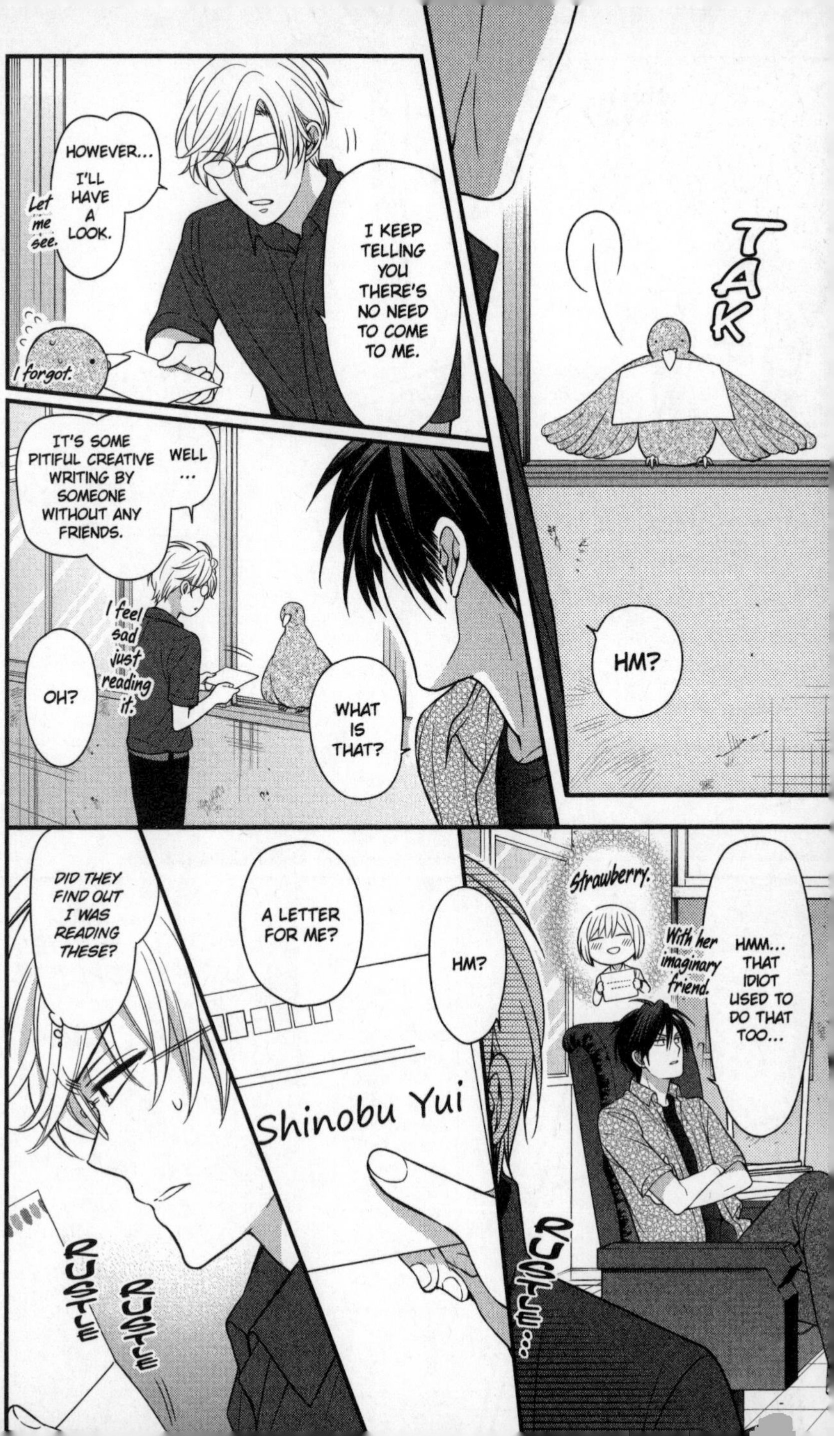
TAK
I KEEP TELLING YOU THERE'S NO NEED TO COME TO ME.
HOWEVER... I'LL HAVE A LOOK.
Let me see.
I forgot.
HM?
WHAT IS THAT?
OH?
WELL...
IT'S SOME PITIFUL CREATIVE WRITING BY SOMEONE WITHOUT ANY FRIENDS.
I feel sad just reading it.
HMM... THAT IDIOT USED TO DO THAT TOO...
With her imaginary friend.
Strawberry.
RUSTLE...
HM?
A LETTER FOR ME?
Shinobu Yui
DID THEY FIND OUT I WAS READING THESE?
RUSTLE RUSTLE

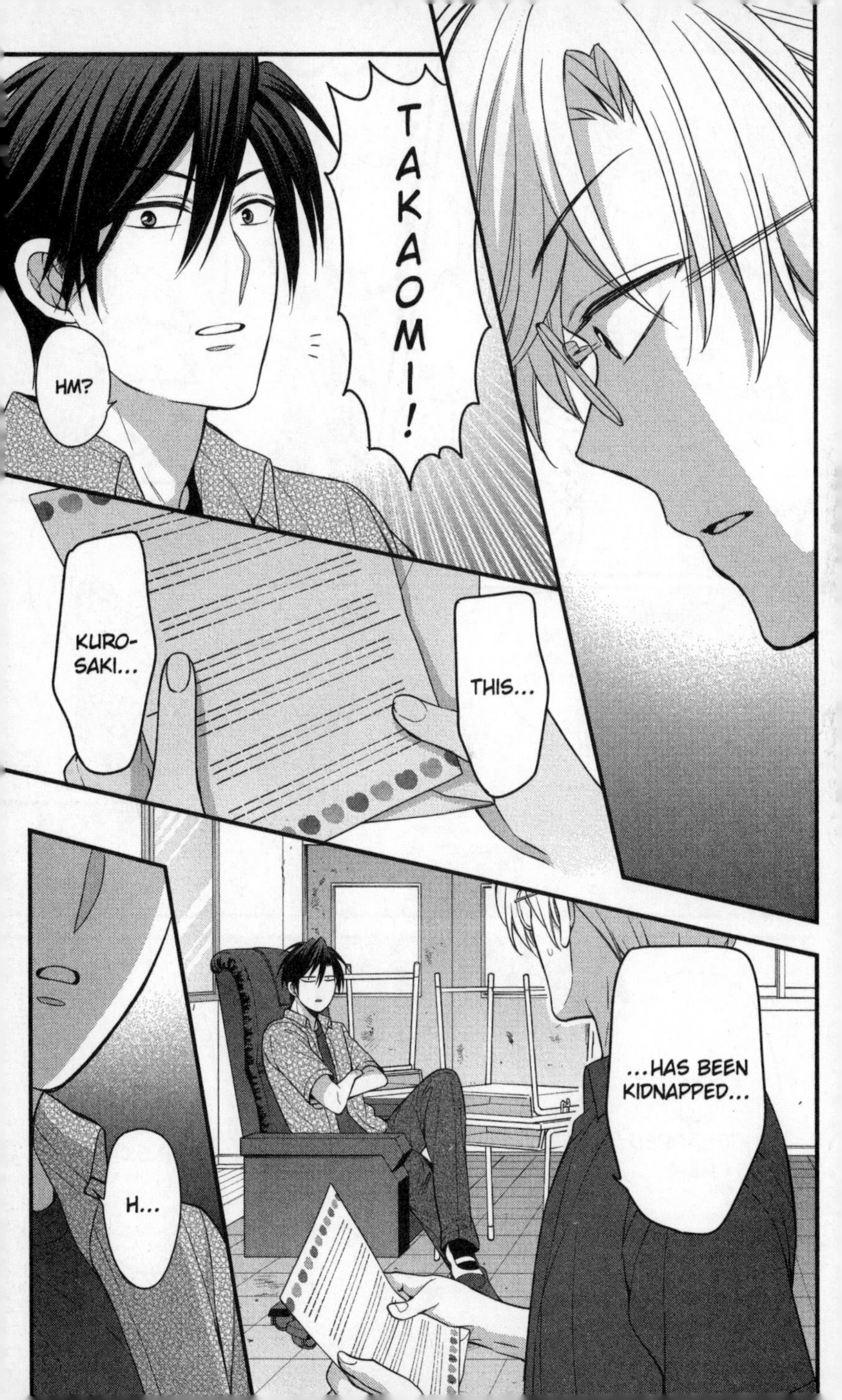
TAKAOMI!
HM?
THIS...
KURO-SAKI...
...HAS BEEN KIDNAPPED...
H...

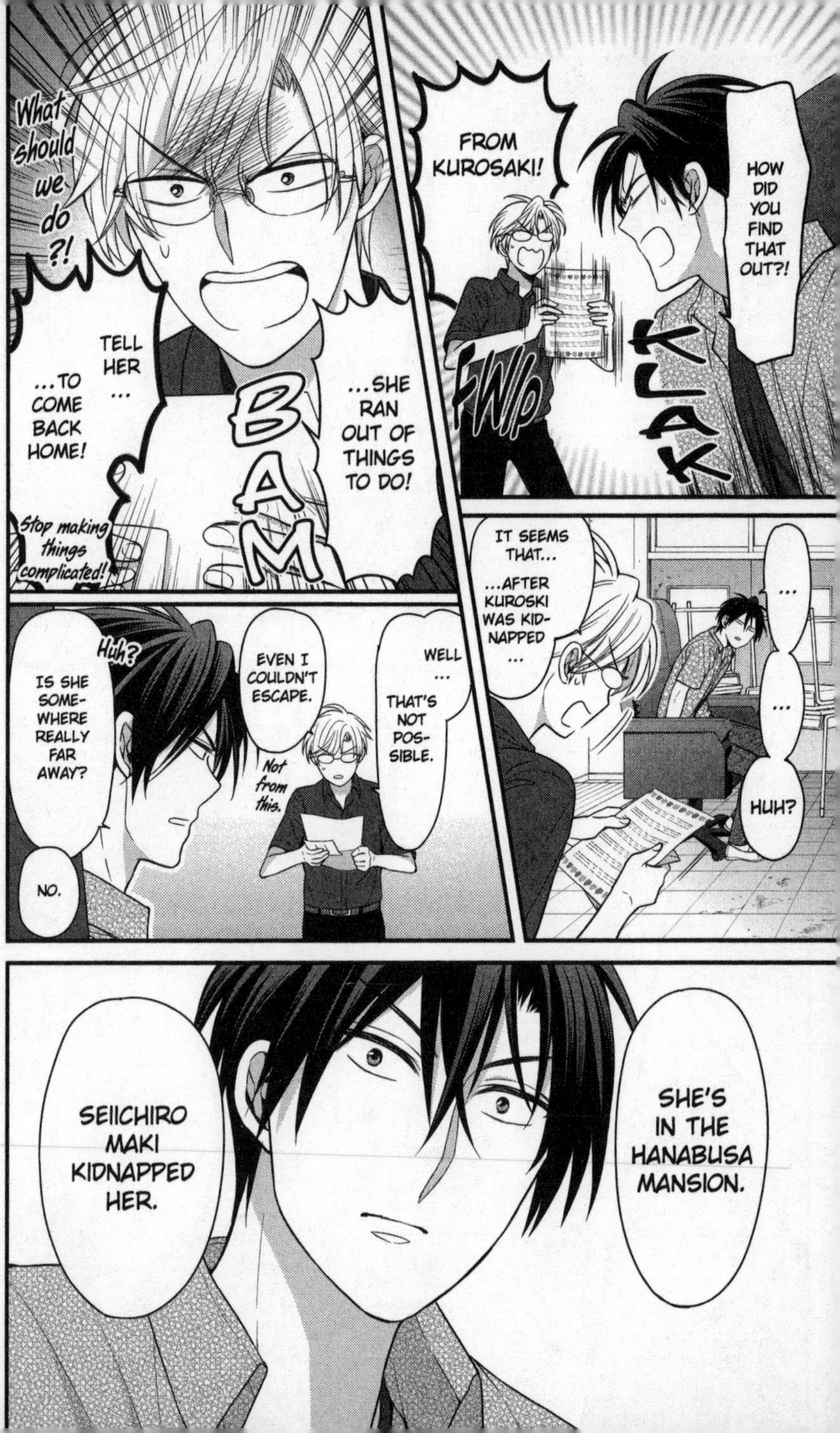
HOW DID YOU FIND THAT OUT?!
KLAK
FROM KUROSAKI!
FWIP
...SHE RAN OUT OF THINGS TO DO!
BAM
What should we do?!
TELL HER...
...TO COME BACK HOME!
Stop making things complicated!
...
...
HUH?
IT SEEMS THAT...
...AFTER KUROSKI WAS KIDNAPPED...
WELL... THAT'S NOT POSSIBLE.
EVEN I COULDN'T ESCAPE.
Not from this.
Huh?
IS SHE SOMEWHERE REALLY FAR AWAY?
NO.
SHE'S IN THE HANABUSA MANSION.
SEIICHIRO MAKI KIDNAPPED HER.

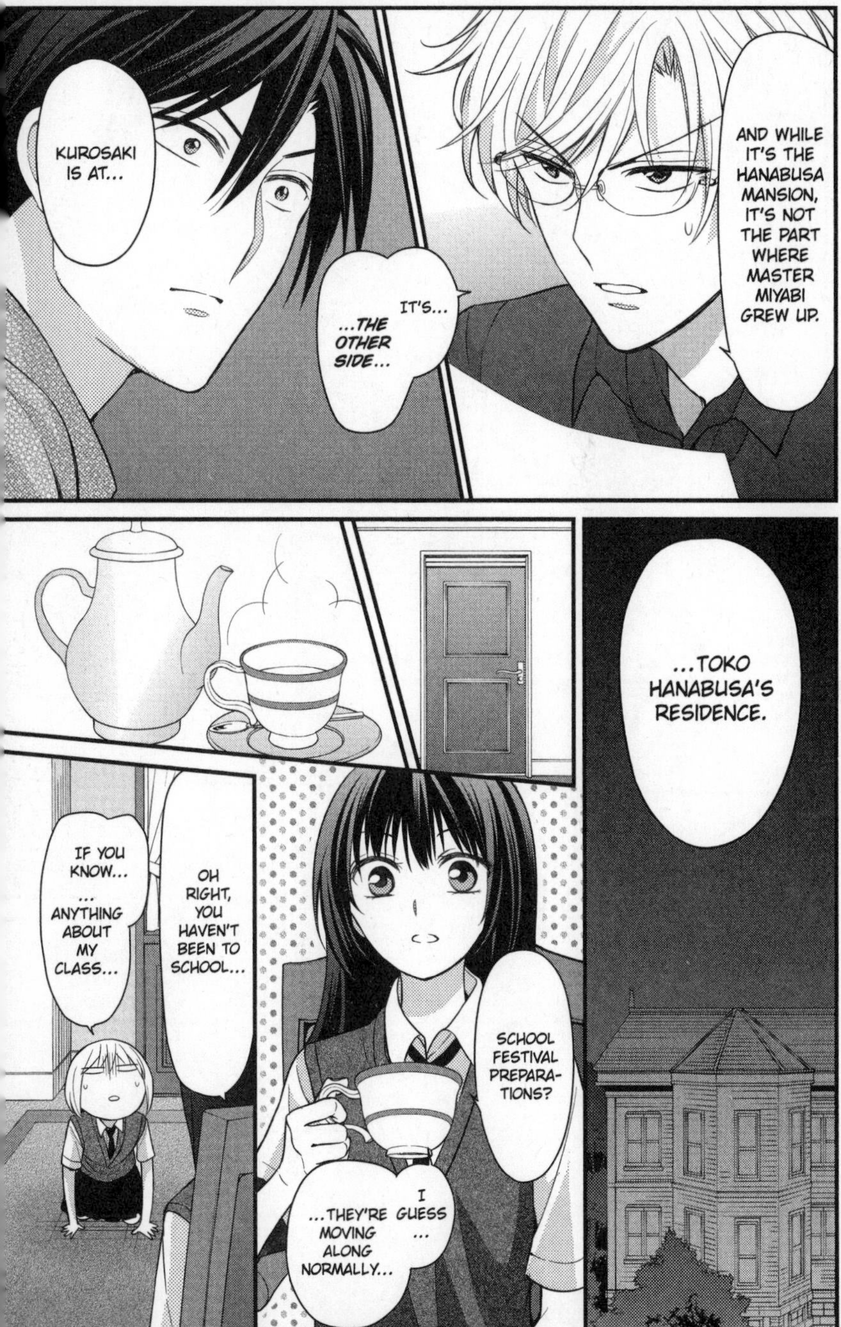
AND WHILE IT'S THE HANABUSA MANSION, IT'S NOT THE PART WHERE MASTER MIYABI GREW UP.
KUROSAKI IS AT...
IT'S... ...THE OTHER SIDE...
...TOKO HANABUSA'S RESIDENCE.
SCHOOL FESTIVAL PREPARATIONS?
I GUESS...
...THEY'RE MOVING ALONG NORMALLY...
OH RIGHT, YOU HAVEN'T BEEN TO SCHOOL...
IF YOU KNOW... ...ANYTHING ABOUT MY CLASS...

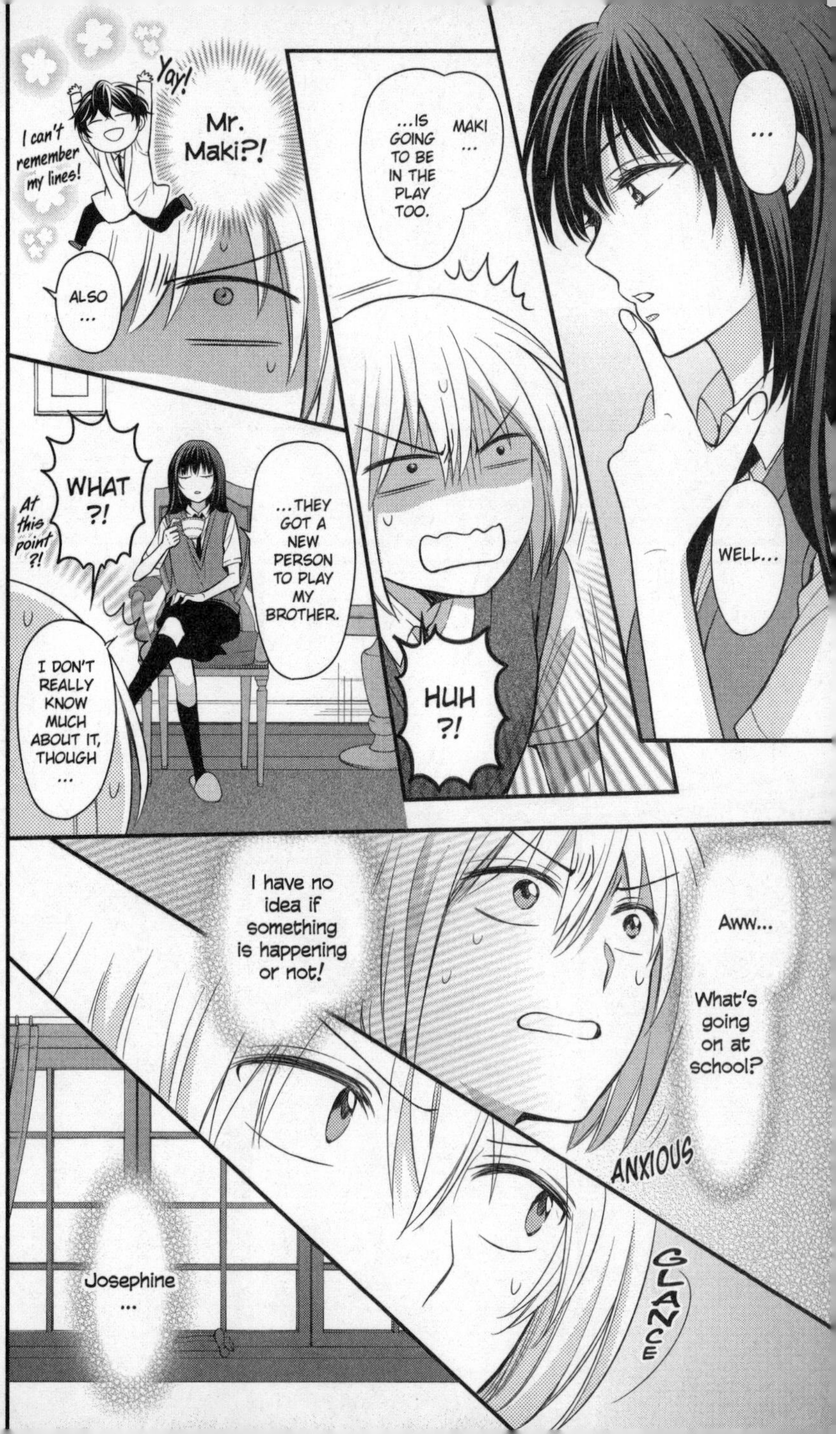
...
WELL...
MAKI...
...IS GOING TO BE IN THE PLAY TOO.
HUH?!
Mr. Maki?!
Yay!
I can't remember my lines!
ALSO...
...THEY GOT A NEW PERSON TO PLAY MY BROTHER.
WHAT?!
At this point?!
I DON'T REALLY KNOW MUCH ABOUT IT, THOUGH...
Aww...
What's going on at school?
I have no idea if something is happening or not!
ANXIOUS
GLANCE
Josephine...

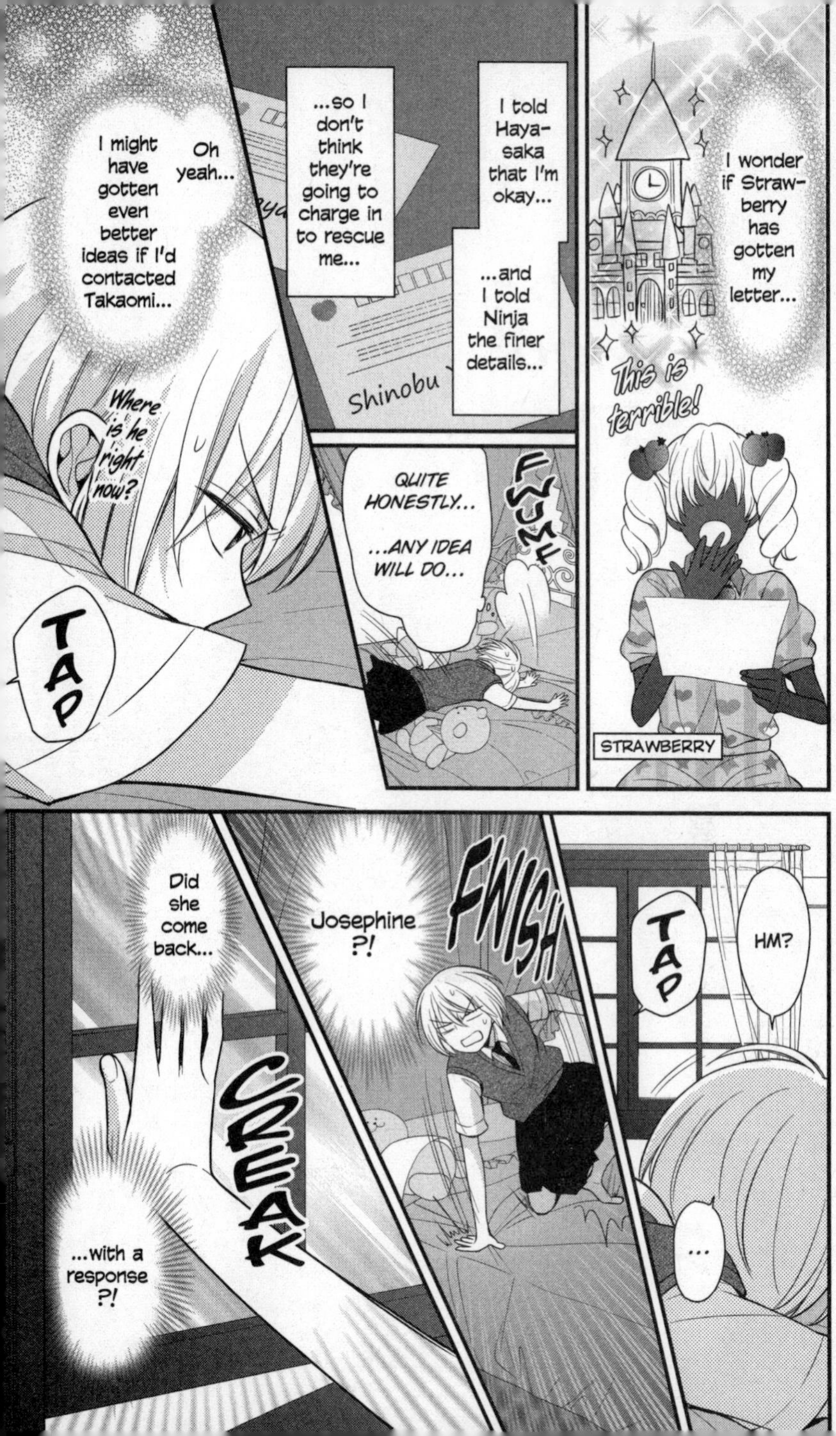
I wonder if Strawberry has gotten my letter...
This is terrible!
STRAWBERRY
I told Hayasaka that I'm okay...
...and I told Ninja the finer details...
...so I don't think they're going to charge in to rescue me...
Shinobu
FWUMF
QUITE HONESTLY...
...ANY IDEA WILL DO...
Oh yeah...
I might have gotten even better ideas if I'd contacted Takaomi...
Where is he right now?
TAP
HM?
TAP
...
FWISH
Josephine?!
Did she come back...
CREAK
...with a response?!

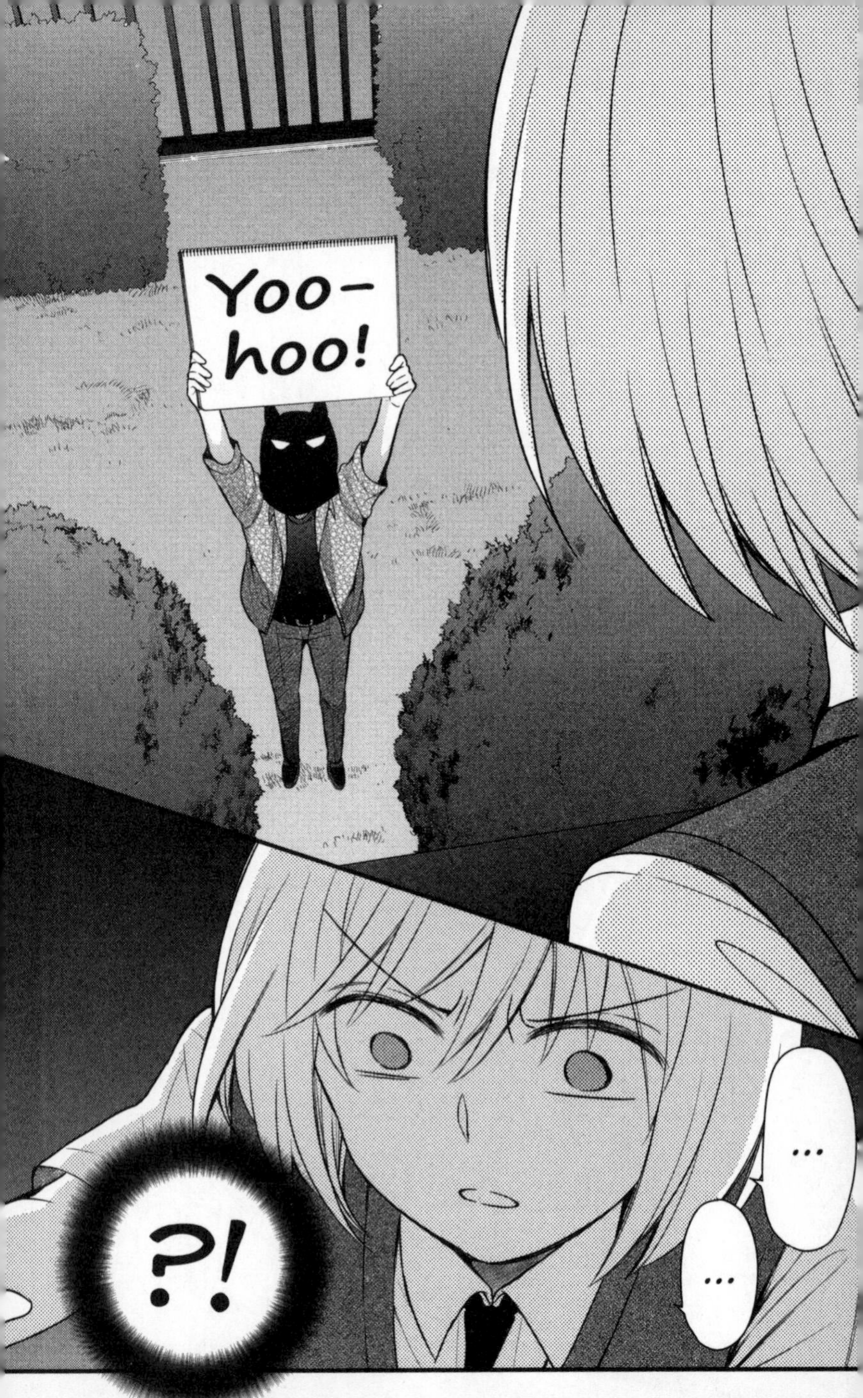
Yoo-hoo!
...
...
?!

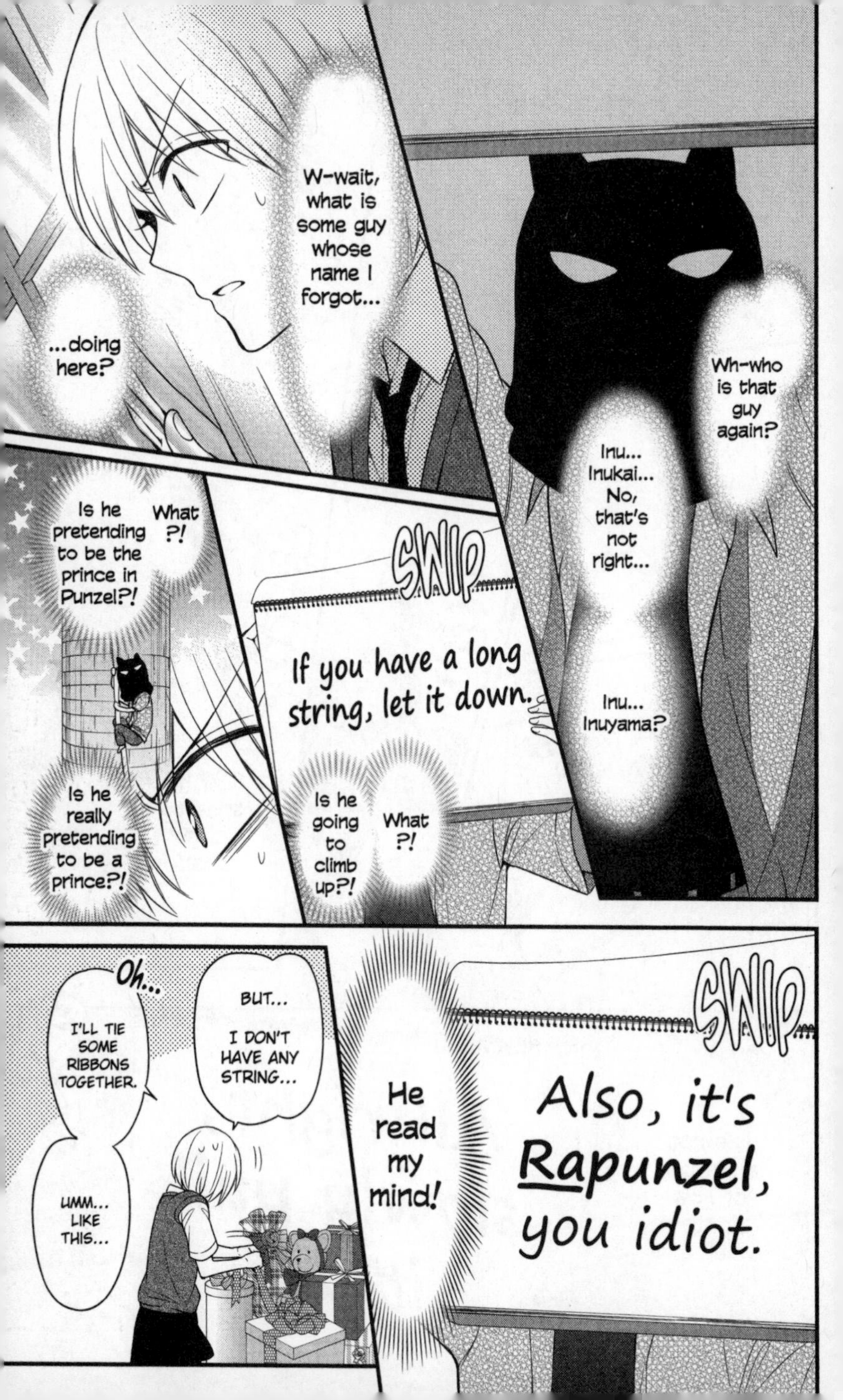
W-wait, what is some guy whose name I forgot...
...doing here?
Wh-who is that guy again?
Inu... Inukai... No, that's not right...
Inu... Inuyama?
SWIP
If you have a long string, let it down.
What?!
Is he pretending to be the prince in Punzel?!
What?!
Is he going to climb up?!
Is he really pretending to be a prince?!
SWIP
Also, it's Rapunzel, you idiot.
He read my mind!
Oh...
BUT... I DON'T HAVE ANY STRING...
I'LL TIE SOME RIBBONS TOGETHER.
UMM... LIKE THIS...

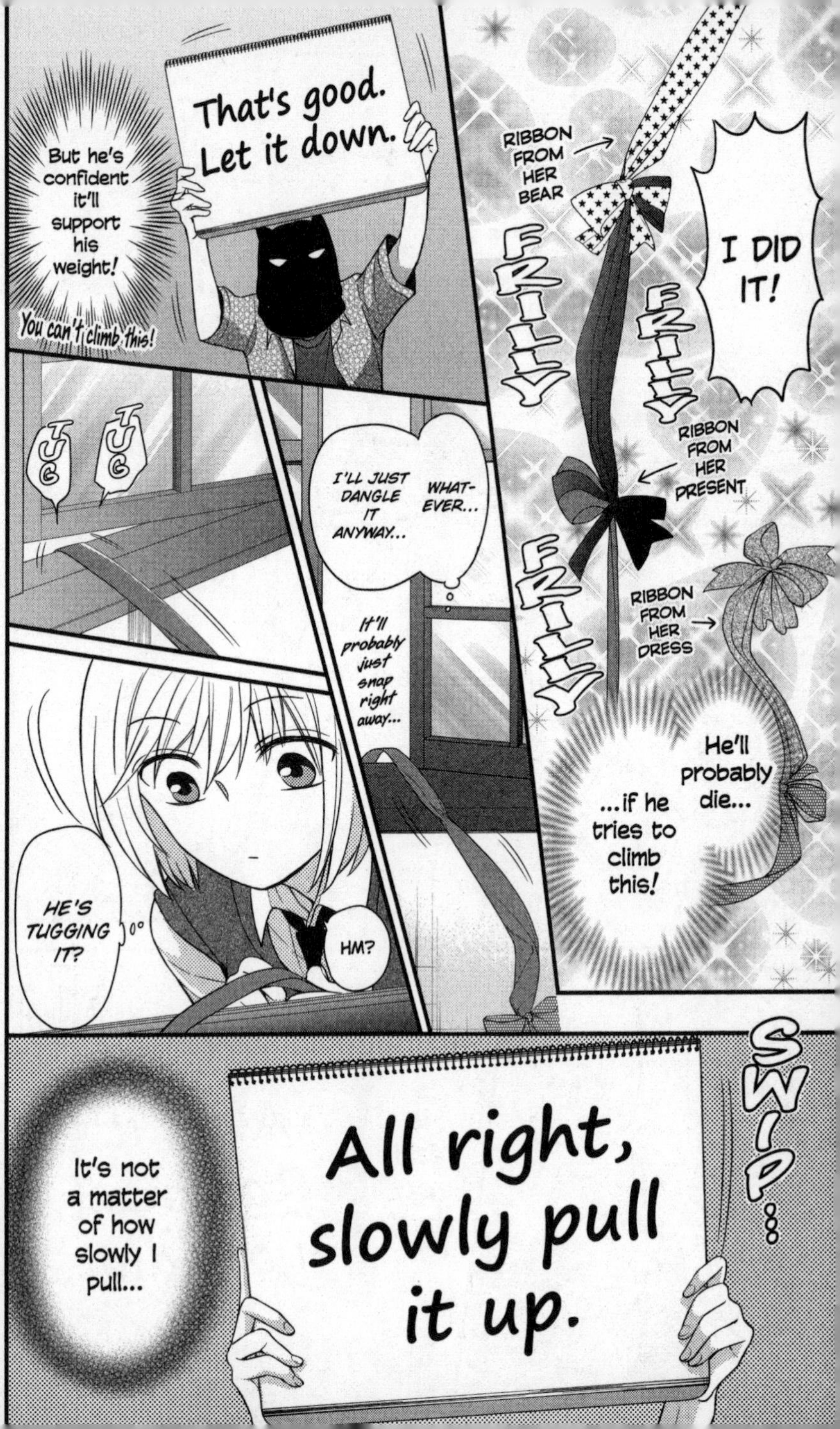
I DID IT!
RIBBON FROM HER BEAR
FRILLY
FRILLY
RIBBON FROM HER PRESENT
FRILLY
RIBBON FROM HER DRESS
He'll probably die...
...if he tries to climb this!
That's good. Let it down.
But he's confident it'll support his weight!
You can't climb this!
WHAT-EVER...
I'LL JUST DANGLE IT ANYWAY...
It'll probably just snap right away...
TUG
TUG
HM?
HE'S TUGGING IT?
SWIP...
All right, slowly pull it up.
It's not a matter of how slowly I pull...

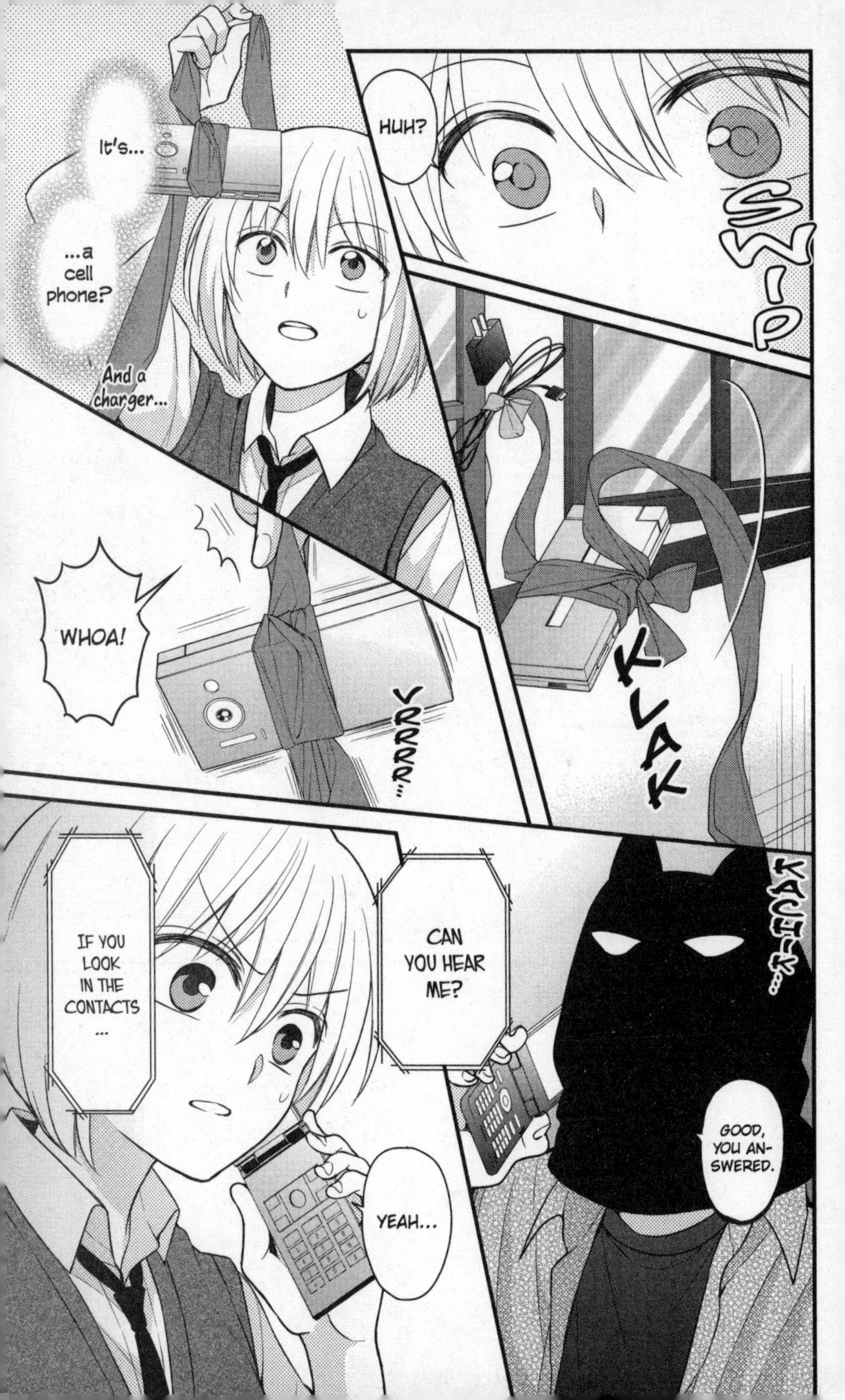
HUH?
SWIP
KLAK
It's...
...a cell phone?
And a charger...
WHOA!
VRRRR...
KACHIK...
CAN YOU HEAR ME?
GOOD, YOU AN-SWERED.
YEAH...
IF YOU LOOK IN THE CONTACTS ...

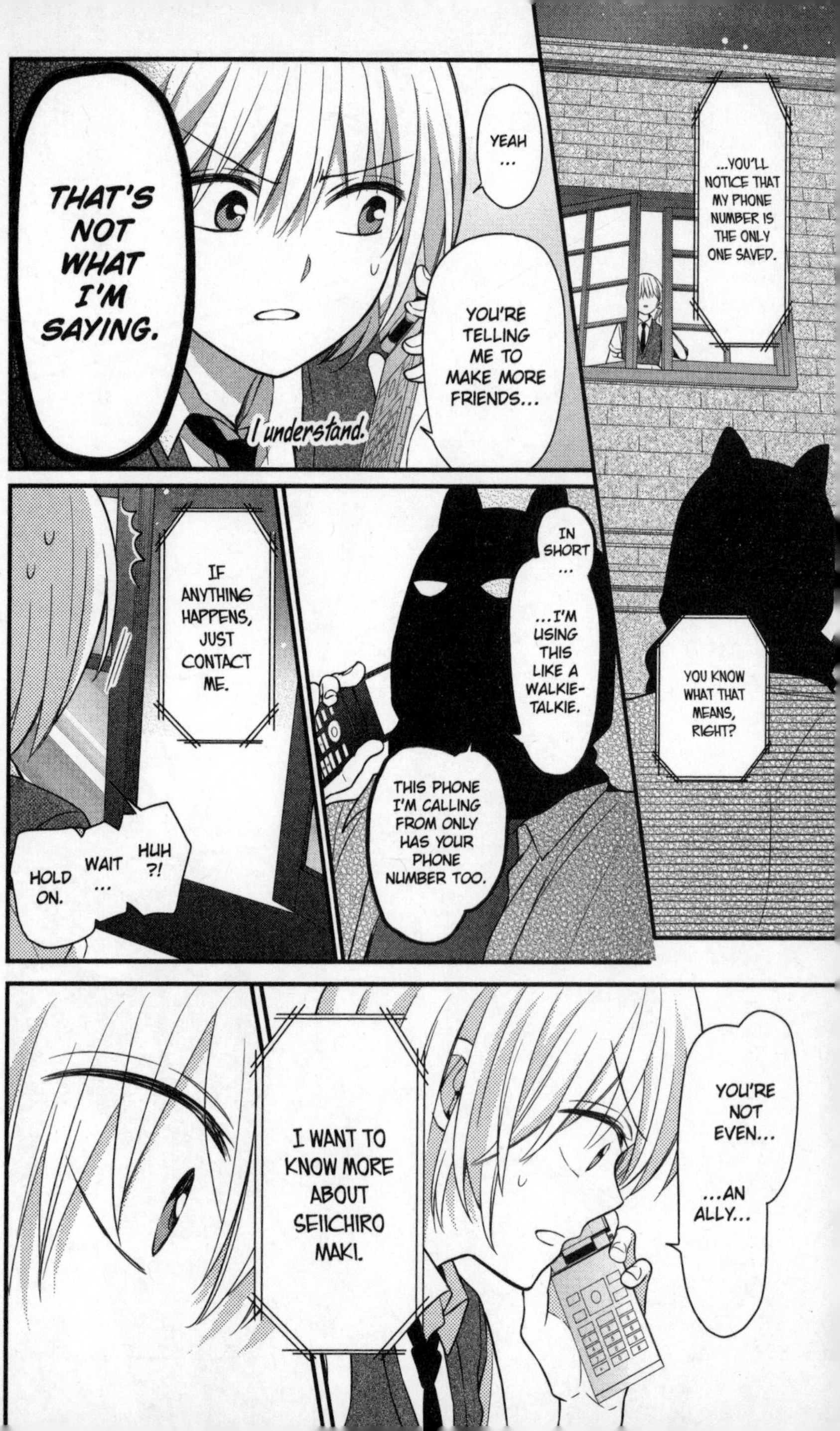
...YOU'LL NOTICE THAT MY PHONE NUMBER IS THE ONLY ONE SAVED.
YOU KNOW WHAT THAT MEANS, RIGHT?
YEAH...
YOU'RE TELLING ME TO MAKE MORE FRIENDS...
I understand.
THAT'S NOT WHAT I'M SAYING.
IN SHORT...
...I'M USING THIS LIKE A WALKIE-TALKIE.
THIS PHONE I'M CALLING FROM ONLY HAS YOUR PHONE NUMBER TOO.
IF ANYTHING HAPPENS, JUST CONTACT ME.
HUH?!
WAIT...
HOLD ON.
YOU'RE NOT EVEN...
...AN ALLY...
I WANT TO KNOW MORE ABOUT SEIICHIRO MAKI.

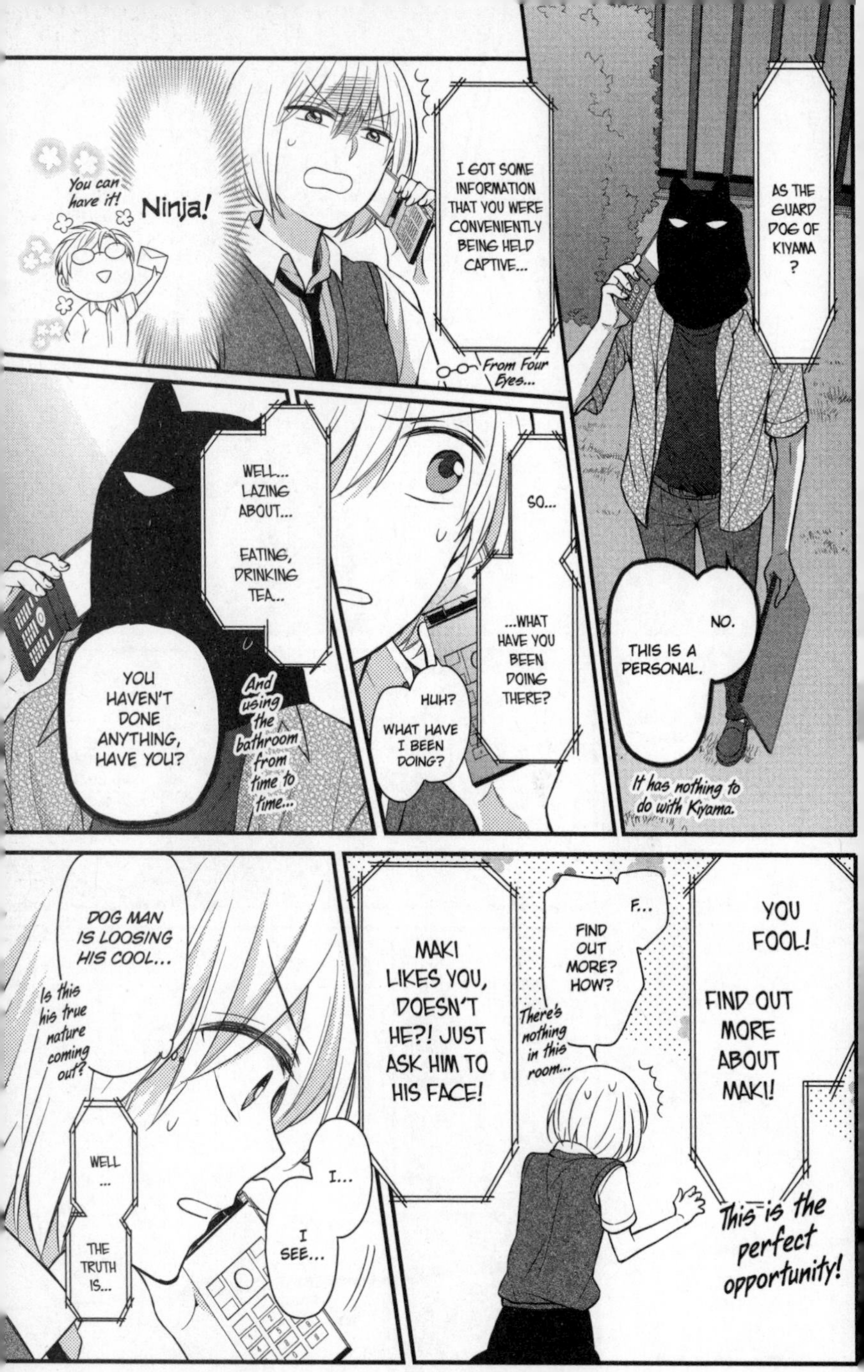
AS THE GUARD DOG OF KIYAMA ?
NO.
THIS IS A PERSONAL.
It has nothing to do with Kiyama.
I GOT SOME INFORMATION THAT YOU WERE CONVENIENTLY BEING HELD CAPTIVE...
From Four Eyes...
Ninja!
You can have it!
SO...
...WHAT HAVE YOU BEEN DOING THERE?
HUH? WHAT HAVE I BEEN DOING?
WELL... LAZING ABOUT...
EATING, DRINKING TEA...
And using the bathroom from time to time...
YOU HAVEN'T DONE ANYTHING, HAVE YOU?
YOU FOOL!
FIND OUT MORE ABOUT MAKI!
F...
FIND OUT MORE? HOW?
There's nothing in this room...
This is the perfect opportunity!
MAKI LIKES YOU, DOESN'T HE?! JUST ASK HIM TO HIS FACE!
I...
I SEE...
WELL ...
THE TRUTH IS...
DOG MAN IS LOOSING HIS COOL...
Is this his true nature coming out?

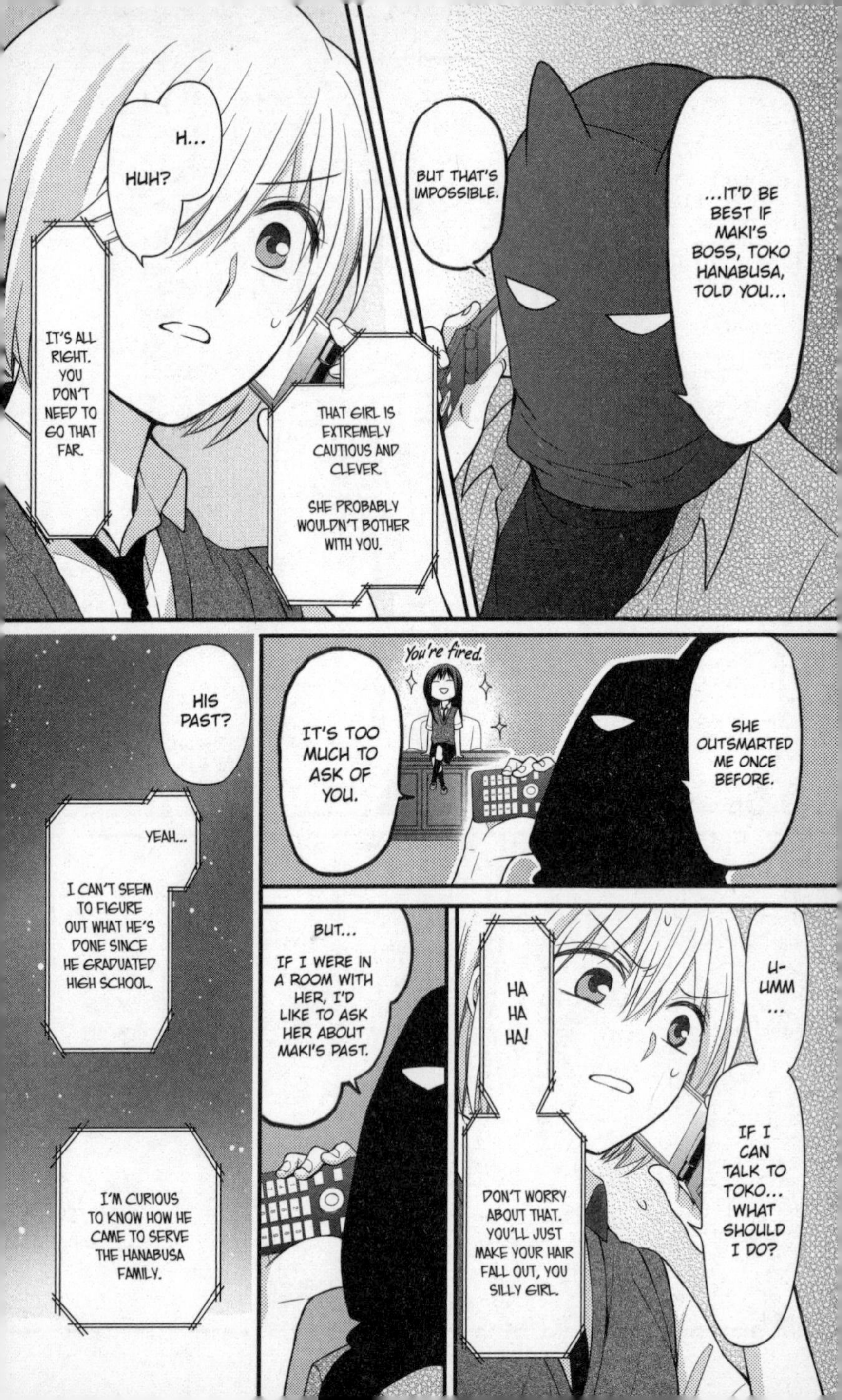
...IT'D BE BEST IF MAKI'S BOSS, TOKO HANABUSA, TOLD YOU...
BUT THAT'S IMPOSSIBLE.
H... HUH?
THAT GIRL IS EXTREMELY CAUTIOUS AND CLEVER. SHE PROBABLY WOULDN'T BOTHER WITH YOU.
IT'S ALL RIGHT. YOU DON'T NEED TO GO THAT FAR.
SHE OUTSMARTED ME ONCE BEFORE.
You're fired.
IT'S TOO MUCH TO ASK OF YOU.
U-UMM...
IF I CAN TALK TO TOKO... WHAT SHOULD I DO?
HA HA HA!
DON'T WORRY ABOUT THAT. YOU'LL JUST MAKE YOUR HAIR FALL OUT, YOU SILLY GIRL.
BUT... IF I WERE IN A ROOM WITH HER, I'D LIKE TO ASK HER ABOUT MAKI'S PAST.
HIS PAST?
YEAH... I CAN'T SEEM TO FIGURE OUT WHAT HE'S DONE SINCE HE GRADUATED HIGH SCHOOL.
I'M CURIOUS TO KNOW HOW HE CAME TO SERVE THE HANABUSA FAMILY.

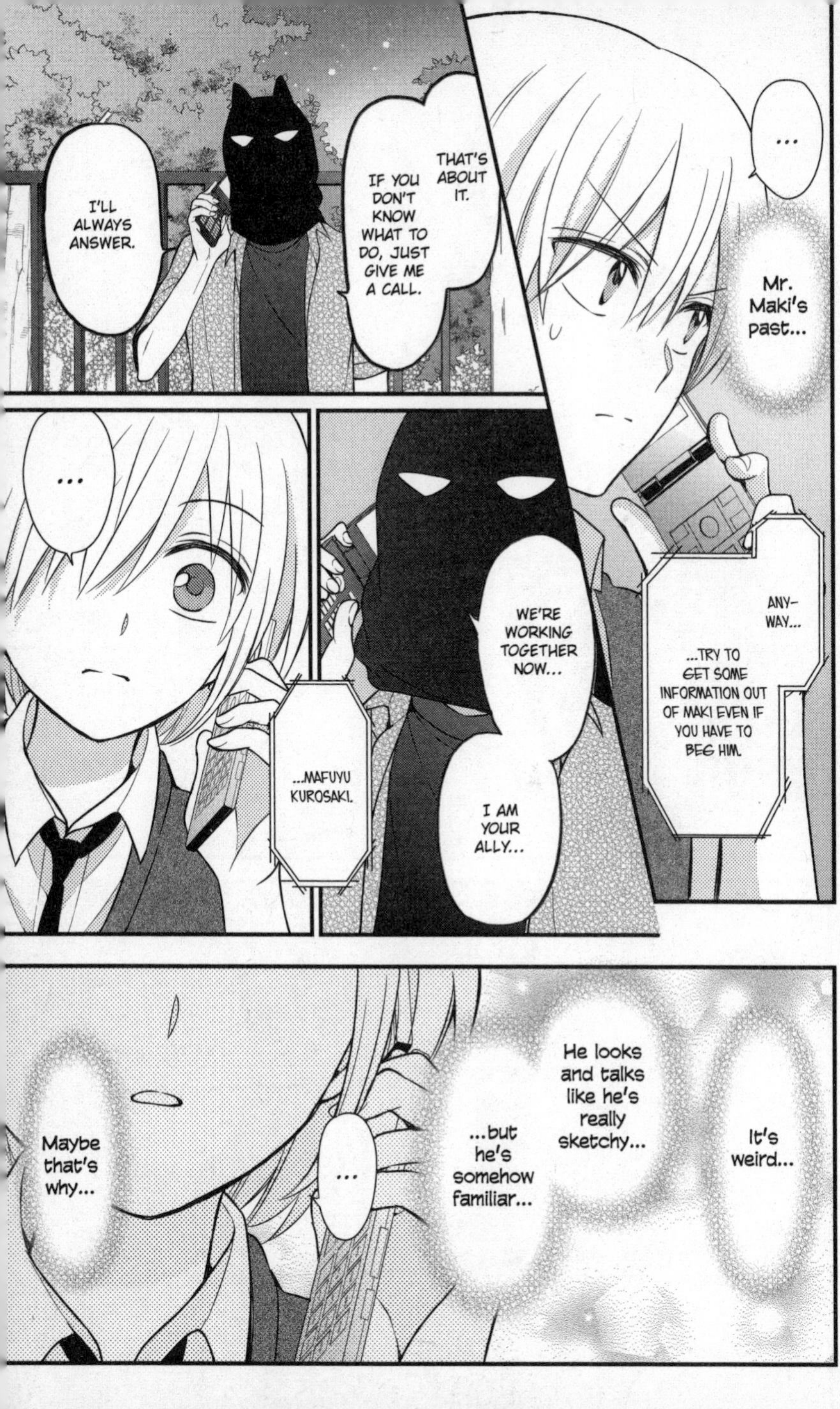
...
Mr. Maki's past...
ANYWAY...
...TRY TO GET SOME INFORMATION OUT OF MAKI EVEN IF YOU HAVE TO BEG HIM.
THAT'S ABOUT IT.
IF YOU DON'T KNOW WHAT TO DO, JUST GIVE ME A CALL.
I'LL ALWAYS ANSWER.
WE'RE WORKING TOGETHER NOW...
I AM YOUR ALLY...
...MAFUYU KUROSAKI.
...
It's weird...
He looks and talks like he's really sketchy...
...but he's somehow familiar...
...
Maybe that's why...

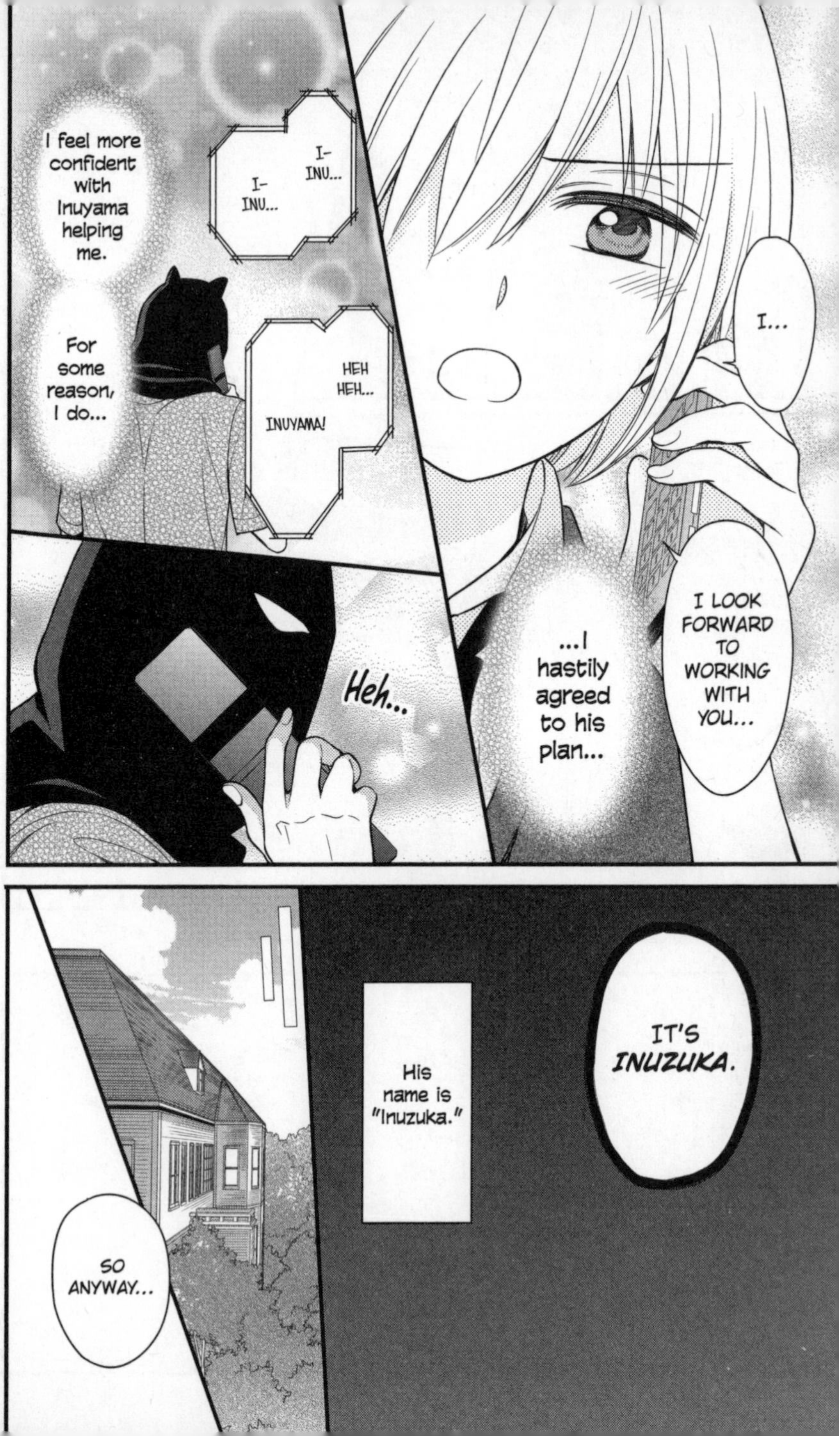
I...
I LOOK FORWARD TO WORKING WITH YOU...
...I hastily agreed to his plan...
I- INU...
I- INU...
I feel more confident with Inuyama helping me.
HEH HEH...
INUYAMA!
For some reason, I do...
Heh...
IT'S INUZUKA.
His name is "Inuzuka."
SO ANYWAY...

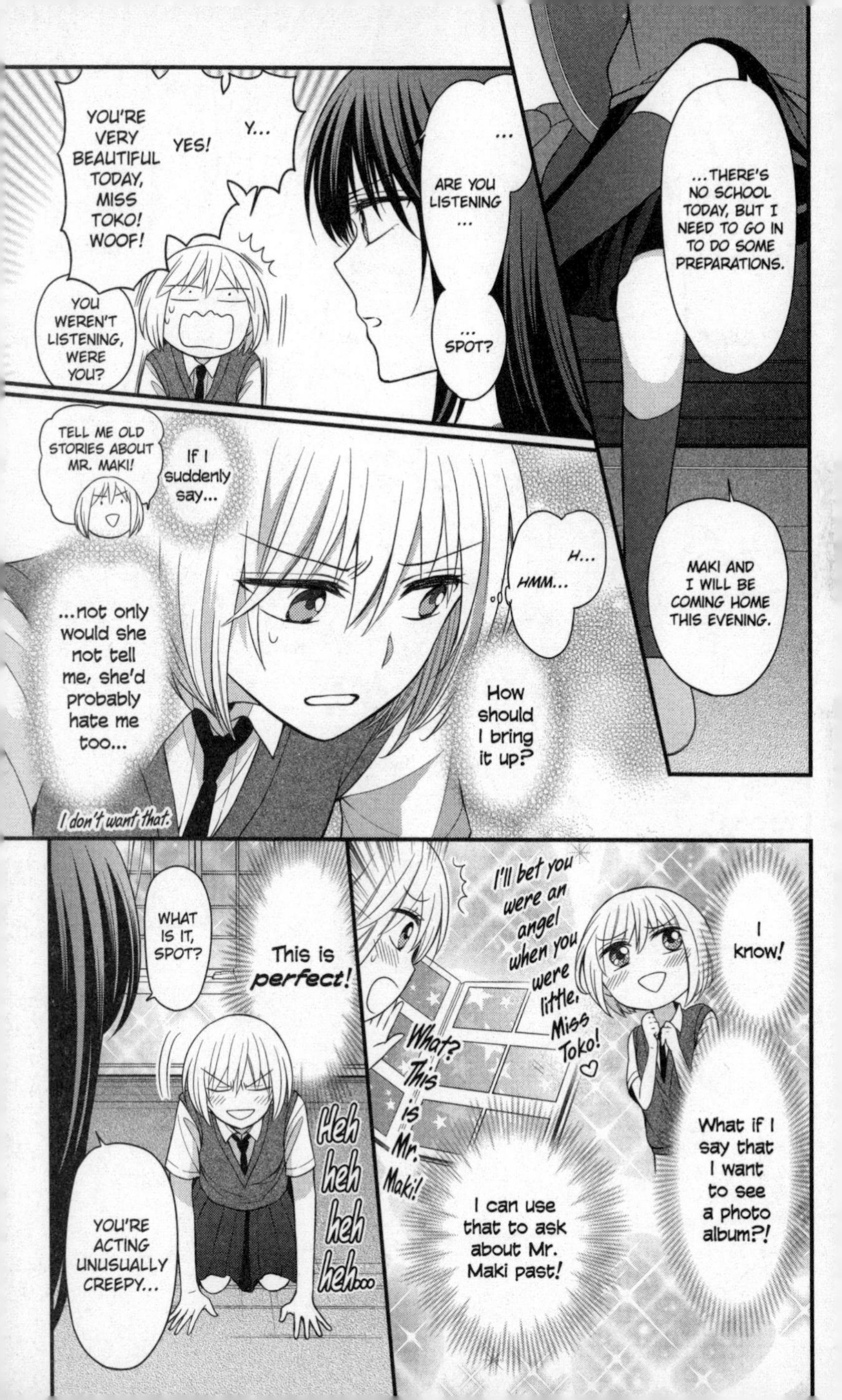
...THERE'S NO SCHOOL TODAY, BUT I NEED TO GO IN TO DO SOME PREPARATIONS.
MAKI AND I WILL BE COMING HOME THIS EVENING.
...
ARE YOU LISTENING ...
... SPOT?
Y... YES!
YOU'RE VERY BEAUTIFUL TODAY, MISS TOKO! WOOF!
YOU WEREN'T LISTENING, WERE YOU?
H... HMM...
How should I bring it up?
If I suddenly say...
TELL ME OLD STORIES ABOUT MR. MAKI!
...not only would she not tell me, she'd probably hate me too...
I don't want that.
I know!
What if I say that I want to see a photo album?!
I'll bet you were an angel when you were little, Miss Toko! ♡
What? This is Mr. Maki!
I can use that to ask about Mr. Maki past!
This is *perfect*!
WHAT IS IT, SPOT?
Heh heh heh heh...
YOU'RE ACTING UNUSUALLY CREEPY...

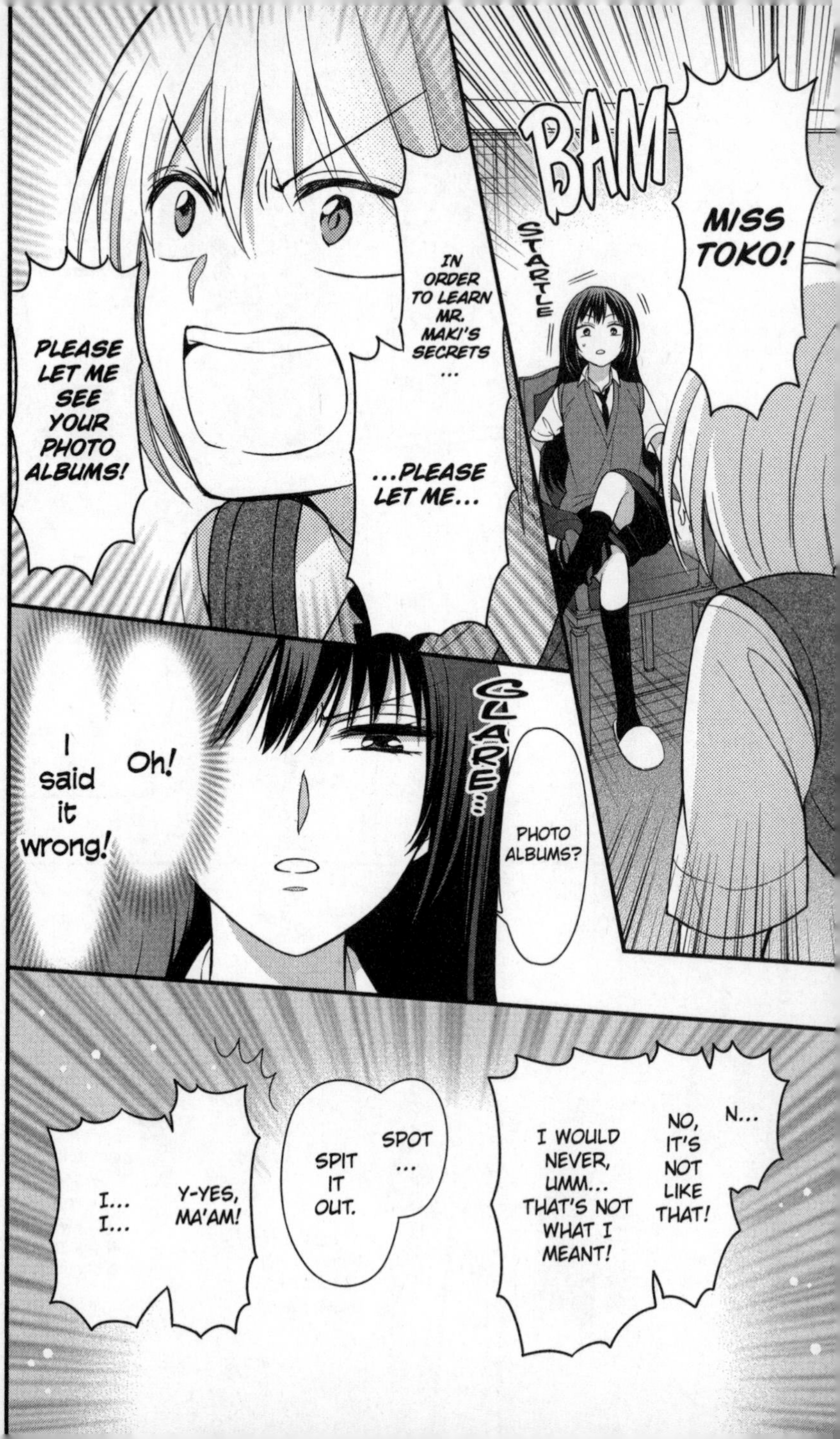
BAM
MISS TOKO!
STARTLE
IN ORDER TO LEARN MR. MAKI'S SECRETS...
...PLEASE LET ME...
PLEASE LET ME SEE YOUR PHOTO ALBUMS!
GLARE...
PHOTO ALBUMS?
Oh!
I said it wrong!
N...
NO, IT'S NOT LIKE THAT!
I WOULD NEVER, UMM... THAT'S NOT WHAT I MEANT!
SPOT...
SPIT IT OUT.
Y-YES, MA'AM!
I... I...

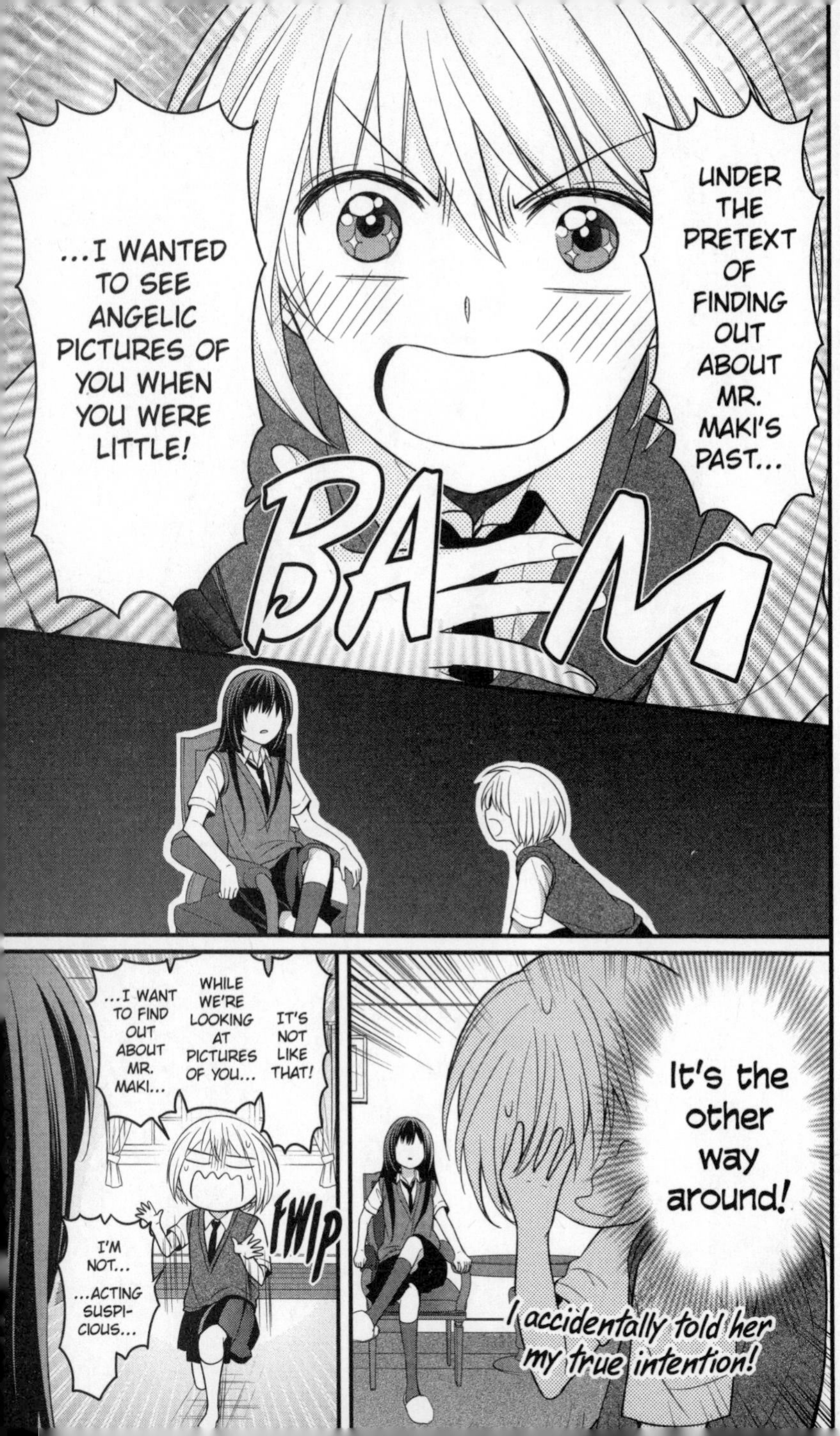
UNDER THE PRETEXT OF FINDING OUT ABOUT MR. MAKI'S PAST...
...I WANTED TO SEE ANGELIC PICTURES OF YOU WHEN YOU WERE LITTLE!
BA-M
It's the other way around!
I accidentally told her my true intention!
IT'S NOT LIKE THAT!
WHILE WE'RE LOOKING AT PICTURES OF YOU...
...I WANT TO FIND OUT ABOUT MR. MAKI...
FWIP
I'M NOT... ...ACTING SUSPICIOUS...

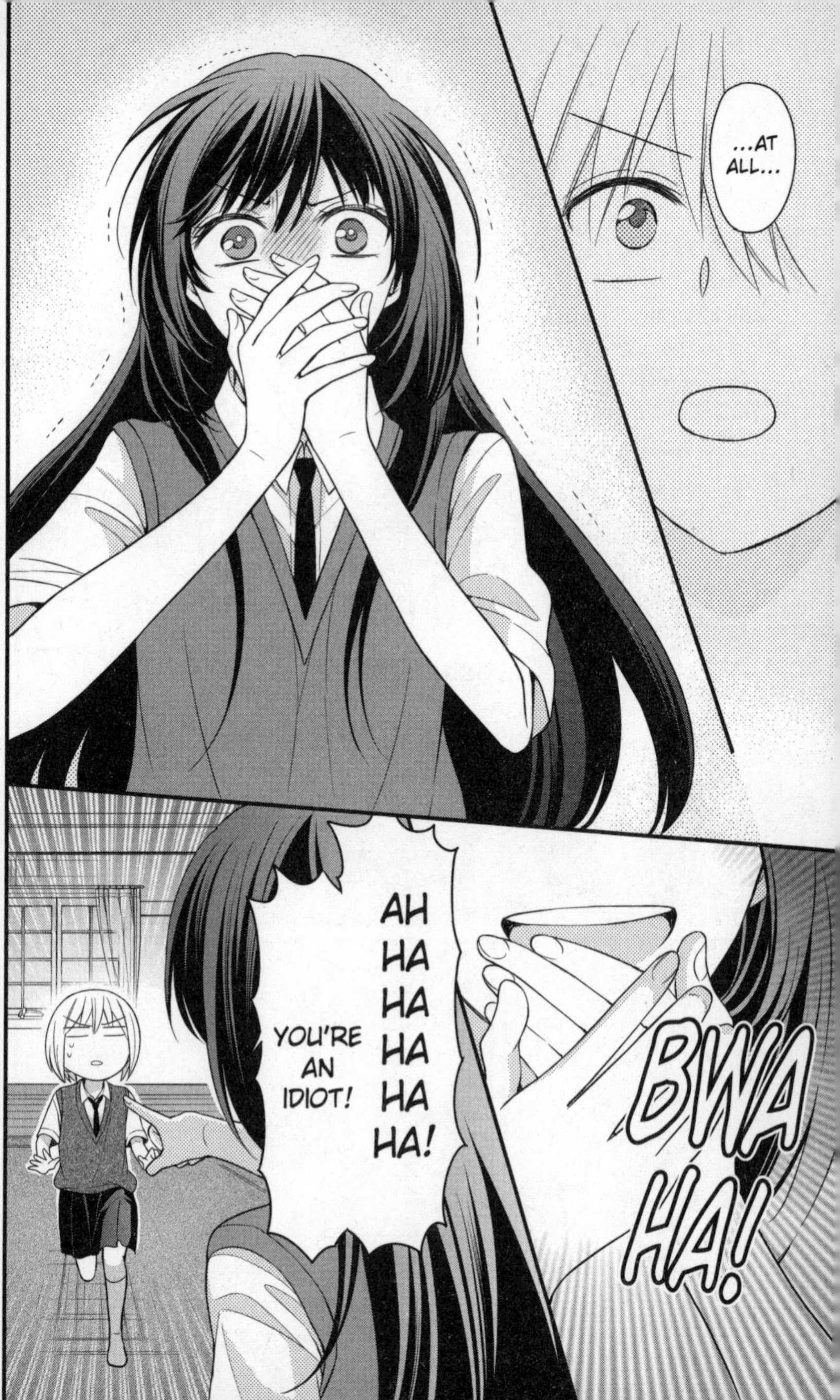
...AT ALL...
BWA HA!
AH HA HA HA HA HA HA!
YOU'RE AN IDIOT!

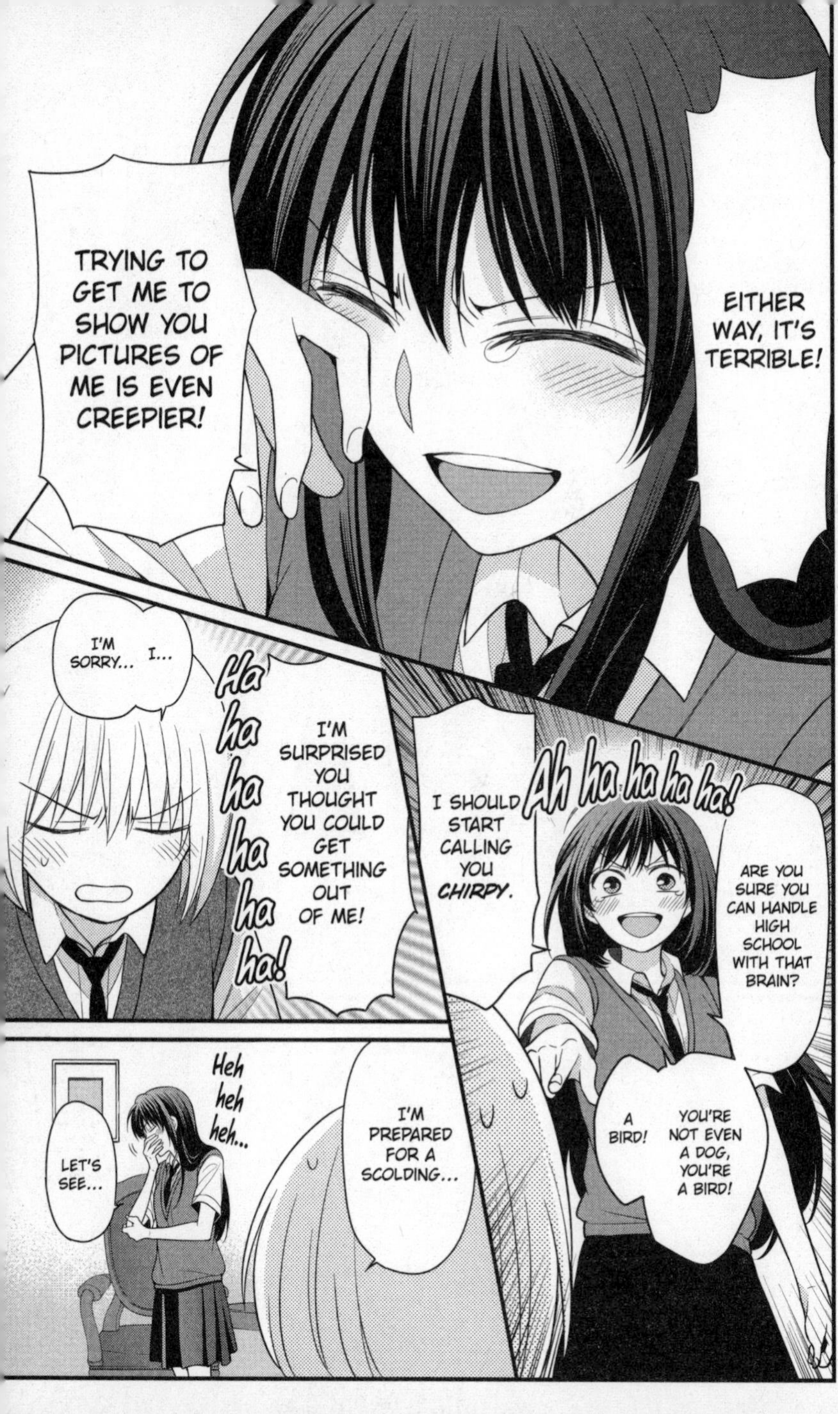
EITHER WAY, IT'S TERRIBLE!
TRYING TO GET ME TO SHOW YOU PICTURES OF ME IS EVEN CREEPIER!
Ah ha ha ha ha!
ARE YOU SURE YOU CAN HANDLE HIGH SCHOOL WITH THAT BRAIN?
I SHOULD START CALLING YOU *CHIRPY*.
YOU'RE NOT EVEN A DOG, YOU'RE A BIRD!
A BIRD!
I'M SURPRISED YOU THOUGHT YOU COULD GET SOMETHING OUT OF ME!
Ha ha ha ha ha ha!
I'M SORRY... I...
I'M PREPARED FOR A SCOLDING...
Heh heh heh...
LET'S SEE...

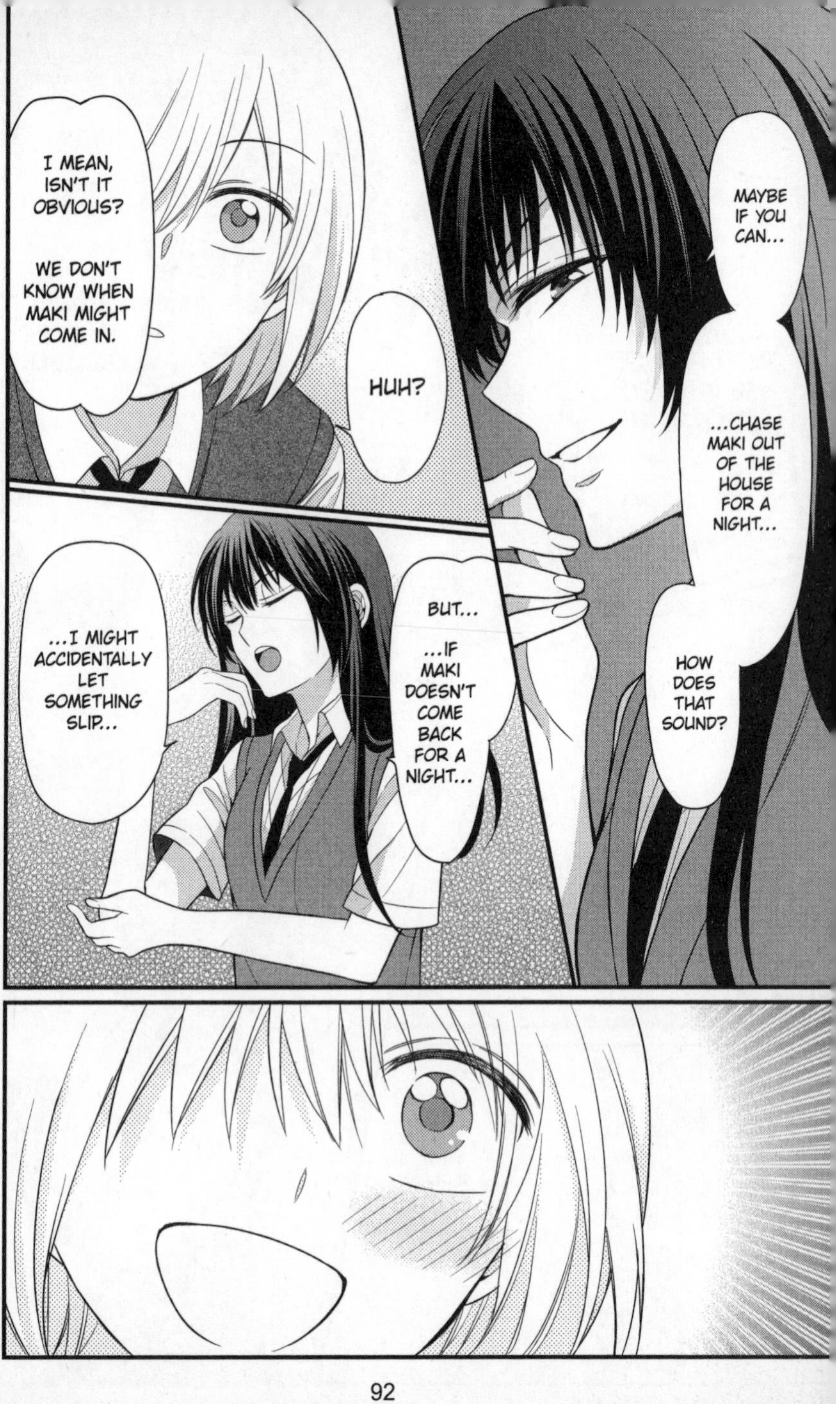

MAYBE IF YOU CAN...
...CHASE MAKI OUT OF THE HOUSE FOR A NIGHT...
HOW DOES THAT SOUND?
HUH?
I MEAN, ISN'T IT OBVIOUS?
WE DON'T KNOW WHEN MAKI MIGHT COME IN.
BUT...
...IF MAKI DOESN'T COME BACK FOR A NIGHT...
...I MIGHT ACCIDENTALLY LET SOMETHING SLIP...

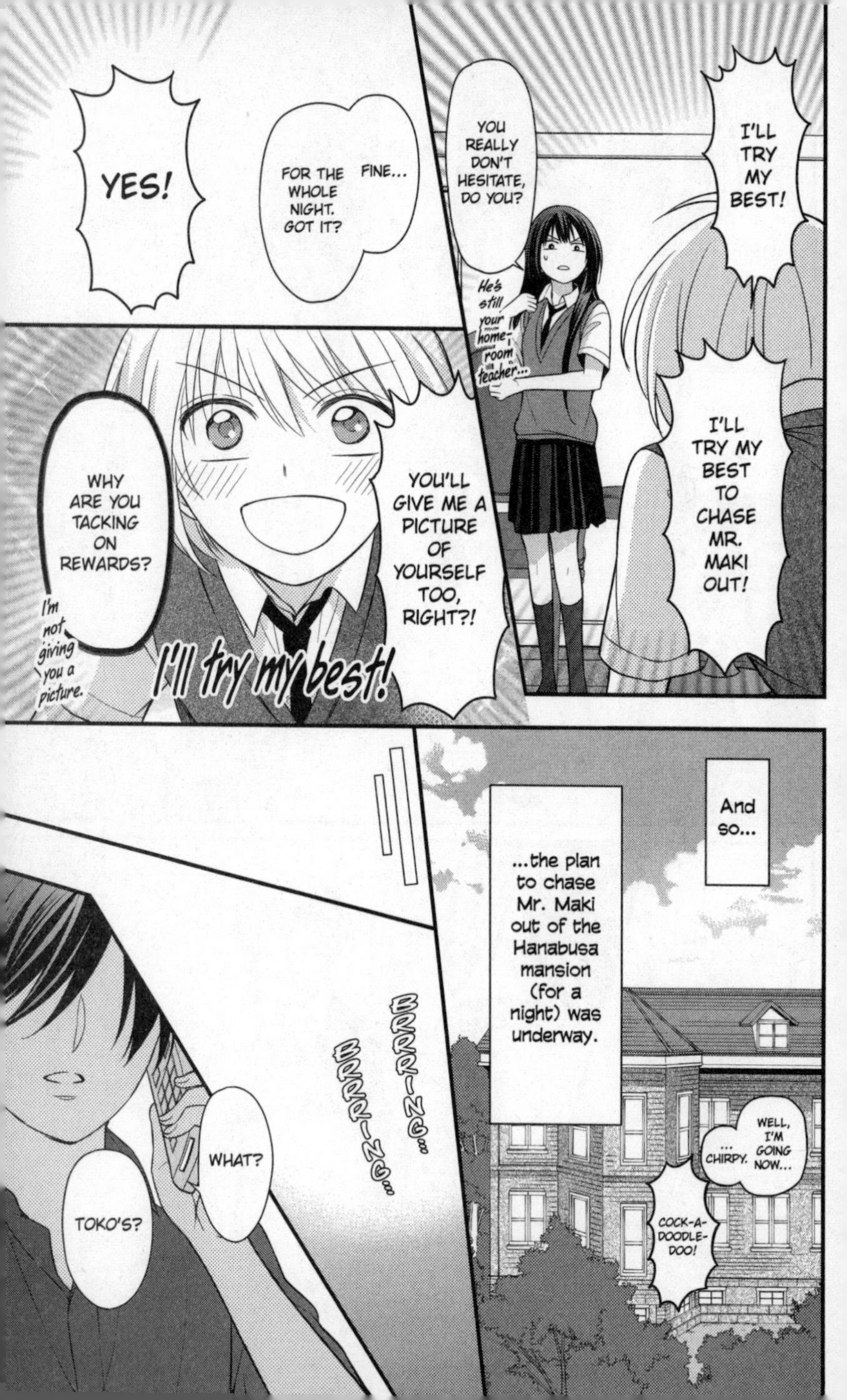
I'LL TRY MY BEST!
YOU REALLY DON'T HESITATE, DO YOU?
He's still your homeroom teacher...
I'LL TRY MY BEST TO CHASE MR. MAKI OUT!
FINE... FOR THE WHOLE NIGHT. GOT IT?
YES!
YOU'LL GIVE ME A PICTURE OF YOURSELF TOO, RIGHT?!
WHY ARE YOU TACKING ON REWARDS?
I'm not giving you a picture.
I'll try my best!
And so...
...the plan to chase Mr. Maki out of the Hanabusa mansion (for a night) was underway.
WELL, I'M GOING NOW...
...CHIRPY.
COCK-A-DOODLE-DOO!
BRRR-ING... BRRR-ING...
WHAT?
TOKO'S?

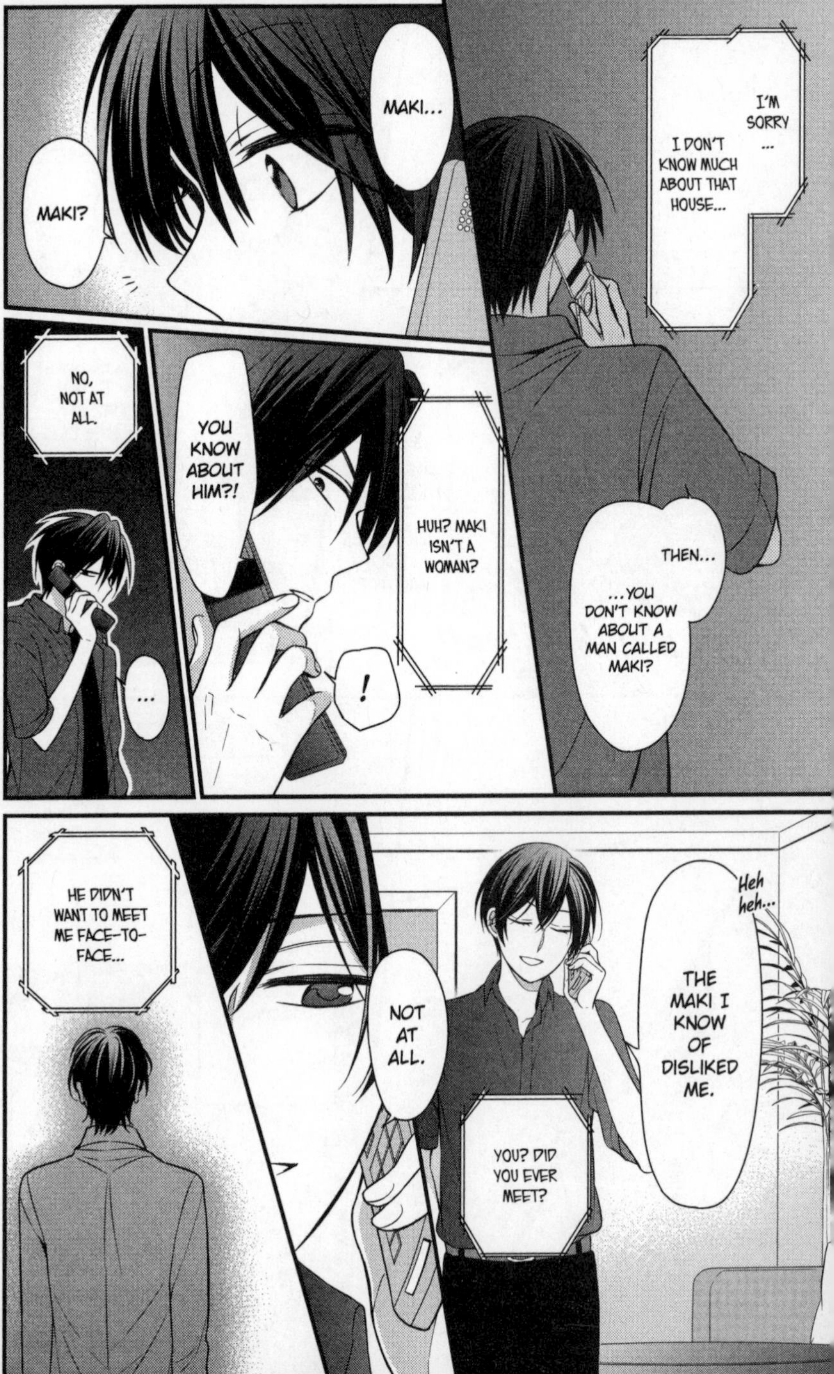
I'M SORRY ...
I DON'T KNOW MUCH ABOUT THAT HOUSE...
THEN...
...YOU DON'T KNOW ABOUT A MAN CALLED MAKI?
MAKI...
MAKI?
!
HUH? MAKI ISN'T A WOMAN?
YOU KNOW ABOUT HIM?!
NO, NOT AT ALL.
...
Heh heh...
THE MAKI I KNOW OF DISLIKED ME.
YOU? DID YOU EVER MEET?
NOT AT ALL.
HE DIDN'T WANT TO MEET ME FACE-TO-FACE...

Chapter 150

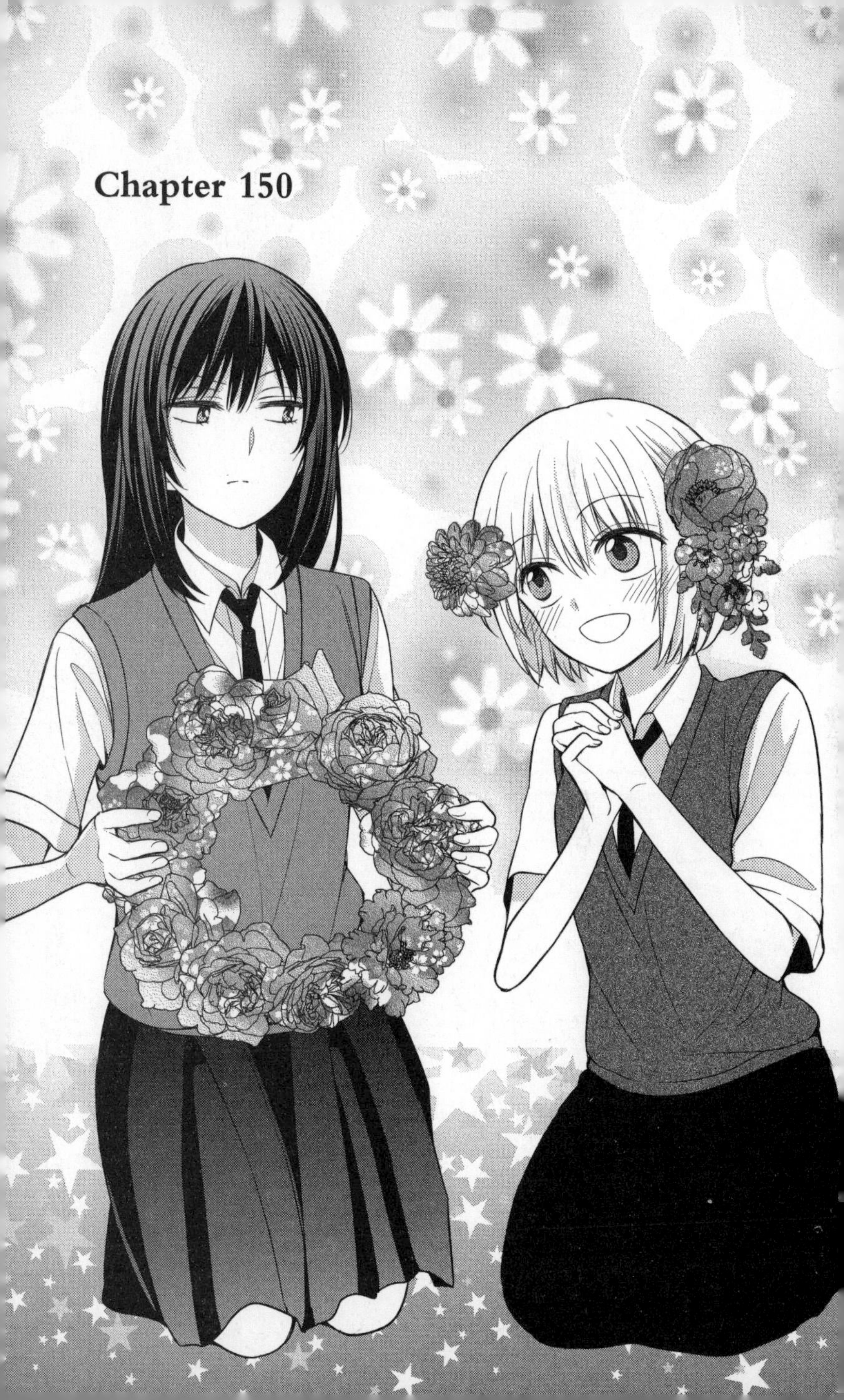

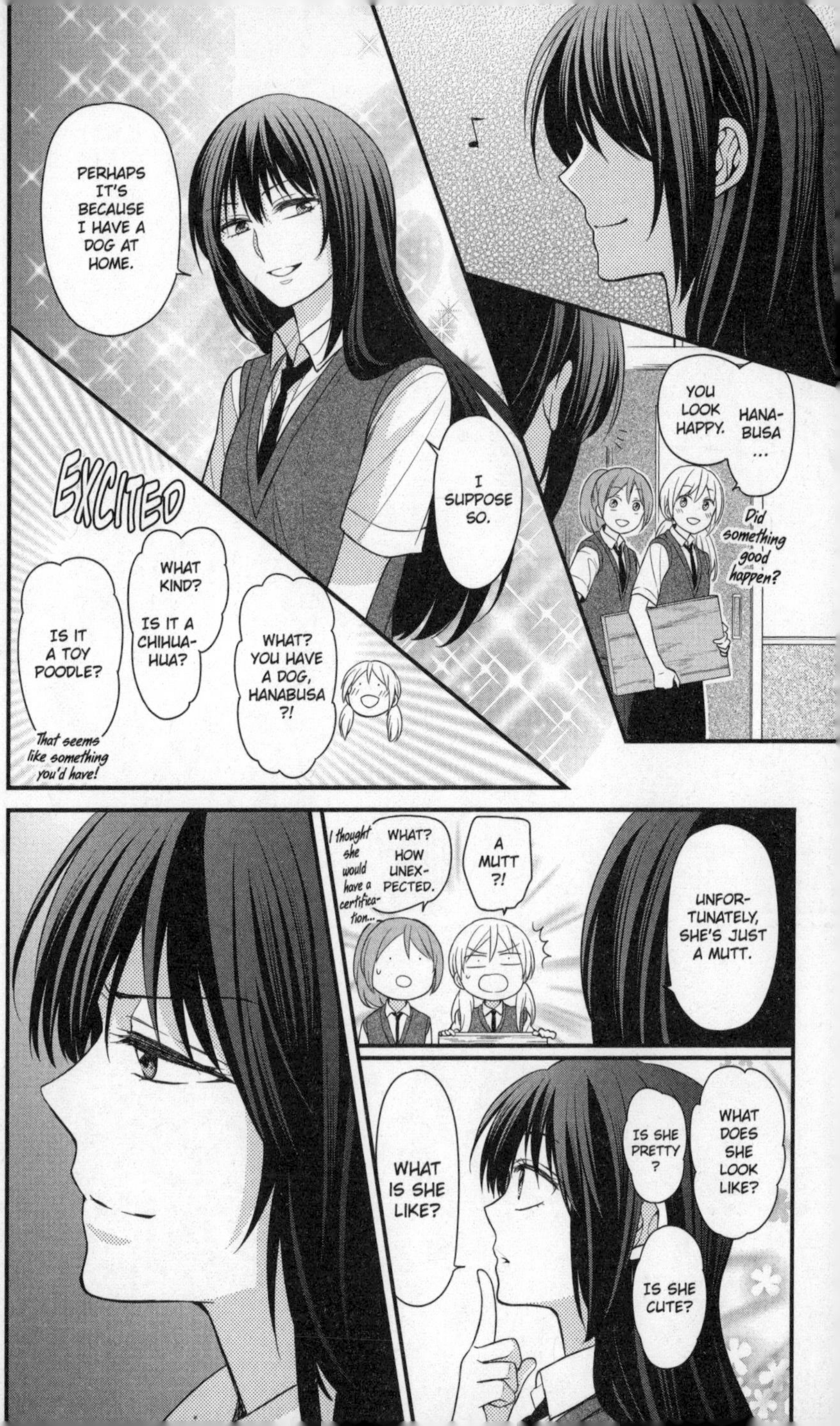
HANA-BUSA...
YOU LOOK HAPPY.
Did something good happen?
I SUPPOSE SO.
PERHAPS IT'S BECAUSE I HAVE A DOG AT HOME.
EXCITED
WHAT? YOU HAVE A DOG, HANABUSA?!
WHAT KIND? IS IT A CHIHUAHUA?
IS IT A TOY POODLE?
That seems like something you'd have!
UNFORTUNATELY, SHE'S JUST A MUTT.
A MUTT?!
WHAT? HOW UNEXPECTED.
I thought she would have a certification...
WHAT DOES SHE LOOK LIKE?
IS SHE PRETTY?
IS SHE CUTE?
WHAT IS SHE LIKE?

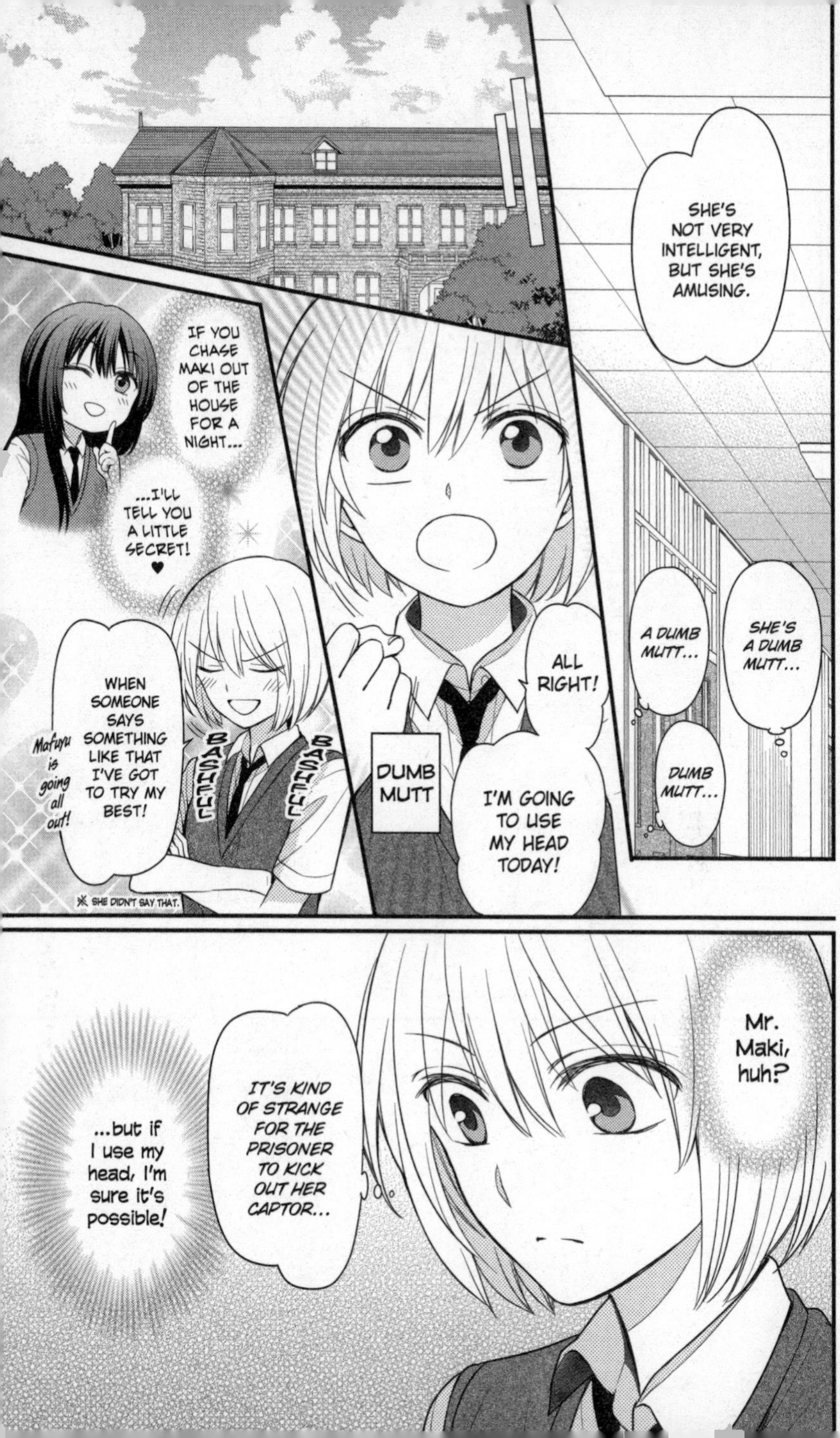
SHE'S NOT VERY INTELLIGENT, BUT SHE'S AMUSING.
SHE'S A DUMB MUTT...
A DUMB MUTT...
DUMB MUTT...
ALL RIGHT!
I'M GOING TO USE MY HEAD TODAY!
DUMB MUTT
IF YOU CHASE MAKI OUT OF THE HOUSE FOR A NIGHT...
...I'LL TELL YOU A LITTLE SECRET! ♥
WHEN SOMEONE SAYS SOMETHING LIKE THAT I'VE GOT TO TRY MY BEST!
BASHFUL
BASHFUL
Mafuyu is going all out!
※ SHE DIDN'T SAY THAT.
Mr. Maki, huh?
IT'S KIND OF STRANGE FOR THE PRISONER TO KICK OUT HER CAPTOR...
...but if I use my head, I'm sure it's possible!

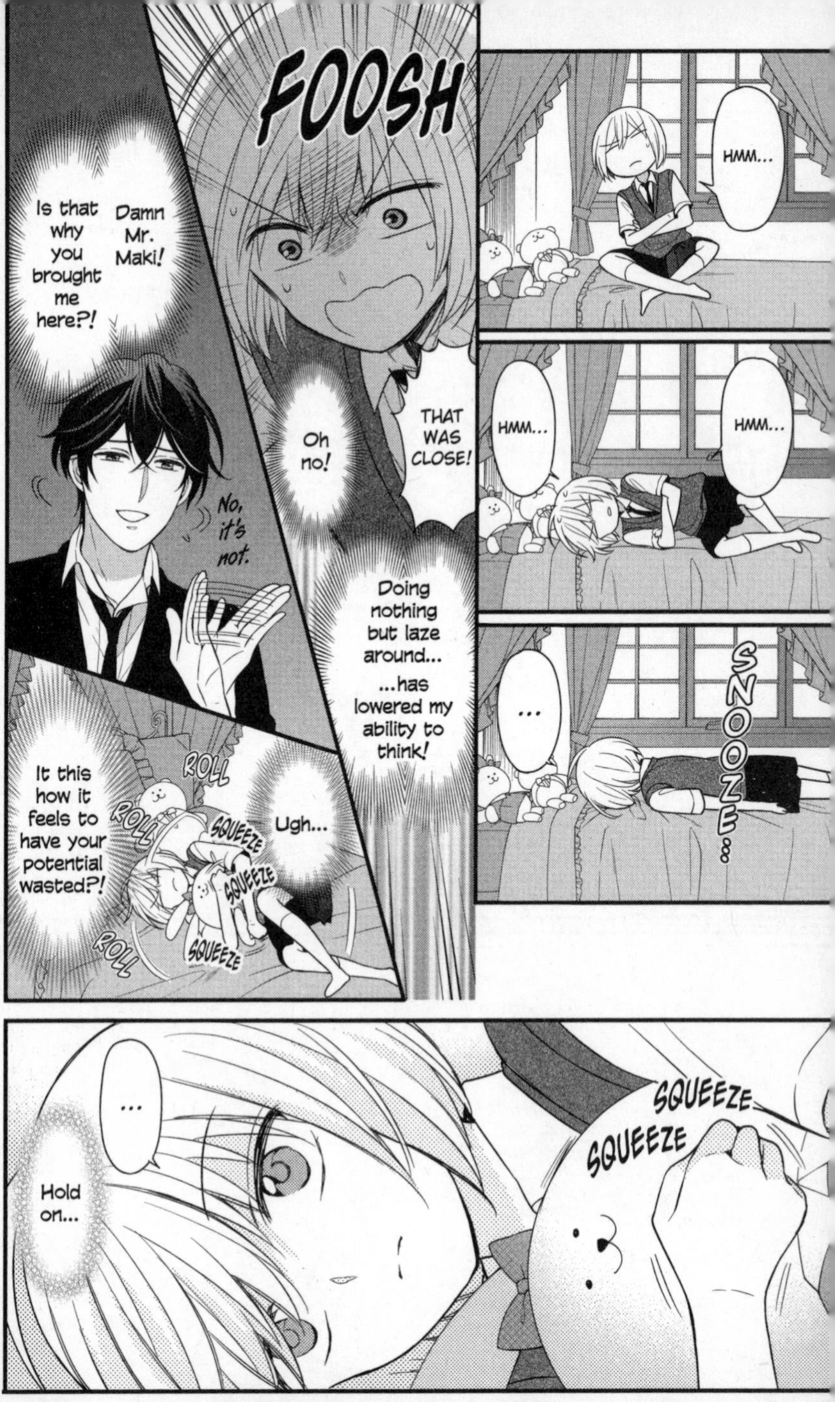
HMM...
HMM...
HMM...
...
SNOOZE...
FOOSH
THAT WAS CLOSE!
Oh no!
Doing nothing but laze around...
...has lowered my ability to think!
Ugh...
Damn Mr. Maki!
Is that why you brought me here?!
No, it's not.
It this how it feels to have your potential wasted?!
ROLL
ROLL
SQUEEZE
SQUEEZE
ROLL
SQUEEZE
...
Hold on...
SQUEEZE
SQUEEZE

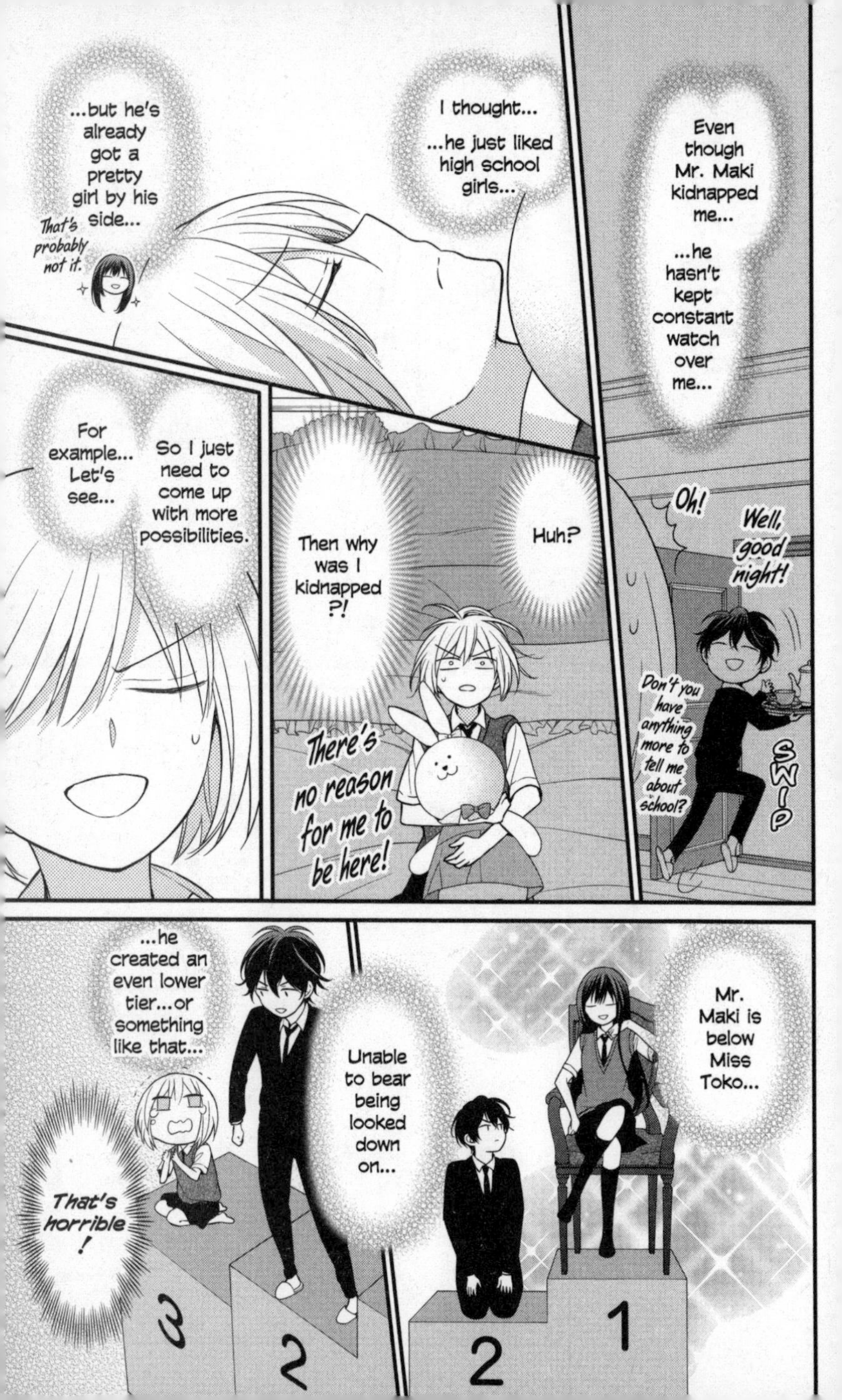

Even though Mr. Maki kidnapped me...
...he hasn't kept constant watch over me...
Oh!
Well, good night!
Don't you have anything more to tell me about school?
SWIP
I thought...
...he just liked high school girls...
...but he's already got a pretty girl by his side...
That's probably not it.
Huh?
Then why was I kidnapped ?!
There's no reason for me to be here!
So I just need to come up with more possibilities.
For example... Let's see...
Mr. Maki is below Miss Toko...
1
2
Unable to bear being looked down on...
...he created an even lower tier...or something like that...
2
3
That's horrible!

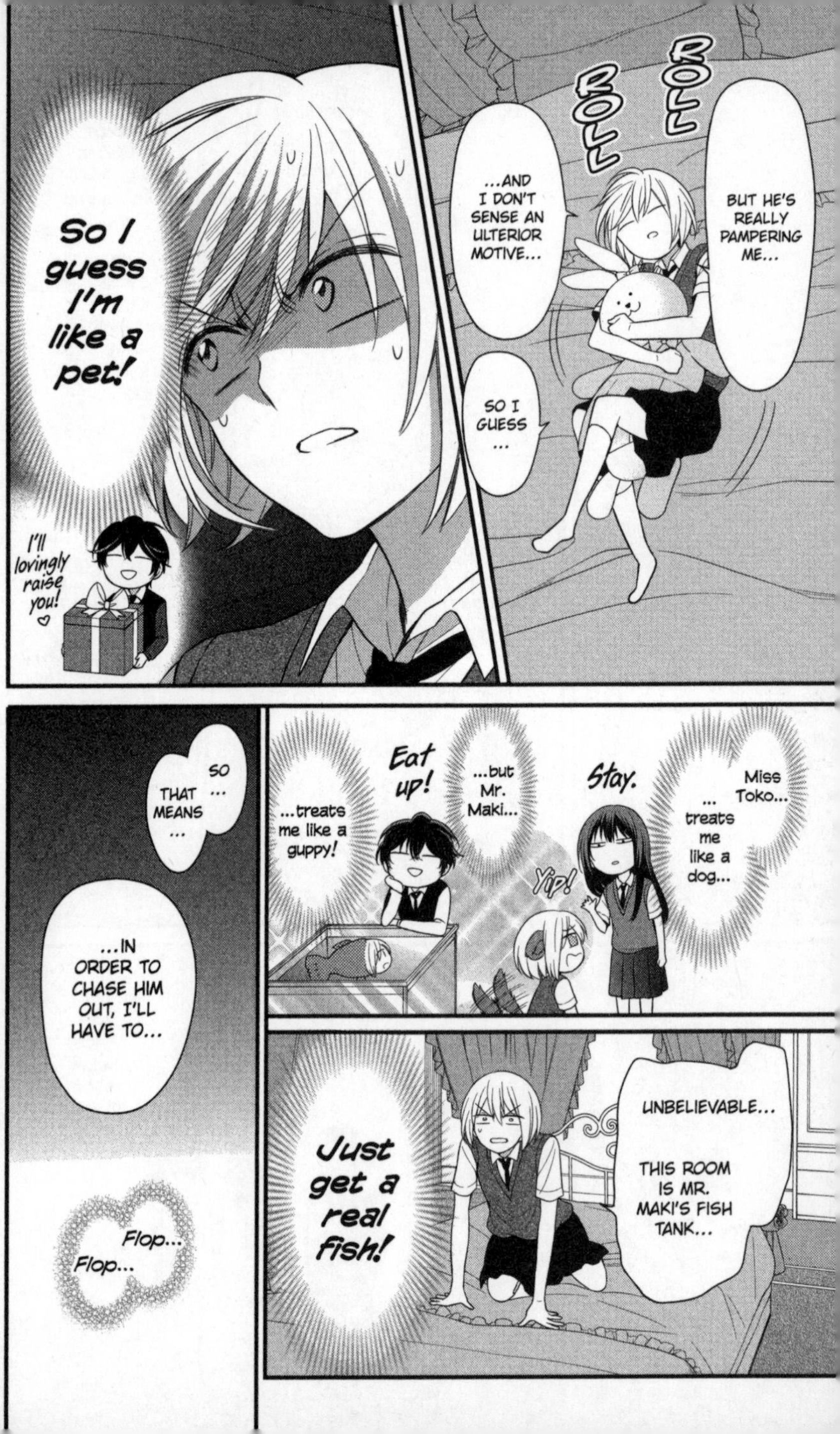
ROLL
ROLL
BUT HE'S REALLY PAMPERING ME...
...AND I DON'T SENSE AN ULTERIOR MOTIVE...
SO I GUESS...
So I guess I'm like a pet!
I'll lovingly raise you! ♡
Miss Toko... ...treats me like a dog...
Stay.
Yip!
...but Mr. Maki...
Eat up!
...treats me like a guppy!
UNBELIEVABLE...
THIS ROOM IS MR. MAKI'S FISH TANK...
Just get a real fish!
SO... THAT MEANS...
...IN ORDER TO CHASE HIM OUT, I'LL HAVE TO...
Flop... Flop...

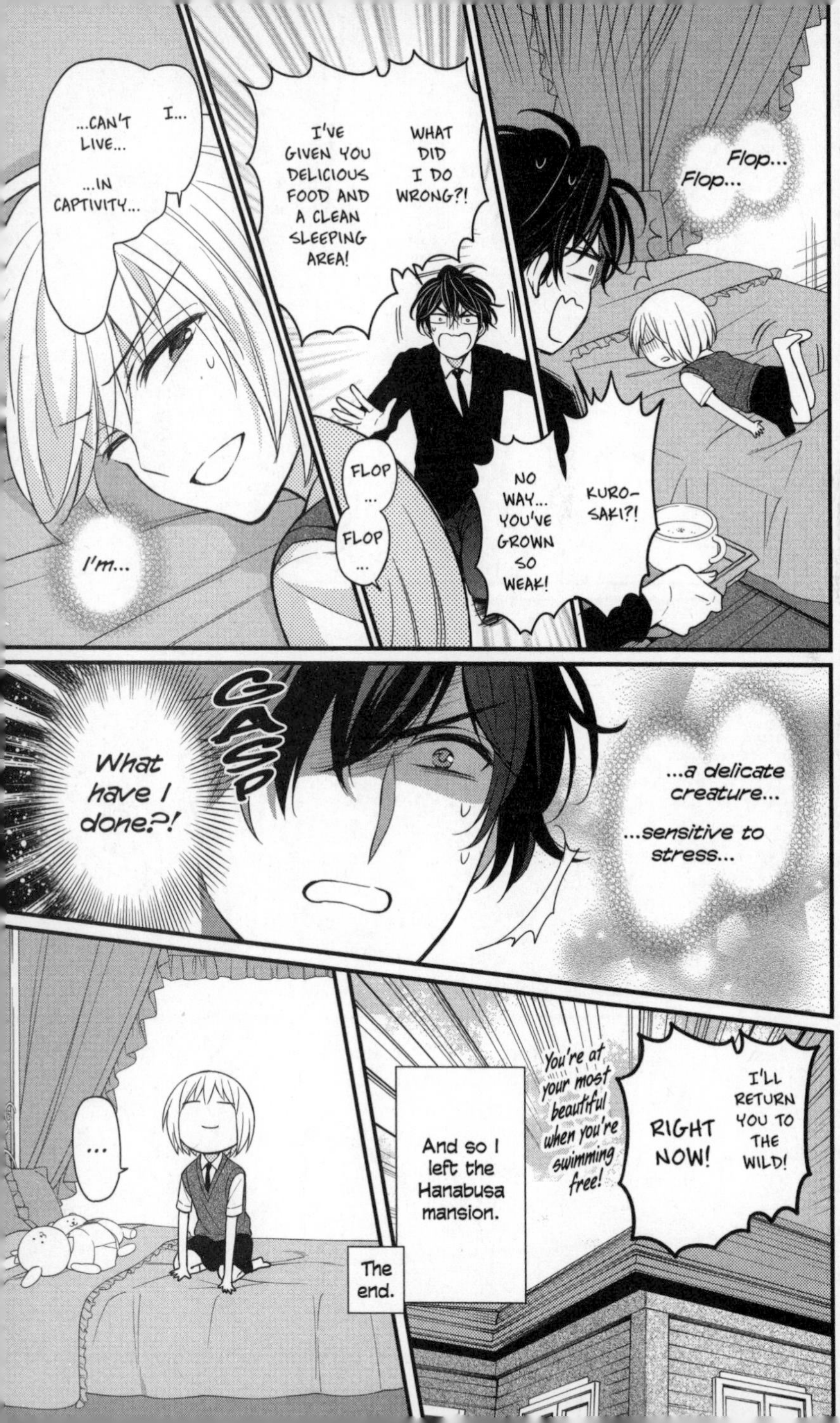
Flop... Flop...
KURO-SAKI?!
NO WAY... YOU'VE GROWN SO WEAK!
WHAT DID I DO WRONG?!
I'VE GIVEN YOU DELICIOUS FOOD AND A CLEAN SLEEPING AREA!
FLOP ... FLOP ...
I...
...CAN'T LIVE...
...IN CAPTIVITY...
I'm...
...a delicate creature...
...sensitive to stress...
GASP
What have I done?!
I'LL RETURN YOU TO THE WILD!
RIGHT NOW!
You're at your most beautiful when you're swimming free!
And so I left the Hanabusa mansion.
...
The end.

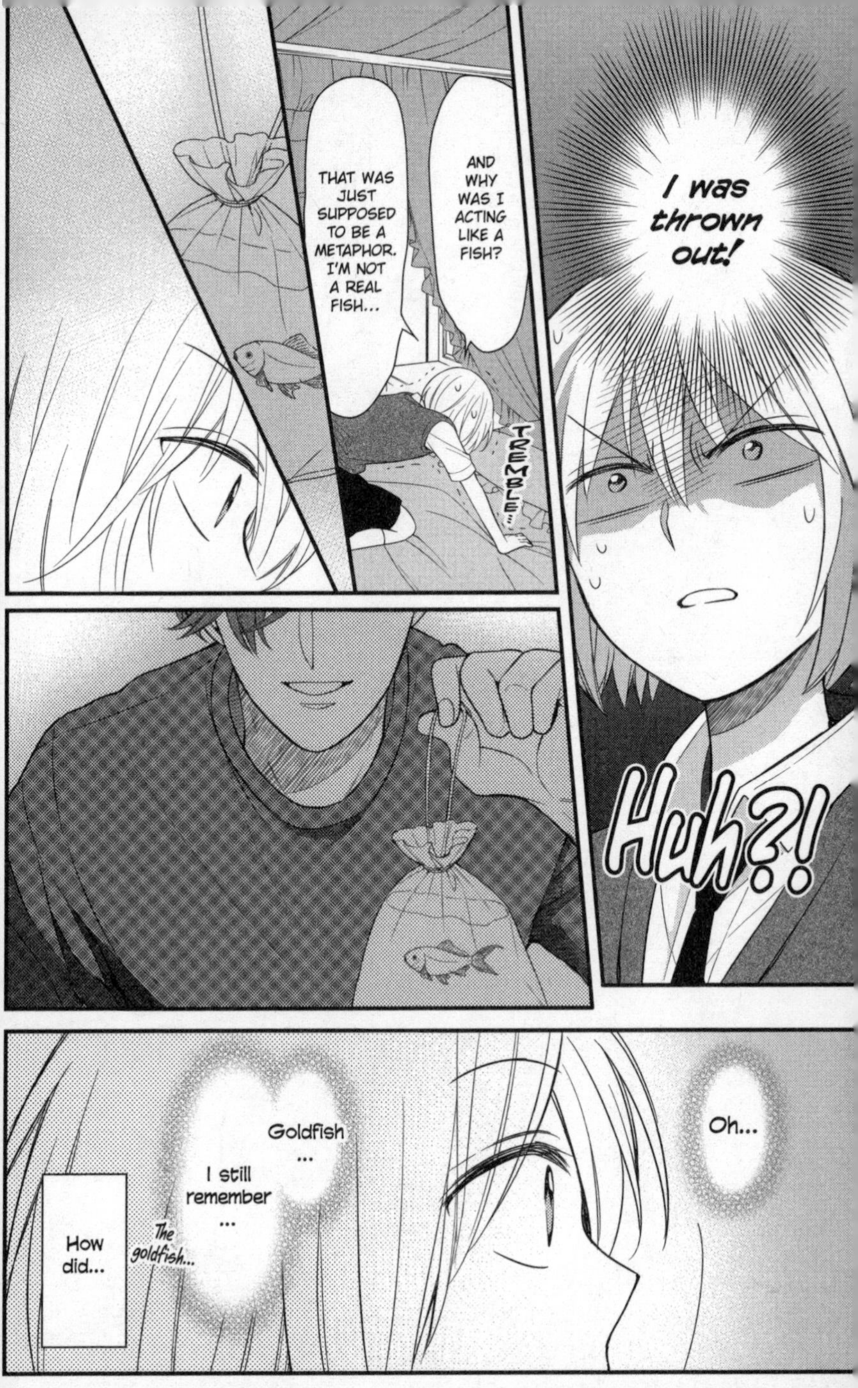
I was thrown out!
Huh?!
AND WHY WAS I ACTING LIKE A FISH?
THAT WAS JUST SUPPOSED TO BE A METAPHOR. I'M NOT A REAL FISH...
TREMBLE...
Oh...
Goldfish...
I still remember...
The goldfish...
How did...

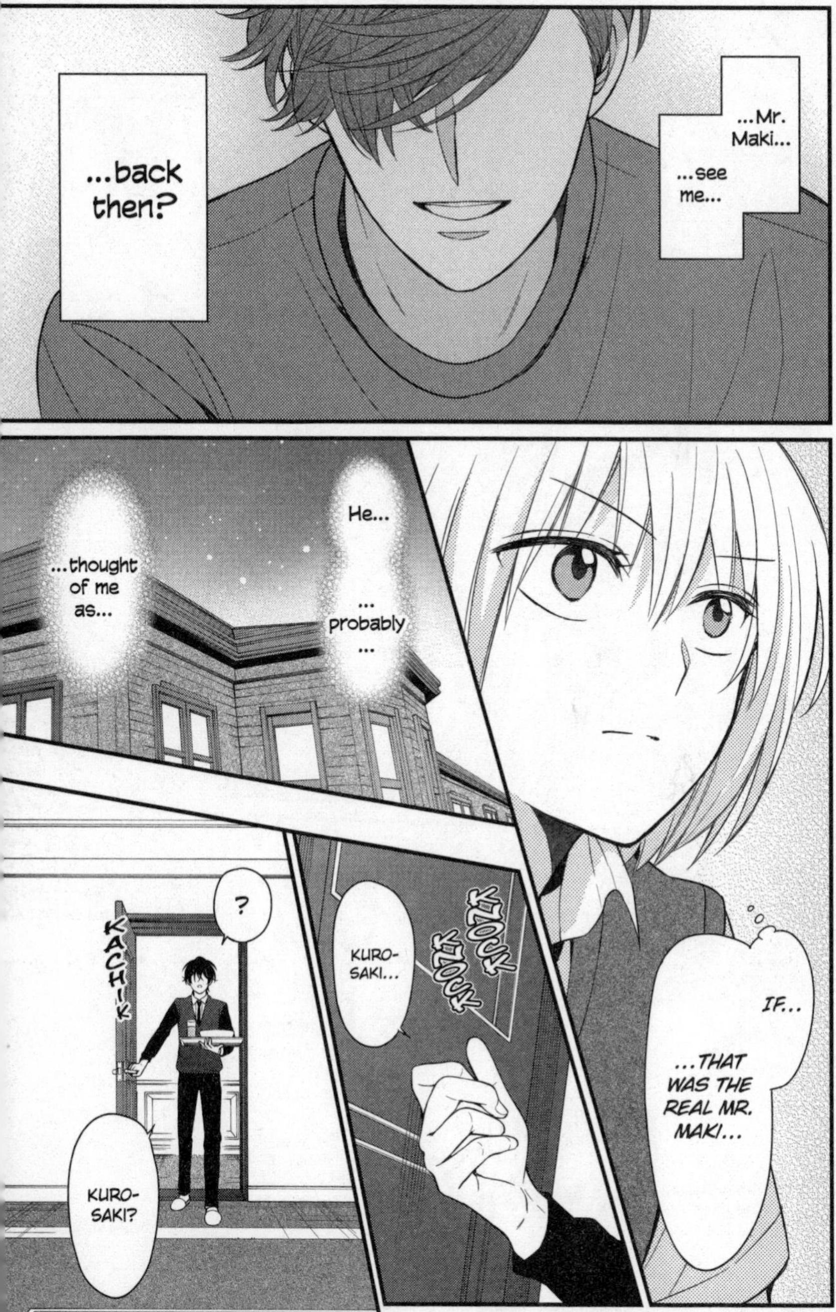
...Mr. Maki... ...see me...
...back then?
IF... ...THAT WAS THE REAL MR. MAKI...
He... ...probably...
...thought of me as...
KLOCK KLOCK
KURO-SAKI...
KACHIK
?
KURO-SAKI?

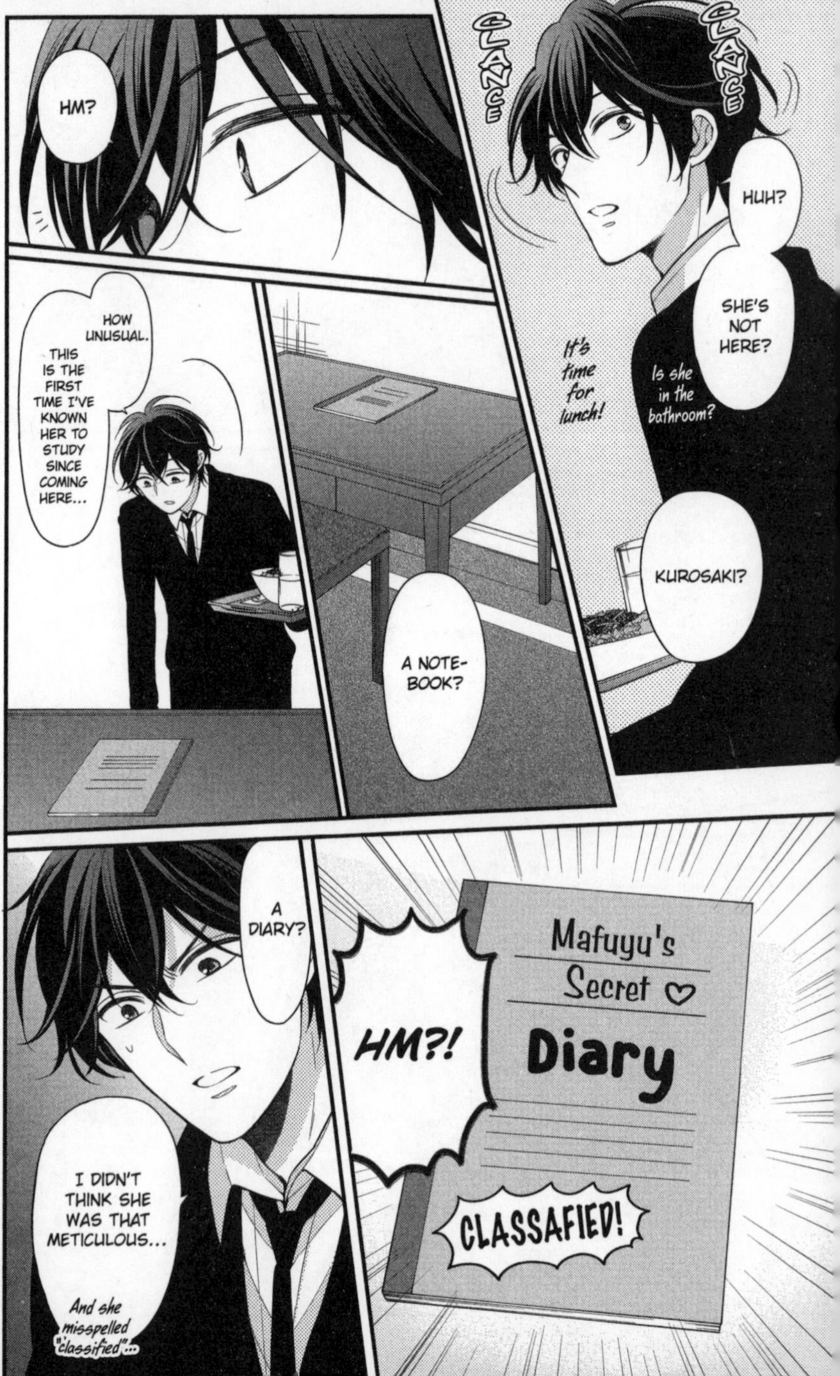
GLANCE
GLANCE
HUH?
SHE'S NOT HERE?
Is she in the bathroom?
It's time for lunch!
KUROSAKI?
HM?
A NOTE-BOOK?
HOW UNUSUAL.
THIS IS THE FIRST TIME I'VE KNOWN HER TO STUDY SINCE COMING HERE...
HM?!
Mafuyu's Secret ♡ Diary
CLASSAFIED!
A DIARY?
I DIDN'T THINK SHE WAS THAT METICULOUS...
And she misspelled "classified"...

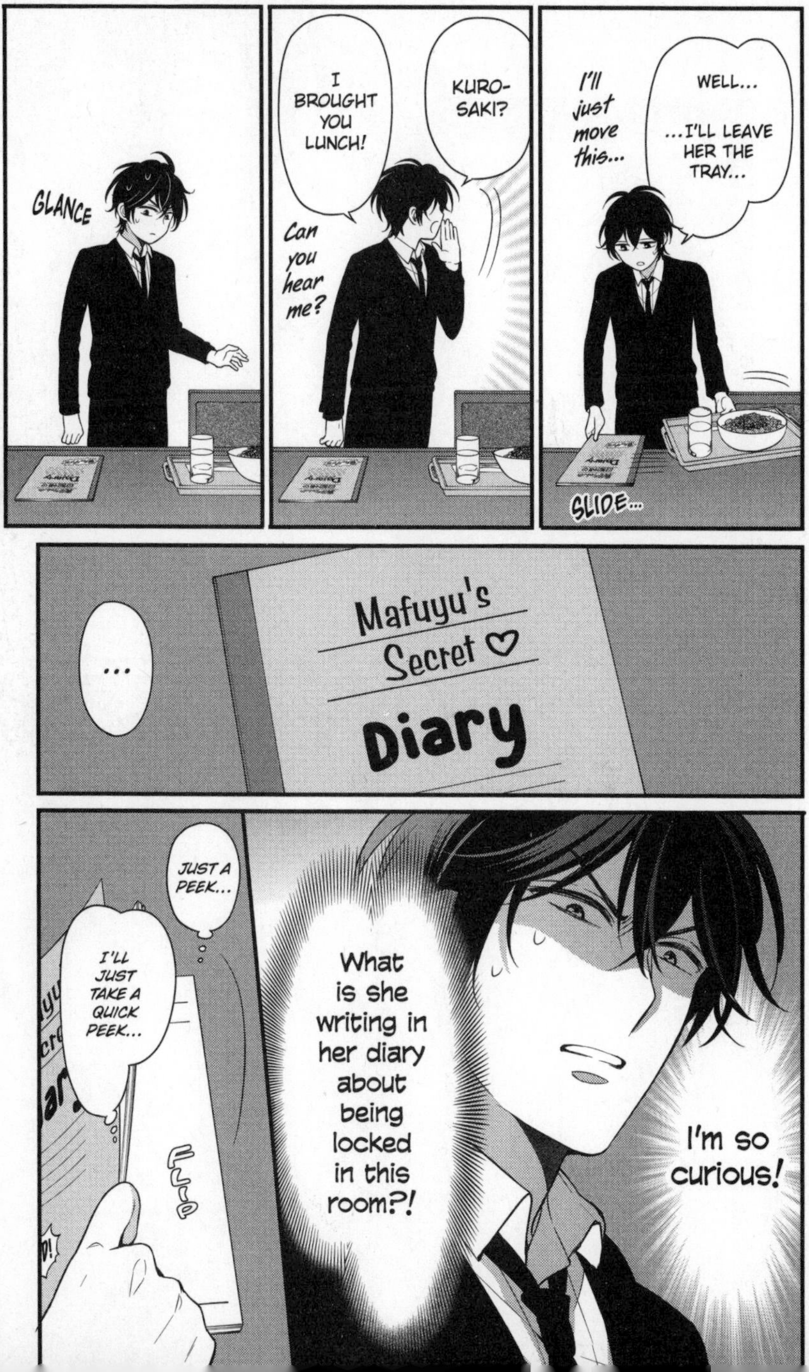
WELL...
...I'LL LEAVE HER THE TRAY...
I'll just move this...
SLIDE...
KURO-SAKI?
I BROUGHT YOU LUNCH!
Can you hear me?
GLANCE
Mafuyu's Secret ♡ Diary
...
I'm so curious!
What is she writing in her diary about being locked in this room?!
JUST A PEEK...
I'LL JUST TAKE A QUICK PEEK...
FLIP

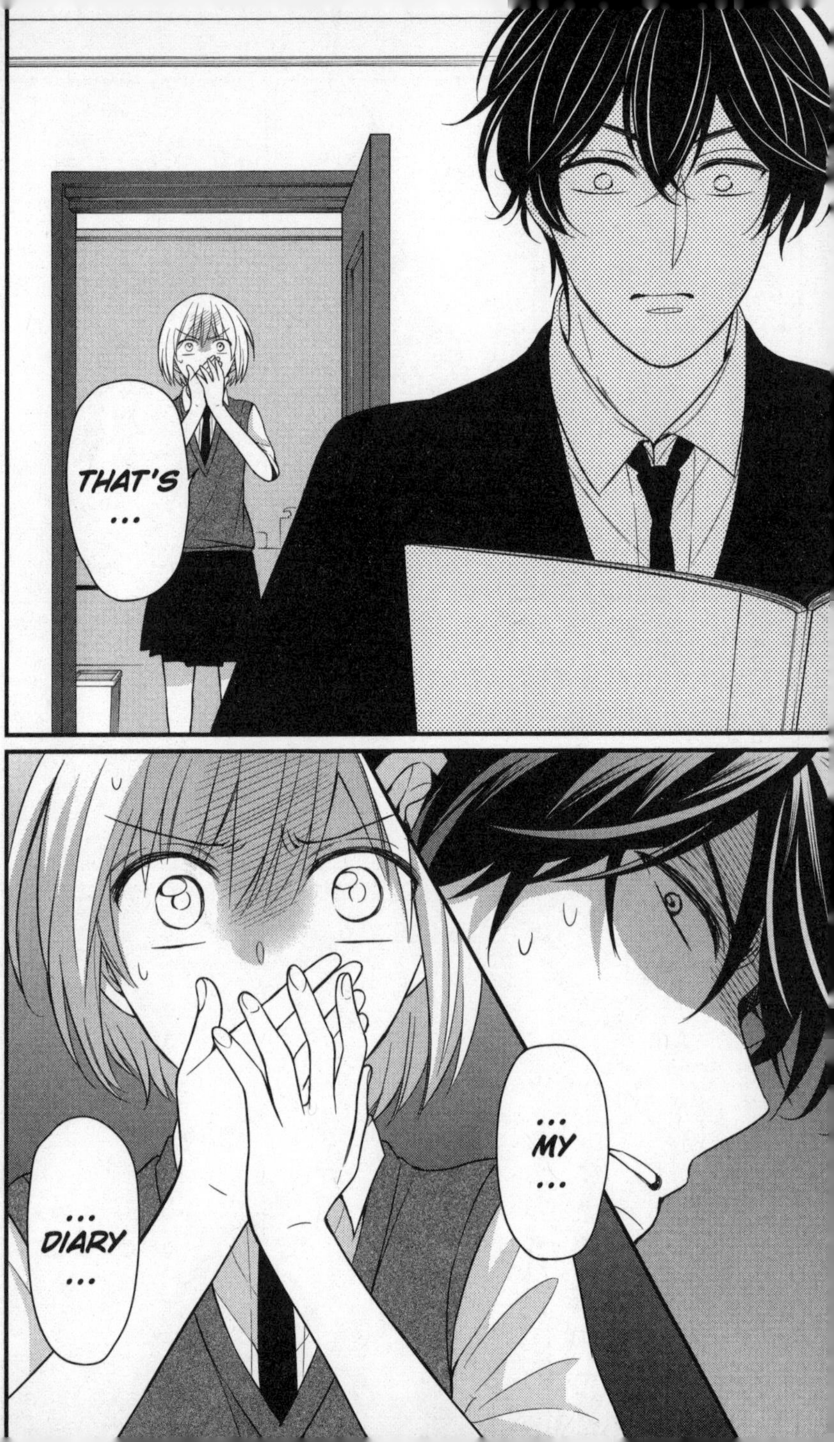
THAT'S ...
... MY ...
... DIARY ...

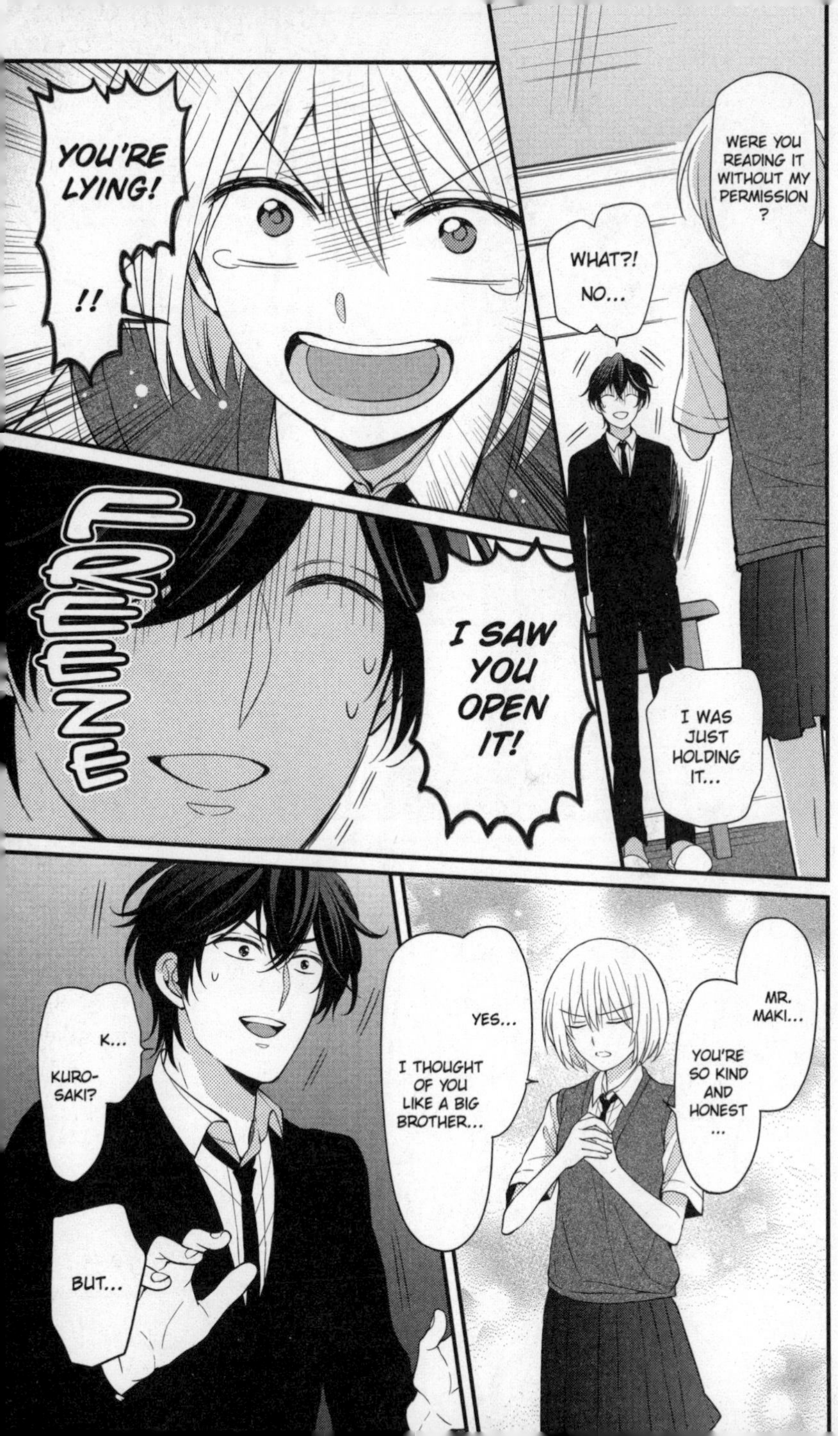
WERE YOU READING IT WITHOUT MY PERMISSION?
WHAT?! NO...
I WAS JUST HOLDING IT...
YOU'RE LYING!
!!
FREEZE
I SAW YOU OPEN IT!
MR. MAKI...
YOU'RE SO KIND AND HONEST...
YES...
I THOUGHT OF YOU LIKE A BIG BROTHER...
K...
KURO-SAKI?
BUT...

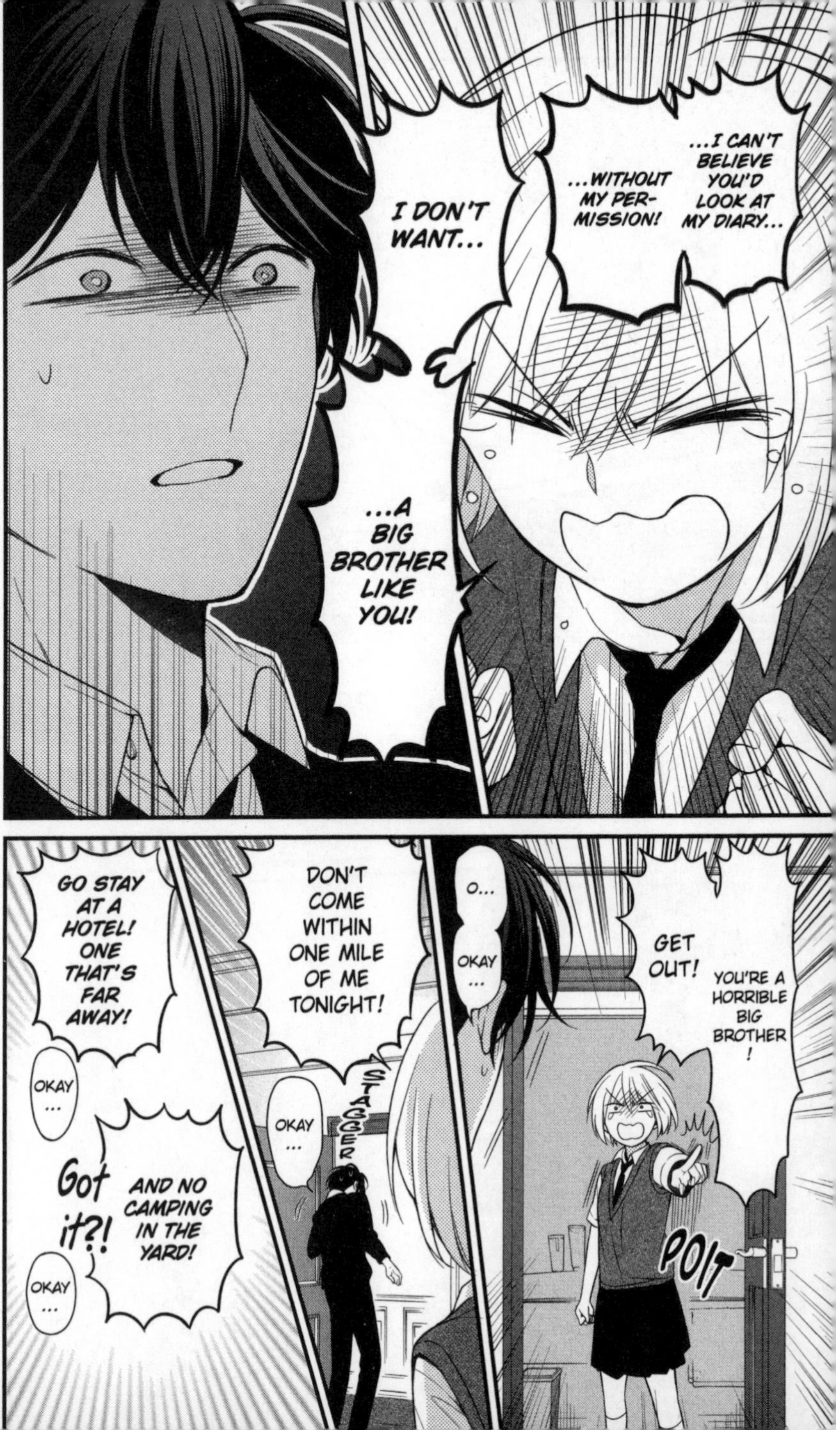
...I CAN'T BELIEVE YOU'D LOOK AT MY DIARY...
...WITHOUT MY PER-MISSION!
I DON'T WANT...
...A BIG BROTHER LIKE YOU!
GET OUT!
YOU'RE A HORRIBLE BIG BROTHER!
POIT
O...
OKAY...
DON'T COME WITHIN ONE MILE OF ME TONIGHT!
STAGGER
OKAY...
GO STAY AT A HOTEL! ONE THAT'S FAR AWAY!
OKAY...
AND NO CAMPING IN THE YARD!
Got it?!
OKAY...

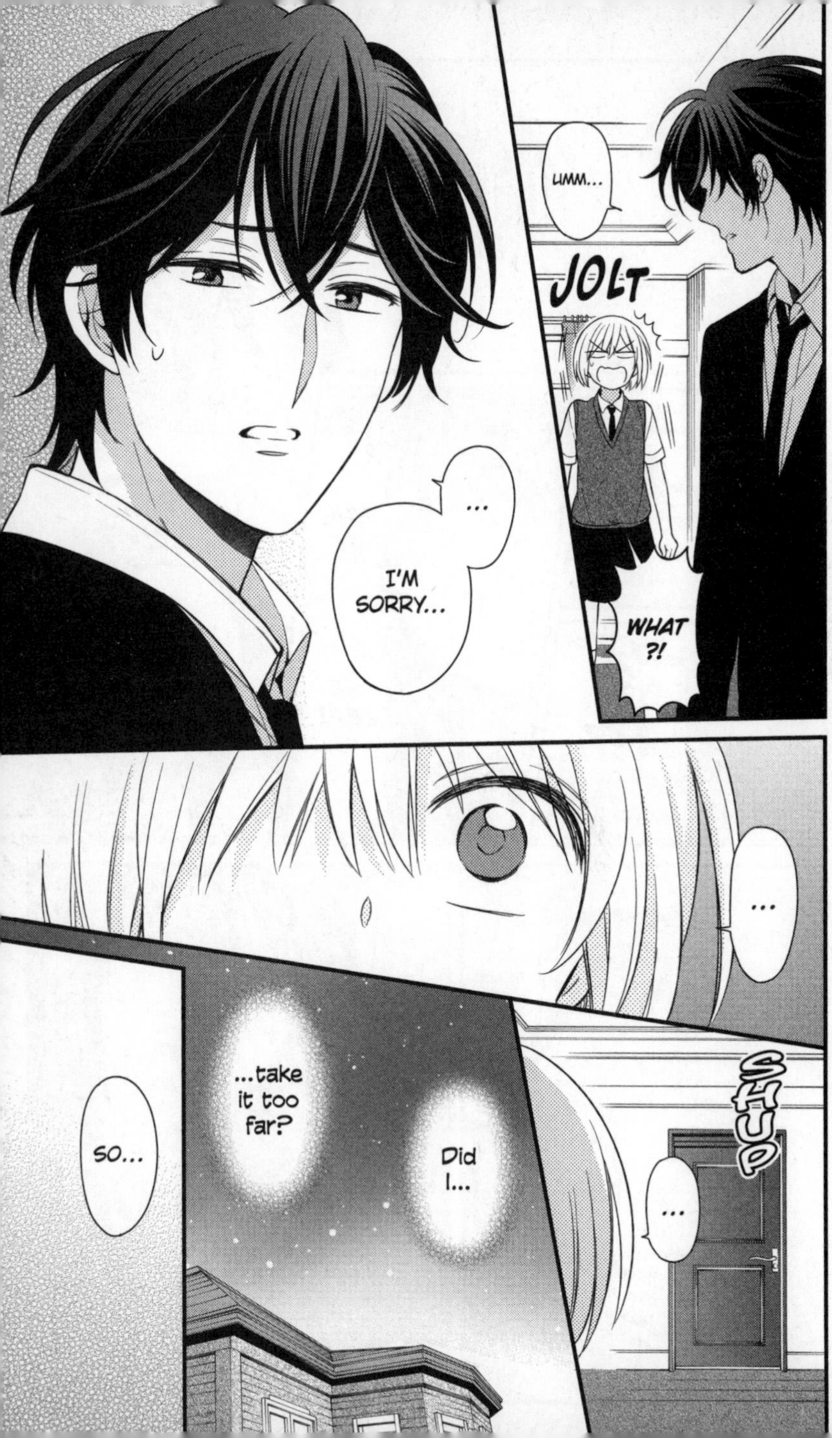
UMM...
JOLT
WHAT ?!
...
I'M SORRY...
...
SHUP
...
Did I...
...take it too far?
SO...

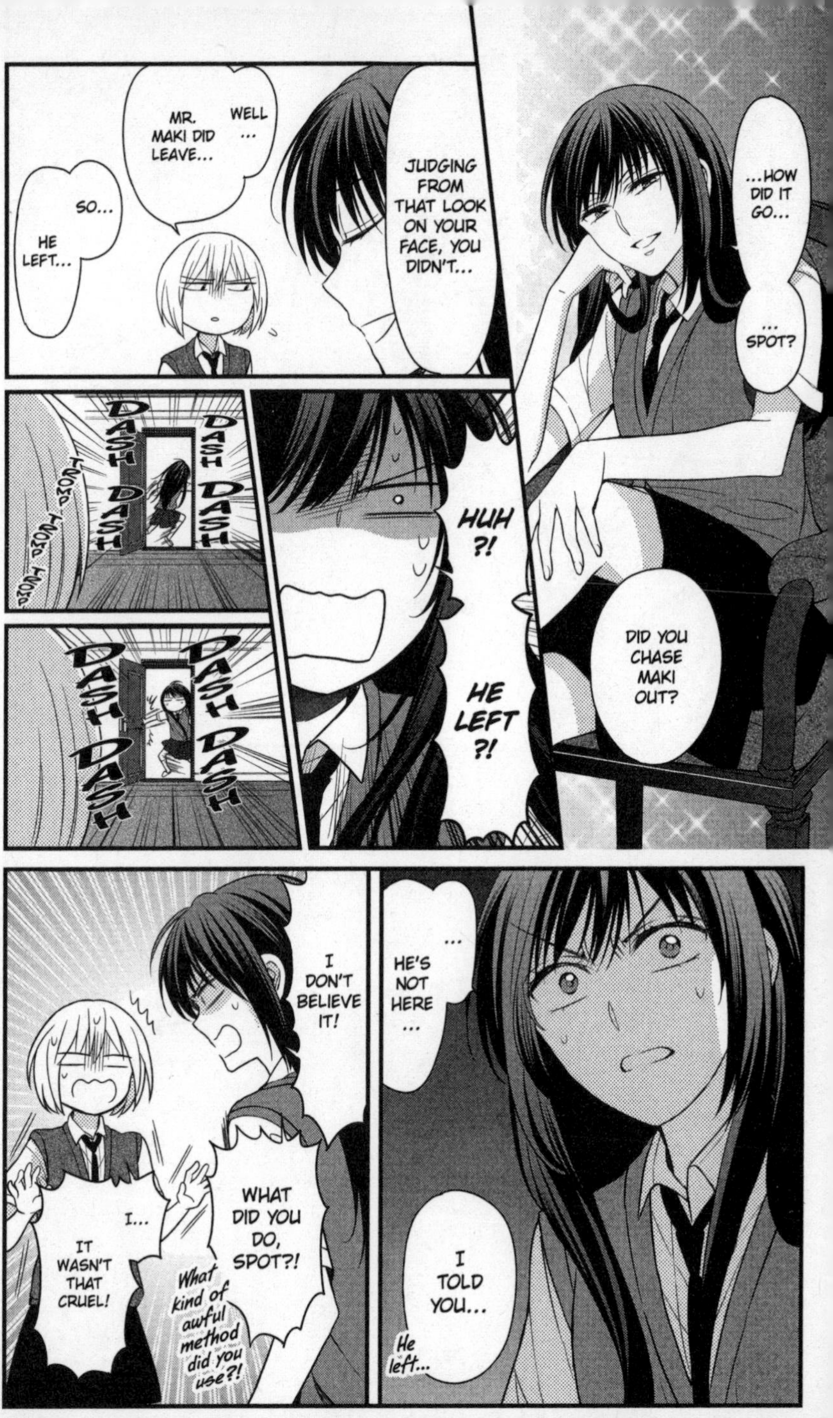
...HOW DID IT GO...
...SPOT?
DID YOU CHASE MAKI OUT?
JUDGING FROM THAT LOOK ON YOUR FACE, YOU DIDN'T...
WELL...
MR. MAKI DID LEAVE...
SO... HE LEFT...
HUH?!
HE LEFT?!
DASH DASH
DASH DASH
TROMP TROMP TROMP
DASH DASH
DASH DASH
...
HE'S NOT HERE...
I TOLD YOU...
He left...
I DON'T BELIEVE IT!
WHAT DID YOU DO, SPOT?!
What kind of awful method did you use?!
I...
IT WASN'T THAT CRUEL!

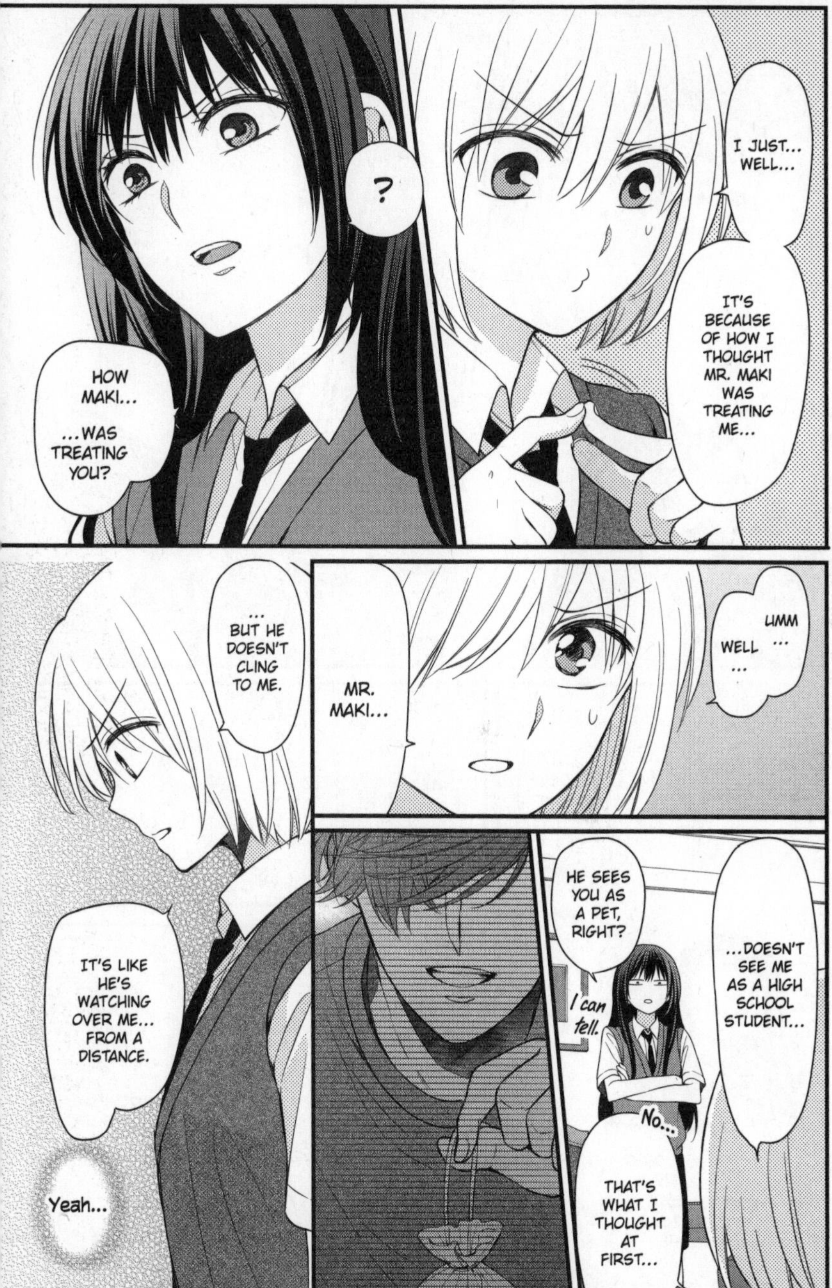
I JUST... WELL...
IT'S BECAUSE OF HOW I THOUGHT MR. MAKI WAS TREATING ME...
?
HOW MAKI... ...WAS TREATING YOU?
UMM... WELL...
MR. MAKI...
...DOESN'T SEE ME AS A HIGH SCHOOL STUDENT...
HE SEES YOU AS A PET, RIGHT?
I can tell.
No...
THAT'S WHAT I THOUGHT AT FIRST...
... BUT HE DOESN'T CLING TO ME.
IT'S LIKE HE'S WATCHING OVER ME... FROM A DISTANCE.
Yeah...

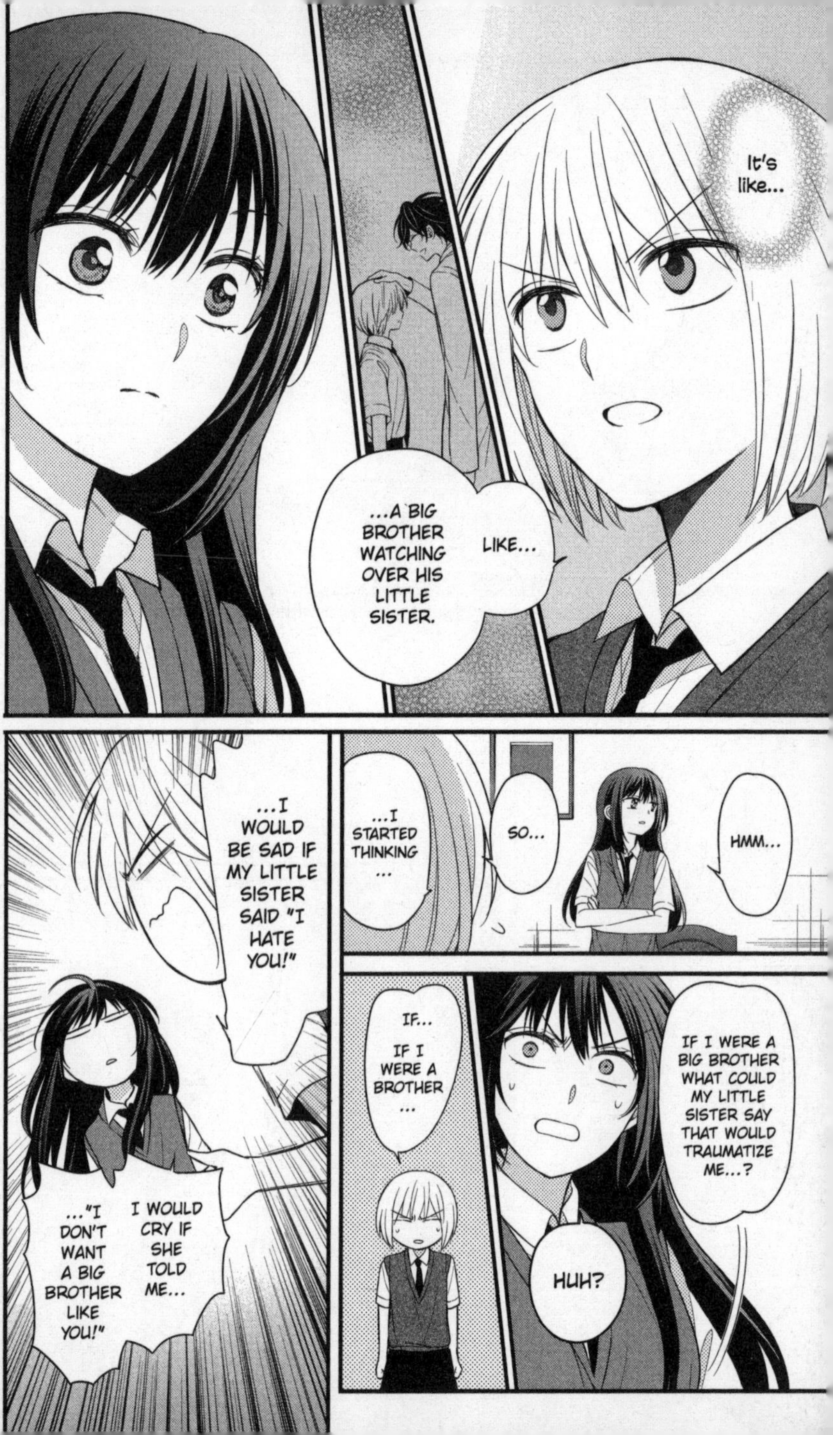
It's like...
LIKE...
...A BIG BROTHER WATCHING OVER HIS LITTLE SISTER.
HMM...
SO...
...I STARTED THINKING...
IF I WERE A BIG BROTHER WHAT COULD MY LITTLE SISTER SAY THAT WOULD TRAUMATIZE ME...?
IF... IF I WERE A BROTHER...
HUH?
...I WOULD BE SAD IF MY LITTLE SISTER SAID "I HATE YOU!"
I WOULD CRY IF SHE TOLD ME...
..."I DON'T WANT A BIG BROTHER LIKE YOU!"

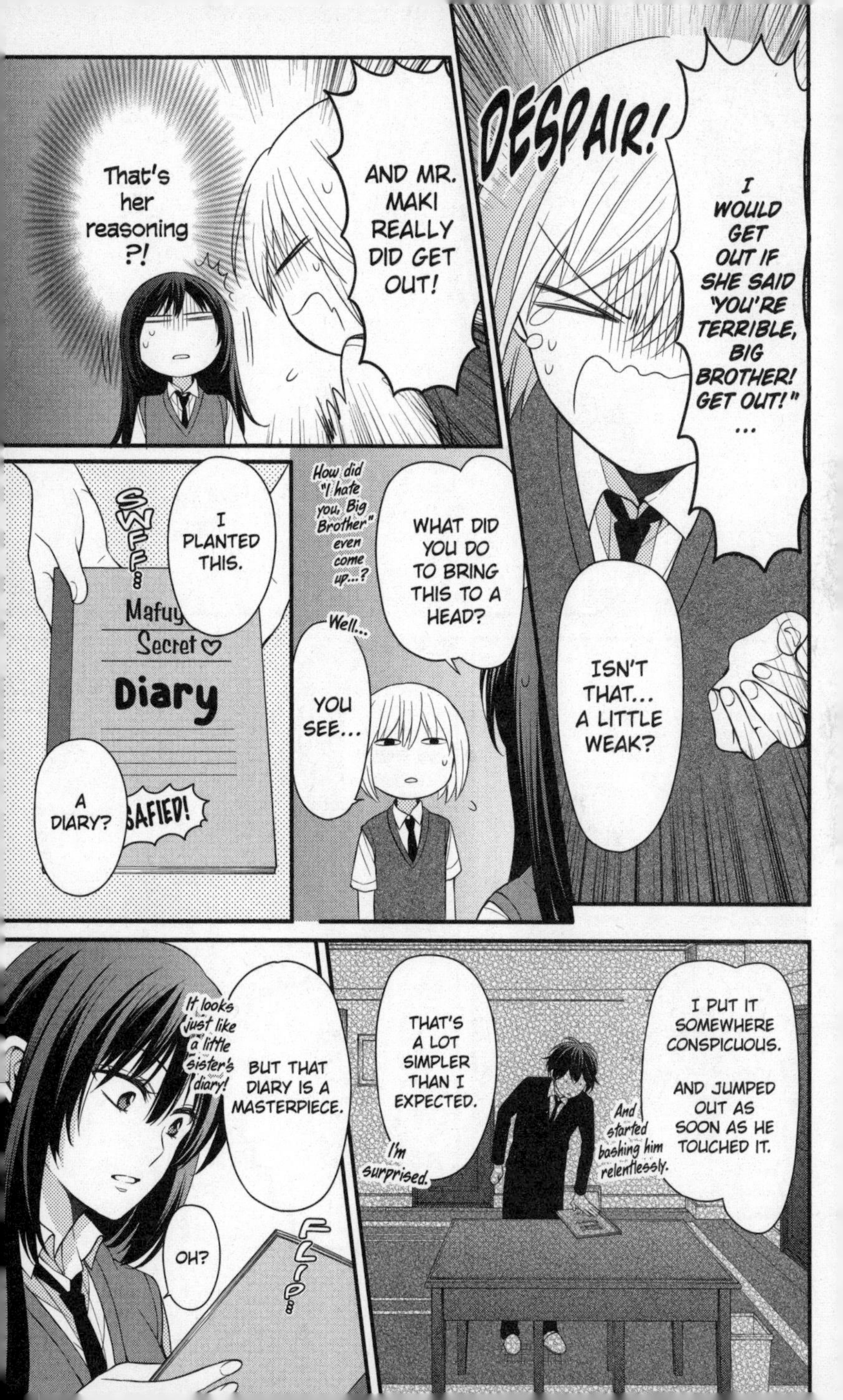
DESPAIR!
I WOULD GET OUT IF SHE SAID "YOU'RE TERRIBLE, BIG BROTHER! GET OUT!" ...
ISN'T THAT... A LITTLE WEAK?
AND MR. MAKI REALLY DID GET OUT!
That's her reasoning?!
WHAT DID YOU DO TO BRING THIS TO A HEAD?
How did "I hate you, Big Brother" even come up...?
Well...
YOU SEE...
I PLANTED THIS.
SWFF
Mafuy
Secret ♡
Diary
SAFIED!
A DIARY?
I PUT IT SOMEWHERE CONSPICUOUS.
AND JUMPED OUT AS SOON AS HE TOUCHED IT.
And started bashing him relentlessly.
THAT'S A LOT SIMPLER THAN I EXPECTED.
I'm surprised.
BUT THAT DIARY IS A MASTERPIECE.
It looks just like a little sister's diary!
OH?
FLIP

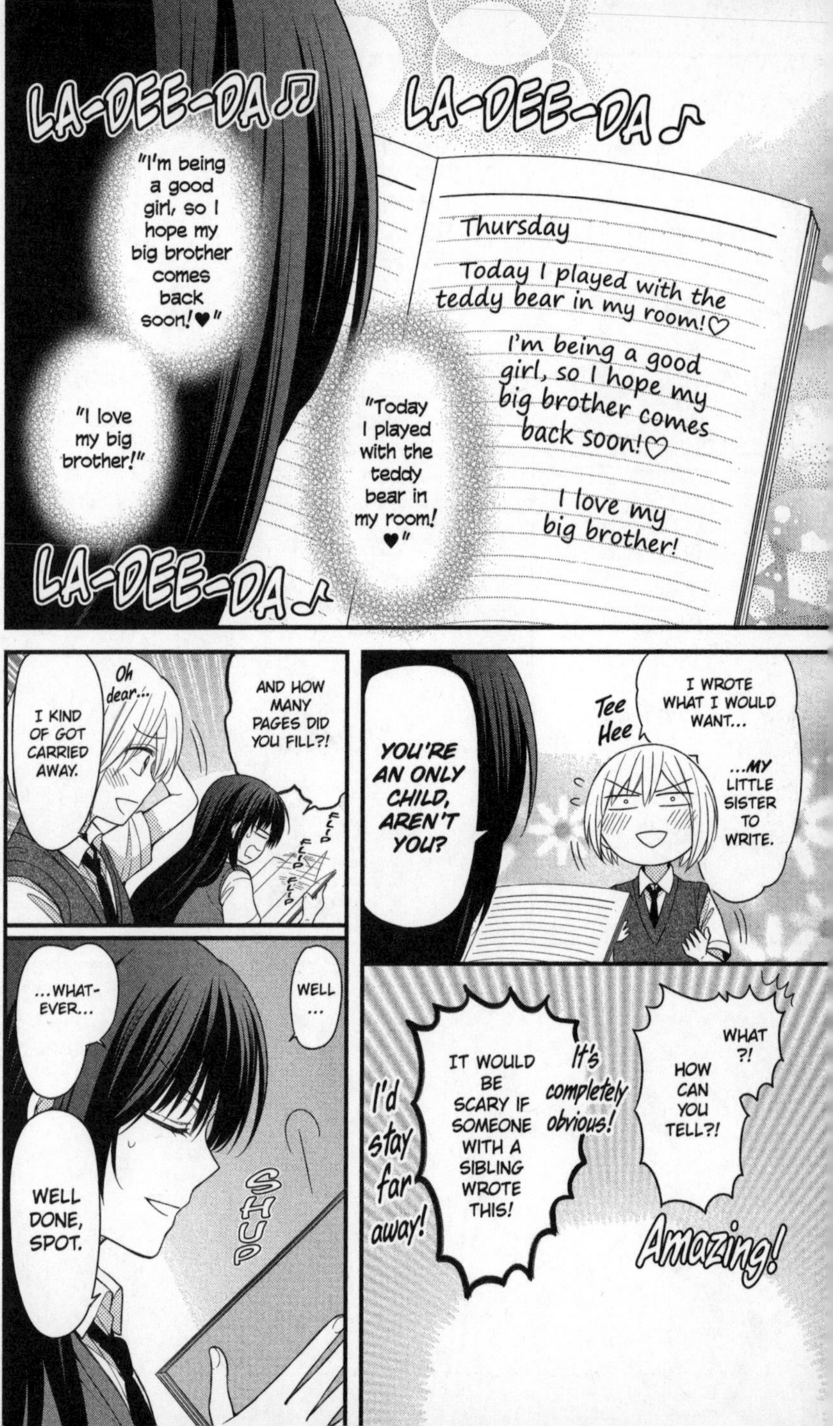
LA-DEE-DA♪
Thursday
Today I played with the teddy bear in my room!♡
I'm being a good girl, so I hope my big brother comes back soon!♡
I love my big brother!
"Today I played with the teddy bear in my room! ♥"
LA-DEE-DA♫
"I'm being a good girl, so I hope my big brother comes back soon! ♥"
"I love my big brother!"
LA-DEE-DA♪
Tee Hee
I WROTE WHAT I WOULD WANT...
...MY LITTLE SISTER TO WRITE.
YOU'RE AN ONLY CHILD, AREN'T YOU?
AND HOW MANY PAGES DID YOU FILL?!
FLIP FLIP FLIP
Oh dear...
I KIND OF GOT CARRIED AWAY.
WHAT?!
HOW CAN YOU TELL?!
Amazing!
It's completely obvious!
IT WOULD BE SCARY IF SOMEONE WITH A SIBLING WROTE THIS!
I'd stay far away!
WELL...
...WHAT-EVER...
SHUP
WELL DONE, SPOT.

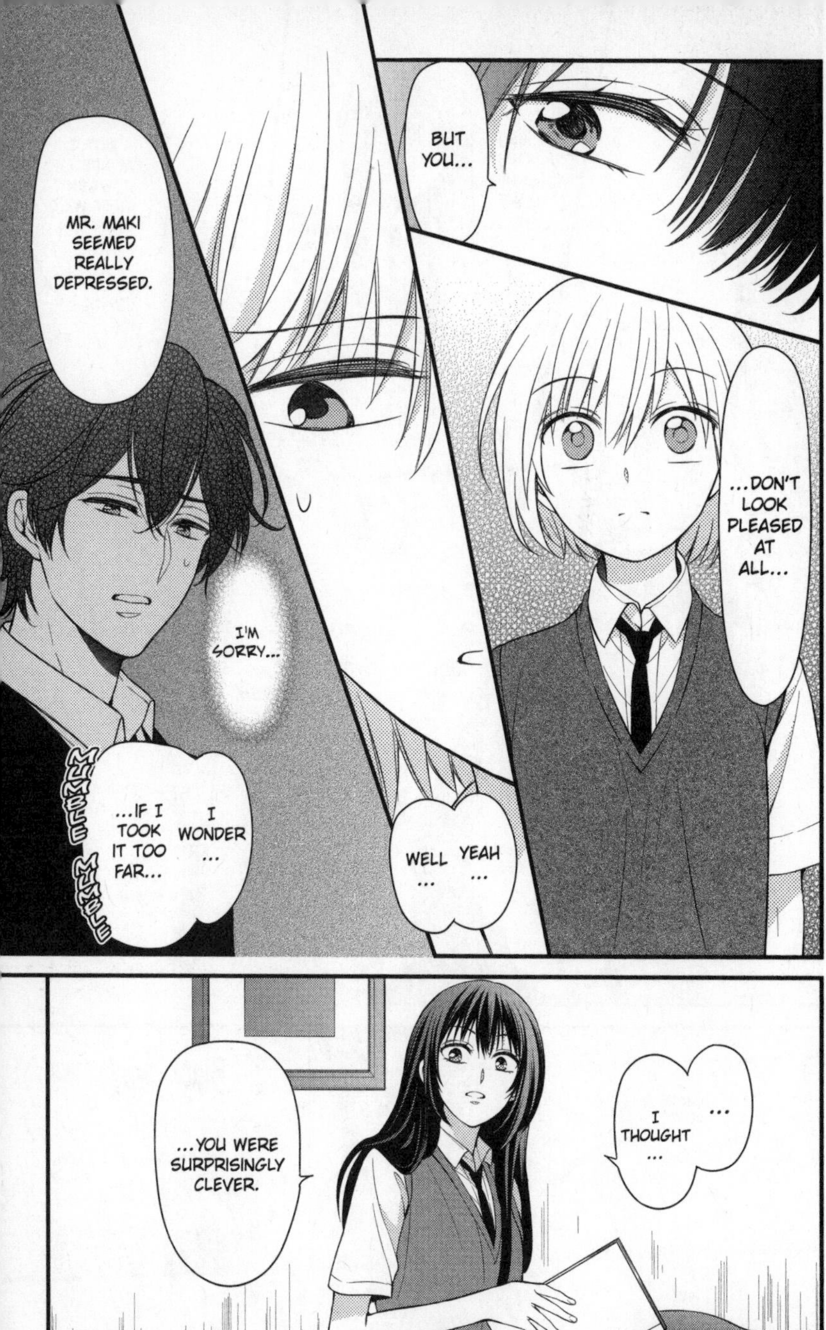
BUT YOU...
...DON'T LOOK PLEASED AT ALL...
WELL... YEAH...
MR. MAKI SEEMED REALLY DEPRESSED.
I'M SORRY...
I WONDER... ...IF I TOOK IT TOO FAR...
MUMBLE MUMBLE
... I THOUGHT...
...YOU WERE SURPRISINGLY CLEVER.

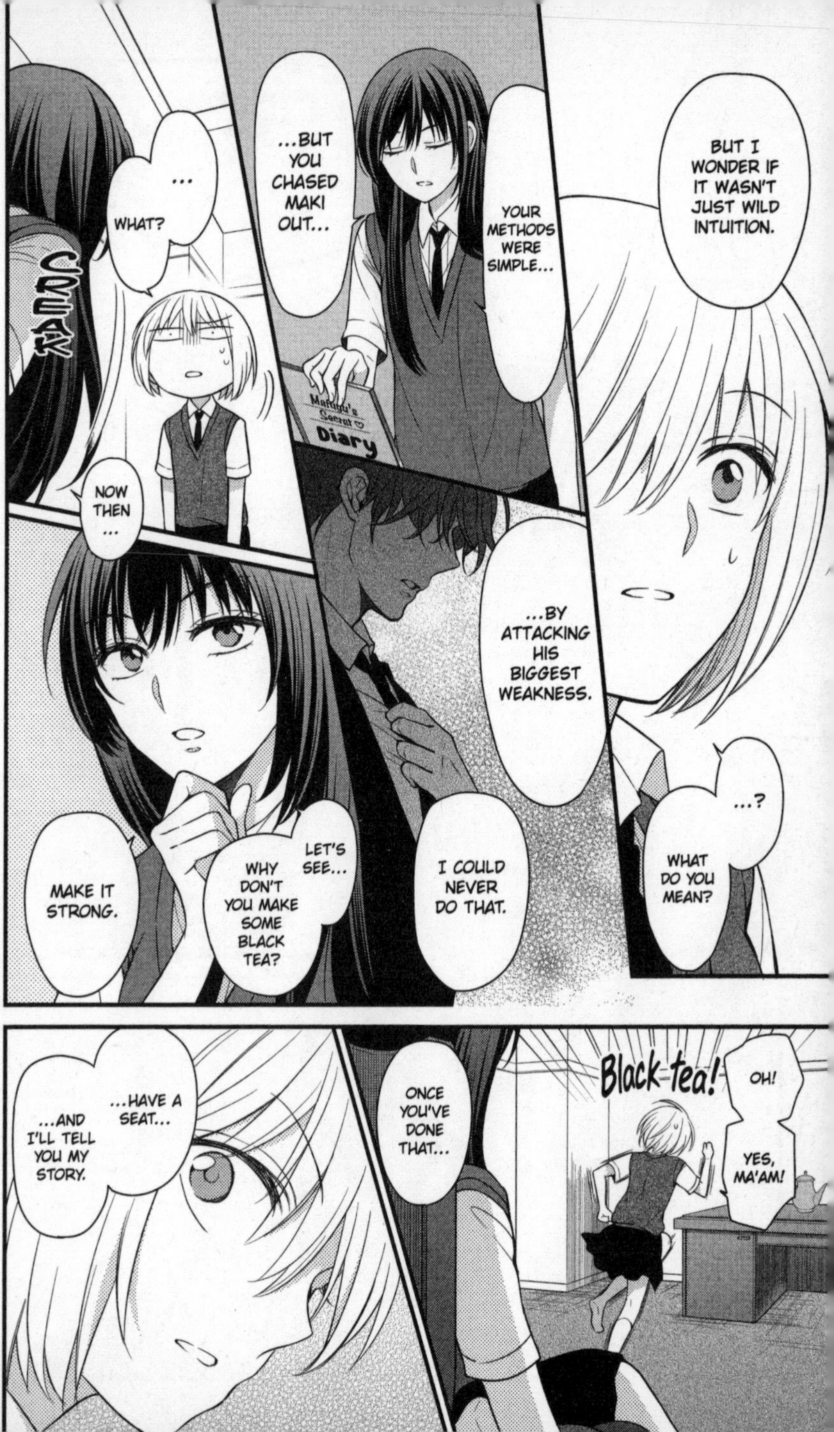
BUT I WONDER IF IT WASN'T JUST WILD INTUITION.
YOUR METHODS WERE SIMPLE...
...BUT YOU CHASED MAKI OUT...
Diary
...
WHAT?
CREAK
...BY ATTACKING HIS BIGGEST WEAKNESS.
...?
WHAT DO YOU MEAN?
I COULD NEVER DO THAT.
NOW THEN ...
LET'S SEE...
WHY DON'T YOU MAKE SOME BLACK TEA?
MAKE IT STRONG.
OH!
YES, MA'AM!
Black-tea!
ONCE YOU'VE DONE THAT...
...HAVE A SEAT...
...AND I'LL TELL YOU MY STORY.

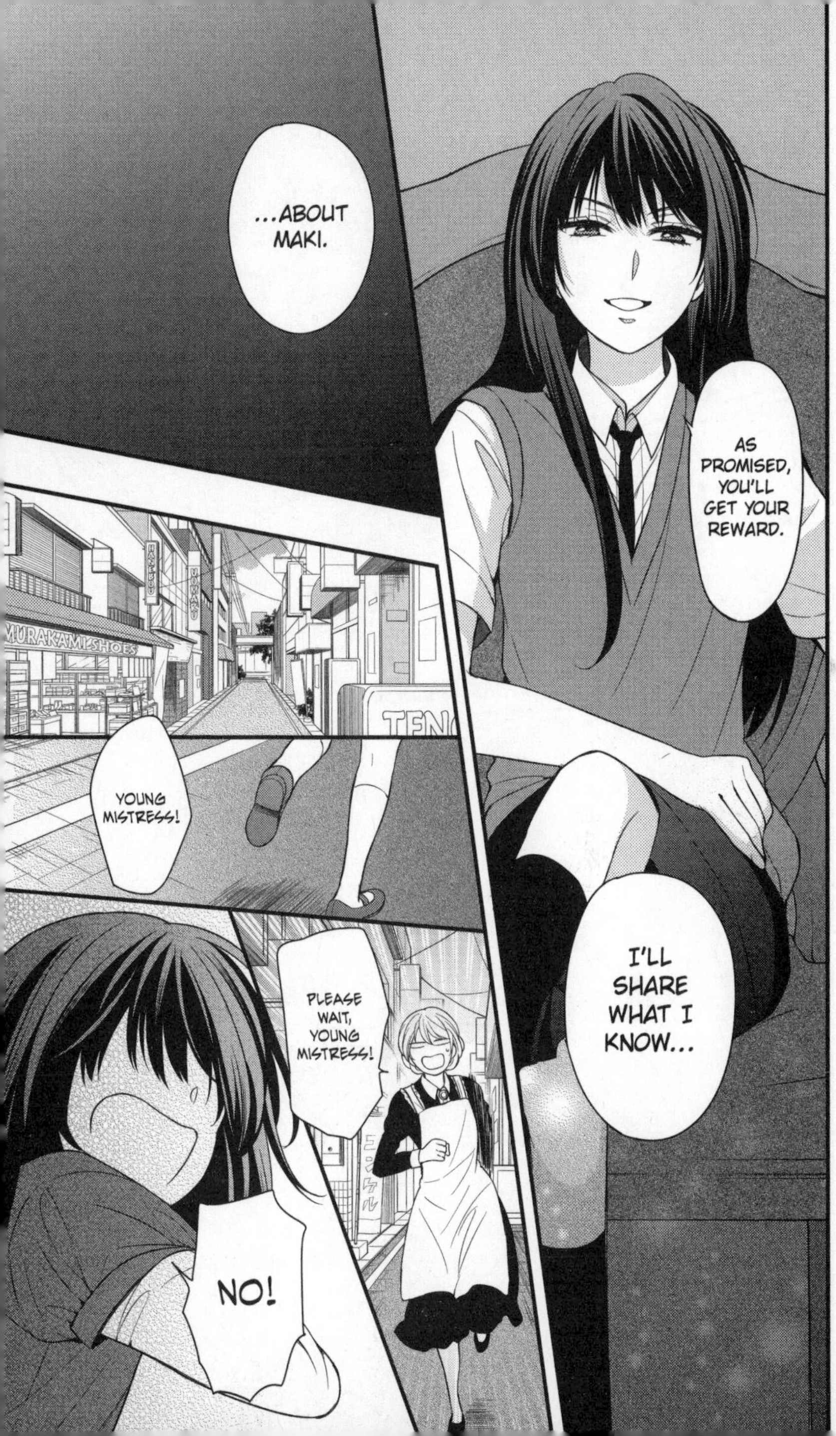
AS PROMISED, YOU'LL GET YOUR REWARD.
I'LL SHARE WHAT I KNOW...
...ABOUT MAKI.
MURAKAMI SHOES
YOUNG MISTRESS!
PLEASE WAIT, YOUNG MISTRESS!
NO!

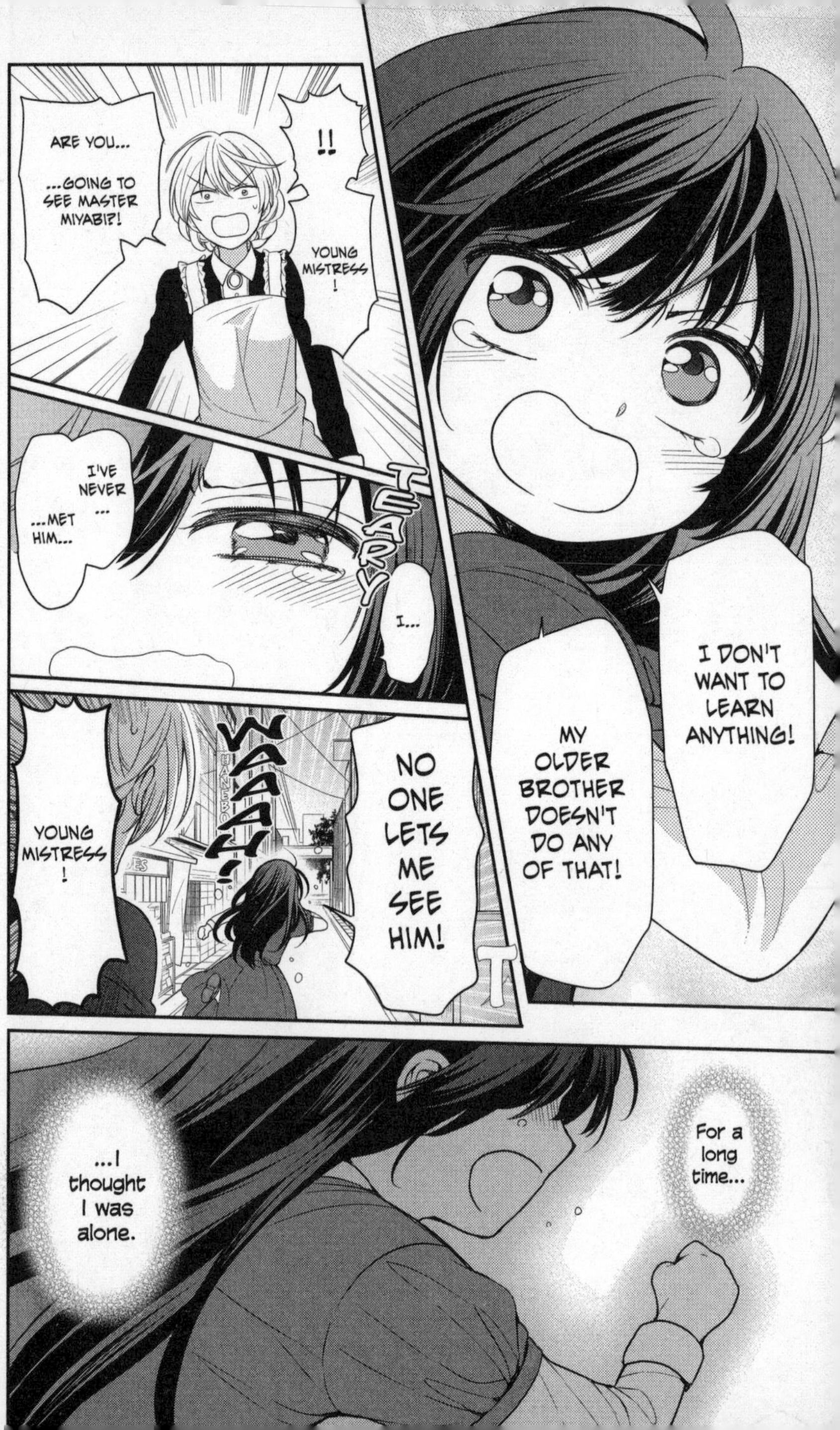
I DON'T WANT TO LEARN ANYTHING!
MY OLDER BROTHER DOESN'T DO ANY OF THAT!
!!
ARE YOU...
...GOING TO SEE MASTER MIYABI?!
YOUNG MISTRESS!
I...
TEARY
I'VE NEVER...
...MET HIM...
NO ONE LETS ME SEE HIM!
WAAAH!
YOUNG MISTRESS!
For a long time...
...I thought I was alone.

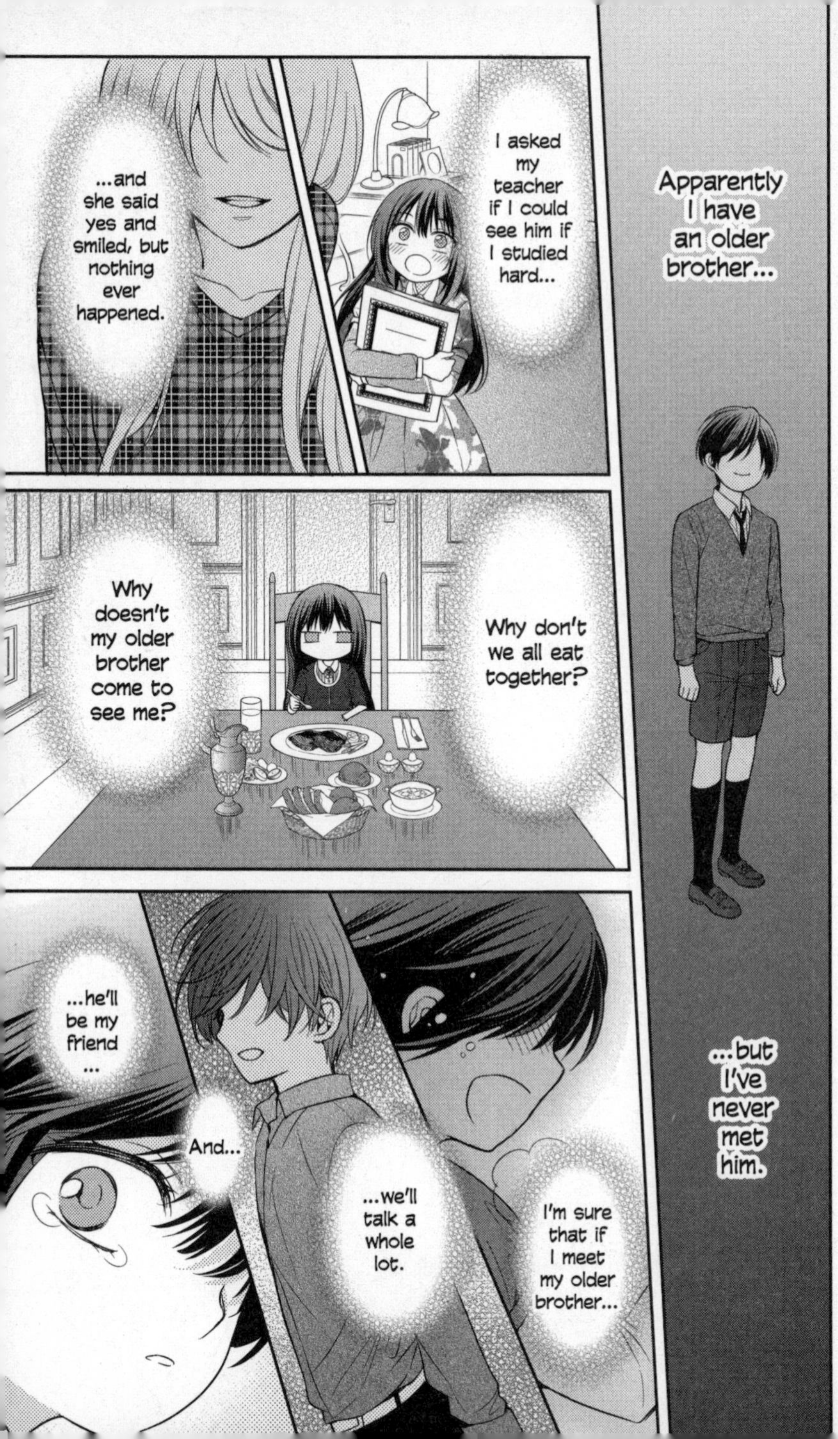
Apparently I have an older brother...
...but I've never met him.
I asked my teacher if I could see him if I studied hard...
...and she said yes and smiled, but nothing ever happened.
Why don't we all eat together?
Why doesn't my older brother come to see me?
I'm sure that if I meet my older brother...
...he'll be my friend ...
And...
...we'll talk a whole lot.

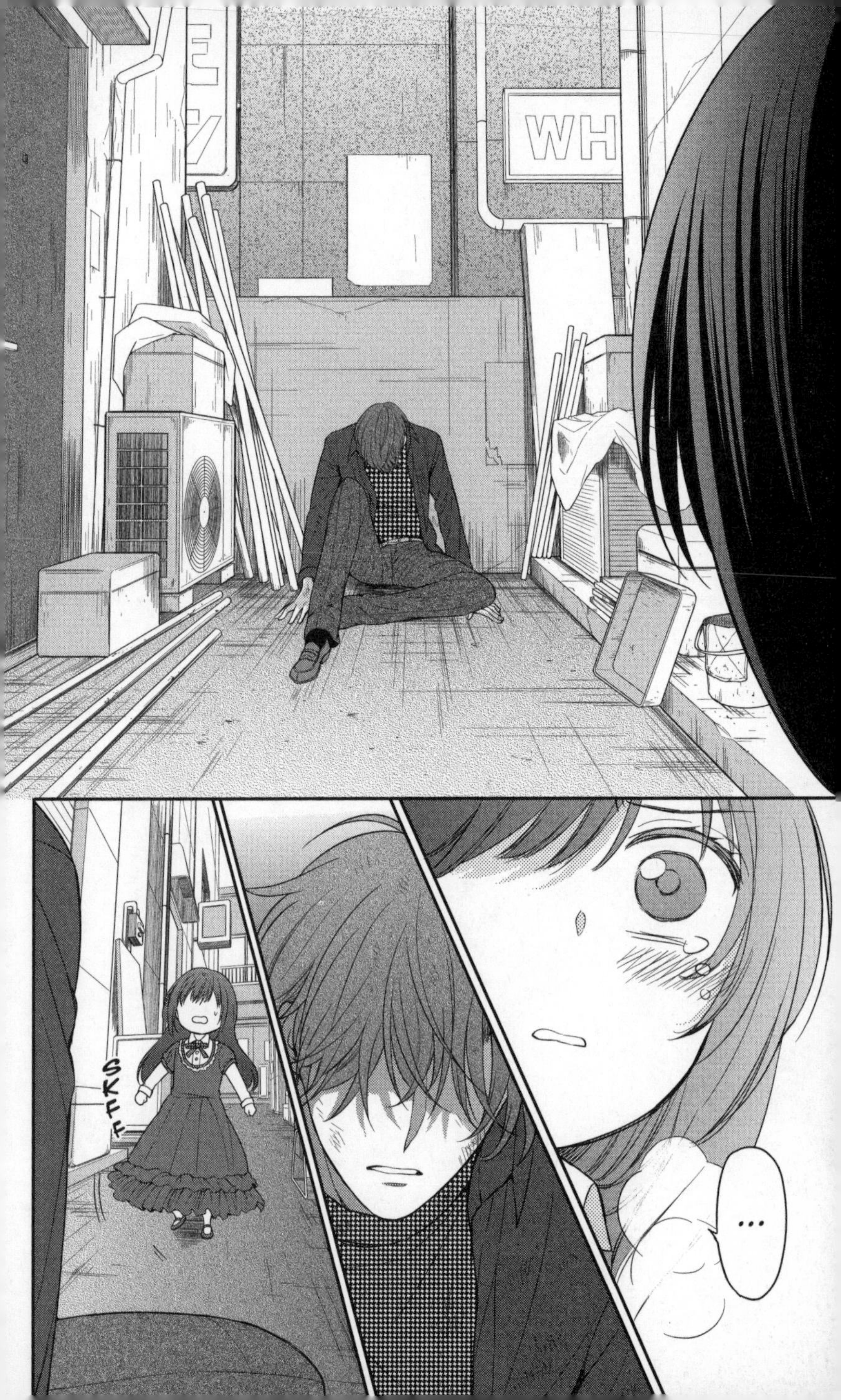

WH
...
SKFF

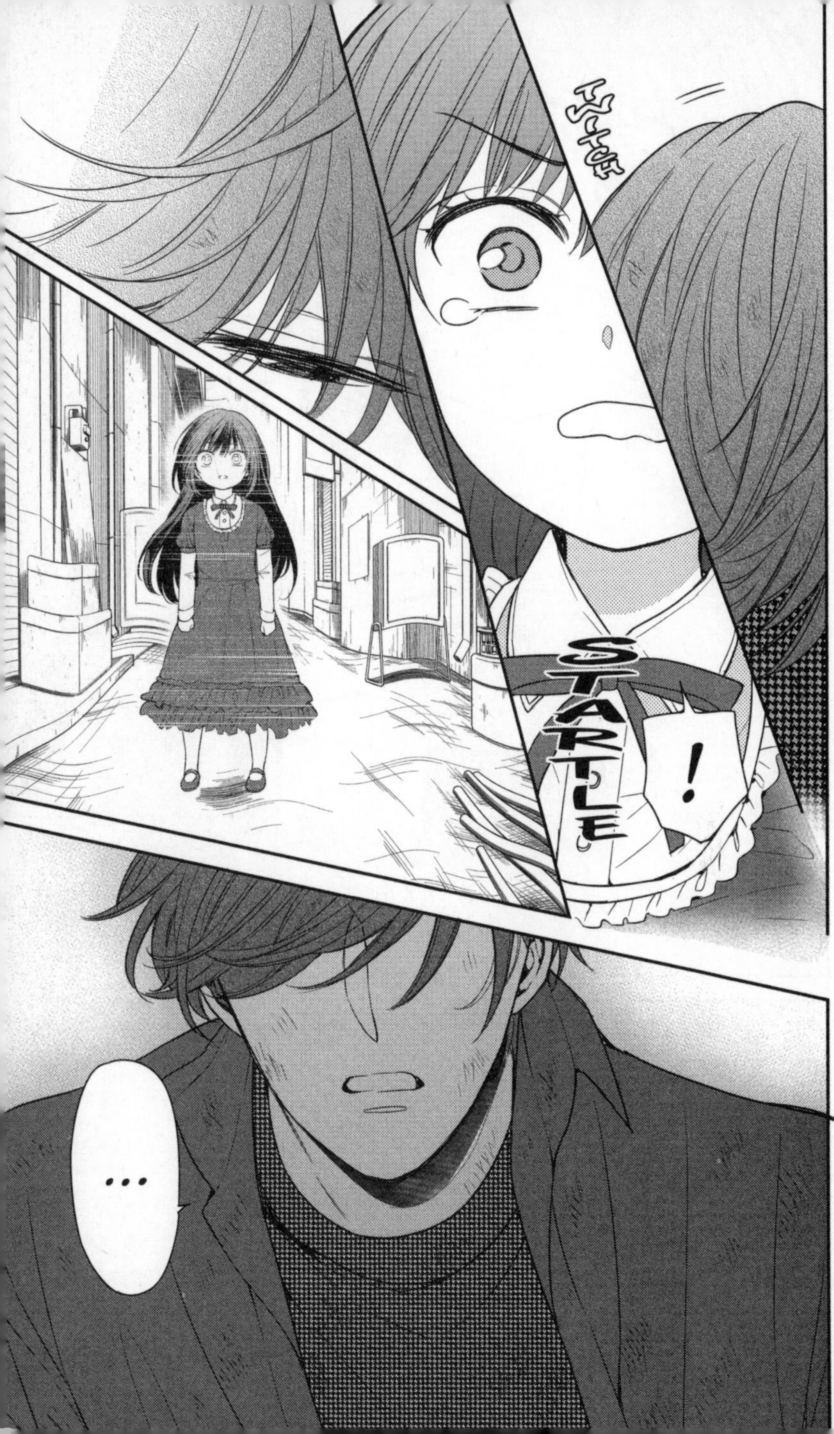
TWITCH
STARTLE
!
...

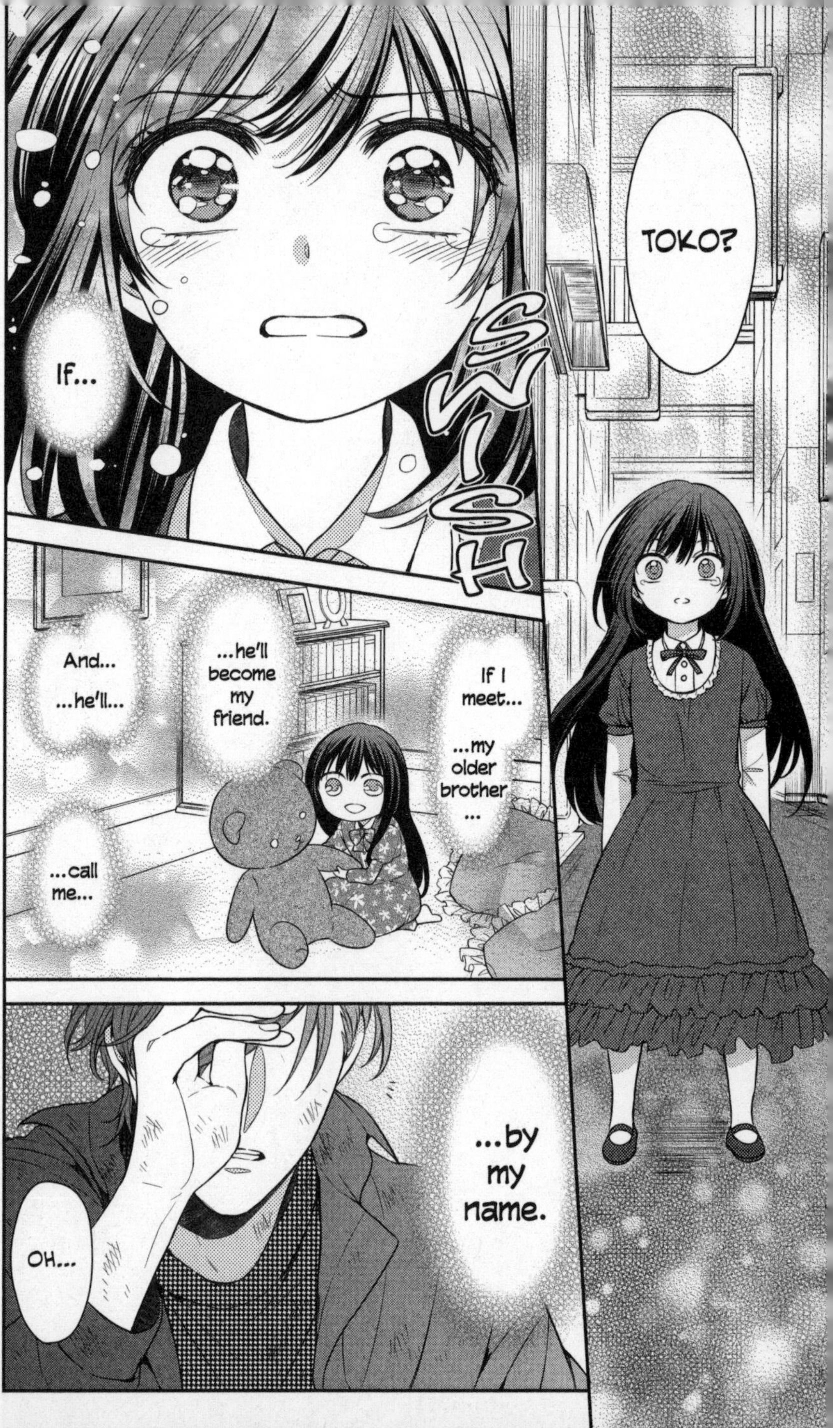
TOKO?
SWISH
If...
If I meet...
...my older brother...
...he'll become my friend.
And... ...he'll...
...call me...
...by my name.
OH...

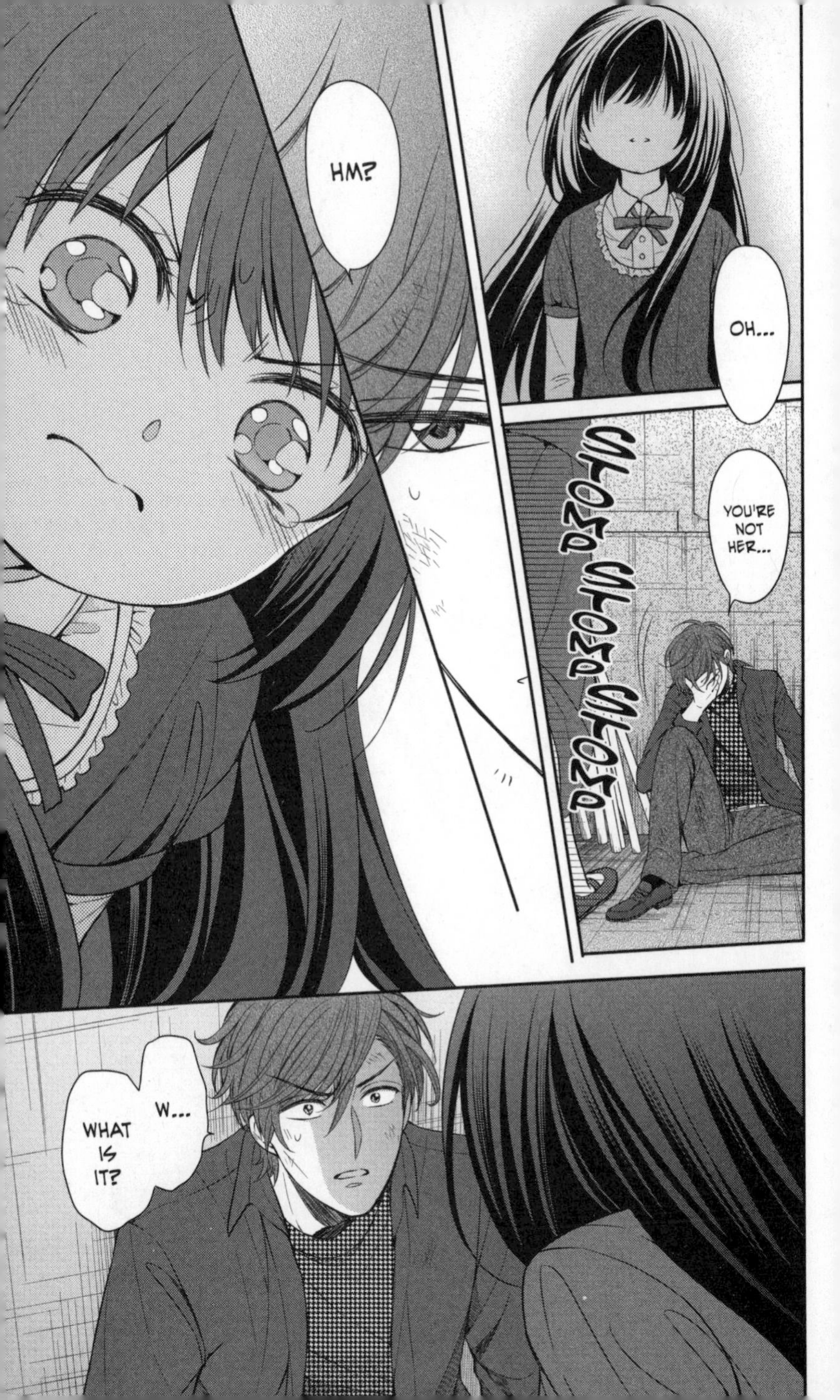
OH...
YOU'RE NOT HER...
STOMP STOMP STOMP
HM?
W...
WHAT IS IT?

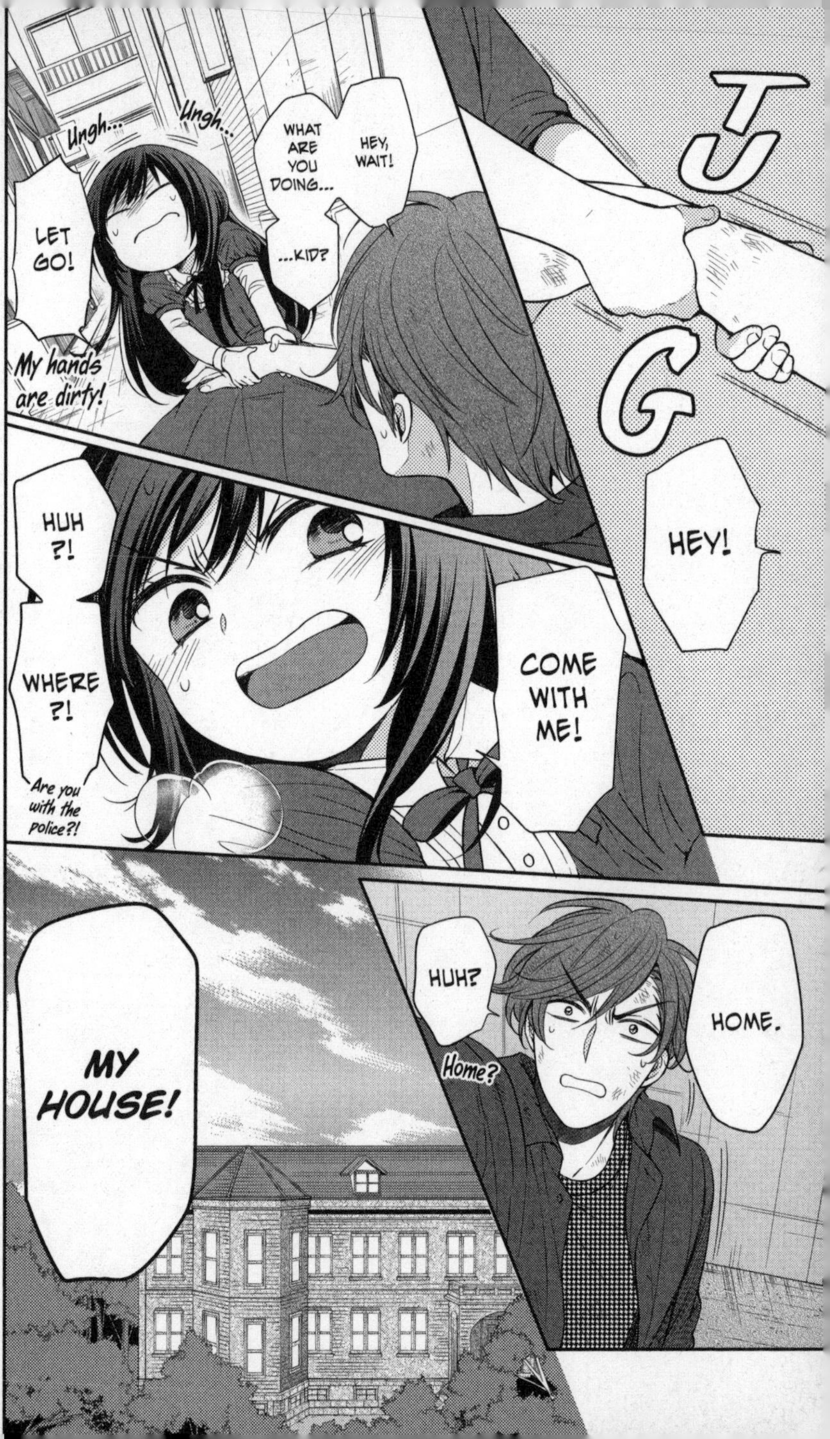
TUG
HEY!
HEY, WAIT!
WHAT ARE YOU DOING...
...KID?
Ungh...
Ungh...
LET GO!
My hands are dirty!
COME WITH ME!
HUH?!
WHERE?!
Are you with the police?!
HOME.
HUH?
Home?
MY HOUSE!

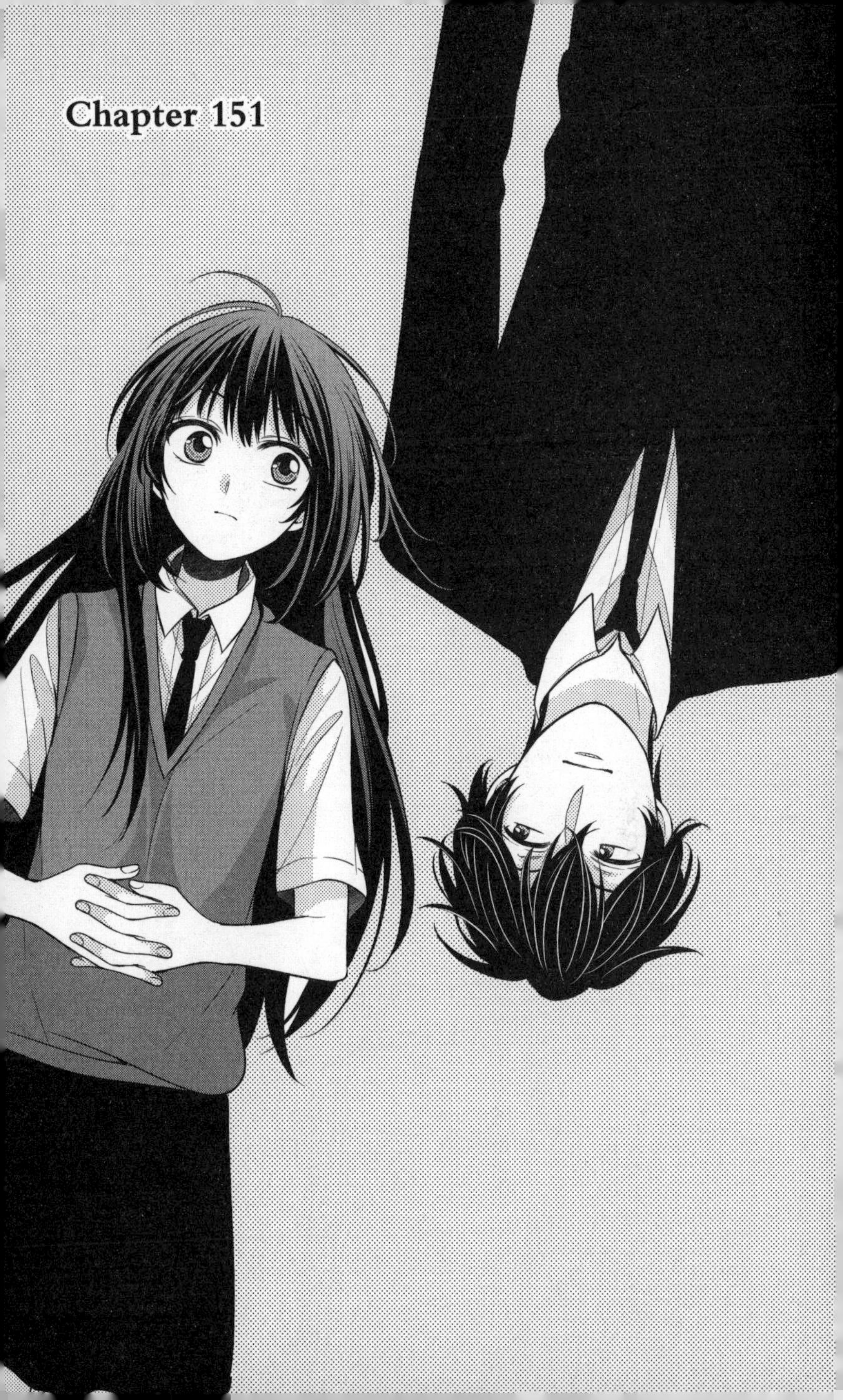
Chapter 151

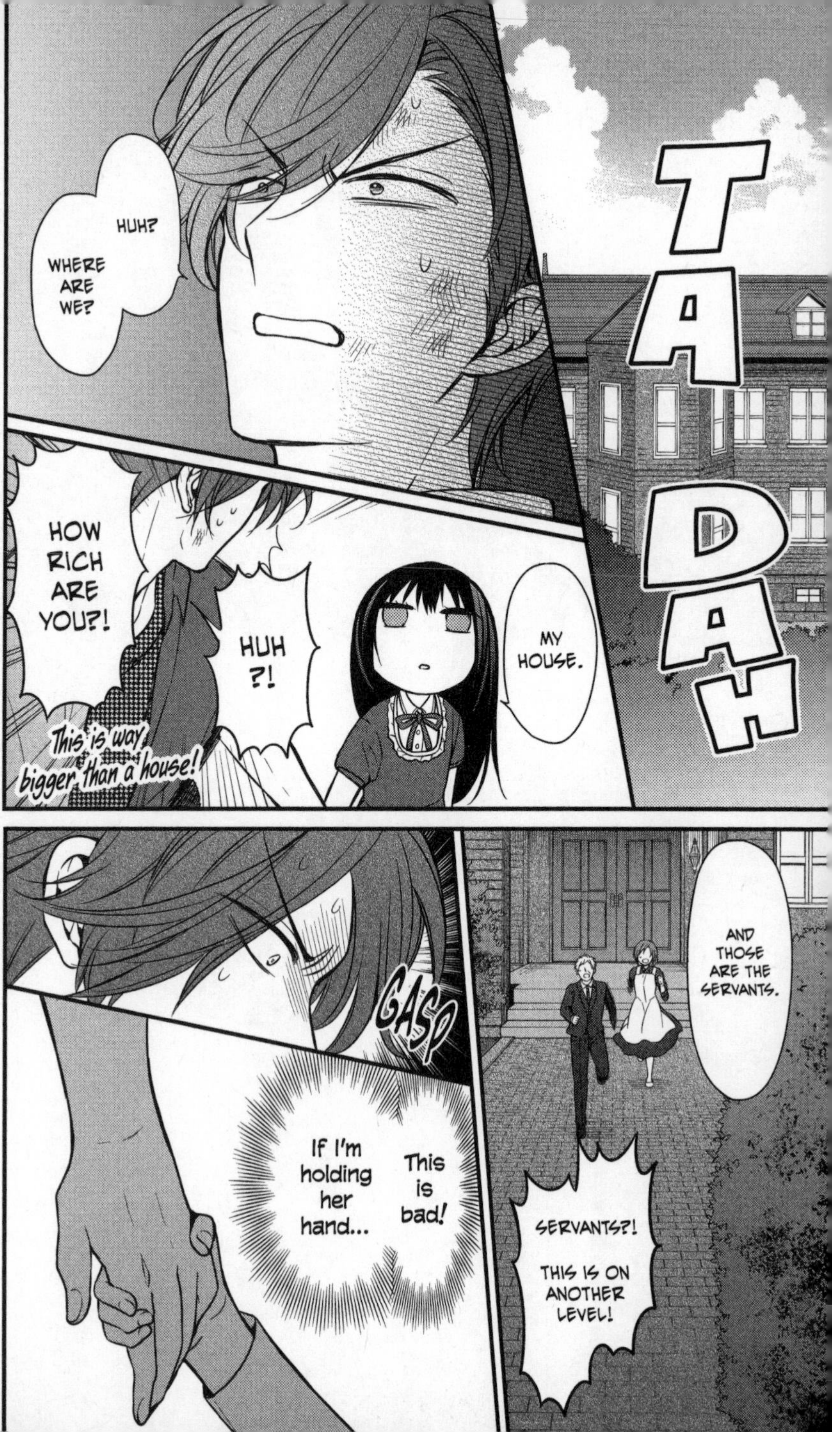
HUH?
WHERE ARE WE?
TA DAH
MY HOUSE.
HUH?!
HOW RICH ARE YOU?!
This is way bigger than a house!
AND THOSE ARE THE SERVANTS.
SERVANTS?!
THIS IS ON ANOTHER LEVEL!
GASP
This is bad!
If I'm holding her hand...

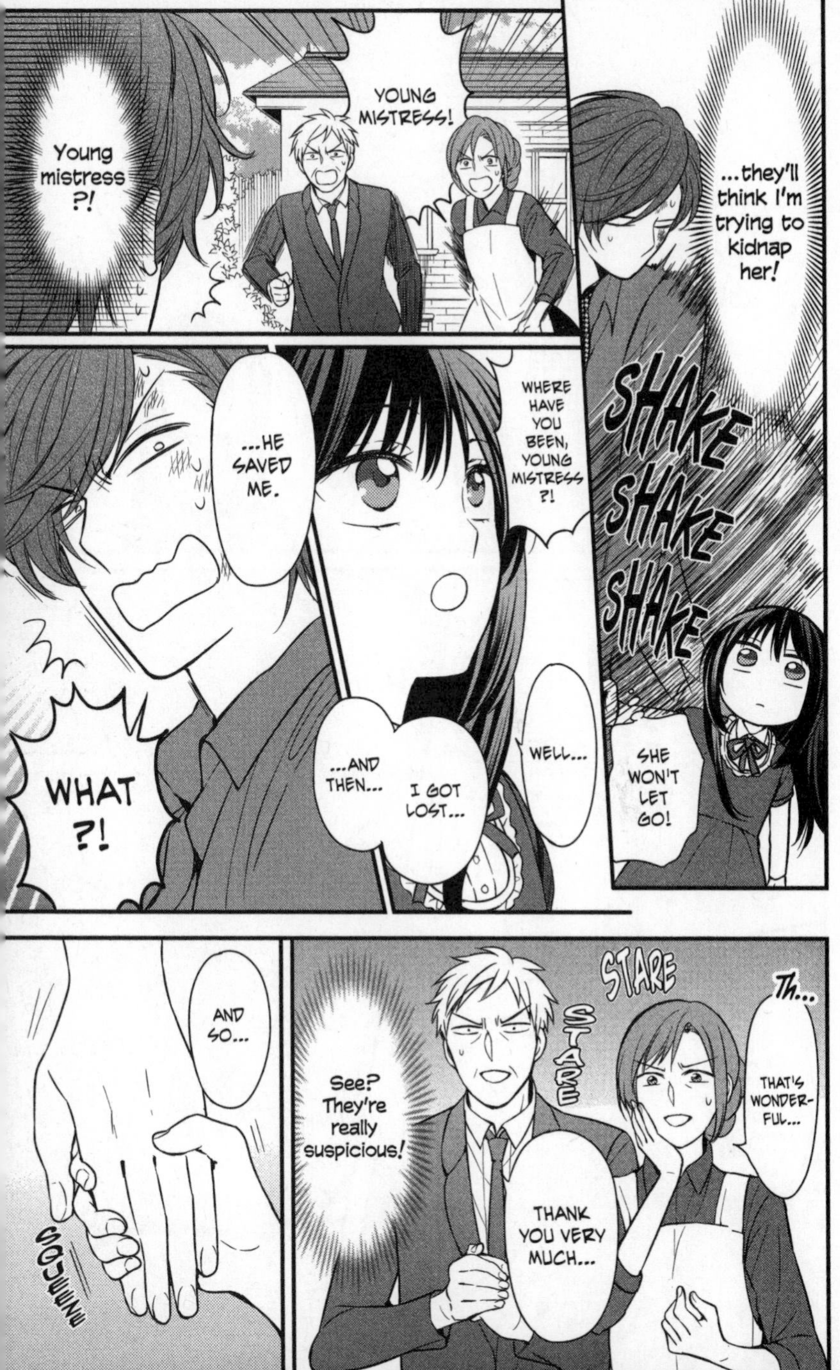
...they'll think I'm trying to kidnap her!
SHAKE SHAKE SHAKE
SHE WON'T LET GO!
YOUNG MISTRESS!
Young mistress?!
WHERE HAVE YOU BEEN, YOUNG MISTRESS?!
WELL...
I GOT LOST...
...AND THEN...
...HE SAVED ME.
WHAT?!
STARE
STARE
Th...
THAT'S WONDERFUL...
See? They're really suspicious!
THANK YOU VERY MUCH...
AND SO...
SQUEEEE

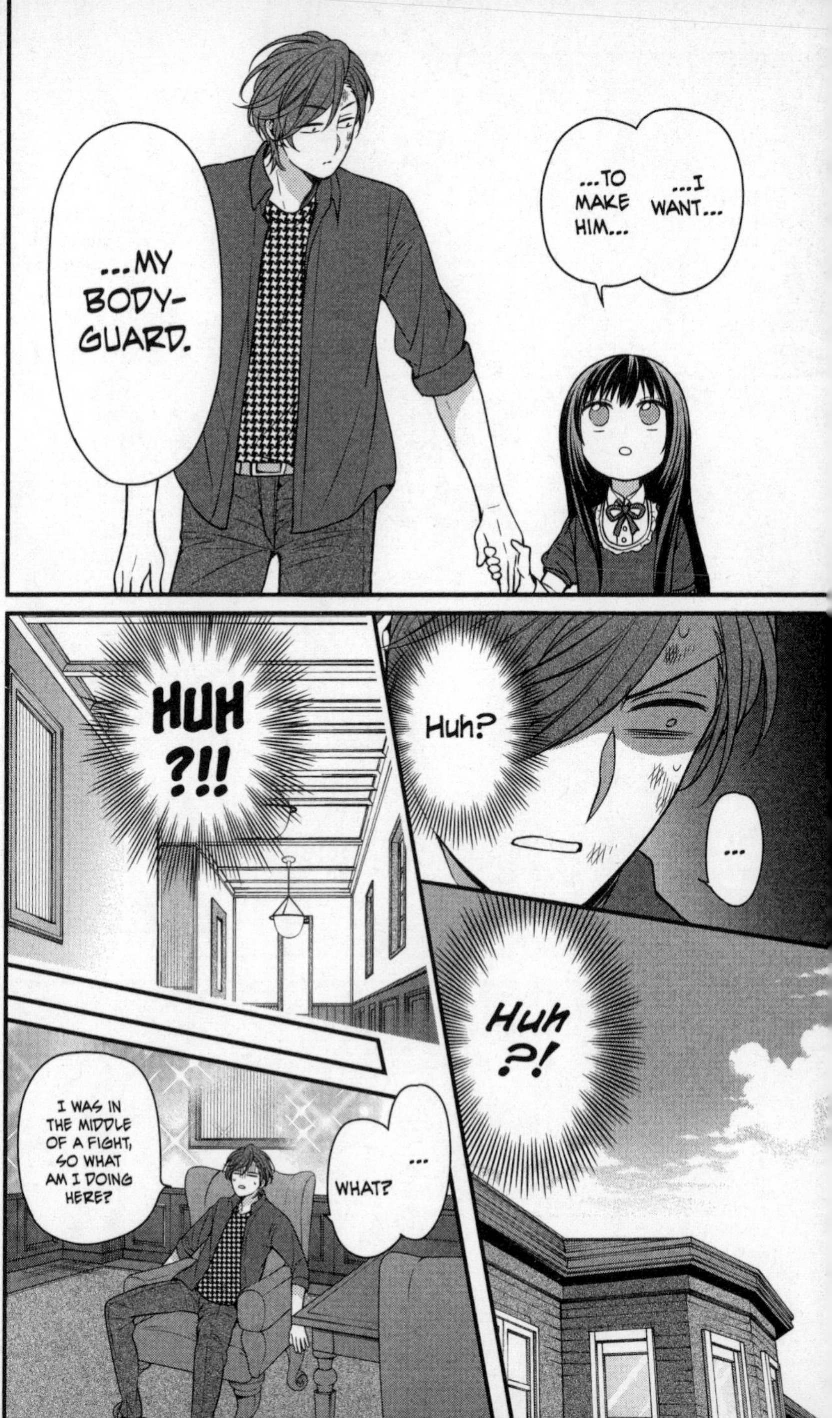
...I WANT... ...TO MAKE HIM...
...MY BODY-GUARD.
Huh?
...
HUH ?!!
Huh ?!
... WHAT?
I WAS IN THE MIDDLE OF A FIGHT, SO WHAT AM I DOING HERE?

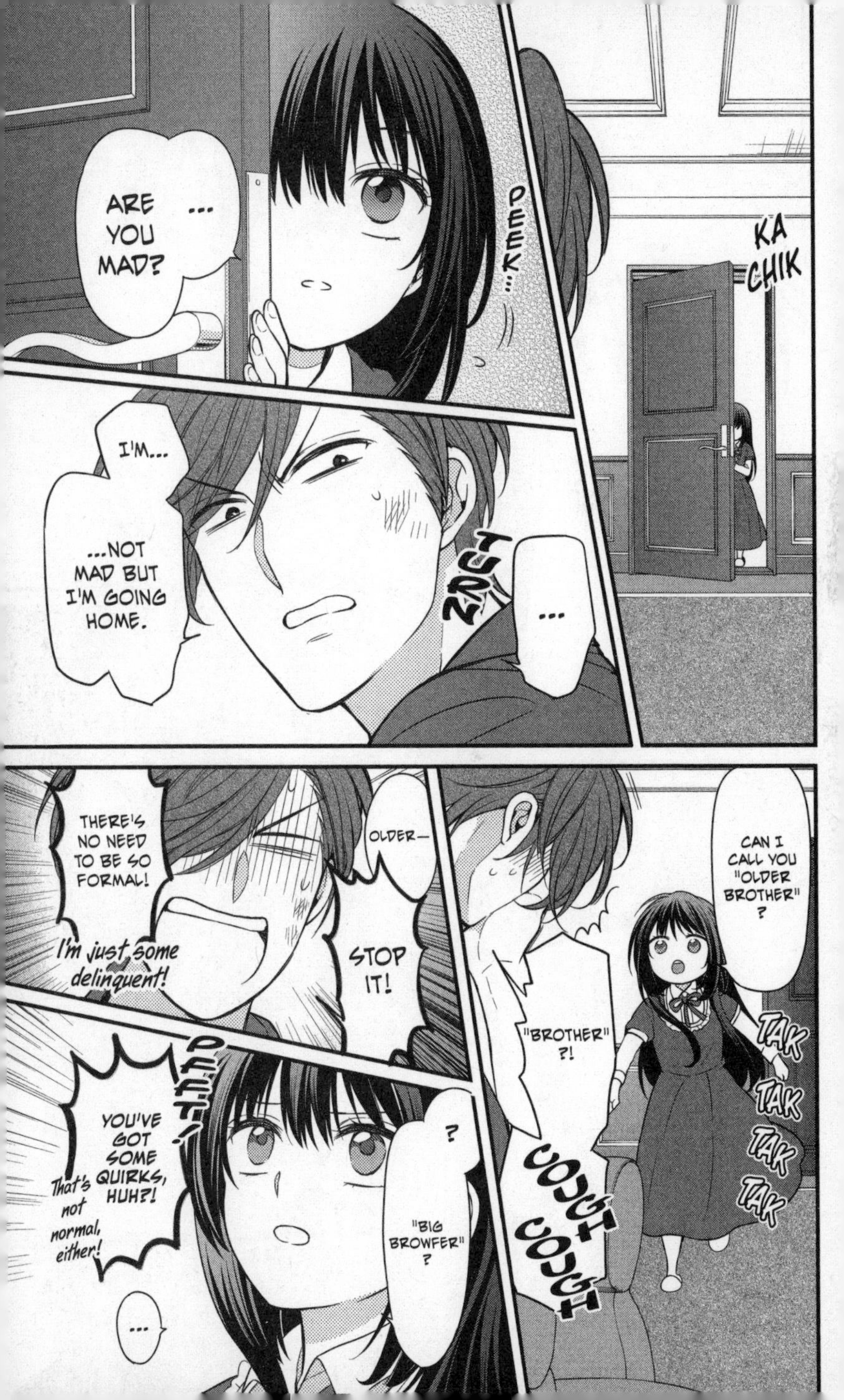
KA CHIK
PEEK...
...
ARE YOU MAD?
TURN
...
I'M...
...NOT MAD BUT I'M GOING HOME.
CAN I CALL YOU "OLDER BROTHER"?
TAK TAK TAK TAK
"BROTHER"?!
COUGH COUGH
OLDER—
STOP IT!
THERE'S NO NEED TO BE SO FORMAL!
I'm just some delinquent!
PFFT!
?
"BIG BROWFER"?
YOU'VE GOT SOME QUIRKS, HUH?!
That's not normal, either!
...

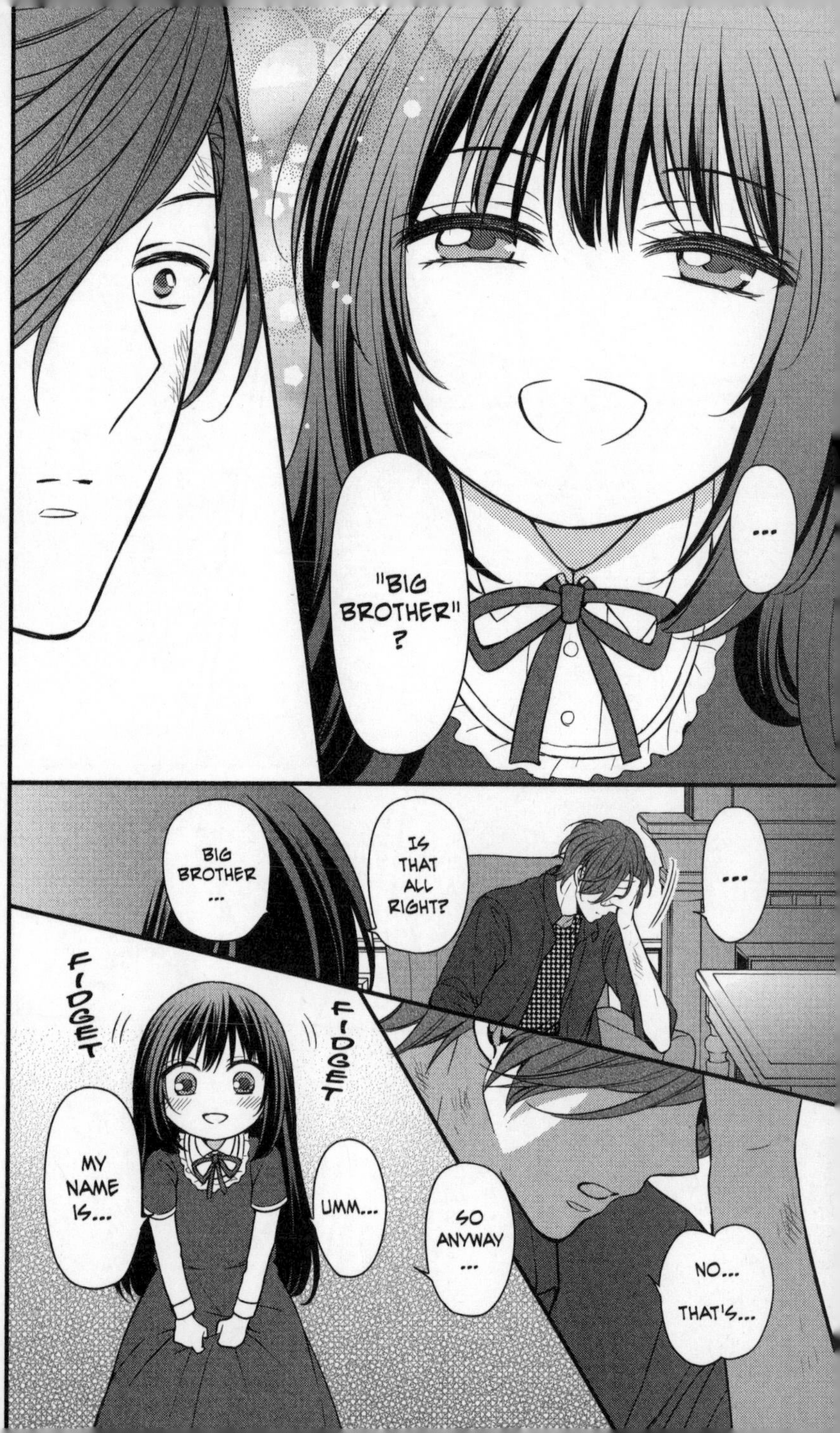
...
"BIG BROTHER"?
...
IS THAT ALL RIGHT?
BIG BROTHER ...
NO... THAT'S...
SO ANYWAY ...
FIDGET
FIDGET
UMM...
MY NAME IS...

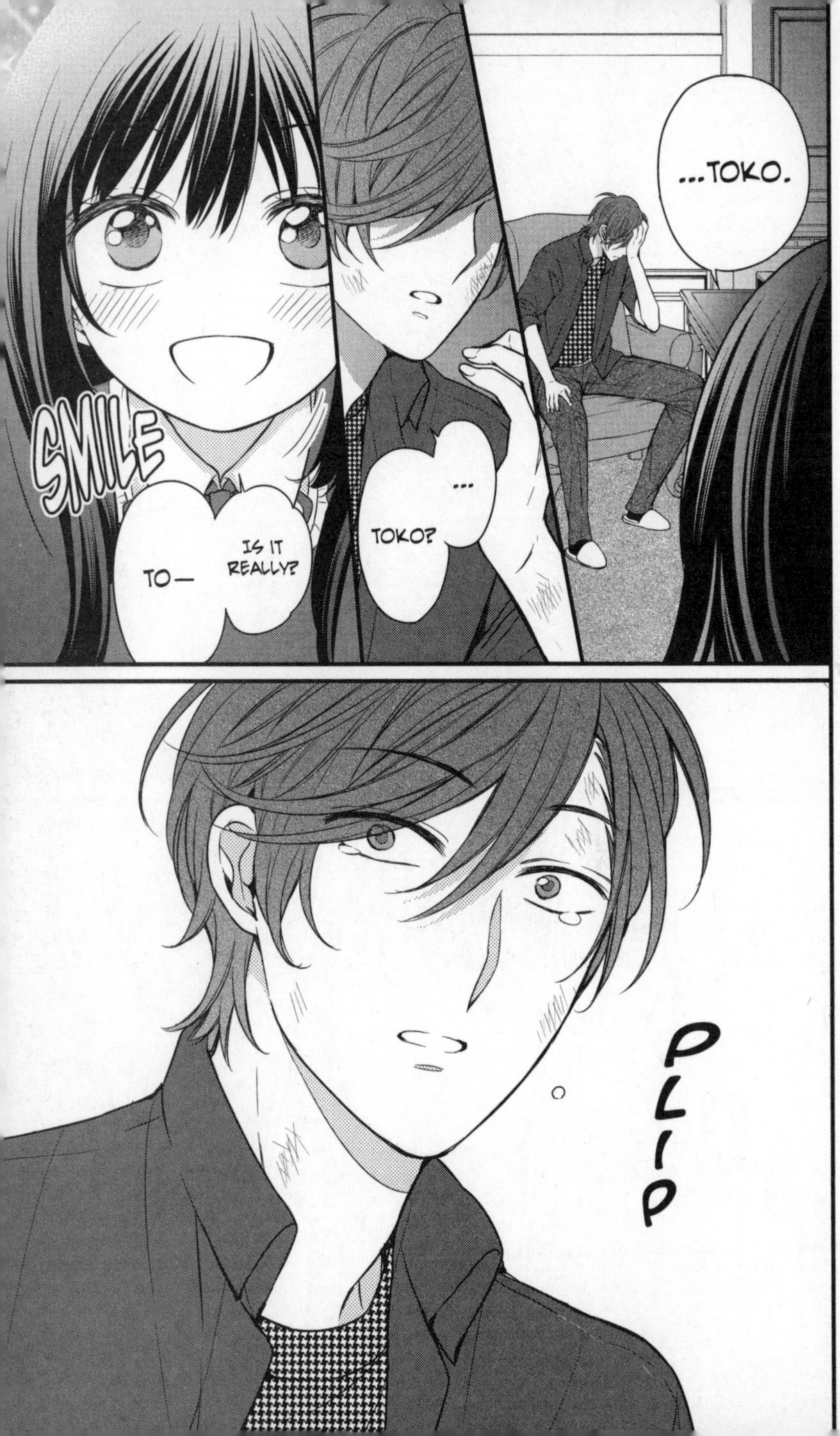
...TOKO.
...
TOKO?
SMILE
IS IT REALLY?
TO—
PLIP

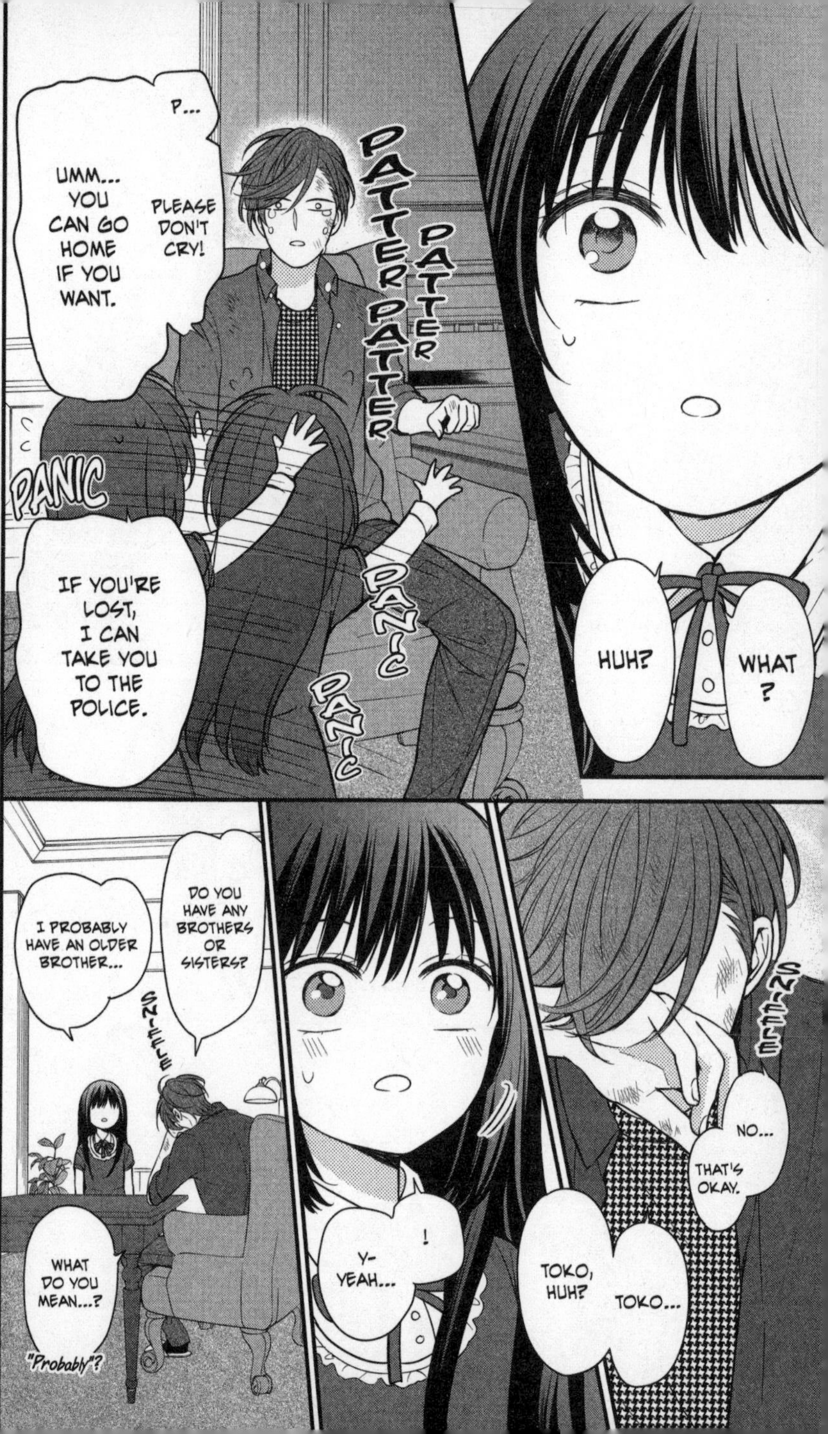
WHAT ?
HUH?
PATTER PATTER
PATTER PATTER
P...
PLEASE DON'T CRY!
UMM... YOU CAN GO HOME IF YOU WANT.
PANIC
IF YOU'RE LOST, I CAN TAKE YOU TO THE POLICE.
PANIC
PANIC
SNIFFLE
NO... THAT'S OKAY.
TOKO...
TOKO, HUH?
!
Y-YEAH...
DO YOU HAVE ANY BROTHERS OR SISTERS?
SNIFFLE
I PROBABLY HAVE AN OLDER BROTHER...
WHAT DO YOU MEAN...?
"Probably"?

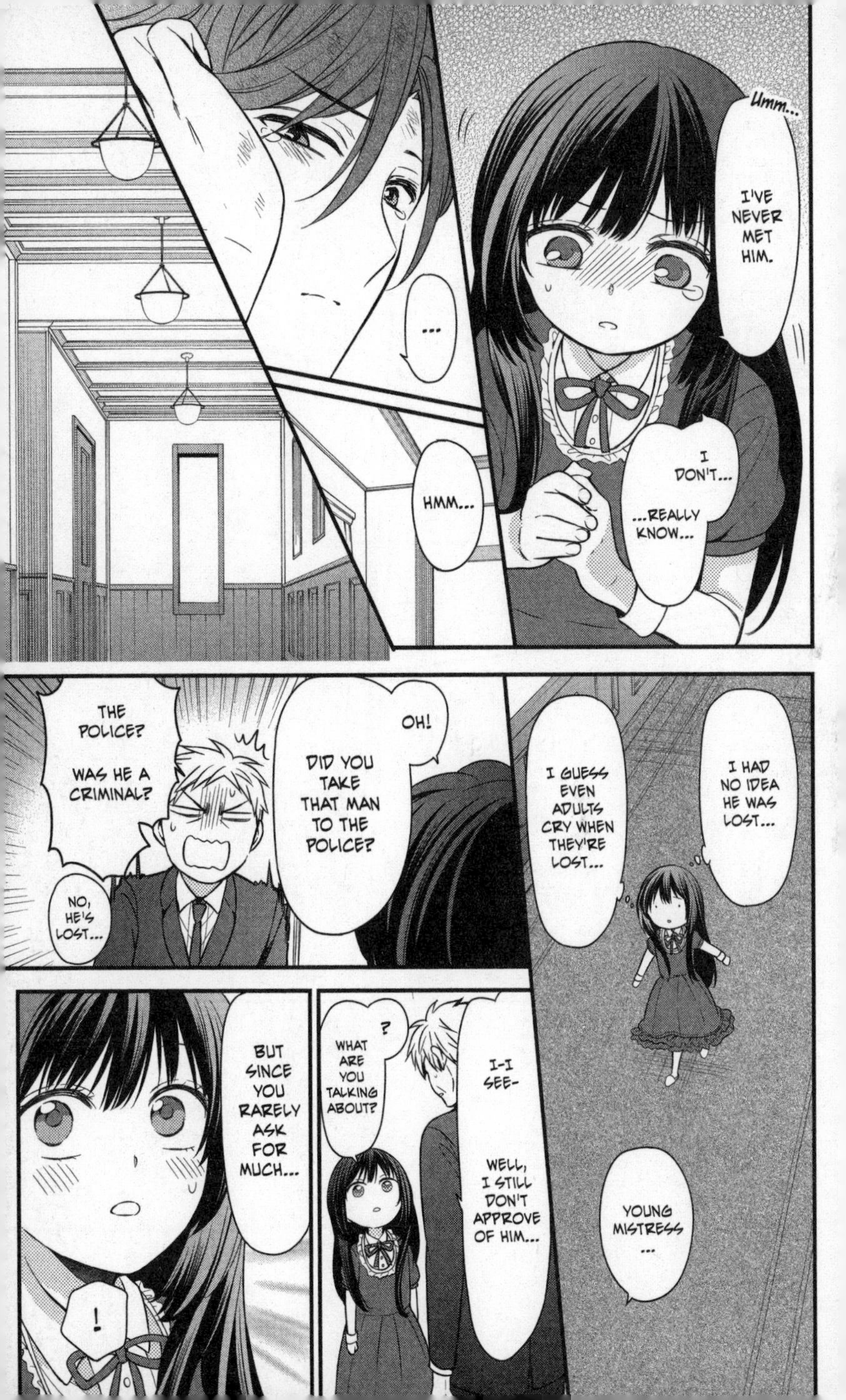
Umm...
I'VE NEVER MET HIM.
I DON'T...
...REALLY KNOW...
...
HMM...
I HAD NO IDEA HE WAS LOST...
I GUESS EVEN ADULTS CRY WHEN THEY'RE LOST...
YOUNG MISTRESS...
OH!
DID YOU TAKE THAT MAN TO THE POLICE?
THE POLICE?
WAS HE A CRIMINAL?
NO, HE'S LOST...
I-I SEE-
WELL, I STILL DON'T APPROVE OF HIM...
?
WHAT ARE YOU TALKING ABOUT?
BUT SINCE YOU RARELY ASK FOR MUCH...
!

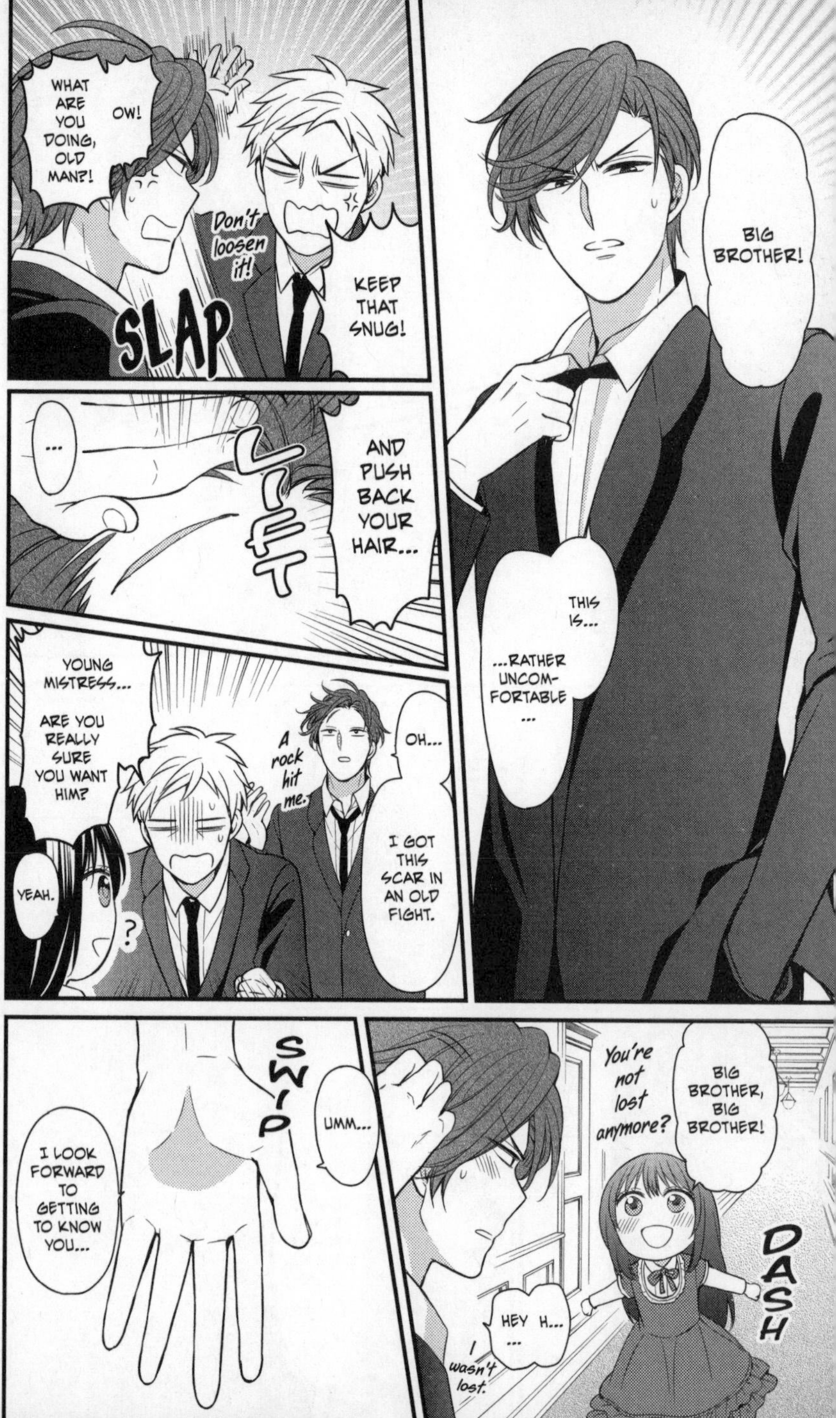
BIG BROTHER!
THIS IS...
...RATHER UNCOMFORTABLE...
KEEP THAT SNUG!
Don't loosen it!
SLAP
OW!
WHAT ARE YOU DOING, OLD MAN?!
AND PUSH BACK YOUR HAIR...
LIFT
...
OH...
I GOT THIS SCAR IN AN OLD FIGHT.
A rock hit me.
YOUNG MISTRESS...
ARE YOU REALLY SURE YOU WANT HIM?
YEAH.
?
BIG BROTHER, BIG BROTHER!
You're not lost anymore?
DASH
HEY H... ...
I wasn't lost.
SWIP
UMM...
I LOOK FORWARD TO GETTING TO KNOW YOU...

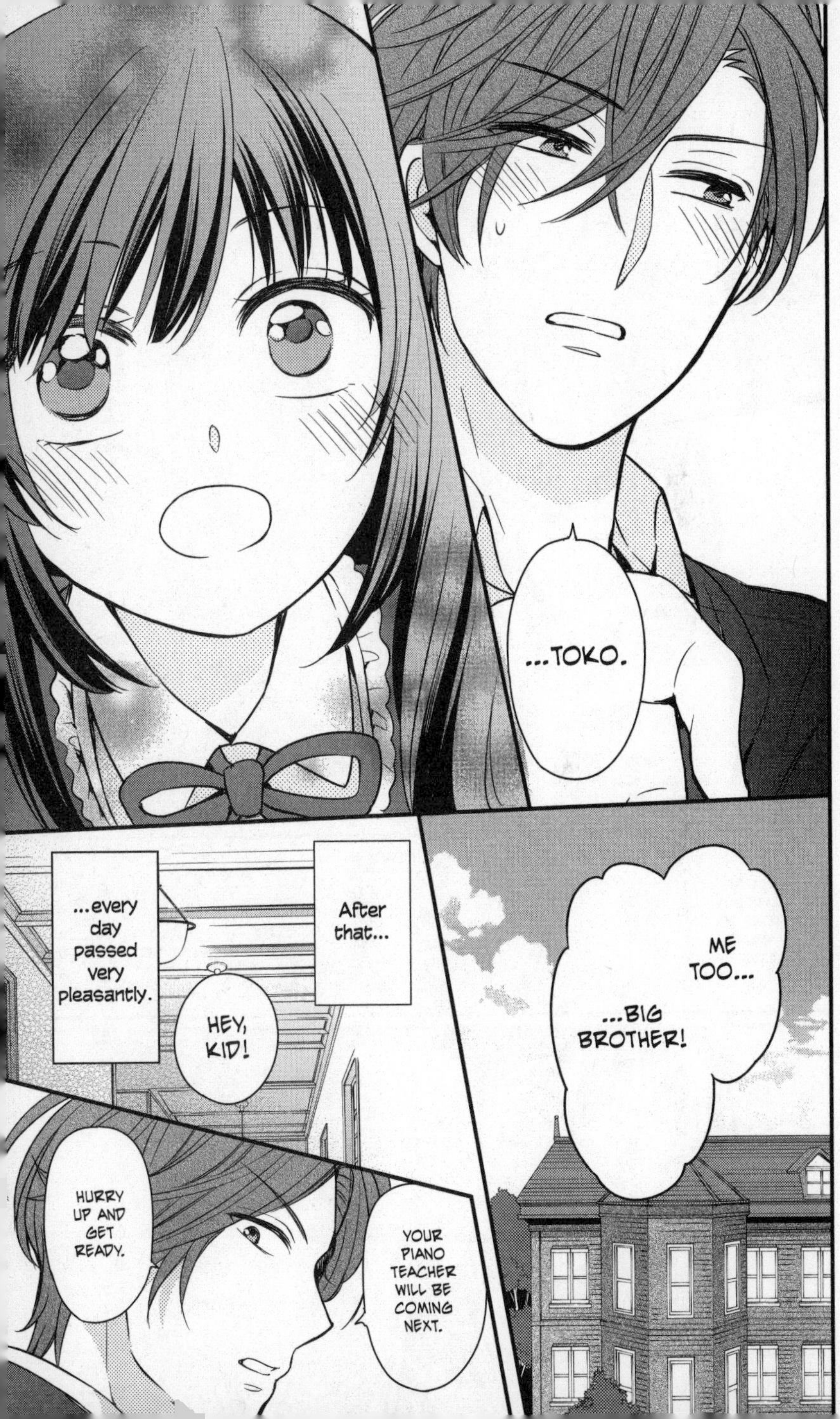
...TOKO.
ME TOO...
...BIG BROTHER!
After that...
...every day passed very pleasantly.
HEY, KID!
YOUR PIANO TEACHER WILL BE COMING NEXT.
HURRY UP AND GET READY.

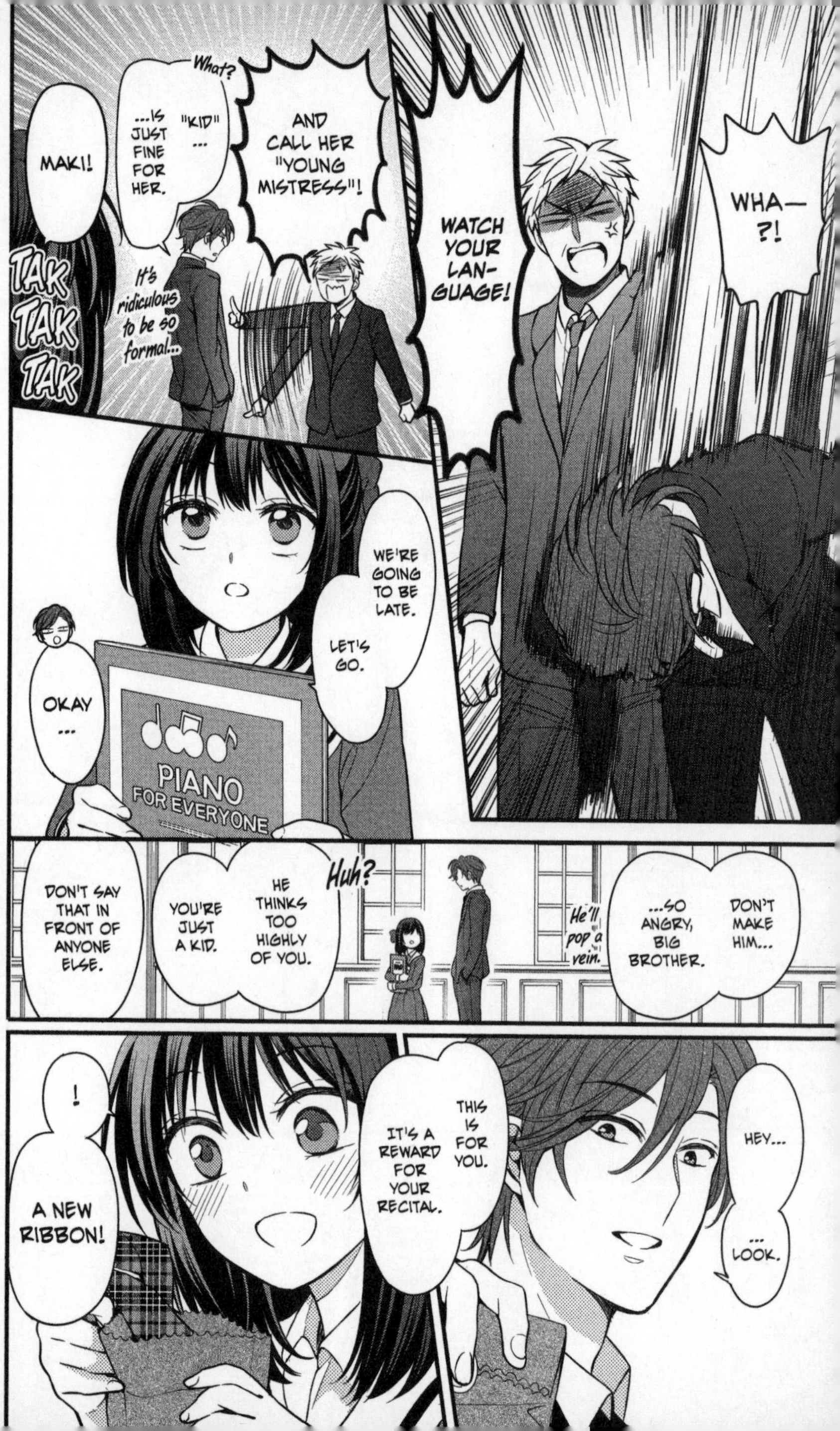
WHA—?!
WATCH YOUR LANGUAGE!
AND CALL HER "YOUNG MISTRESS"!
What?
"KID" ...
...IS JUST FINE FOR HER.
It's ridiculous to be so formal...
MAKI!
TAK TAK TAK
WE'RE GOING TO BE LATE.
LET'S GO.
OKAY ...
PIANO FOR EVERYONE
DON'T MAKE HIM...
...SO ANGRY, BIG BROTHER.
He'll pop a vein.
Huh?
HE THINKS TOO HIGHLY OF YOU.
YOU'RE JUST A KID.
DON'T SAY THAT IN FRONT OF ANYONE ELSE.
HEY...
...LOOK.
THIS IS FOR YOU.
IT'S A REWARD FOR YOUR RECITAL.
!
A NEW RIBBON!

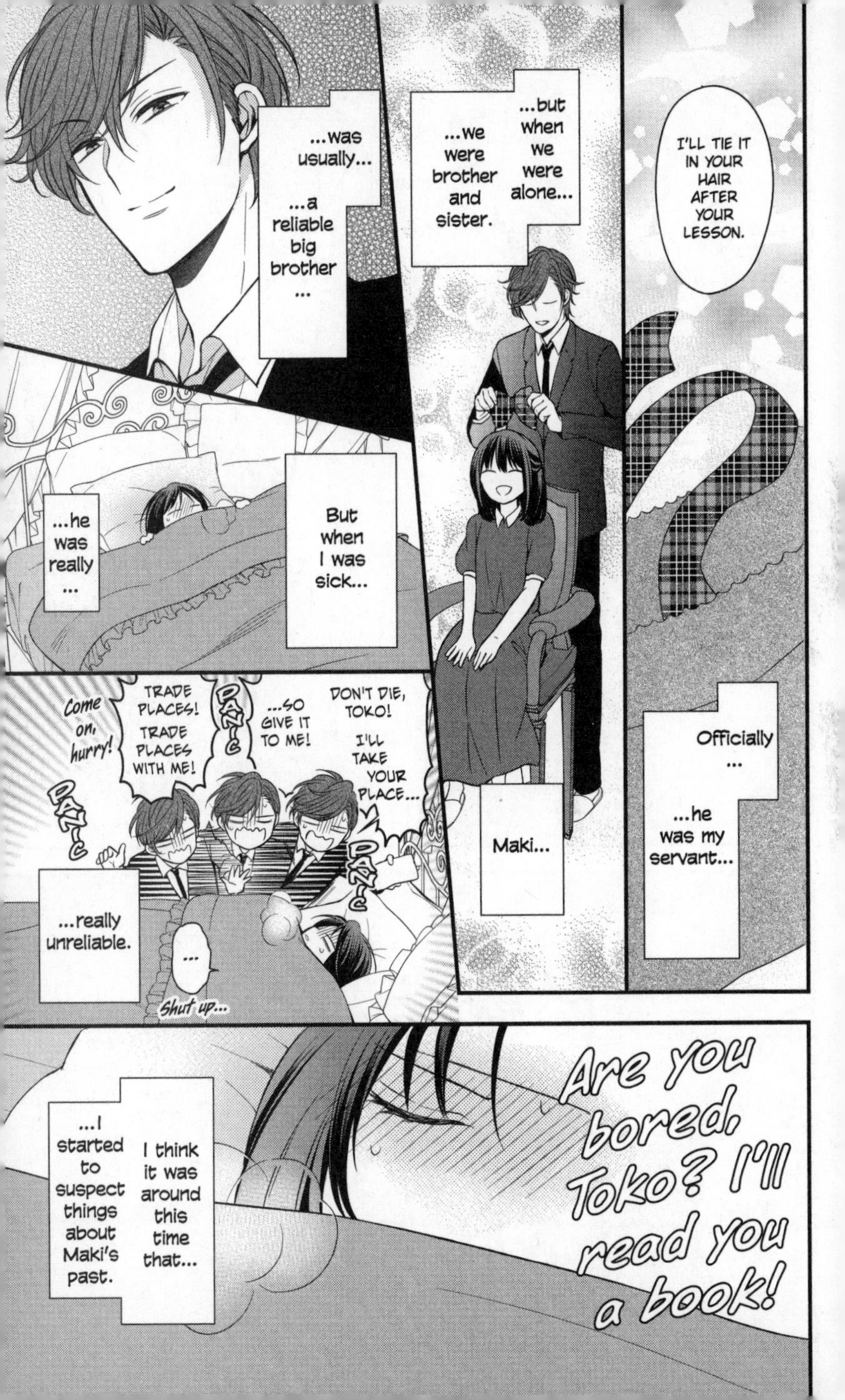
I'LL TIE IT IN YOUR HAIR AFTER YOUR LESSON.
Officially...
...he was my servant...
...but when we were alone...
...we were brother and sister.
Maki...
...was usually...
...a reliable big brother...
But when I was sick...
...he was really...
DON'T DIE, TOKO! I'LL TAKE YOUR PLACE...
...SO GIVE IT TO ME!
TRADE PLACES! TRADE PLACES WITH ME!
Come on, hurry!
PANIC
PANIC
PANIC
...really unreliable.
...
Shut up...
Are you bored, Toko? I'll read you a book!
I think it was around this time that...
...I started to suspect things about Maki's past.

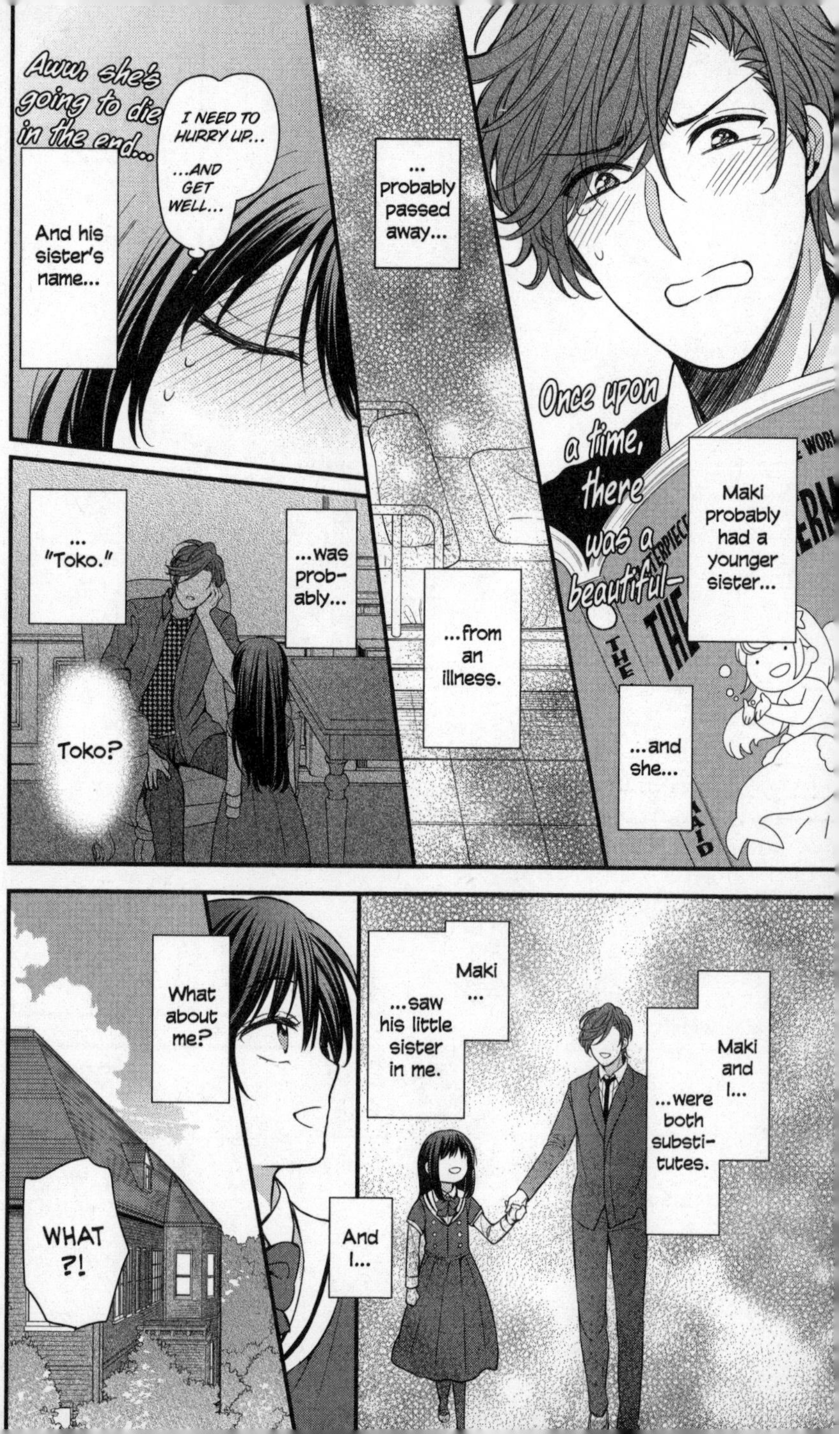
Once upon a time, there was a beautiful—
Maki probably had a younger sister...
...and she...
...probably passed away...
...from an illness.
Aww, she's going to die in the end...
I NEED TO HURRY UP... ...AND GET WELL...
And his sister's name...
... "Toko."
...was probably...
Toko?
Maki... ...saw his little sister in me.
Maki and I... ...were both substitutes.
And I...
What about me?
WHAT?!

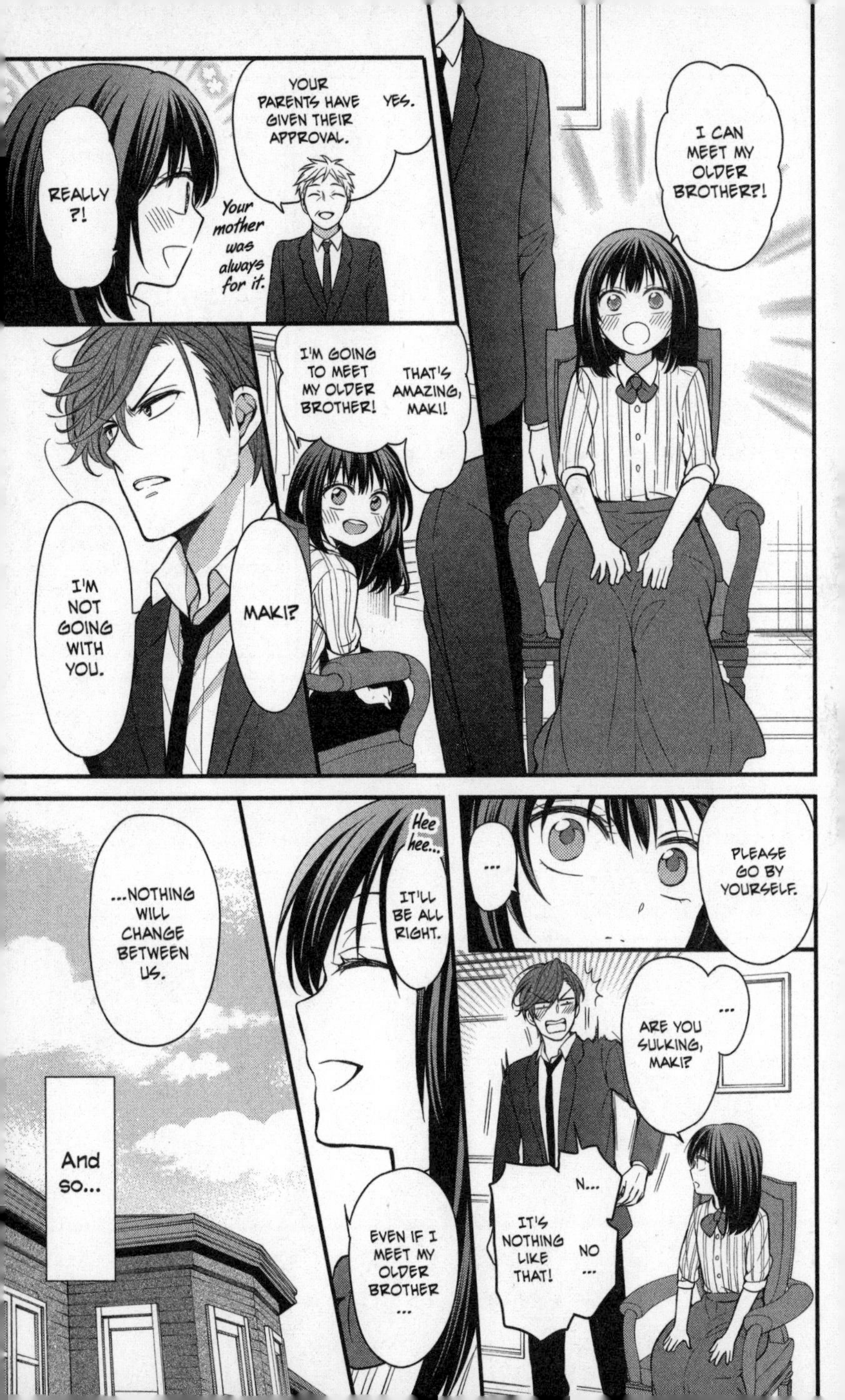
I CAN MEET MY OLDER BROTHER?!
YES.
YOUR PARENTS HAVE GIVEN THEIR APPROVAL.
Your mother was always for it.
REALLY?!
THAT'S AMAZING, MAKI!
I'M GOING TO MEET MY OLDER BROTHER!
MAKI?
I'M NOT GOING WITH YOU.
PLEASE GO BY YOURSELF.
...
...
ARE YOU SULKING, MAKI?
N... NO...
IT'S NOTHING LIKE THAT!
Hee hee...
IT'LL BE ALL RIGHT.
EVEN IF I MEET MY OLDER BROTHER...
...NOTHING WILL CHANGE BETWEEN US.
And so...

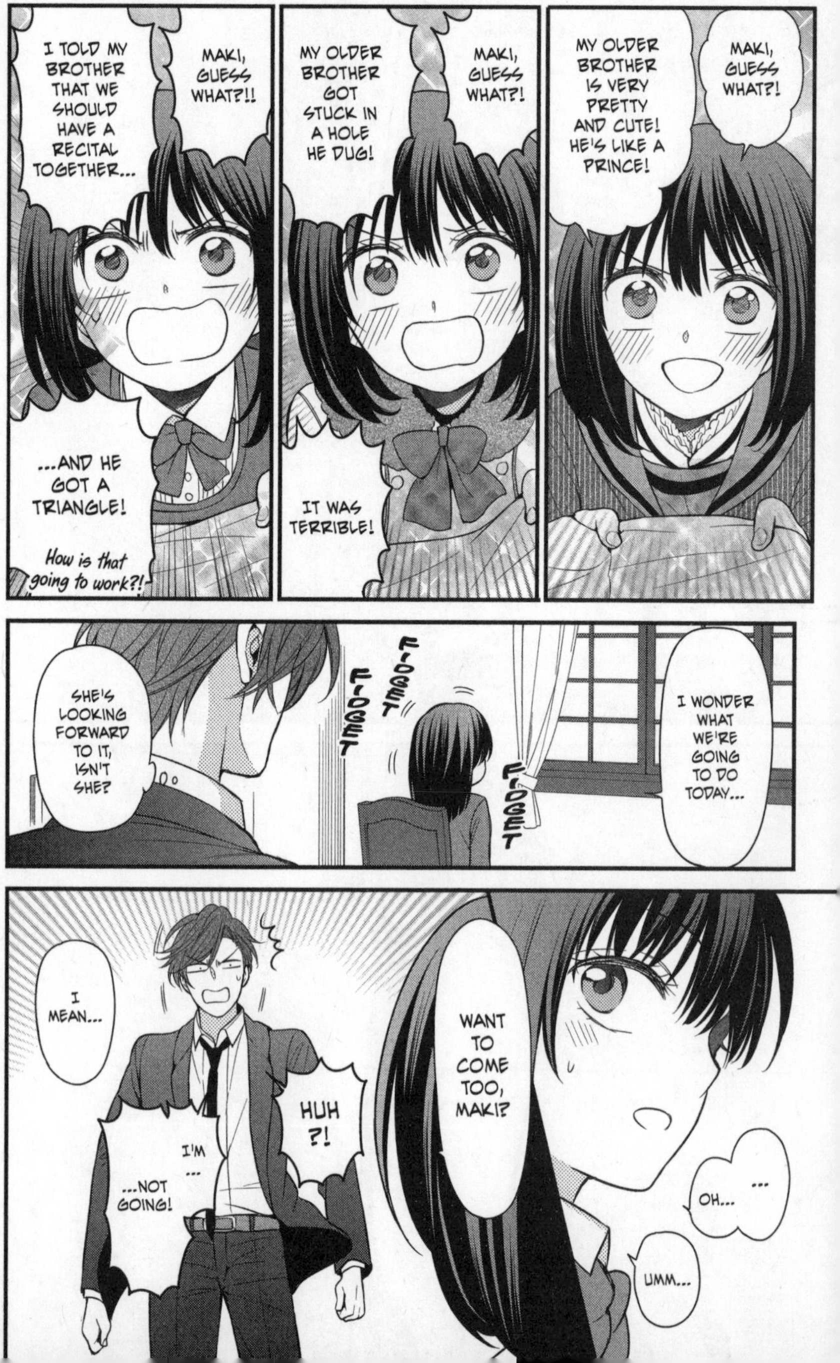
MAKI, GUESS WHAT?!
MY OLDER BROTHER IS VERY PRETTY AND CUTE! HE'S LIKE A PRINCE!
MAKI, GUESS WHAT?!
MY OLDER BROTHER GOT STUCK IN A HOLE HE DUG!
IT WAS TERRIBLE!
MAKI, GUESS WHAT?!!
I TOLD MY BROTHER THAT WE SHOULD HAVE A RECITAL TOGETHER...
...AND HE GOT A TRIANGLE!
How is that going to work?!
I WONDER WHAT WE'RE GOING TO DO TODAY...
FIDGET
FIDGET
FIDGET
SHE'S LOOKING FORWARD TO IT, ISN'T SHE?
WANT TO COME TOO, MAKI?
...
OH...
UMM...
HUH?!
I MEAN...
I'M ...
...NOT GOING!

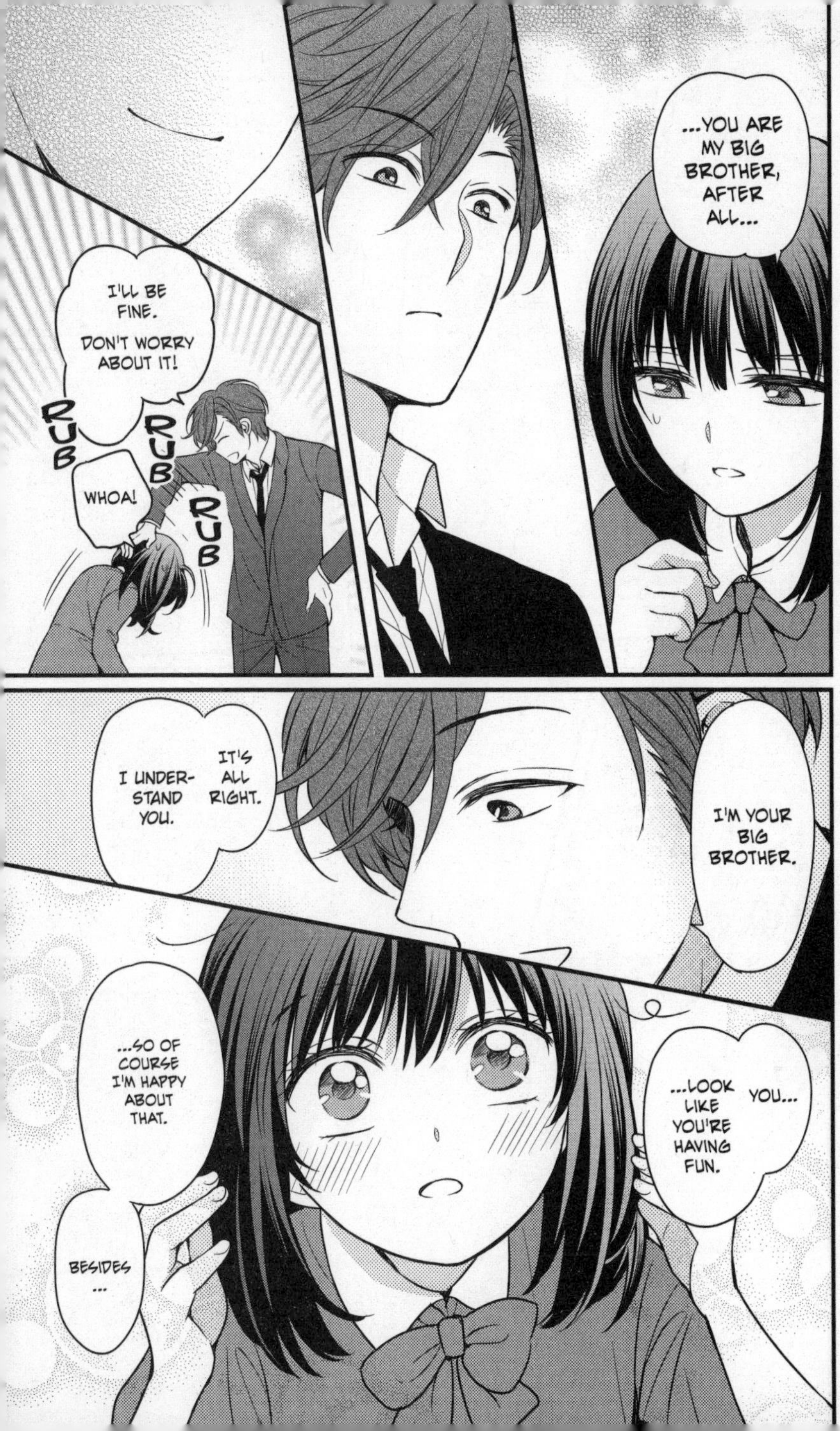
...YOU ARE MY BIG BROTHER, AFTER ALL...
I'LL BE FINE.
DON'T WORRY ABOUT IT!
RUB
RUB
RUB
WHOA!
I'M YOUR BIG BROTHER.
IT'S ALL RIGHT.
I UNDER-STAND YOU.
YOU...
...LOOK LIKE YOU'RE HAVING FUN.
...SO OF COURSE I'M HAPPY ABOUT THAT.
BESIDES...

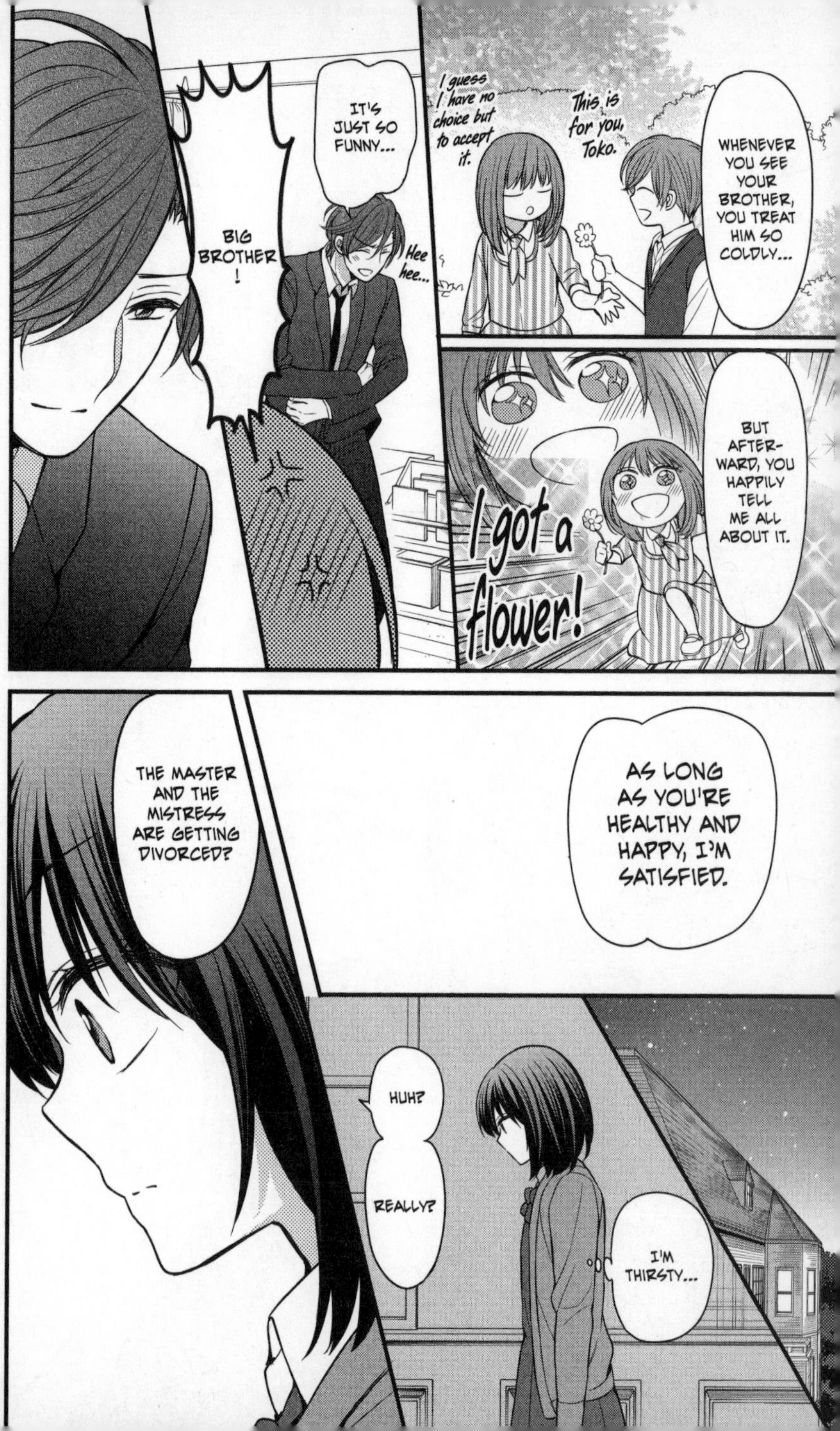
WHENEVER YOU SEE YOUR BROTHER, YOU TREAT HIM SO COLDLY...
This is for you, Toko.
I guess I have no choice but to accept it.
BUT AFTER-WARD, YOU HAPPILY TELL ME ALL ABOUT IT.
I got a flower!
IT'S JUST SO FUNNY...
Hee hee...
BIG BROTHER!
AS LONG AS YOU'RE HEALTHY AND HAPPY, I'M SATISFIED.
THE MASTER AND THE MISTRESS ARE GETTING DIVORCED?
I'M THIRSTY...
HUH?
REALLY?

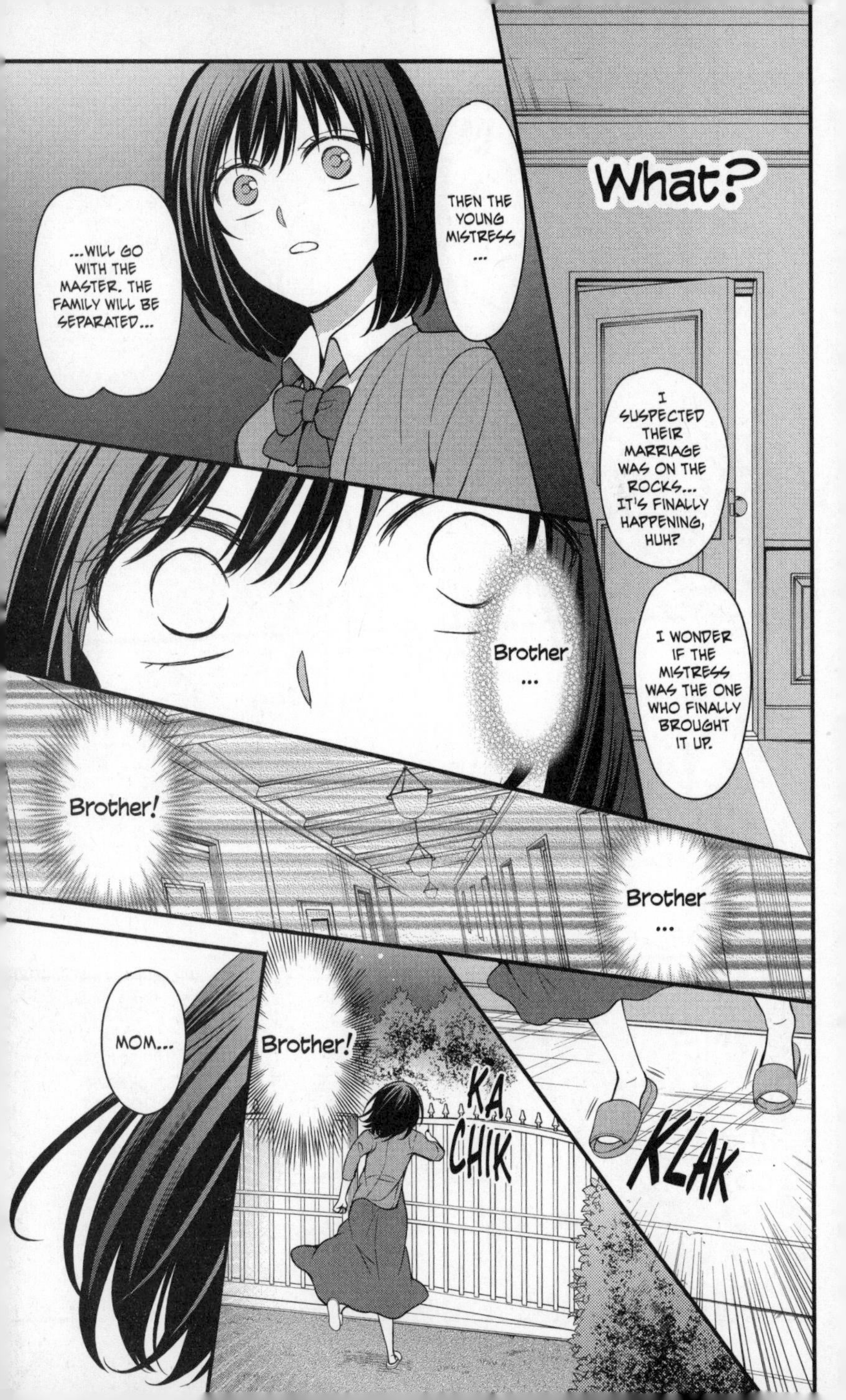
What?
I SUSPECTED THEIR MARRIAGE WAS ON THE ROCKS... IT'S FINALLY HAPPENING, HUH?
I WONDER IF THE MISTRESS WAS THE ONE WHO FINALLY BROUGHT IT UP.
THEN THE YOUNG MISTRESS...
...WILL GO WITH THE MASTER. THE FAMILY WILL BE SEPARATED...
Brother...
Brother...
Brother!
KLAK
KA CHIK
Brother!
MOM...

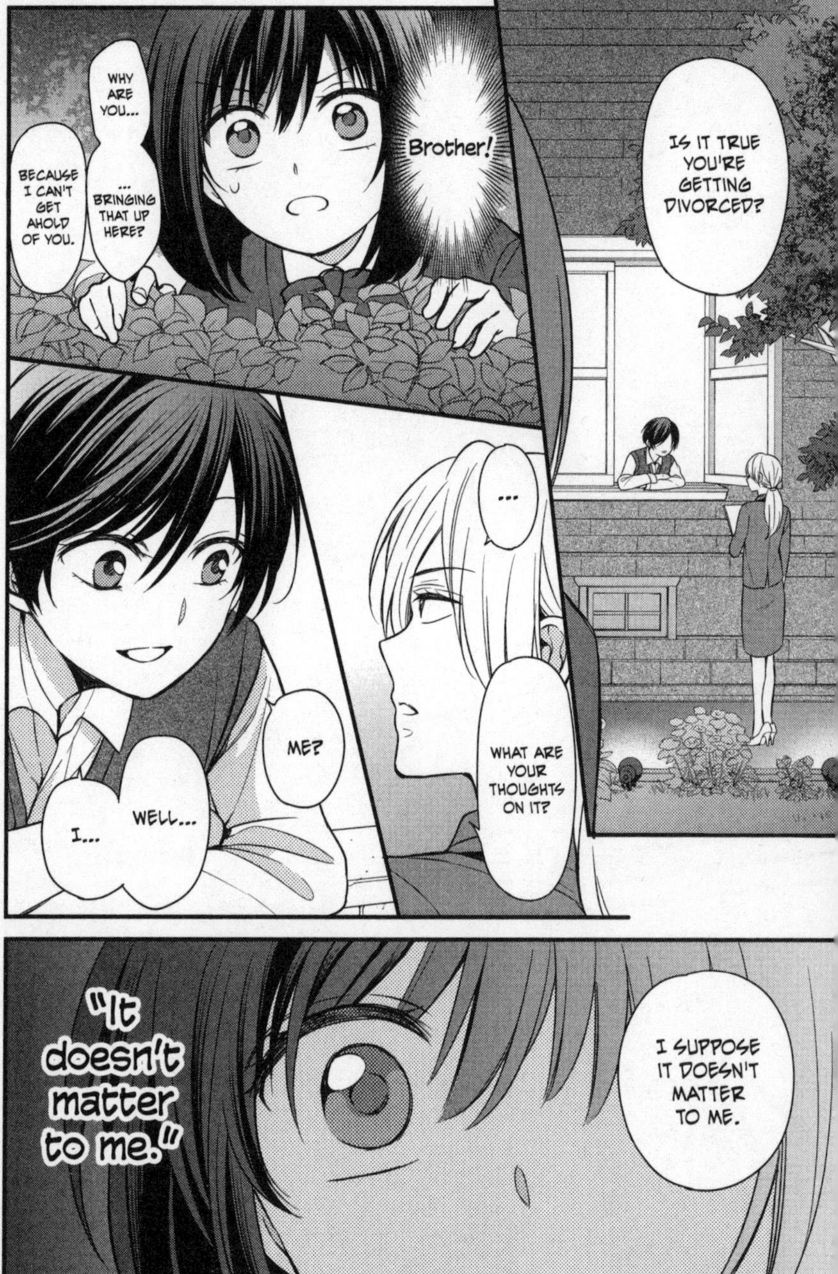
IS IT TRUE YOU'RE GETTING DIVORCED?
Brother!
WHY ARE YOU...
... BRINGING THAT UP HERE?
BECAUSE I CAN'T GET AHOLD OF YOU.
...
WHAT ARE YOUR THOUGHTS ON IT?
ME?
WELL... I...
I SUPPOSE IT DOESN'T MATTER TO ME.
"It doesn't matter to me."

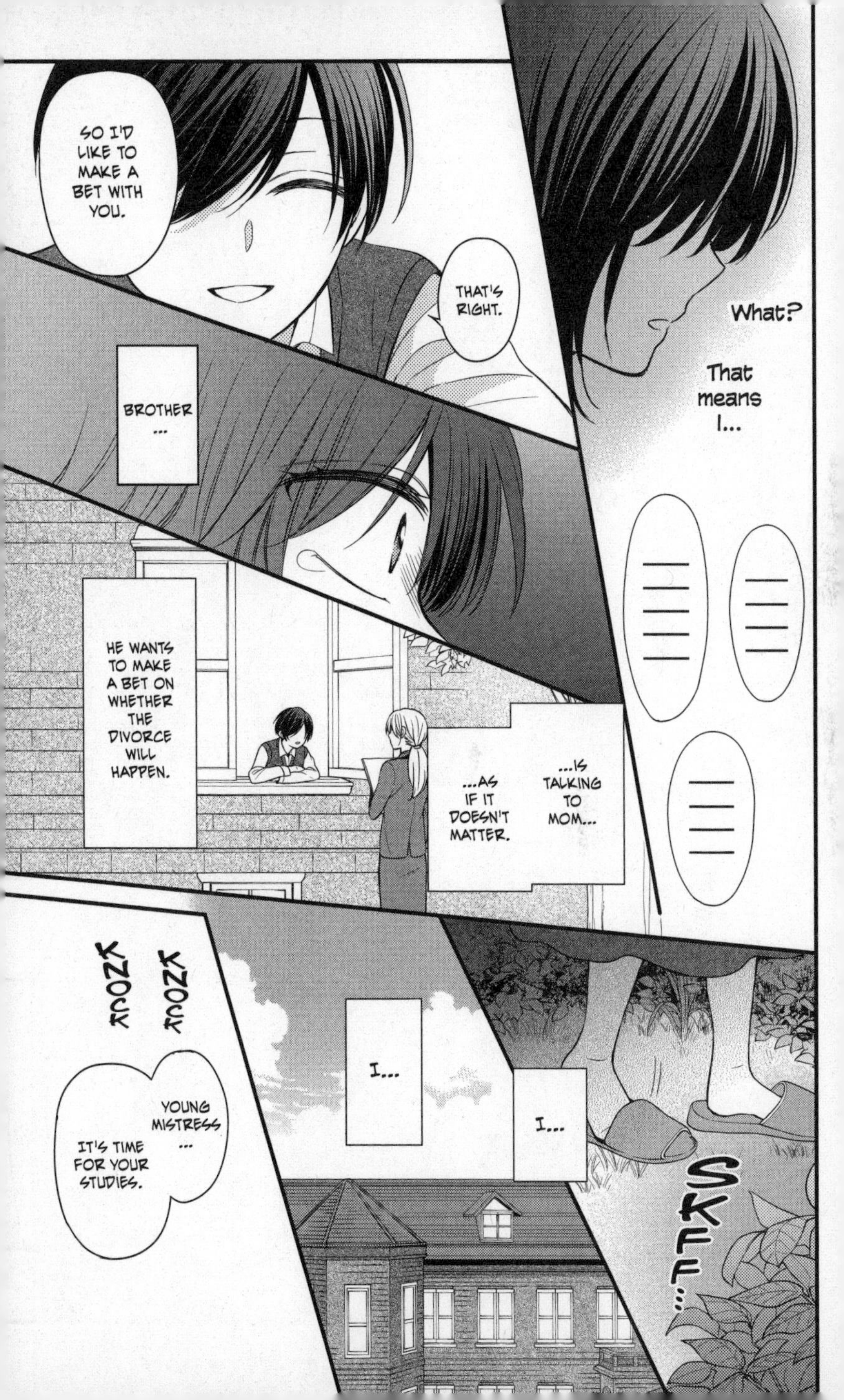

What?
That means I...
——
——
——
SO I'D LIKE TO MAKE A BET WITH YOU.
THAT'S RIGHT.
BROTHER...
...IS TALKING TO MOM...
...AS IF IT DOESN'T MATTER.
HE WANTS TO MAKE A BET ON WHETHER THE DIVORCE WILL HAPPEN.
SKFF...
I...
I...
KNOCK KNOCK
YOUNG MISTRESS...
IT'S TIME FOR YOUR STUDIES.

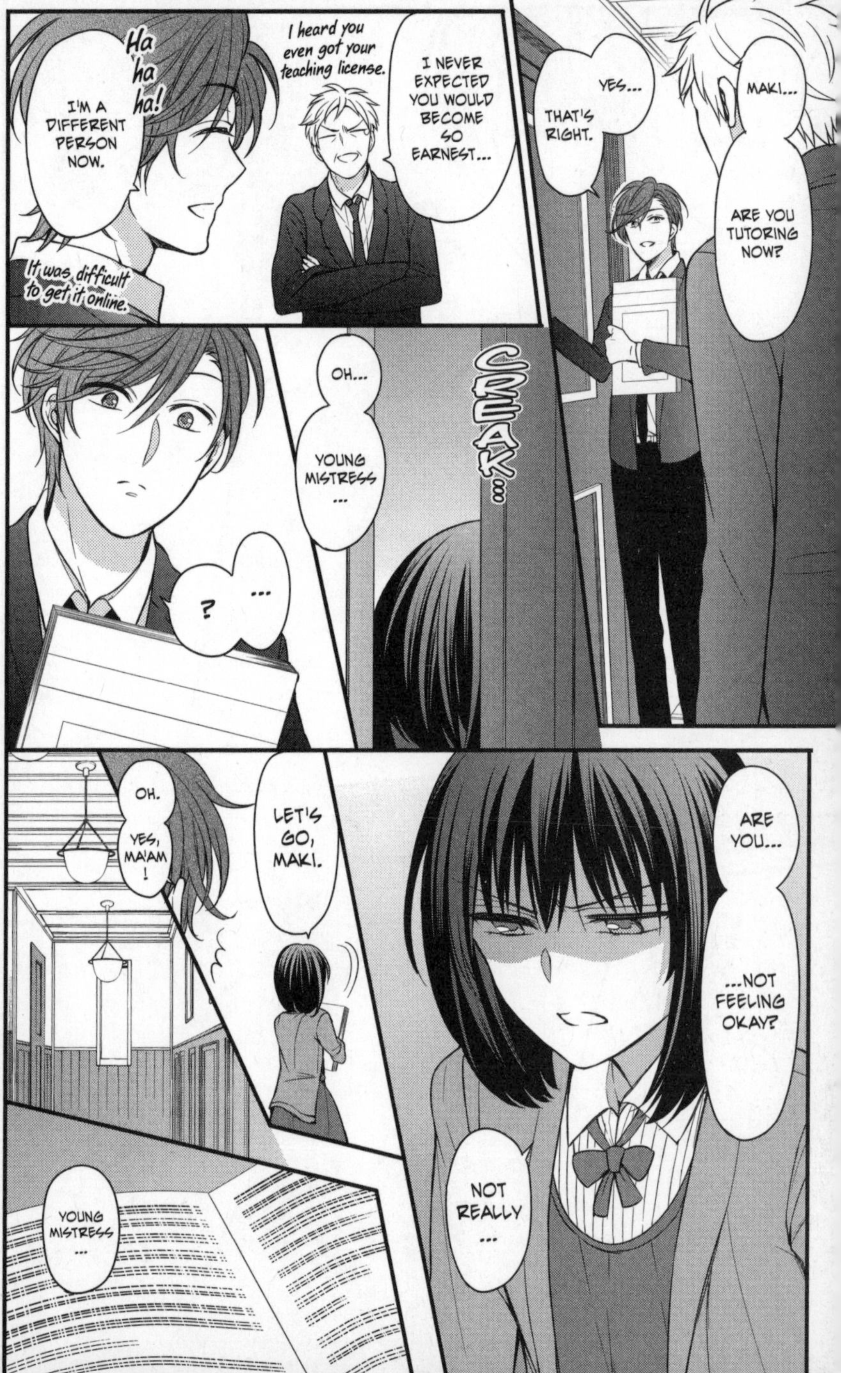
MAKI...
ARE YOU TUTORING NOW?
YES...
THAT'S RIGHT.
I NEVER EXPECTED YOU WOULD BECOME SO EARNEST...
I heard you even got your teaching license.
Ha ha ha!
I'M A DIFFERENT PERSON NOW.
It was difficult to get it online.
CREAK...
OH...
YOUNG MISTRESS...
...
?
ARE YOU...
...NOT FEELING OKAY?
NOT REALLY...
LET'S GO, MAKI.
OH.
YES, MA'AM!
YOUNG MISTRESS...

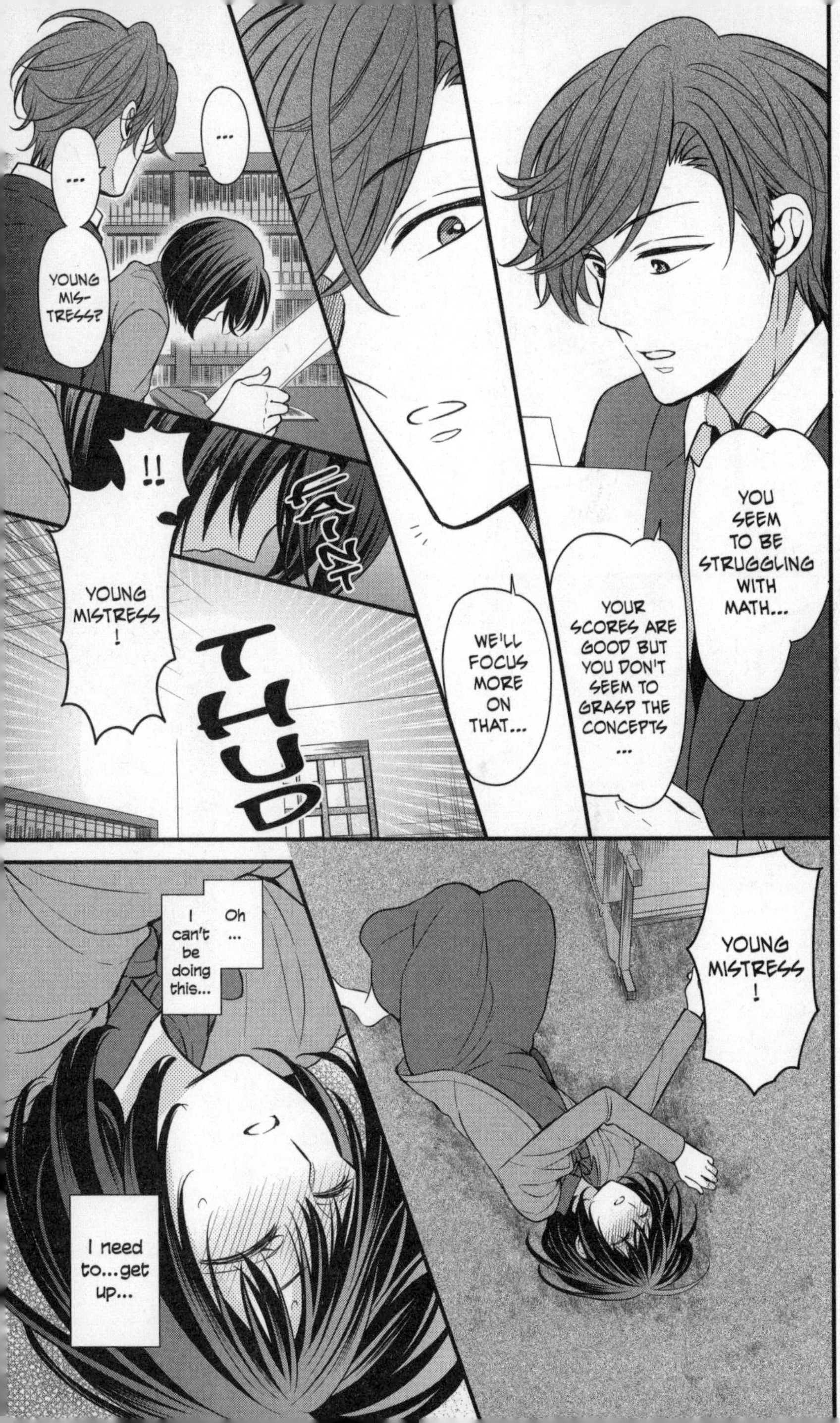
YOU SEEM TO BE STRUGGLING WITH MATH...
YOUR SCORES ARE GOOD BUT YOU DON'T SEEM TO GRASP THE CONCEPTS ...
WE'LL FOCUS MORE ON THAT...
...
...
YOUNG MIS-TRESS?
!!
YOUNG MISTRESS !
THUD
YOUNG MISTRESS !
Oh ... I can't be doing this...
I need to...get up...

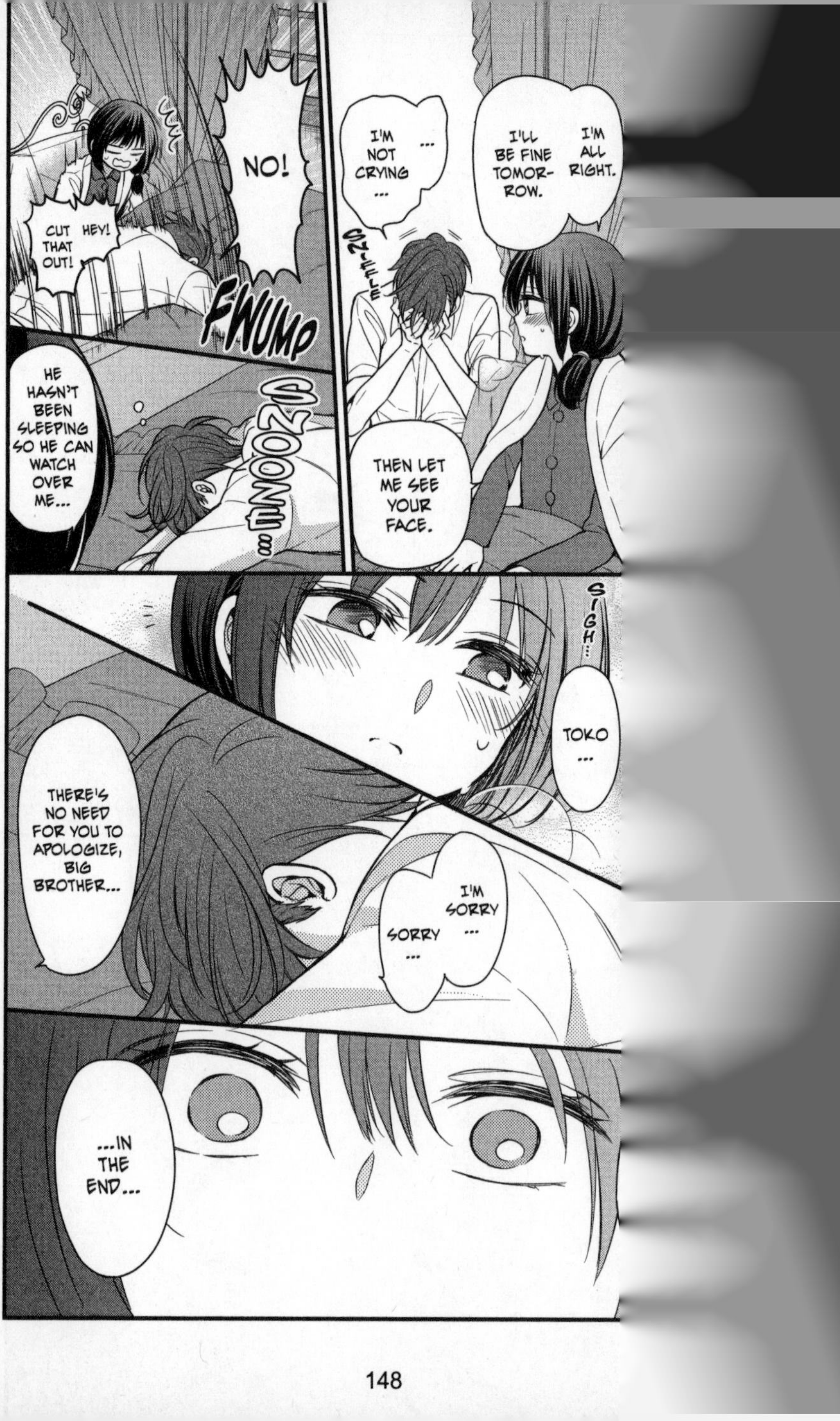
I'M ALL RIGHT.
I'LL BE FINE TOMORROW.
I'M NOT CRYING...
...
SNIFFLE
THEN LET ME SEE YOUR FACE.
NO!
HEY! CUT THAT OUT!
FWUMP
SNOOZE...
HE HASN'T BEEN SLEEPING SO HE CAN WATCH OVER ME...
SIGH...
TOKO...
I'M SORRY...
SORRY...
THERE'S NO NEED FOR YOU TO APOLOGIZE, BIG BROTHER...
...IN THE END...

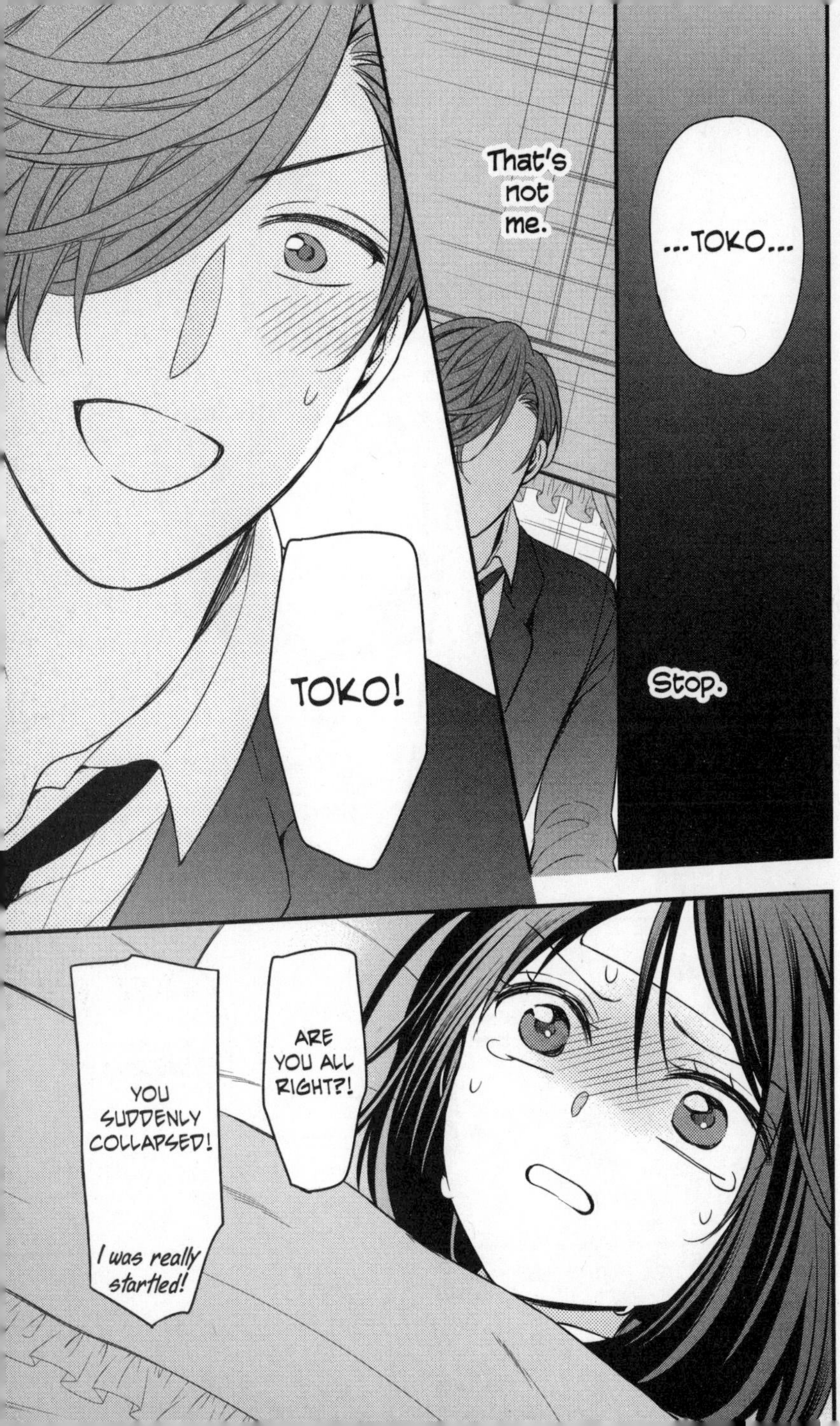
...TOKO...
Stop.
That's not me.
TOKO!
ARE YOU ALL RIGHT?!
YOU SUDDENLY COLLAPSED!
I was really startled!

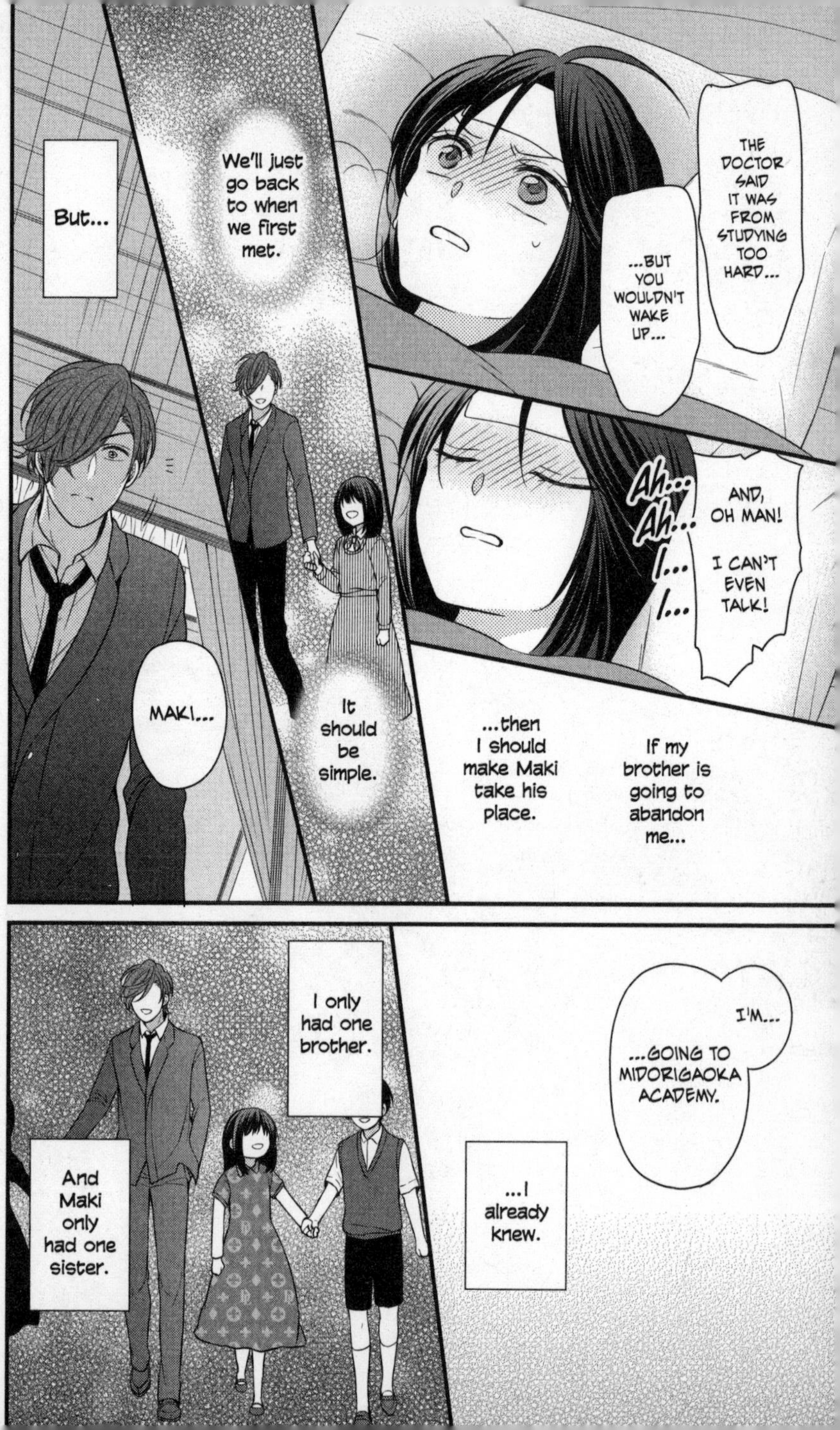
THE DOCTOR SAID IT WAS FROM STUDYING TOO HARD...
...BUT YOU WOULDN'T WAKE UP...
AND, OH MAN!
I CAN'T EVEN TALK!
Ah... Ah... I... I...
If my brother is going to abandon me...
...then I should make Maki take his place.
We'll just go back to when we first met.
It should be simple.
But...
MAKI...
I'M...
...GOING TO MIDORIGAOKA ACADEMY.
...I already knew.
I only had one brother.
And Maki only had one sister.

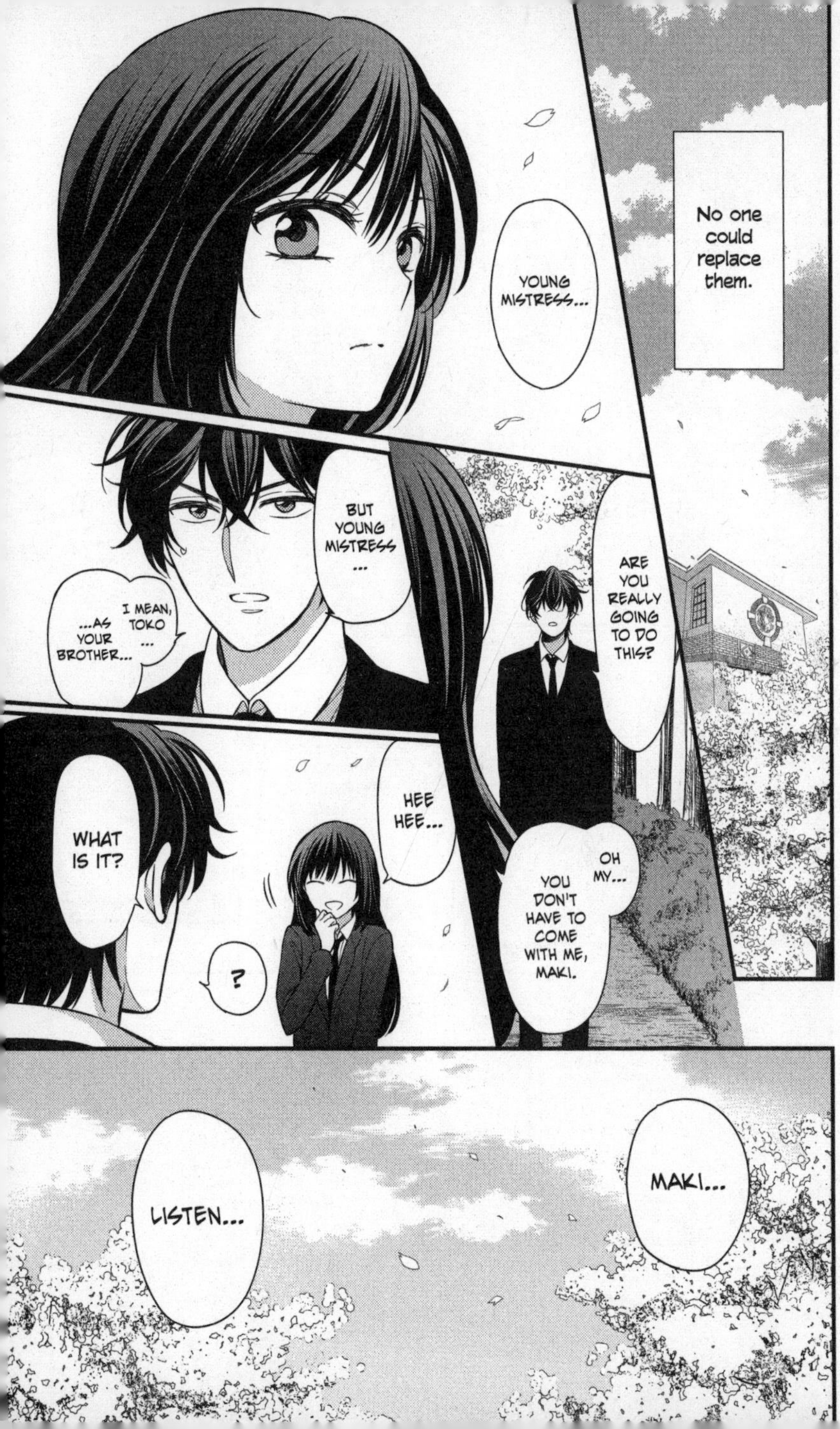
No one could replace them.
YOUNG MISTRESS...
ARE YOU REALLY GOING TO DO THIS?
OH MY...
YOU DON'T HAVE TO COME WITH ME, MAKI.
BUT YOUNG MISTRESS...
I MEAN, TOKO...
...AS YOUR BROTHER...
HEE HEE...
?
WHAT IS IT?
MAKI...
LISTEN...

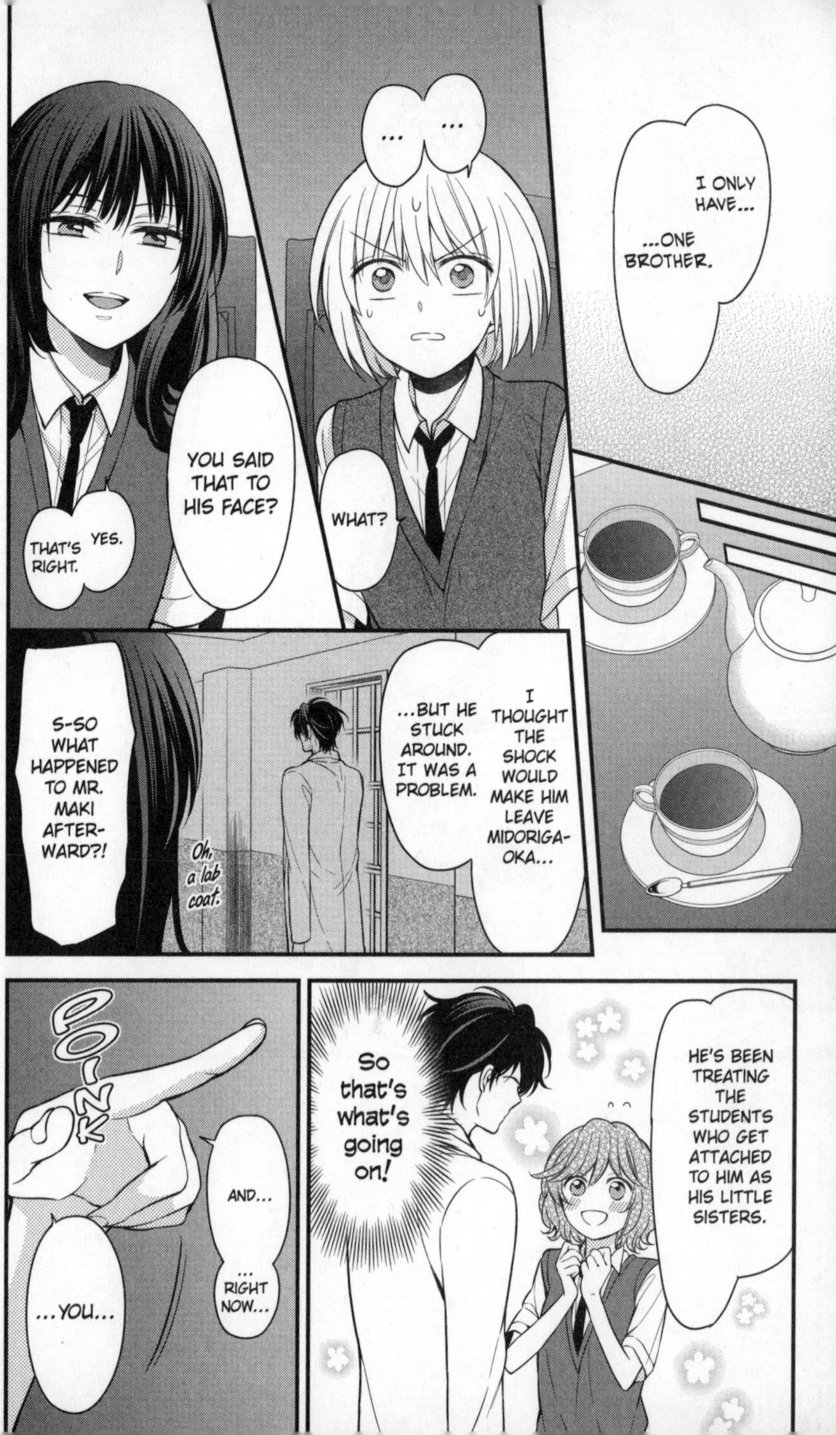
I ONLY HAVE...
...ONE BROTHER.
... ...
WHAT?
YOU SAID THAT TO HIS FACE?
YES. THAT'S RIGHT.
I THOUGHT THE SHOCK WOULD MAKE HIM LEAVE MIDORIGA-OKA...
...BUT HE STUCK AROUND. IT WAS A PROBLEM.
Oh, a lab coat.
S-SO WHAT HAPPENED TO MR. MAKI AFTER-WARD?!
HE'S BEEN TREATING THE STUDENTS WHO GET ATTACHED TO HIM AS HIS LITTLE SISTERS.
So that's what's going on!
... RIGHT NOW...
AND...
...YOU...
POINK

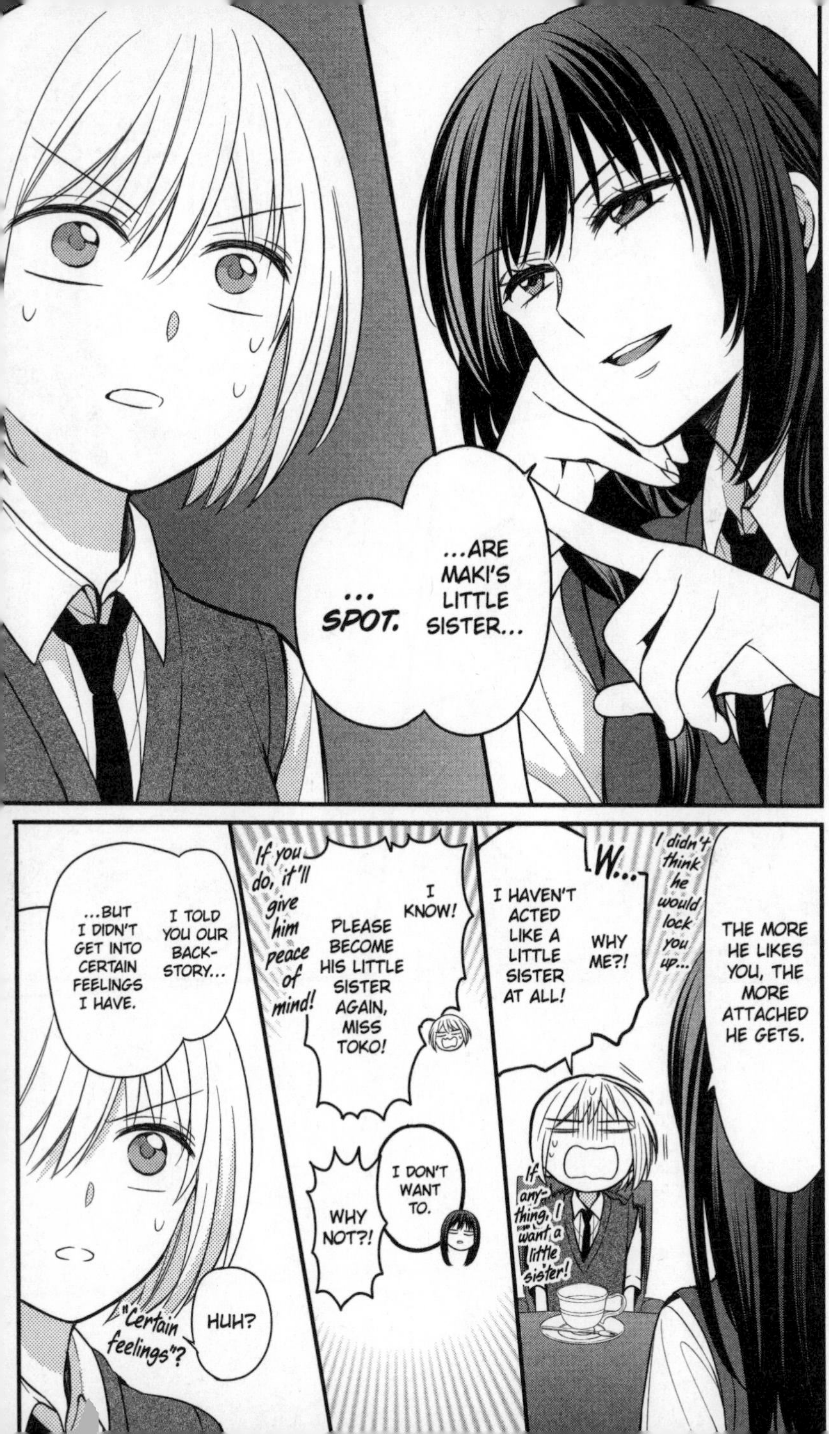
...ARE MAKI'S LITTLE SISTER...
... SPOT.
THE MORE HE LIKES YOU, THE MORE ATTACHED HE GETS.
I didn't think he would lock you up...
W...
WHY ME?!
I HAVEN'T ACTED LIKE A LITTLE SISTER AT ALL!
If anything, I want a little sister!
I KNOW!
PLEASE BECOME HIS LITTLE SISTER AGAIN, MISS TOKO!
If you do, it'll give him peace of mind!
I DON'T WANT TO.
WHY NOT?!
I TOLD YOU OUR BACK-STORY...
...BUT I DIDN'T GET INTO CERTAIN FEELINGS I HAVE.
HUH?
"Certain feelings"?

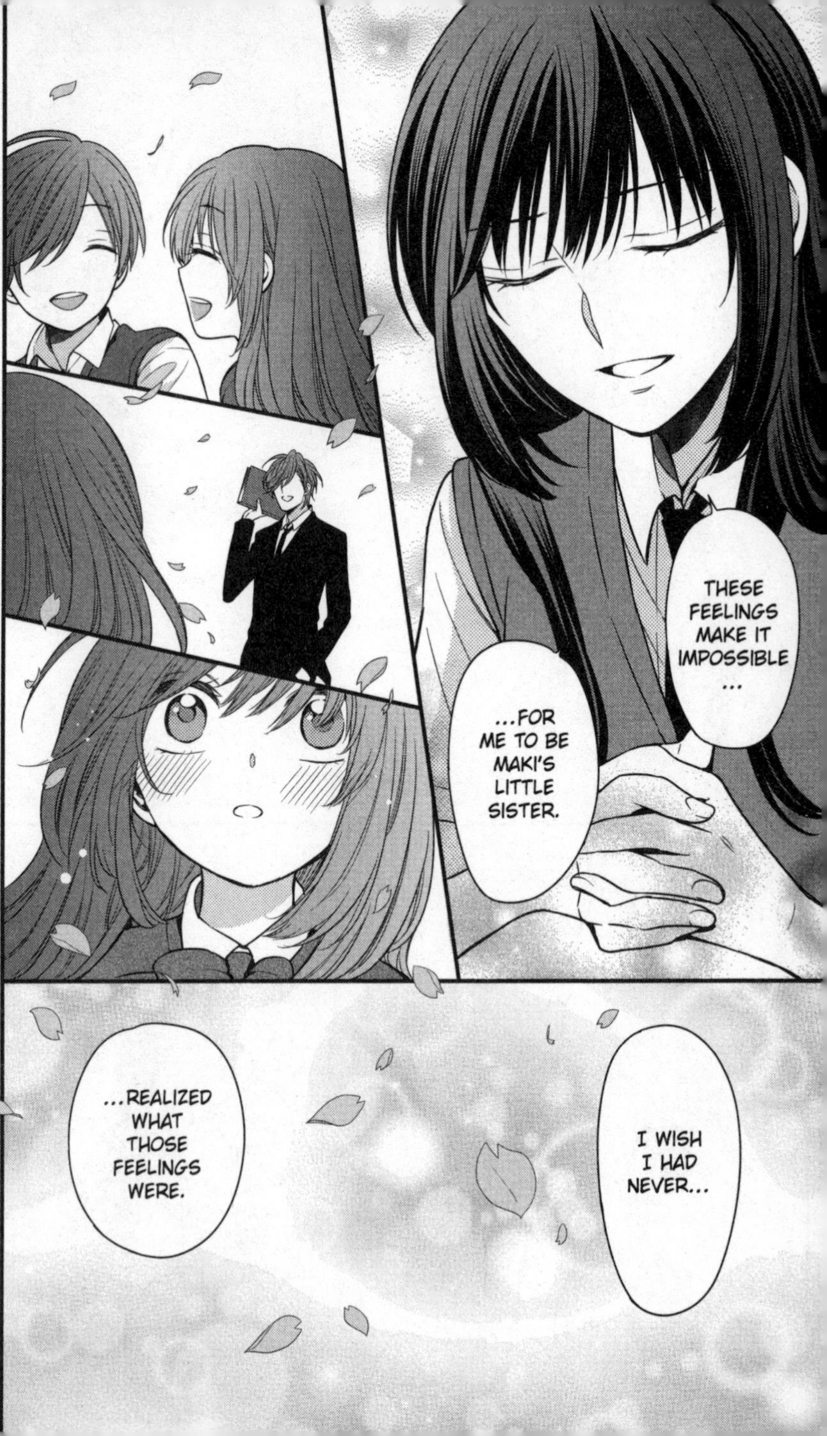
THESE FEELINGS MAKE IT IMPOSSIBLE ...
...FOR ME TO BE MAKI'S LITTLE SISTER.
I WISH I HAD NEVER...
...REALIZED WHAT THOSE FEELINGS WERE.

Chapter 152

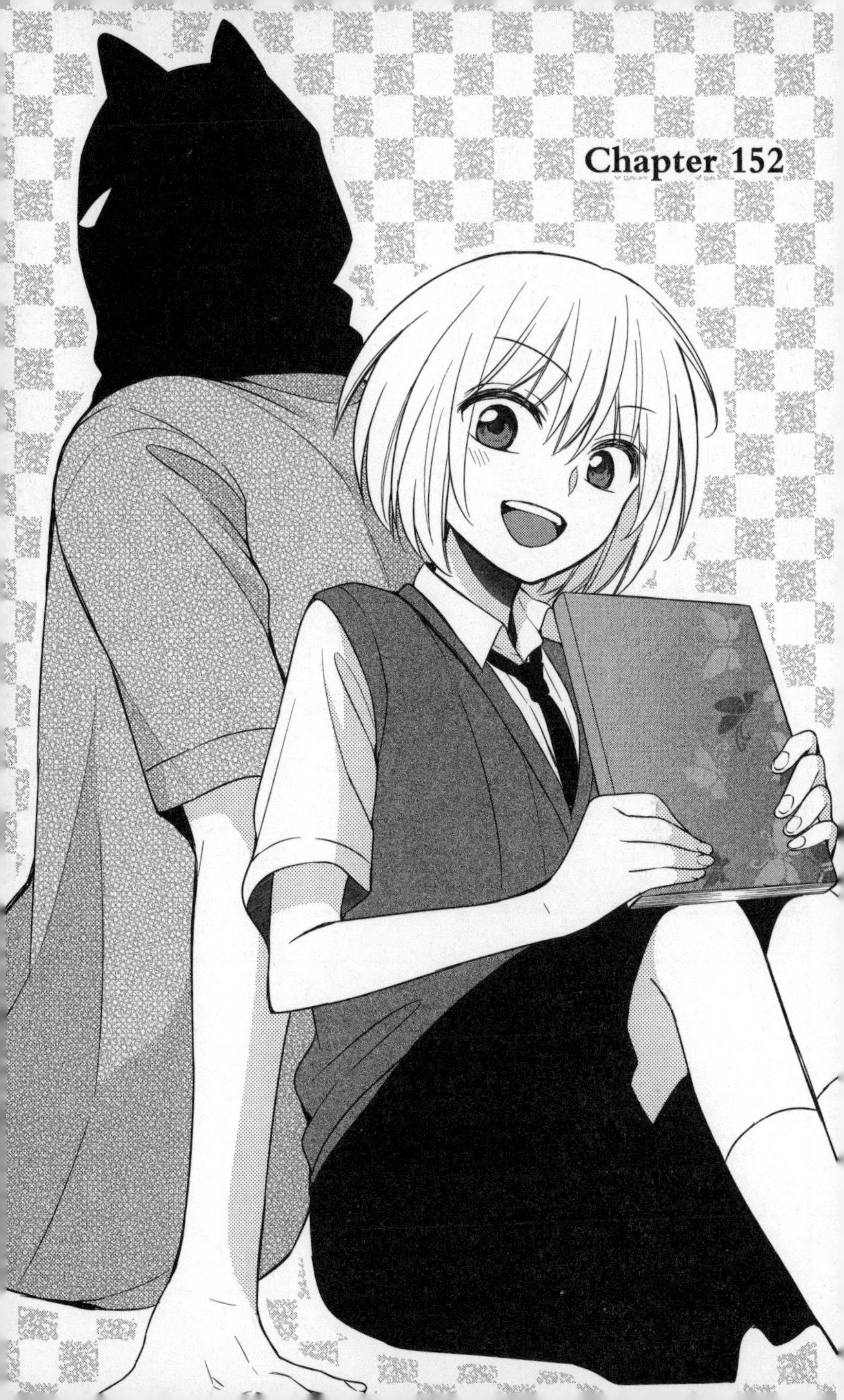

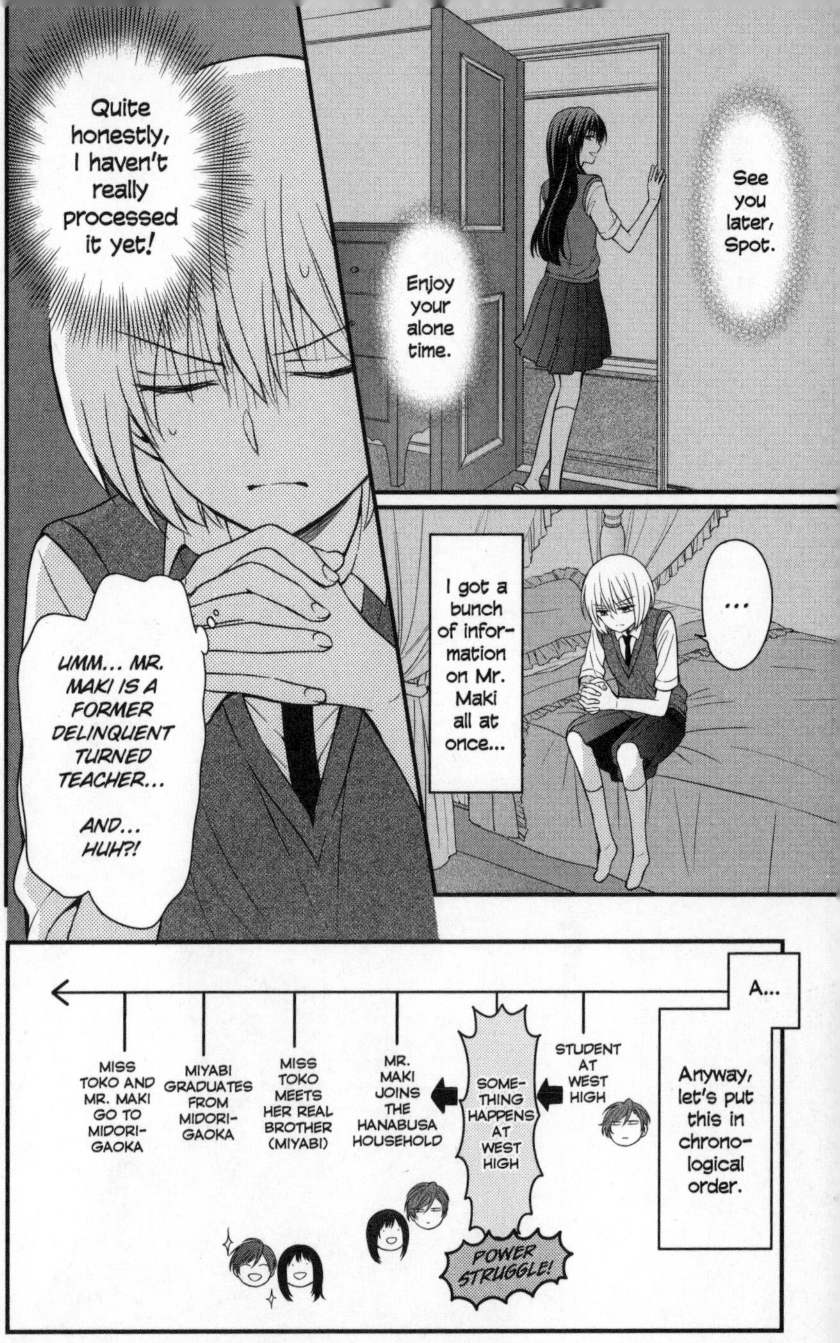
See you later, Spot.
Enjoy your alone time.
...
I got a bunch of information on Mr. Maki all at once...
Quite honestly, I haven't really processed it yet!
UMM... MR. MAKI IS A FORMER DELINQUENT TURNED TEACHER...
AND... HUH?!
A...
Anyway, let's put this in chronological order.
STUDENT AT WEST HIGH
SOMETHING HAPPENS AT WEST HIGH
POWER STRUGGLE!
MR. MAKI JOINS THE HANABUSA HOUSEHOLD
MISS TOKO MEETS HER REAL BROTHER (MIYABI)
MIYABI GRADUATES FROM MIDORI-GAOKA
MISS TOKO AND MR. MAKI GO TO MIDORI-GAOKA

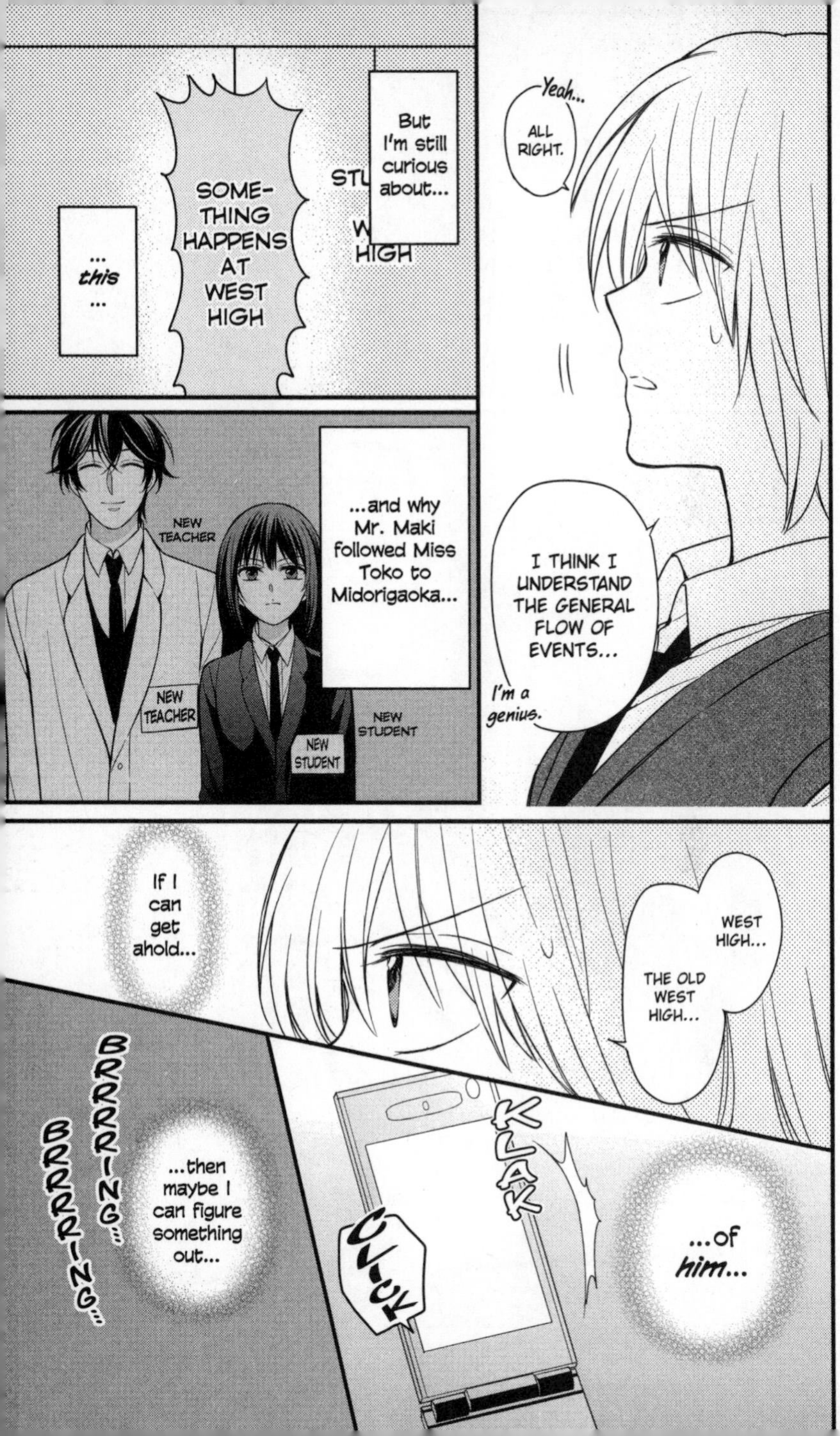
Yeah...
ALL RIGHT.
I THINK I UNDERSTAND THE GENERAL FLOW OF EVENTS...
I'm a genius.
But I'm still curious about...
SOME-THING HAPPENS AT WEST HIGH
... this ...
...and why Mr. Maki followed Miss Toko to Midorigaoka...
NEW STUDENT
NEW STUDENT
NEW TEACHER
NEW TEACHER
WEST HIGH...
THE OLD WEST HIGH...
If I can get ahold...
...of him...
KLAK
CLICK
...then maybe I can figure something out...
BRRRRING...
BRRRRING...

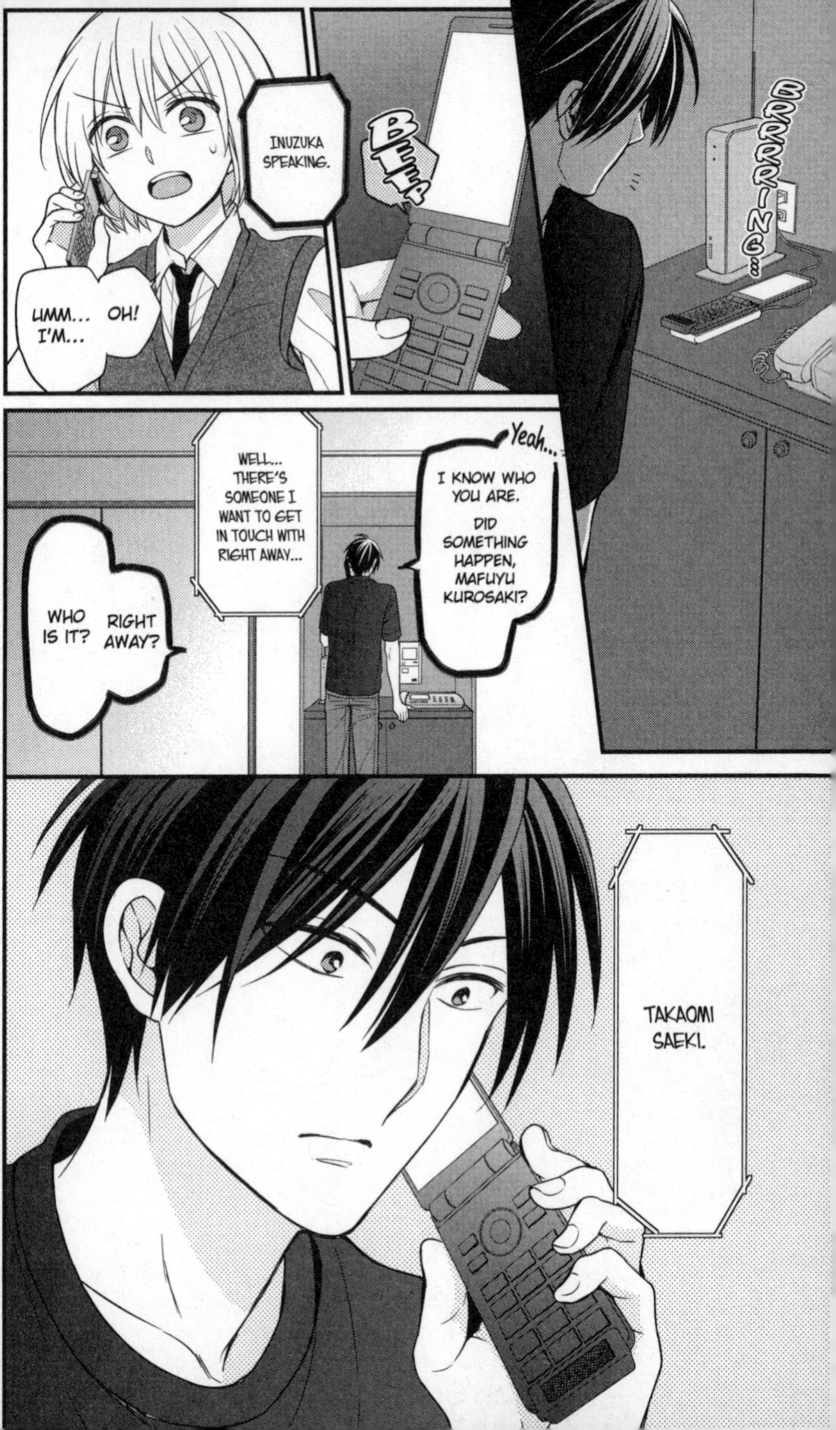
BRRRRING...
BEEP
INUZUKA SPEAKING.
UMM... OH! I'M...
Yeah...
I KNOW WHO YOU ARE.
DID SOMETHING HAPPEN, MAFUYU KUROSAKI?
WELL... THERE'S SOMEONE I WANT TO GET IN TOUCH WITH RIGHT AWAY...
RIGHT AWAY? WHO IS IT?
TAKAOMI SAEKI.

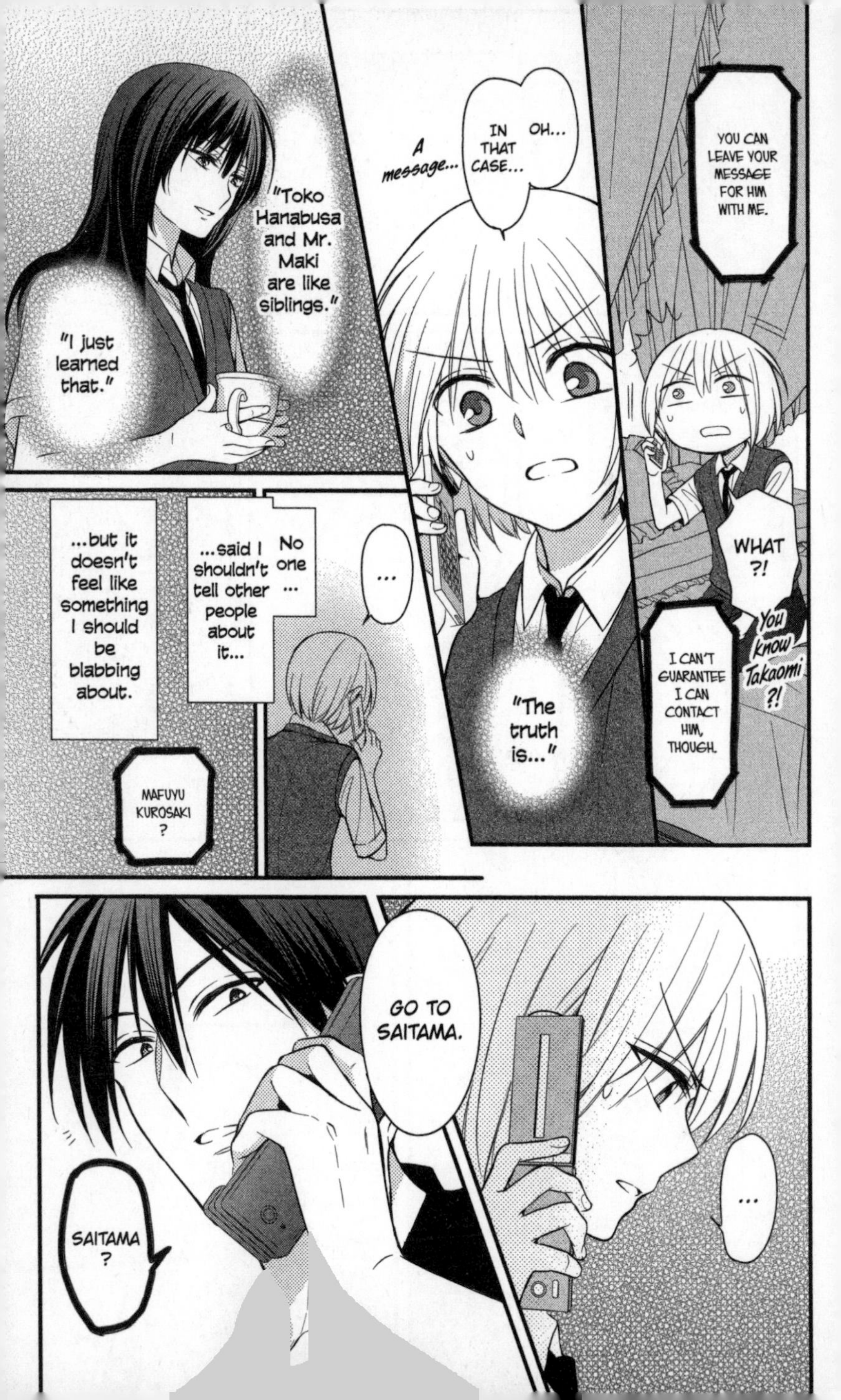
YOU CAN LEAVE YOUR MESSAGE FOR HIM WITH ME.
WHAT?!
You know Takaomi?!
I CAN'T GUARANTEE I CAN CONTACT HIM, THOUGH.
OH... IN THAT CASE...
A message...
"The truth is..."
"Toko Hanabusa and Mr. Maki are like siblings."
"I just learned that."
...
No one ...
...said I shouldn't tell other people about it...
...but it doesn't feel like something I should be blabbing about.
MAFUYU KUROSAKI?
GO TO SAITAMA.
...
SAITAMA?

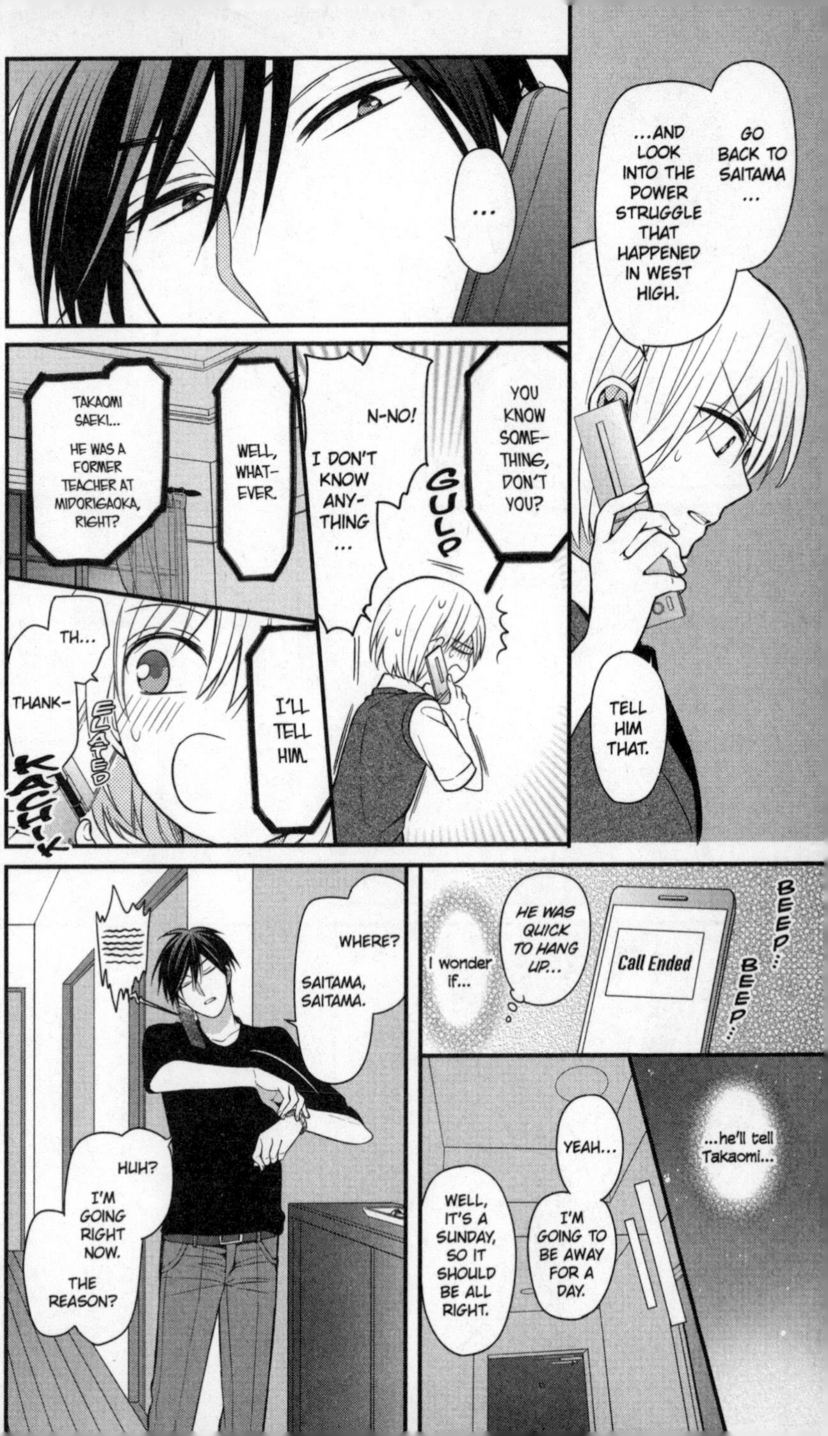
GO BACK TO SAITAMA...
...AND LOOK INTO THE POWER STRUGGLE THAT HAPPENED IN WEST HIGH.
TELL HIM THAT.
...
YOU KNOW SOMETHING, DON'T YOU?
GULP
N-NO!
I DON'T KNOW ANYTHING...
WELL, WHATEVER.
TAKAOMI SAEKI...
HE WAS A FORMER TEACHER AT MIDORIGAOKA, RIGHT?
I'LL TELL HIM.
TH...
THANK-
ELATED
KACHIK
BEEP... BEEP...
Call Ended
HE WAS QUICK TO HANG UP...
I wonder if...
...he'll tell Takaomi...
YEAH...
I'M GOING TO BE AWAY FOR A DAY.
WELL, IT'S A SUNDAY, SO IT SHOULD BE ALL RIGHT.
WHERE?
SAITAMA, SAITAMA.
HUH?
I'M GOING RIGHT NOW.
THE REASON?

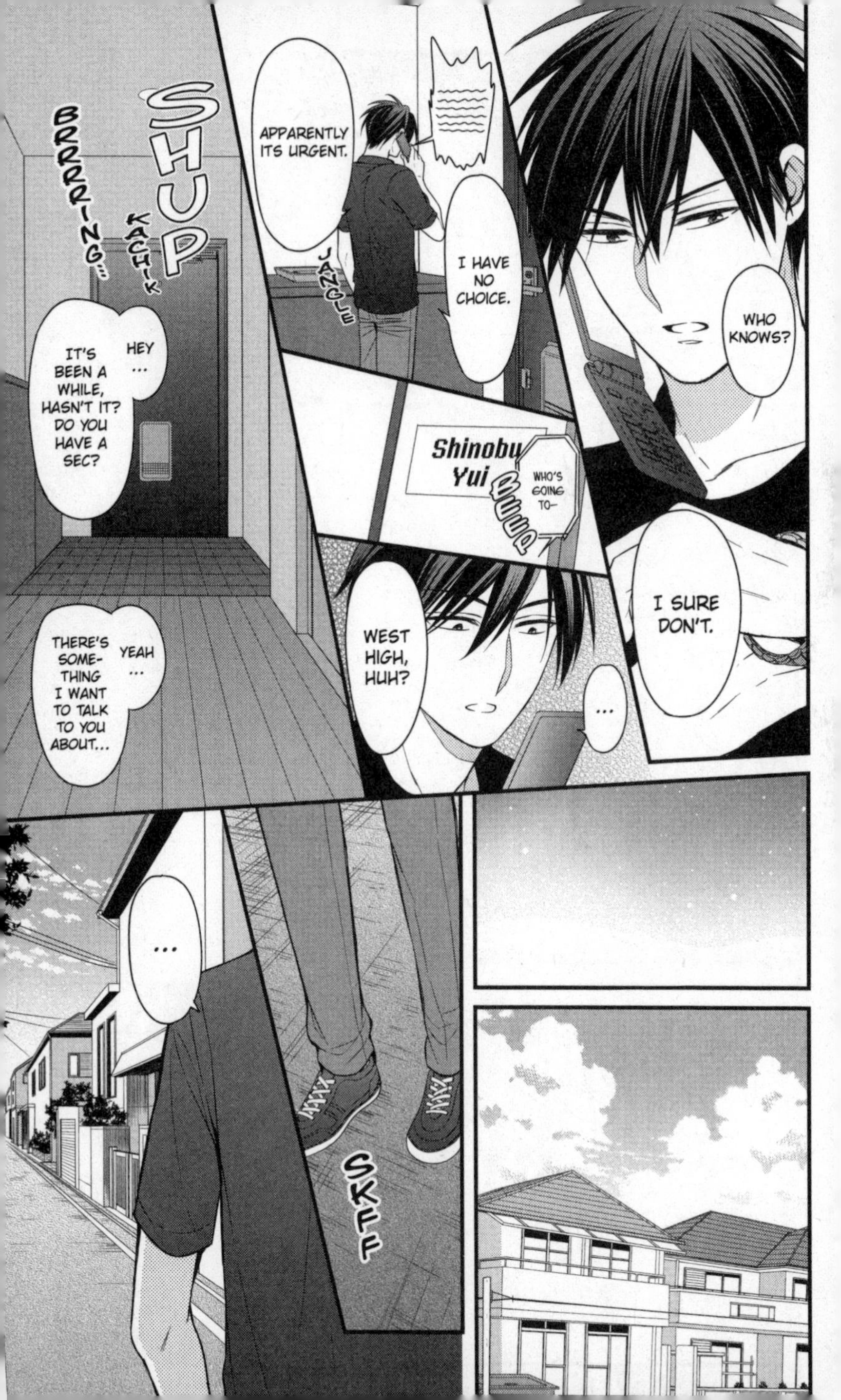
WHO KNOWS?
I HAVE NO CHOICE.
APPARENTLY ITS URGENT.
JANGLE
Shinobu Yui
BEEP
WHO'S GOING TO—
I SURE DON'T.
...
WEST HIGH, HUH?
SHUP
KACHIK
BRRRRING...
HEY...
IT'S BEEN A WHILE, HASN'T IT? DO YOU HAVE A SEC?
YEAH...
THERE'S SOME-THING I WANT TO TALK TO YOU ABOUT...
SKFF
...

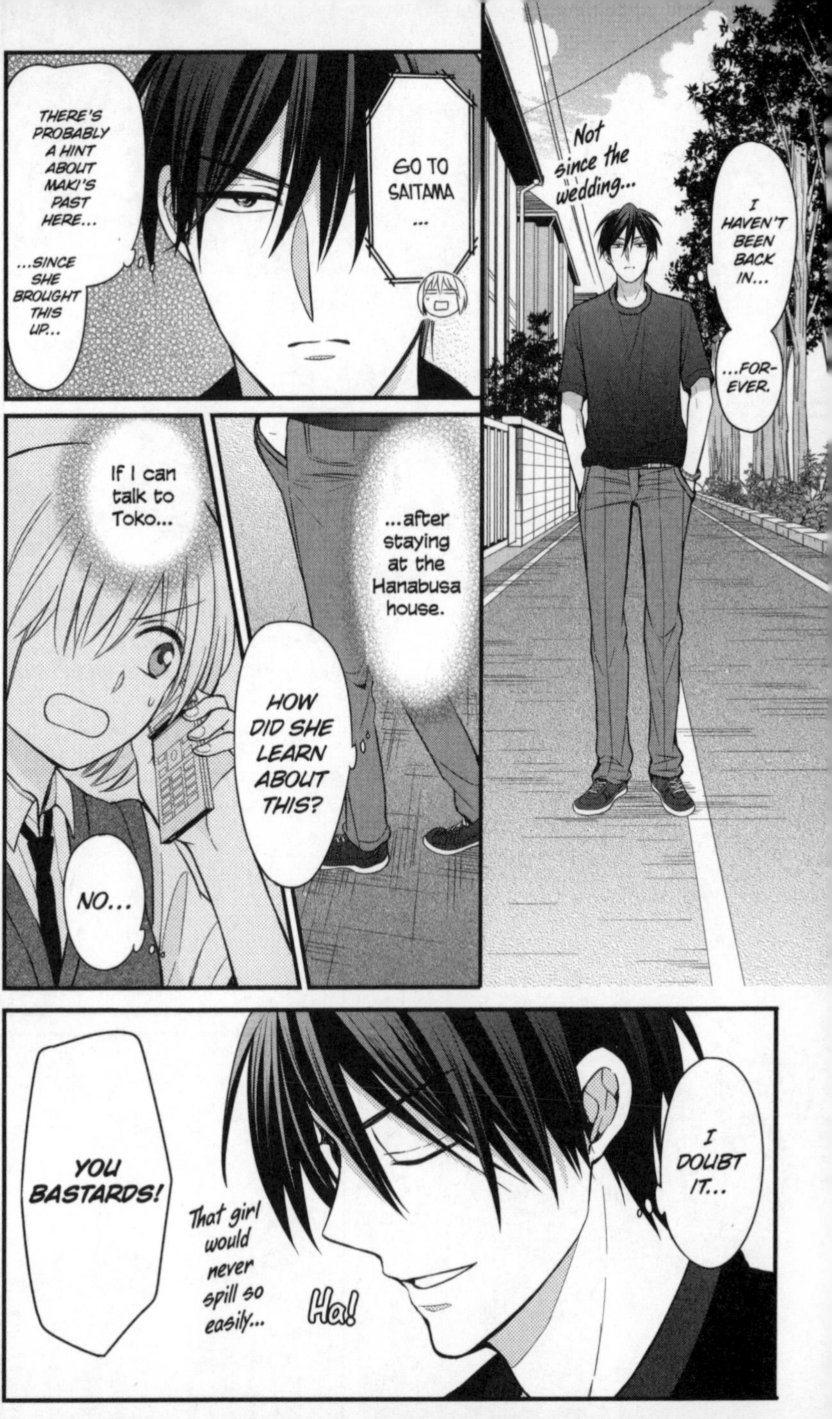
I HAVEN'T BEEN BACK IN...
...FOR-EVER.
Not since the wedding...
GO TO SAITAMA ...
THERE'S PROBABLY A HINT ABOUT MAKI'S PAST HERE...
...SINCE SHE BROUGHT THIS UP...
If I can talk to Toko...
...after staying at the Hanabusa house.
HOW DID SHE LEARN ABOUT THIS?
NO...
I DOUBT IT...
Ha!
That girl would never spill so easily...
YOU BASTARDS!

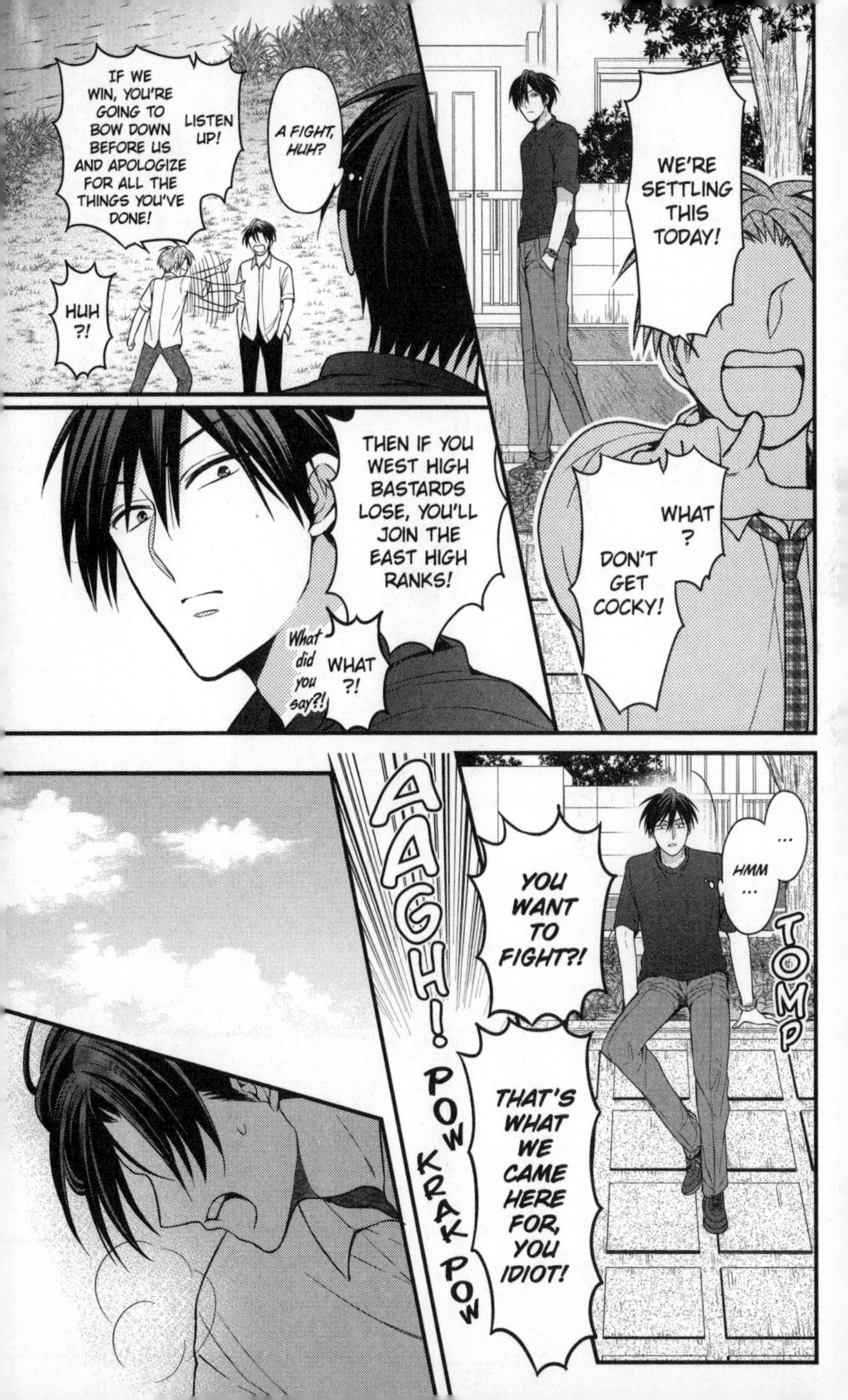
WE'RE SETTLING THIS TODAY!
WHAT?
DON'T GET COCKY!
A FIGHT, HUH?
LISTEN UP!
IF WE WIN, YOU'RE GOING TO BOW DOWN BEFORE US AND APOLOGIZE FOR ALL THE THINGS YOU'VE DONE!
HUH?!
THEN IF YOU WEST HIGH BASTARDS LOSE, YOU'LL JOIN THE EAST HIGH RANKS!
WHAT?!
What did you say?!
... HMM ...
TOMP
YOU WANT TO FIGHT?!
THAT'S WHAT WE CAME HERE FOR, YOU IDIOT!
AAGH!
POW KRAK POW

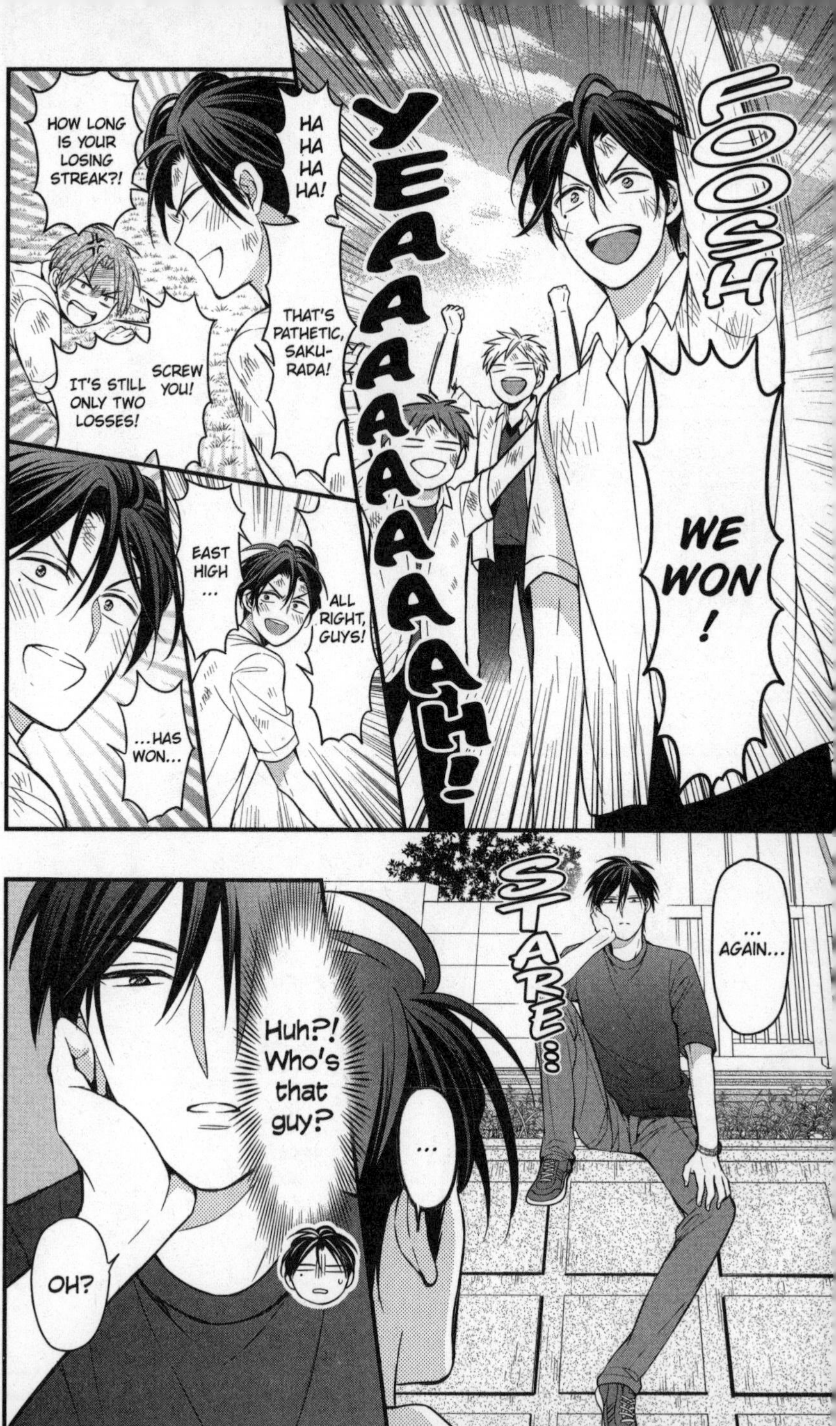
FOOSH
WE WON!
YEAAAAAAAH!
HA HA HA HA!
HOW LONG IS YOUR LOSING STREAK?!
THAT'S PATHETIC, SAKURADA!
SCREW YOU!
IT'S STILL ONLY TWO LOSSES!
ALL RIGHT, GUYS!
EAST HIGH...
...HAS WON...
STARE...
...AGAIN...
Huh?! Who's that guy?
...
OH?

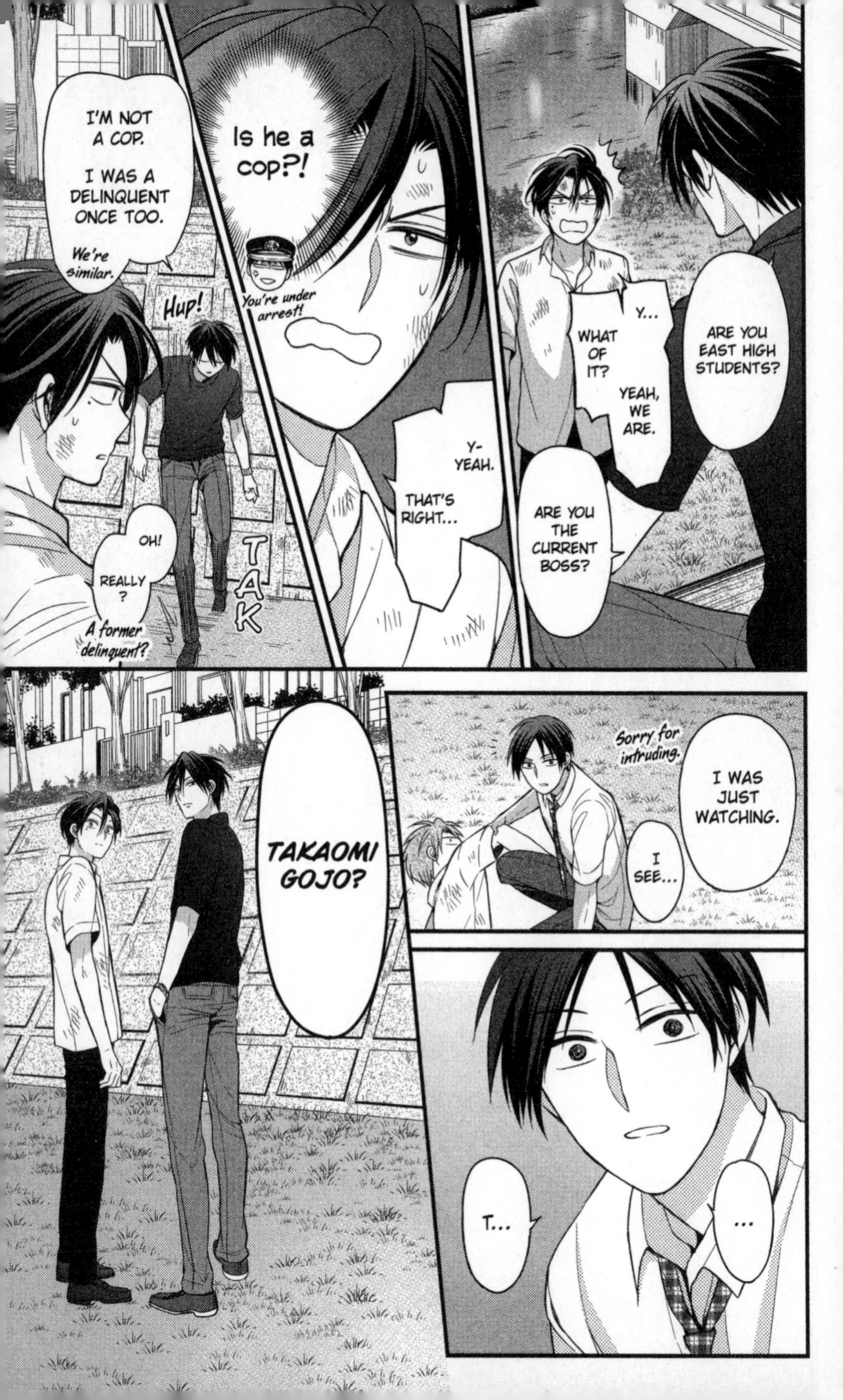
ARE YOU EAST HIGH STUDENTS?
Y... WHAT OF IT?
YEAH, WE ARE.
ARE YOU THE CURRENT BOSS?
Y-YEAH. THAT'S RIGHT...
Is he a cop?!
You're under arrest!
I'M NOT A COP. I WAS A DELINQUENT ONCE TOO.
We're similar.
Hup!
OH! REALLY?
A former delinquent?
TAK
I WAS JUST WATCHING.
Sorry for intruding.
I SEE...
...
T...
TAKAOMI GOJO?

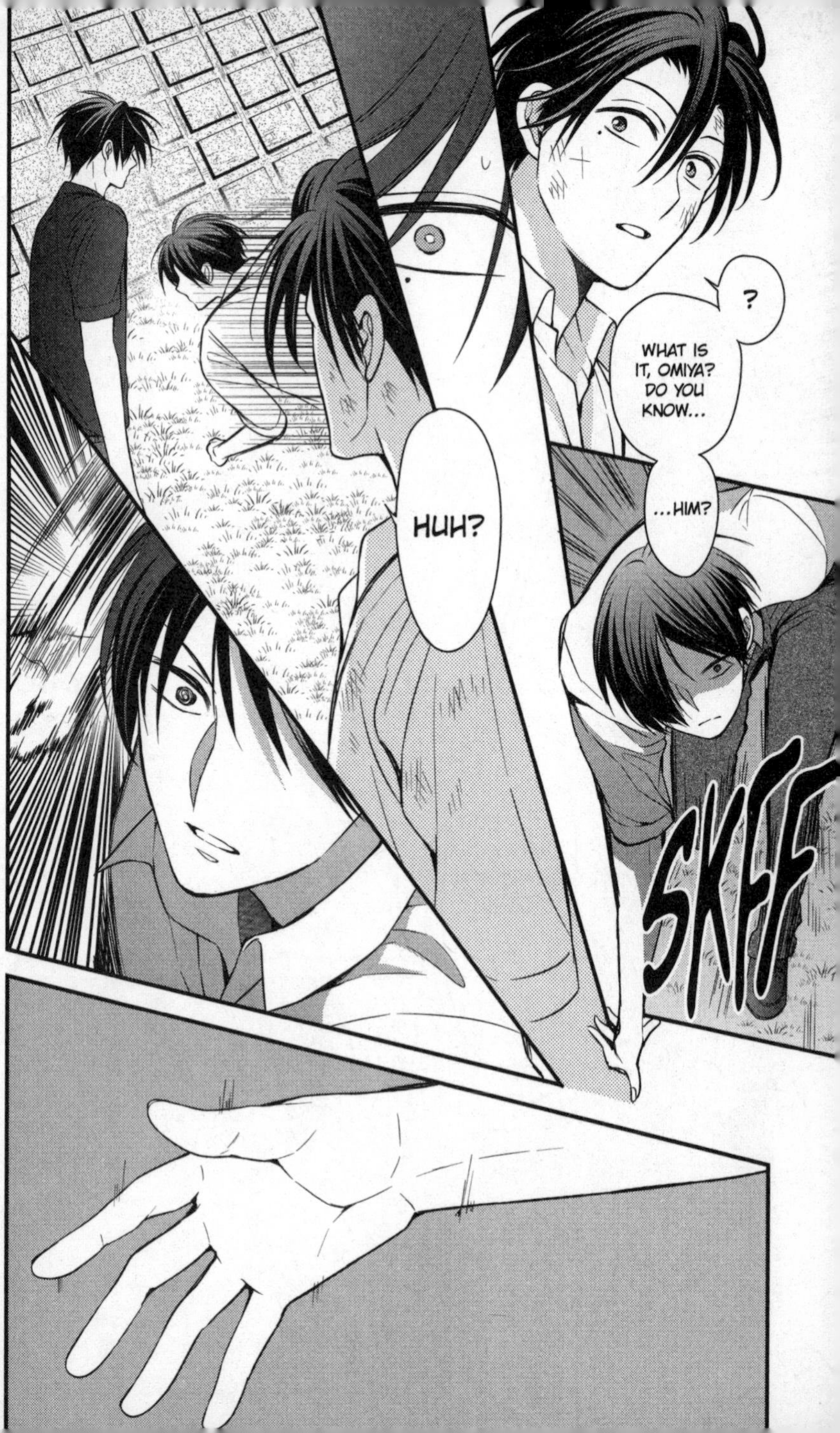
?
WHAT IS IT, OMIYA? DO YOU KNOW...
...HIM?
HUH?
SKFF

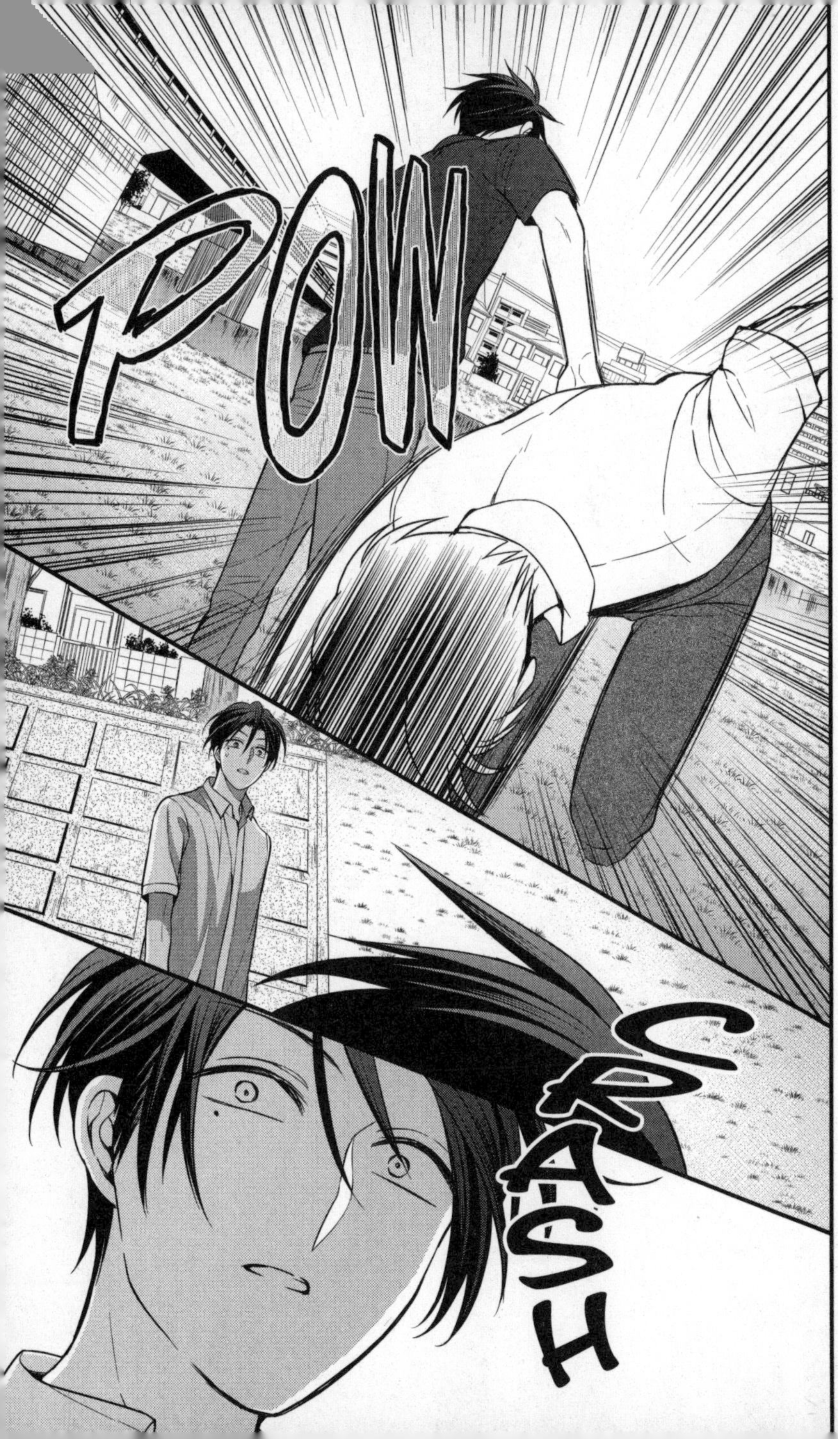
POW
CRASH

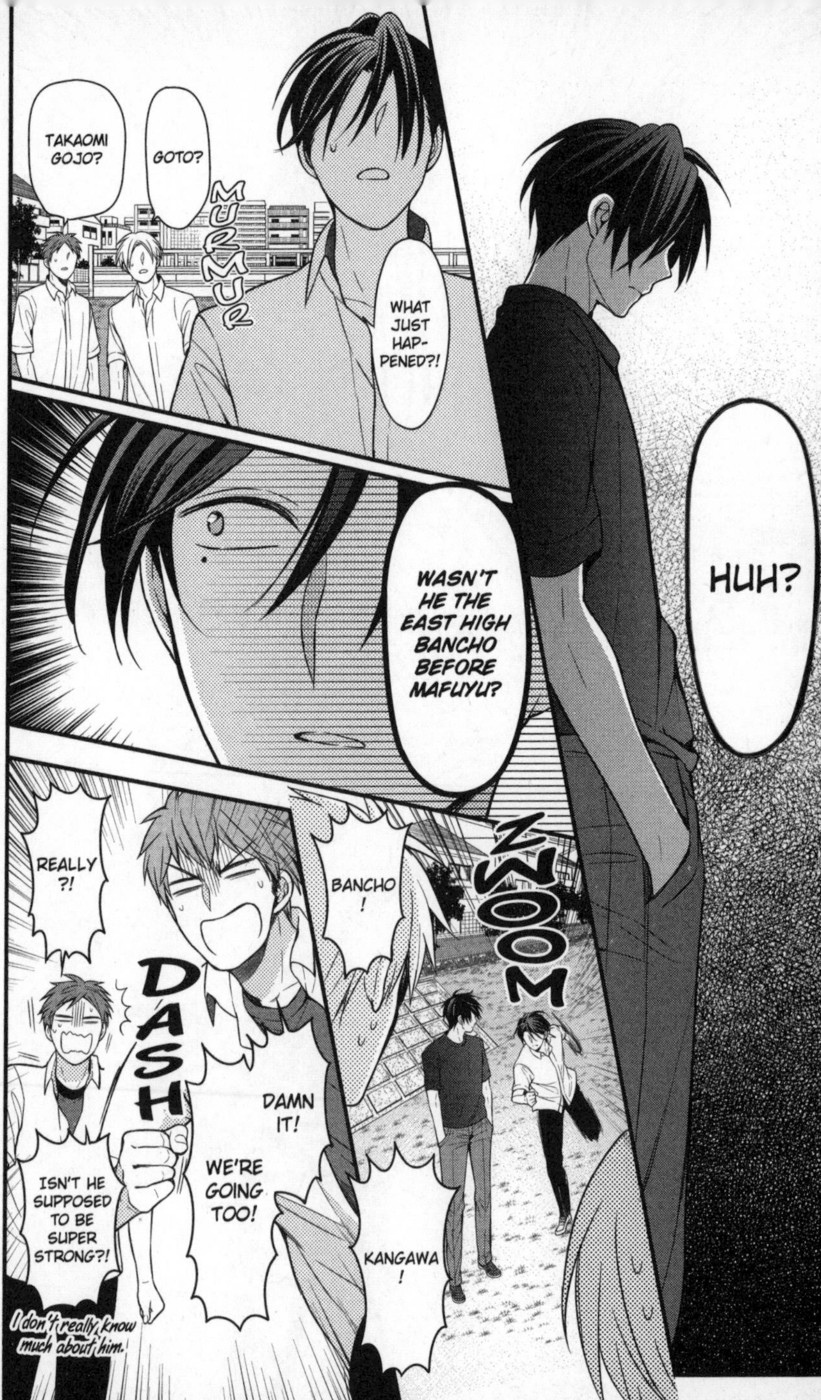
HUH?
GOTO?
TAKAOMI GOJO?
MURMUR
WHAT JUST HAP-PENED?!
WASN'T HE THE EAST HIGH BANCHO BEFORE MAFUYU?
ZWOOM
BANCHO!
REALLY?!
DASH
DAMN IT!
WE'RE GOING TOO!
KANGAWA!
ISN'T HE SUPPOSED TO BE SUPER STRONG?!
I don't really know much about him.

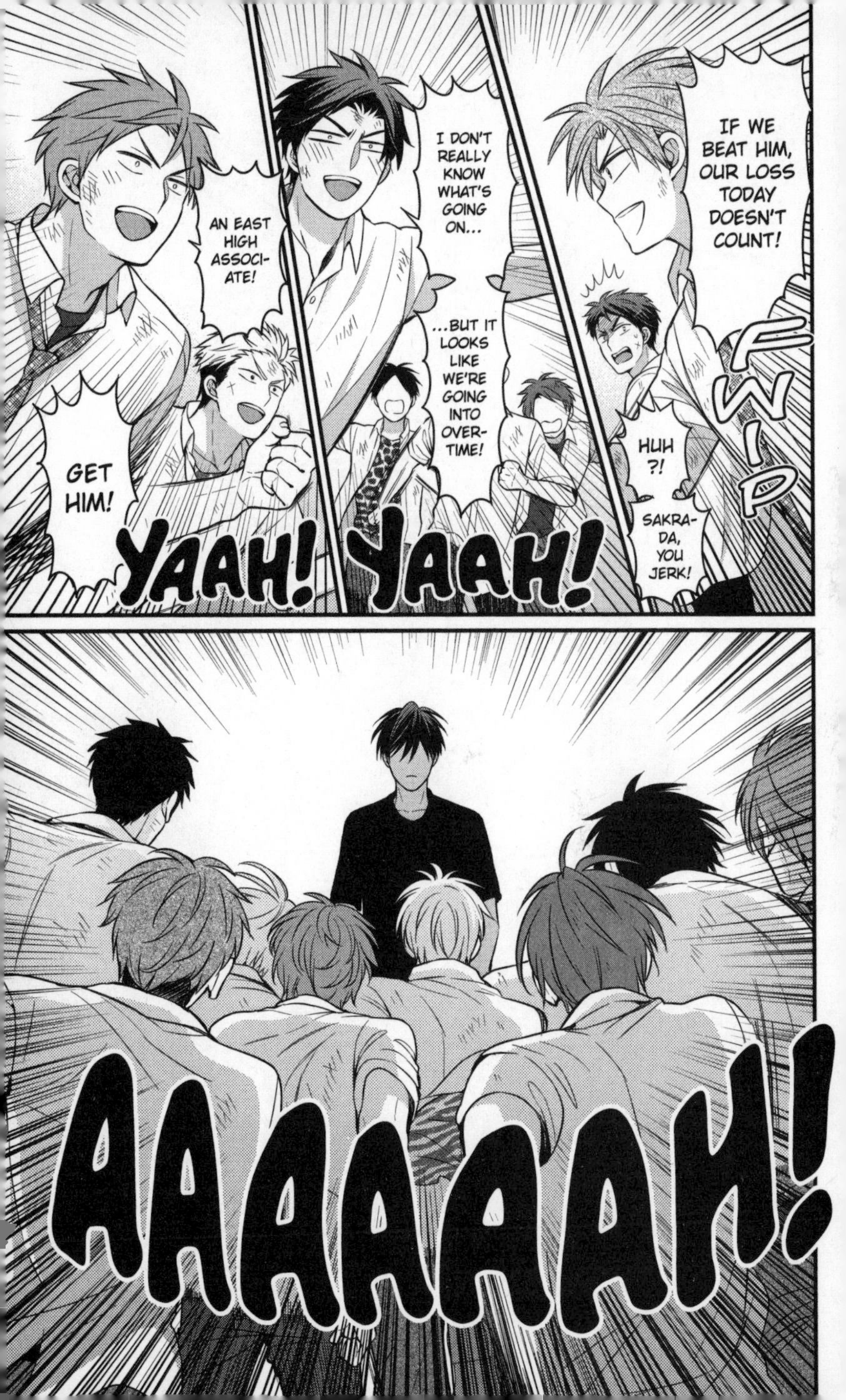
IF WE BEAT HIM, OUR LOSS TODAY DOESN'T COUNT!
FWIP
HUH ?!
SAKRA-DA, YOU JERK!
I DON'T REALLY KNOW WHAT'S GOING ON...
...BUT IT LOOKS LIKE WE'RE GOING INTO OVER-TIME!
YAAAH!
AN EAST HIGH ASSOCI-ATE!
GET HIM!
YAAH!
AAAAAAH!

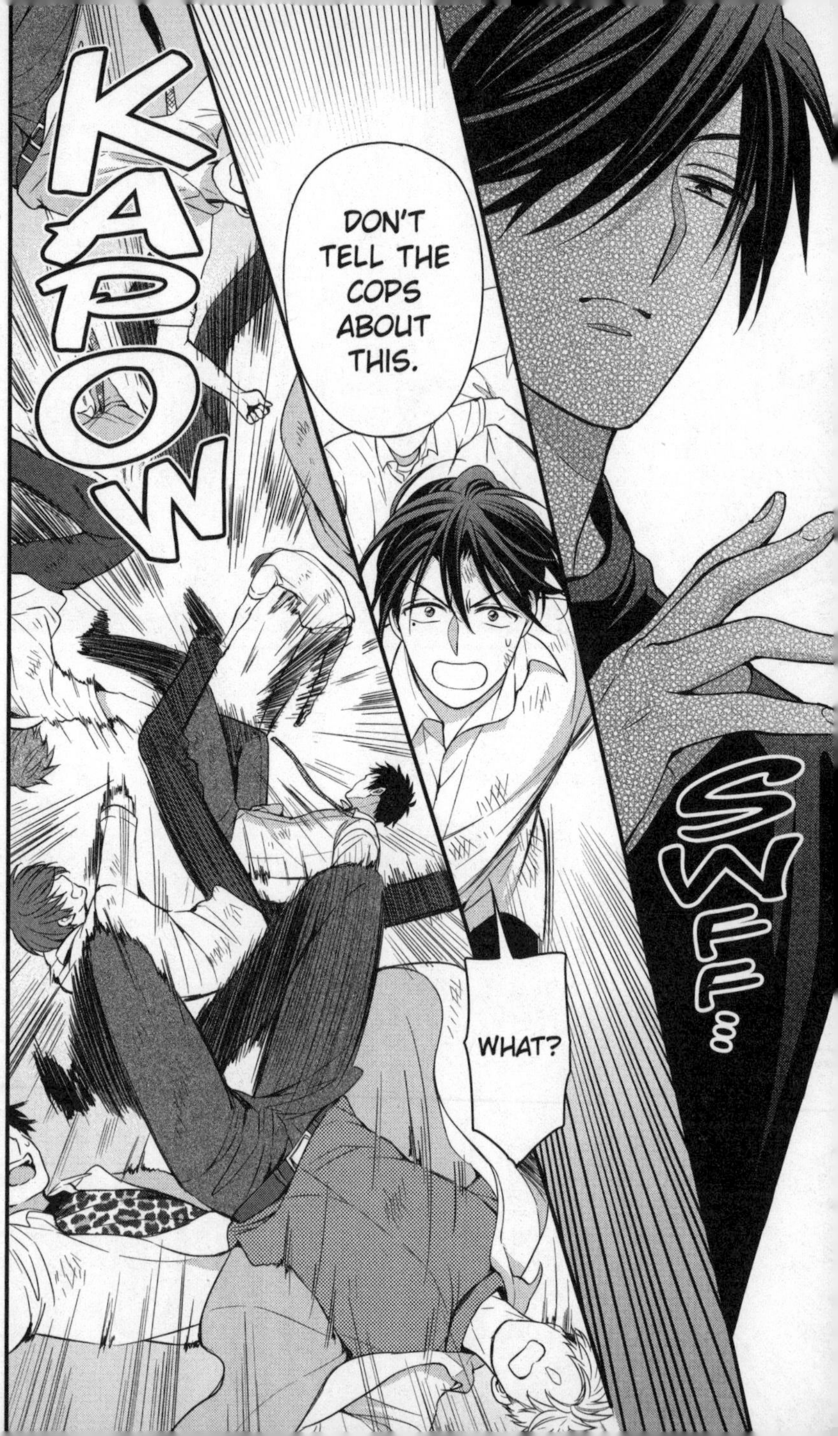
SWFF...
DON'T TELL THE COPS ABOUT THIS.
WHAT?
KAPOW

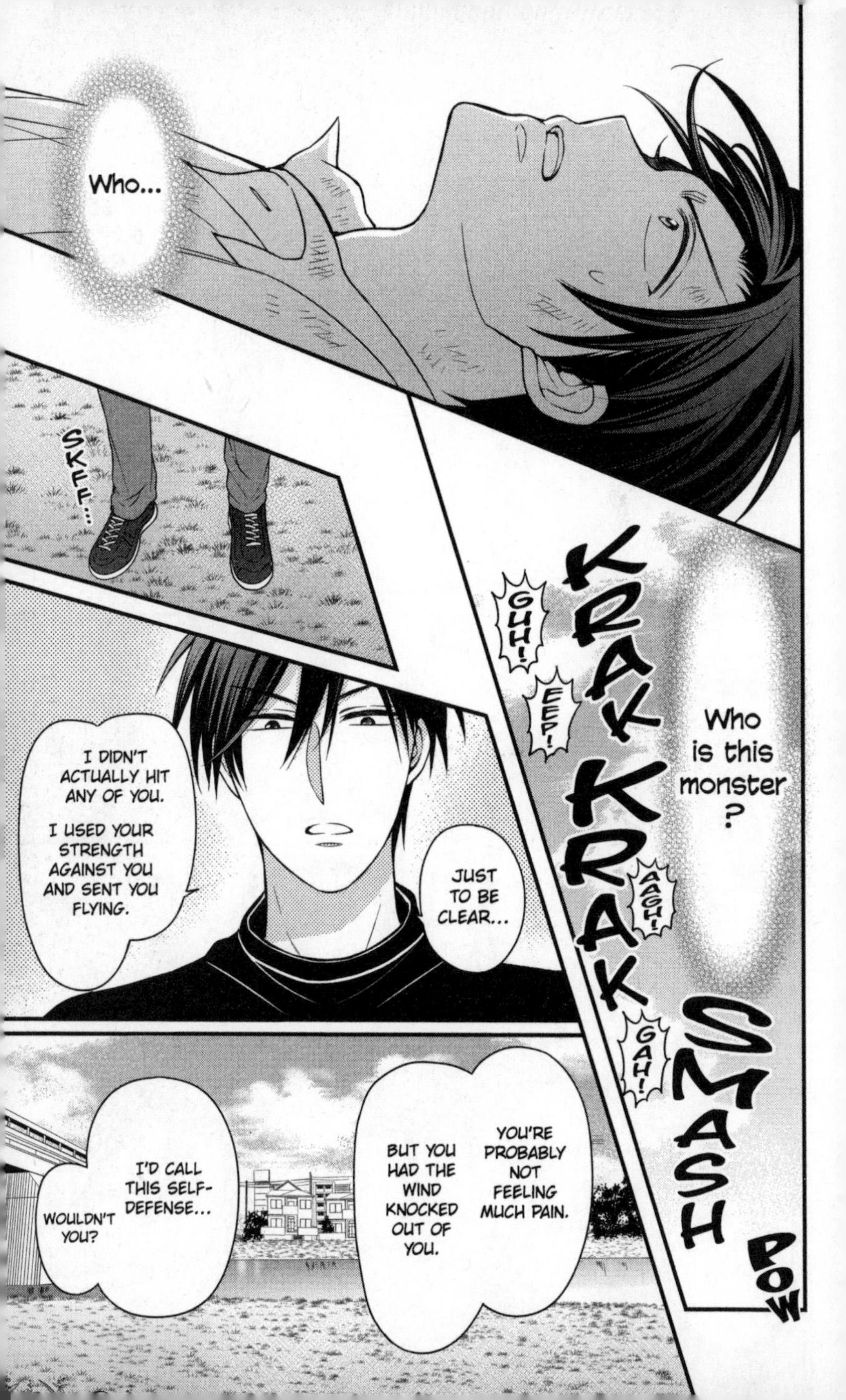
Who...
Who is this monster?
KRAK
GUH!
EEP!
KRAK
AAGH!
GAH!
SMASH
POW
SKFF...
JUST TO BE CLEAR...
I DIDN'T ACTUALLY HIT ANY OF YOU.
I USED YOUR STRENGTH AGAINST YOU AND SENT YOU FLYING.
YOU'RE PROBABLY NOT FEELING MUCH PAIN.
BUT YOU HAD THE WIND KNOCKED OUT OF YOU.
I'D CALL THIS SELF-DEFENSE...
WOULDN'T YOU?

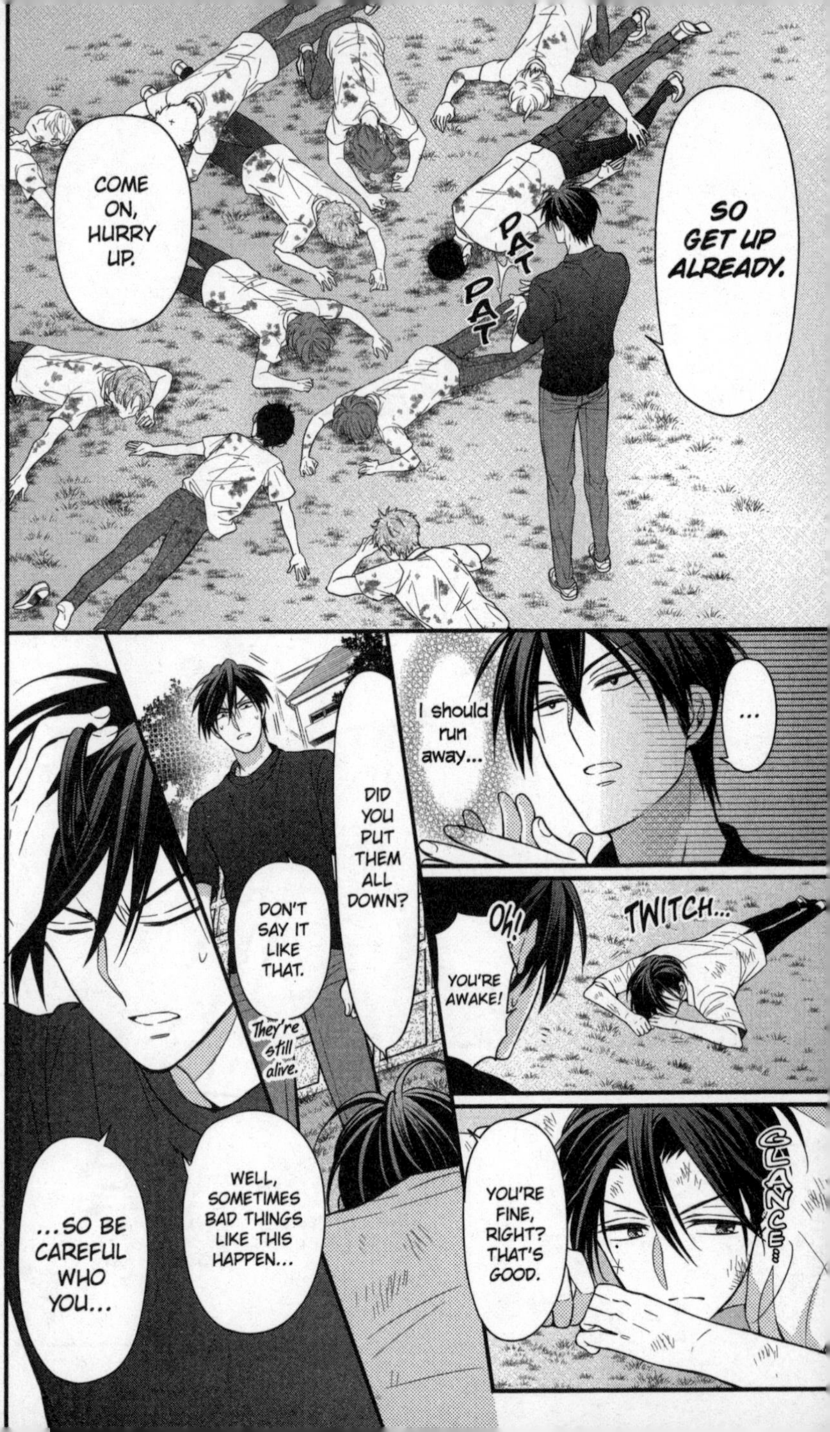
SO GET UP ALREADY.
PAT PAT
COME ON, HURRY UP.
...
I should run away...
TWITCH...
OH!
YOU'RE AWAKE!
GLANCE...
YOU'RE FINE, RIGHT? THAT'S GOOD.
DID YOU PUT THEM ALL DOWN?
DON'T SAY IT LIKE THAT.
They're still alive.
WELL, SOMETIMES BAD THINGS LIKE THIS HAPPEN...
...SO BE CAREFUL WHO YOU...

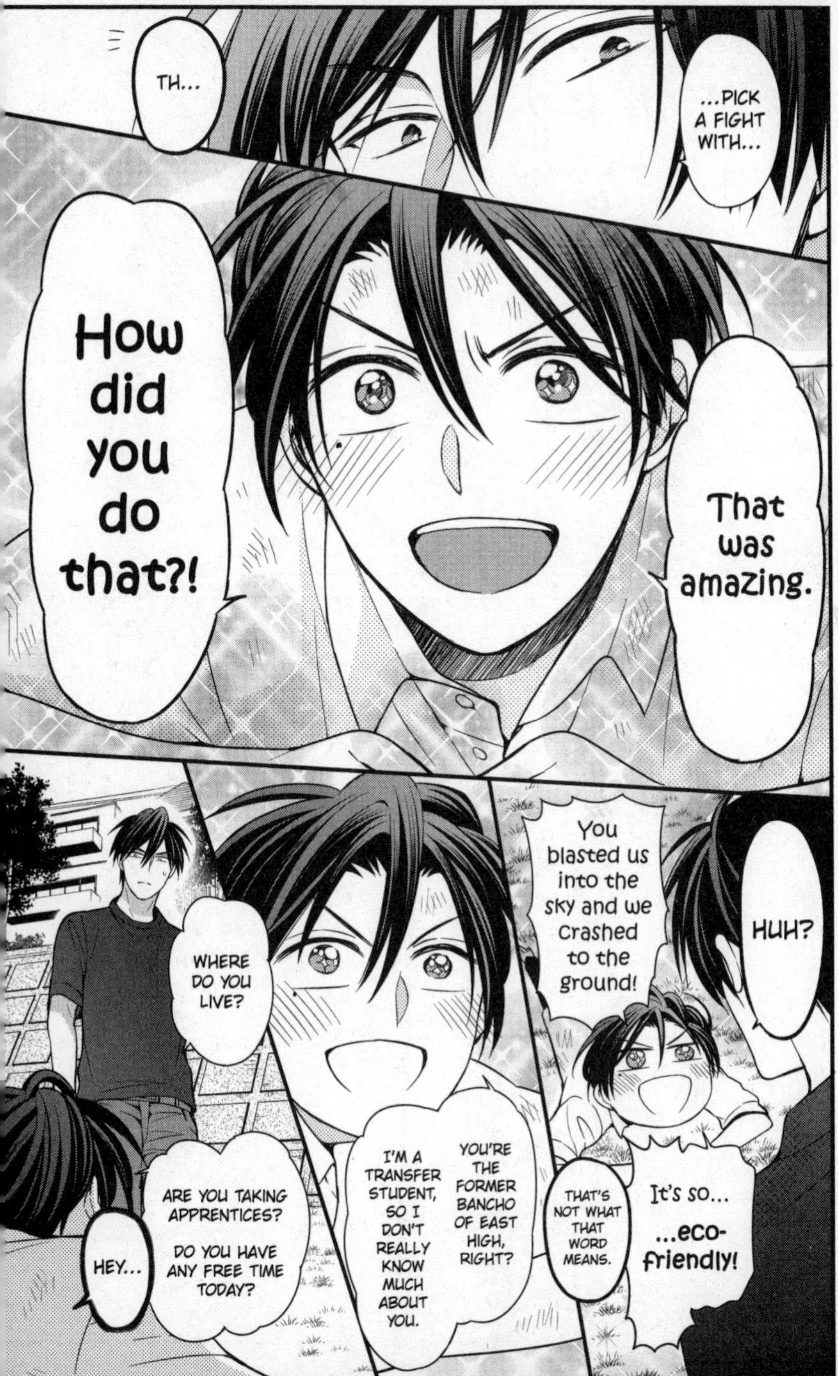
...PICK A FIGHT WITH...
TH...
That was amazing.
How did you do that?!
HUH?
You blasted us into the sky and we crashed to the ground!
It's so... ...eco-friendly!
THAT'S NOT WHAT THAT WORD MEANS.
YOU'RE THE FORMER BANCHO OF EAST HIGH, RIGHT?
I'M A TRANSFER STUDENT, SO I DON'T REALLY KNOW MUCH ABOUT YOU.
WHERE DO YOU LIVE?
ARE YOU TAKING APPRENTICES? DO YOU HAVE ANY FREE TIME TODAY?
HEY...

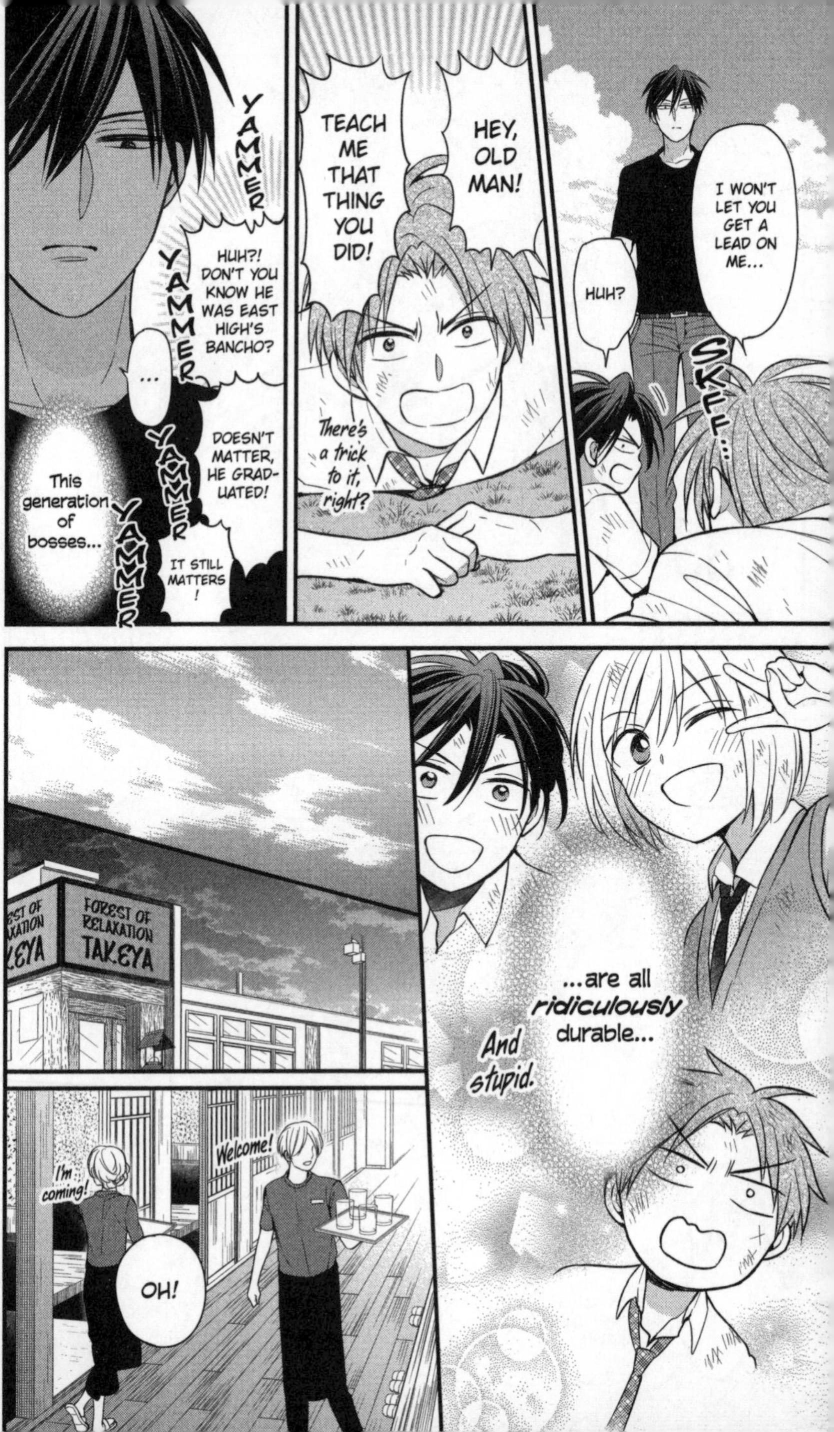
I WON'T LET YOU GET A LEAD ON ME...
HUH?
SKFF...
HEY, OLD MAN!
TEACH ME THAT THING YOU DID!
There's a trick to it, right?
YAMMER
HUH?! DON'T YOU KNOW HE WAS EAST HIGH'S BANCHO?
YAMMER
DOESN'T MATTER, HE GRADUATED!
YAMMER
IT STILL MATTERS!
YAMMER
...
This generation of bosses...
...are all ridiculously durable...
And stupid.
FOREST OF RELAXATION TAKEYA
FOREST OF RELAXATION TAKEYA
Welcome!
I'm coming!
OH!

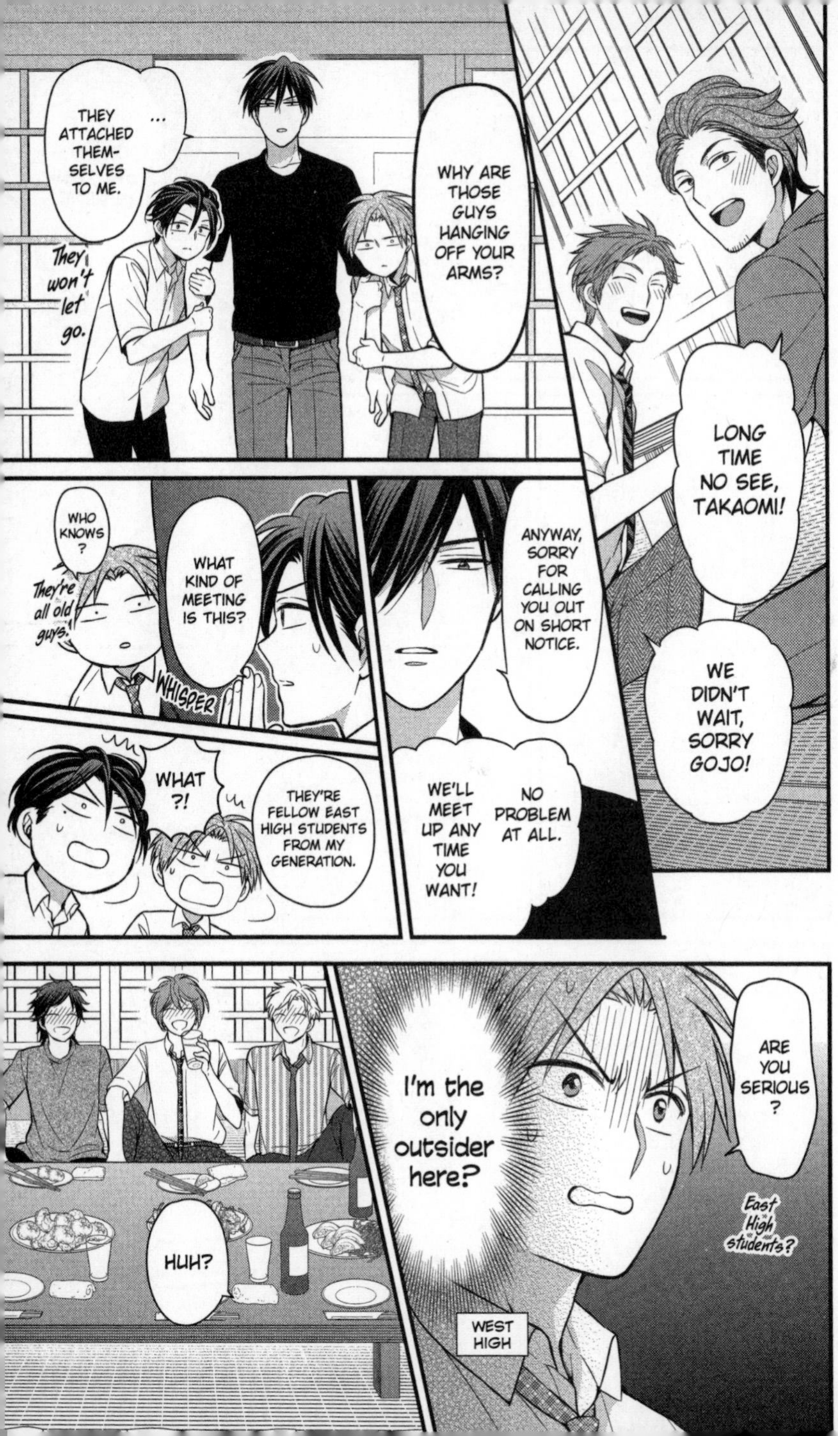

LONG TIME NO SEE, TAKAOMI!
WE DIDN'T WAIT, SORRY GOJO!
WHY ARE THOSE GUYS HANGING OFF YOUR ARMS?
THEY ATTACHED THEM-SELVES TO ME.
...
They won't let go.
ANYWAY, SORRY FOR CALLING YOU OUT ON SHORT NOTICE.
NO PROBLEM AT ALL.
WE'LL MEET UP ANY TIME YOU WANT!
WHAT KIND OF MEETING IS THIS?
WHO KNOWS?
They're all old guys!
WHISPER
THEY'RE FELLOW EAST HIGH STUDENTS FROM MY GENERATION.
WHAT ?!
ARE YOU SERIOUS?
East High students?
I'm the only outsider here?
WEST HIGH
HUH?

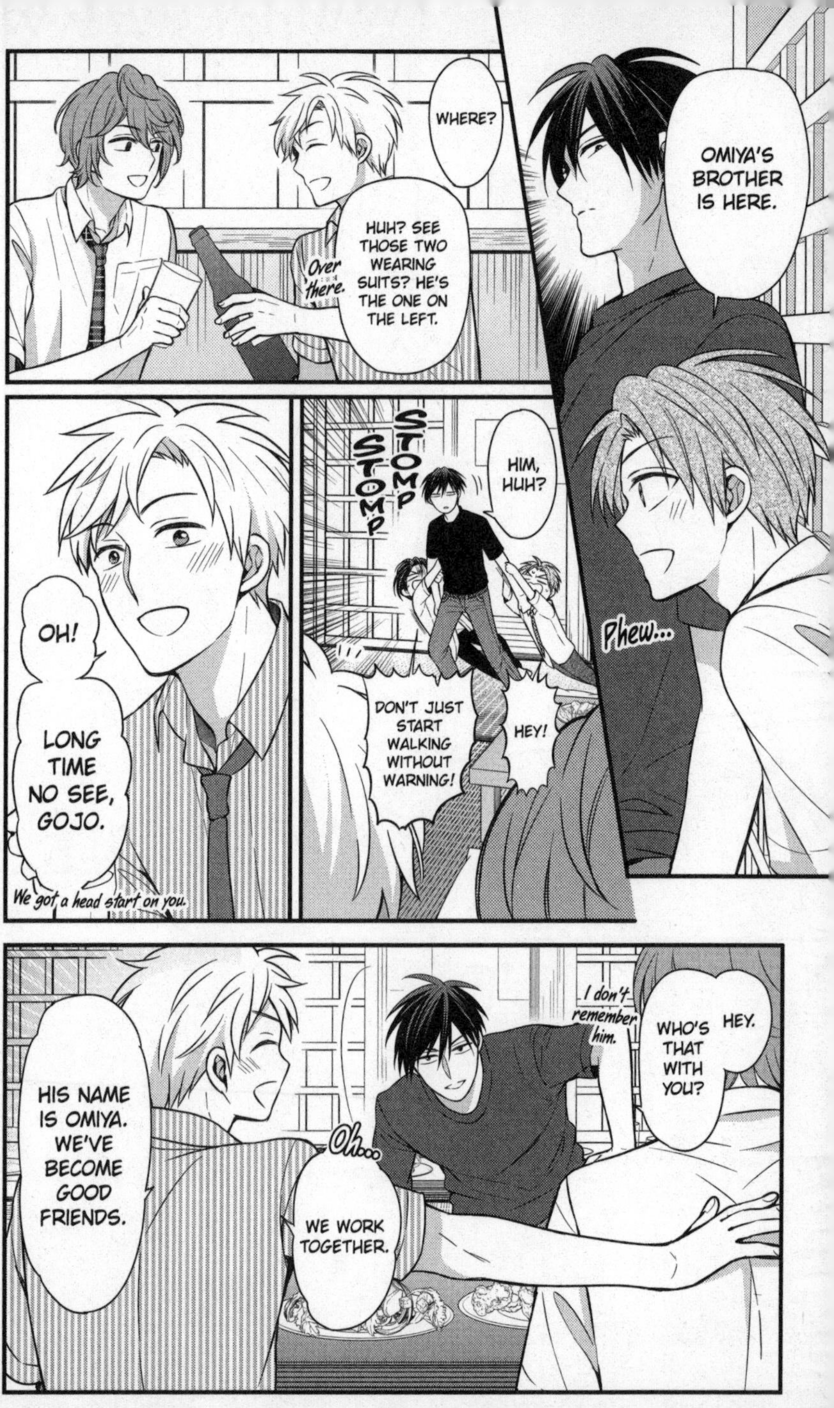
OMIYA'S BROTHER IS HERE.
Phew...
WHERE?
HUH? SEE THOSE TWO WEARING SUITS? HE'S THE ONE ON THE LEFT.
Over there.
STOMP
STOMP
HIM, HUH?
HEY!
DON'T JUST START WALKING WITHOUT WARNING!
OH!
LONG TIME NO SEE, GOJO.
We got a head start on you.
HEY.
WHO'S THAT WITH YOU?
I don't remember him.
Oh...
WE WORK TOGETHER.
HIS NAME IS OMIYA. WE'VE BECOME GOOD FRIENDS.

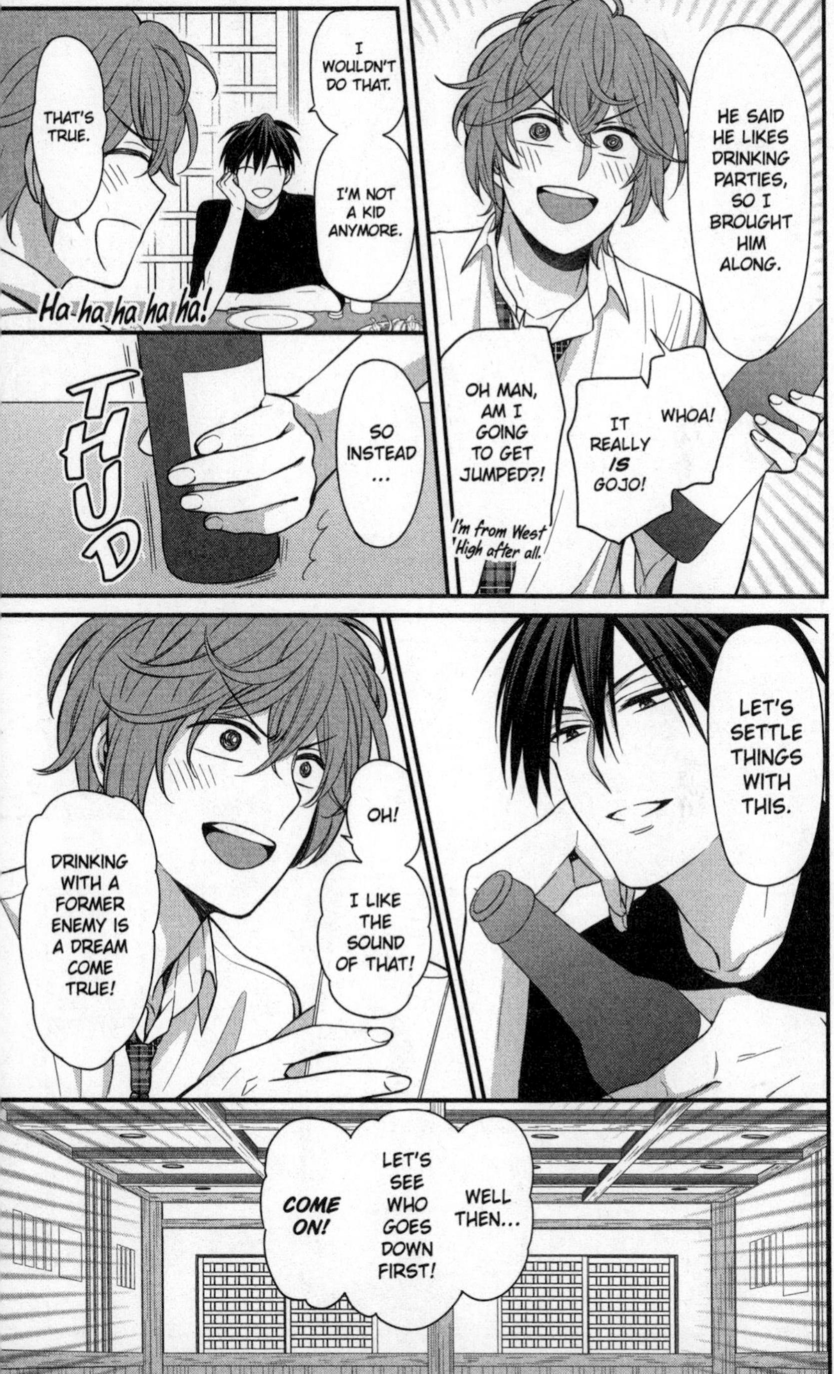
HE SAID HE LIKES DRINKING PARTIES, SO I BROUGHT HIM ALONG.
WHOA!
IT REALLY *IS* GOJO!
OH MAN, AM I GOING TO GET JUMPED?!
I'm from West High after all.
I WOULDN'T DO THAT.
I'M NOT A KID ANYMORE.
THAT'S TRUE.
Ha-ha ha ha ha!
SO INSTEAD...
THUD
LET'S SETTLE THINGS WITH THIS.
OH!
I LIKE THE SOUND OF THAT!
DRINKING WITH A FORMER ENEMY IS A DREAM COME TRUE!
WELL THEN...
LET'S SEE WHO GOES DOWN FIRST!
COME ON!

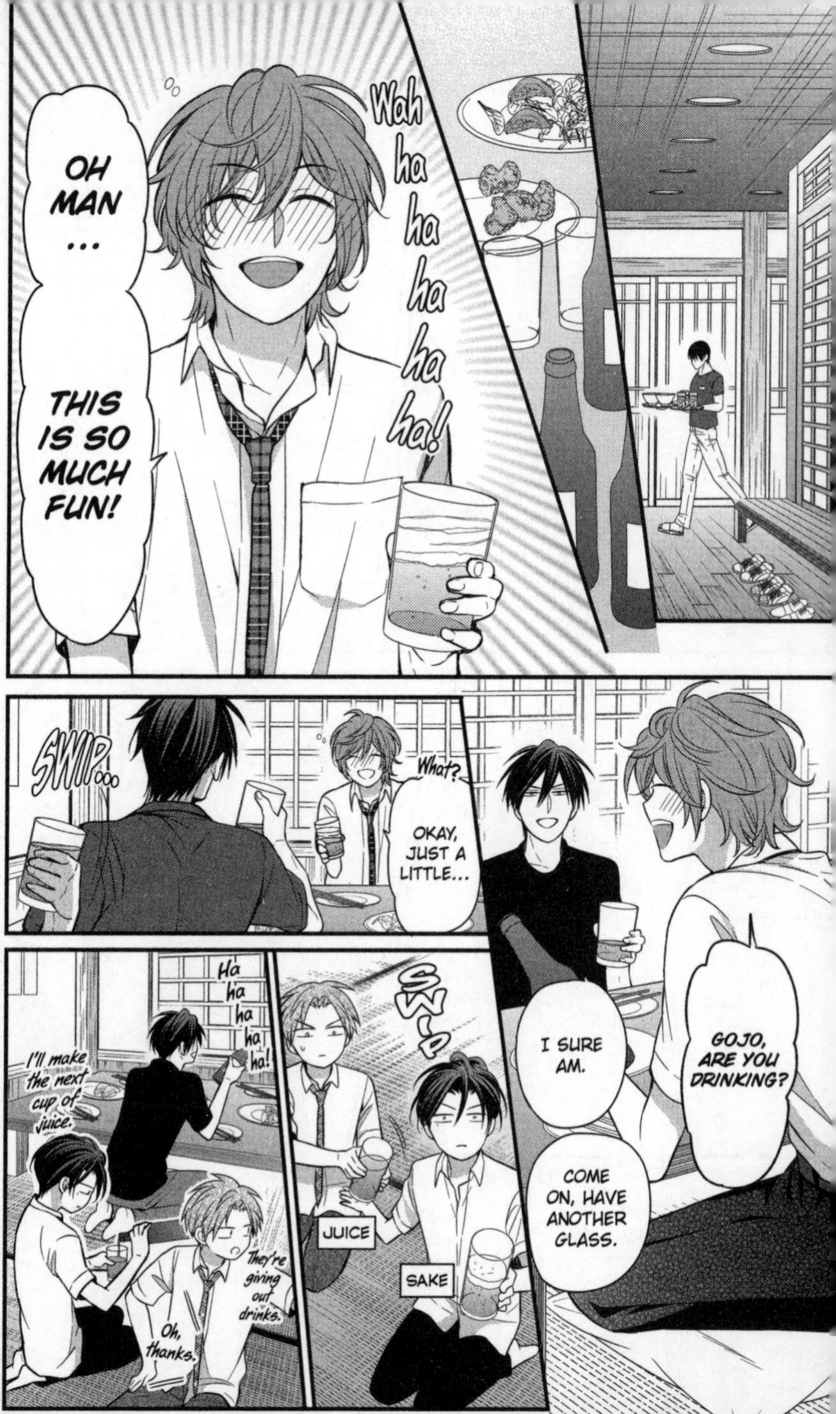
Wah ha ha ha ha ha!
OH MAN ...
THIS IS SO MUCH FUN!
GOJO, ARE YOU DRINKING?
I SURE AM.
COME ON, HAVE ANOTHER GLASS.
What?
OKAY, JUST A LITTLE...
SWIP...
SWIP
JUICE
SAKE
Ha ha ha ha ha!
I'll make the next cup of juice.
They're giving out drinks.
Oh, thanks.

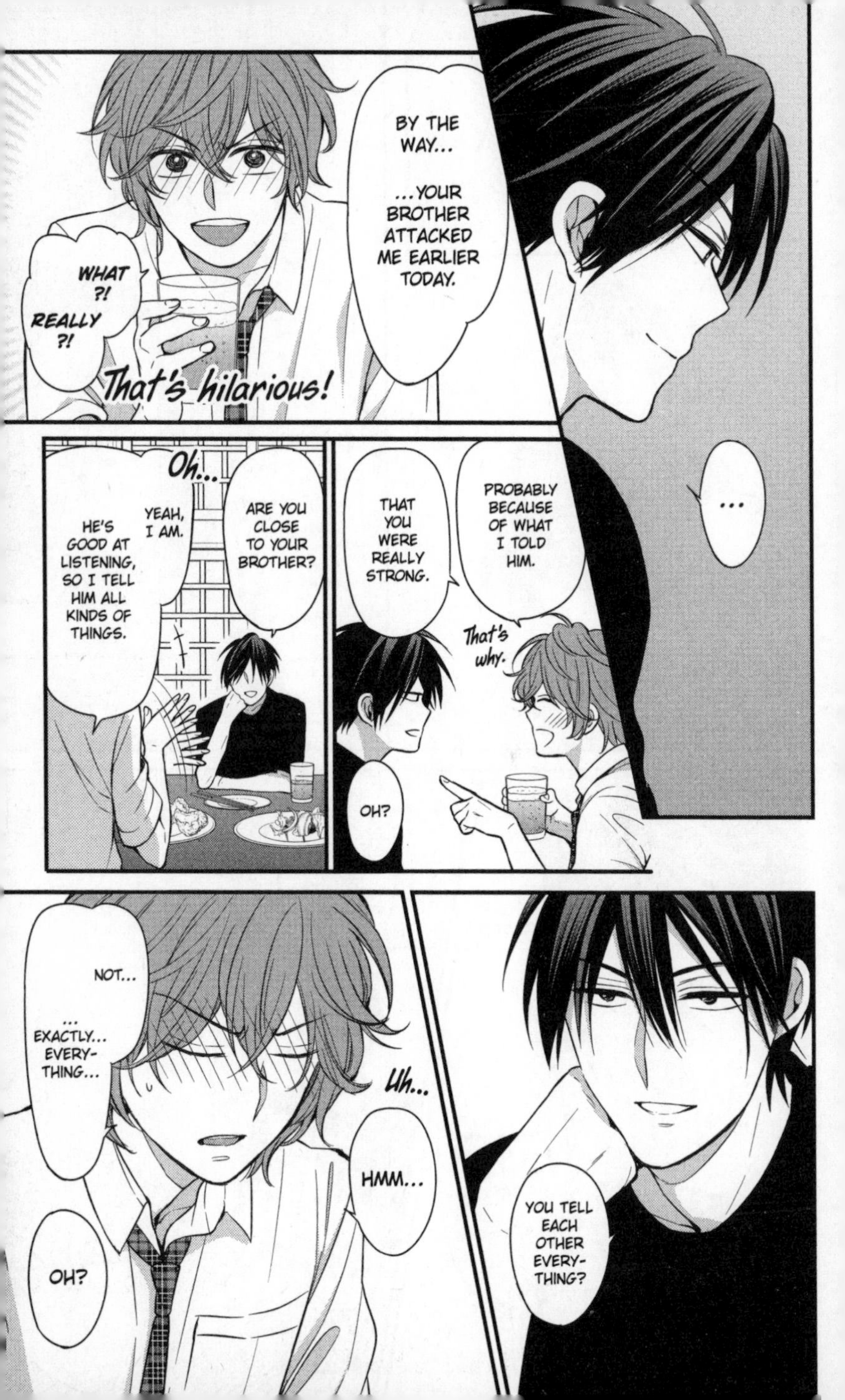
...
BY THE WAY...
...YOUR BROTHER ATTACKED ME EARLIER TODAY.
WHAT?! REALLY?!
That's hilarious!
PROBABLY BECAUSE OF WHAT I TOLD HIM.
THAT YOU WERE REALLY STRONG.
That's why.
OH?
ARE YOU CLOSE TO YOUR BROTHER?
Oh...
YEAH, I AM.
HE'S GOOD AT LISTENING, SO I TELL HIM ALL KINDS OF THINGS.
YOU TELL EACH OTHER EVERY-THING?
Uh...
HMM...
NOT...
...EXACTLY... EVERY-THING...
OH?

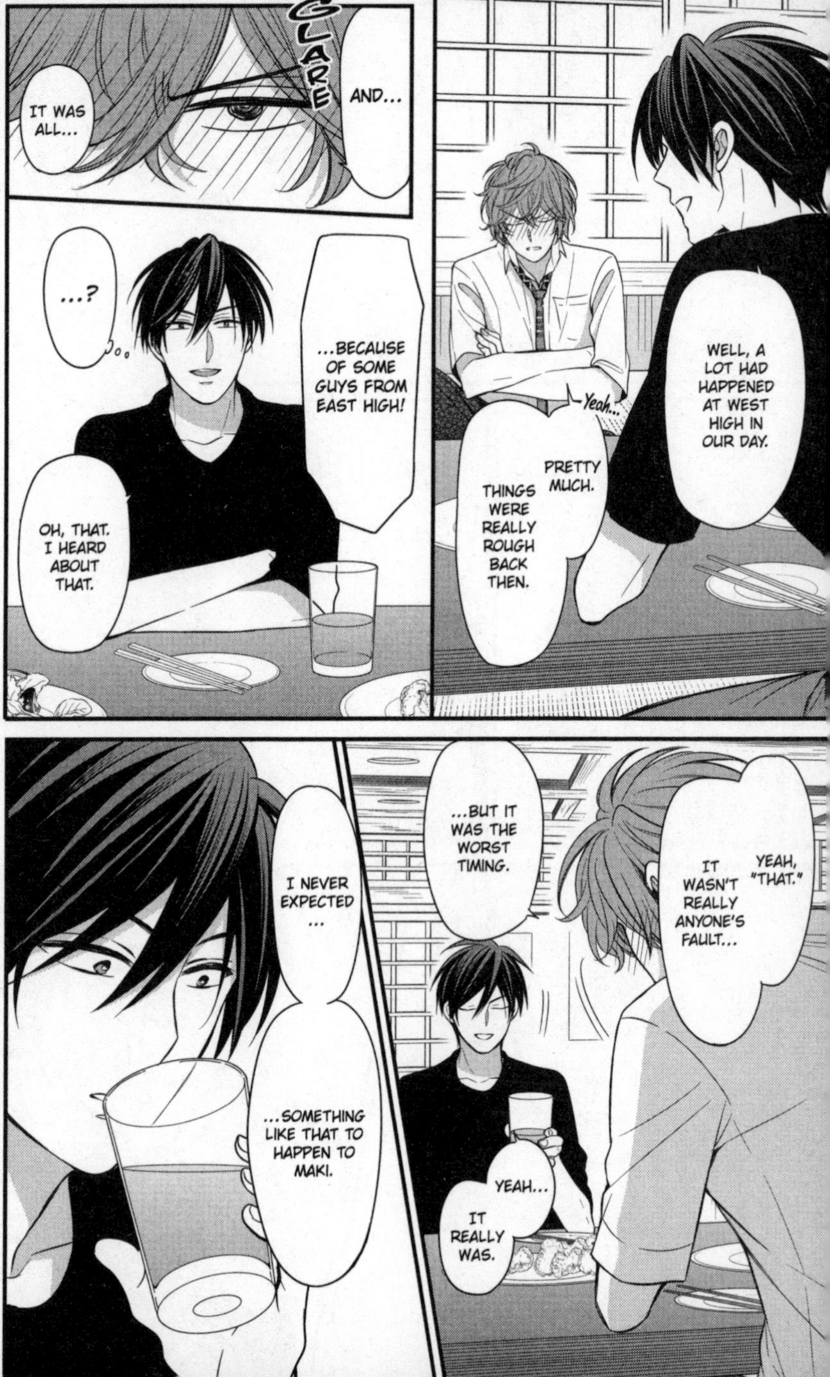
WELL, A LOT HAD HAPPENED AT WEST HIGH IN OUR DAY.
Yeah...
PRETTY MUCH.
THINGS WERE REALLY ROUGH BACK THEN.
AND...
GLARE
IT WAS ALL...
...BECAUSE OF SOME GUYS FROM EAST HIGH!
...?
OH, THAT. I HEARD ABOUT THAT.
YEAH, "THAT."
IT WASN'T REALLY ANYONE'S FAULT...
...BUT IT WAS THE WORST TIMING.
YEAH...
IT REALLY WAS.
I NEVER EXPECTED...
...SOMETHING LIKE THAT TO HAPPEN TO MAKI.

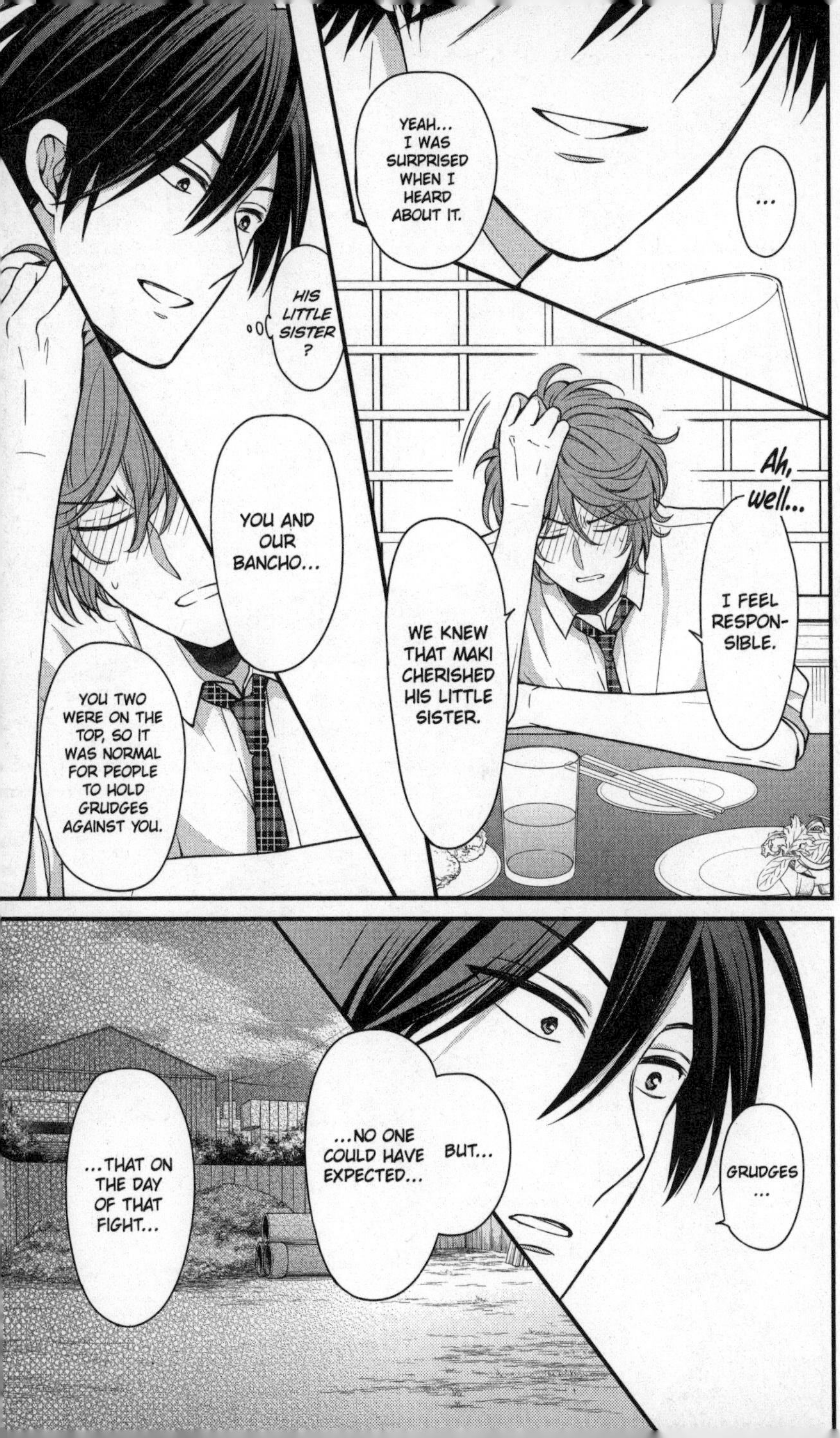
...
YEAH... I WAS SURPRISED WHEN I HEARD ABOUT IT.
HIS LITTLE SISTER?
Ah, well...
I FEEL RESPONSIBLE.
WE KNEW THAT MAKI CHERISHED HIS LITTLE SISTER.
YOU AND OUR BANCHO...
YOU TWO WERE ON THE TOP, SO IT WAS NORMAL FOR PEOPLE TO HOLD GRUDGES AGAINST YOU.
GRUDGES...
BUT...
...NO ONE COULD HAVE EXPECTED...
...THAT ON THE DAY OF THAT FIGHT...

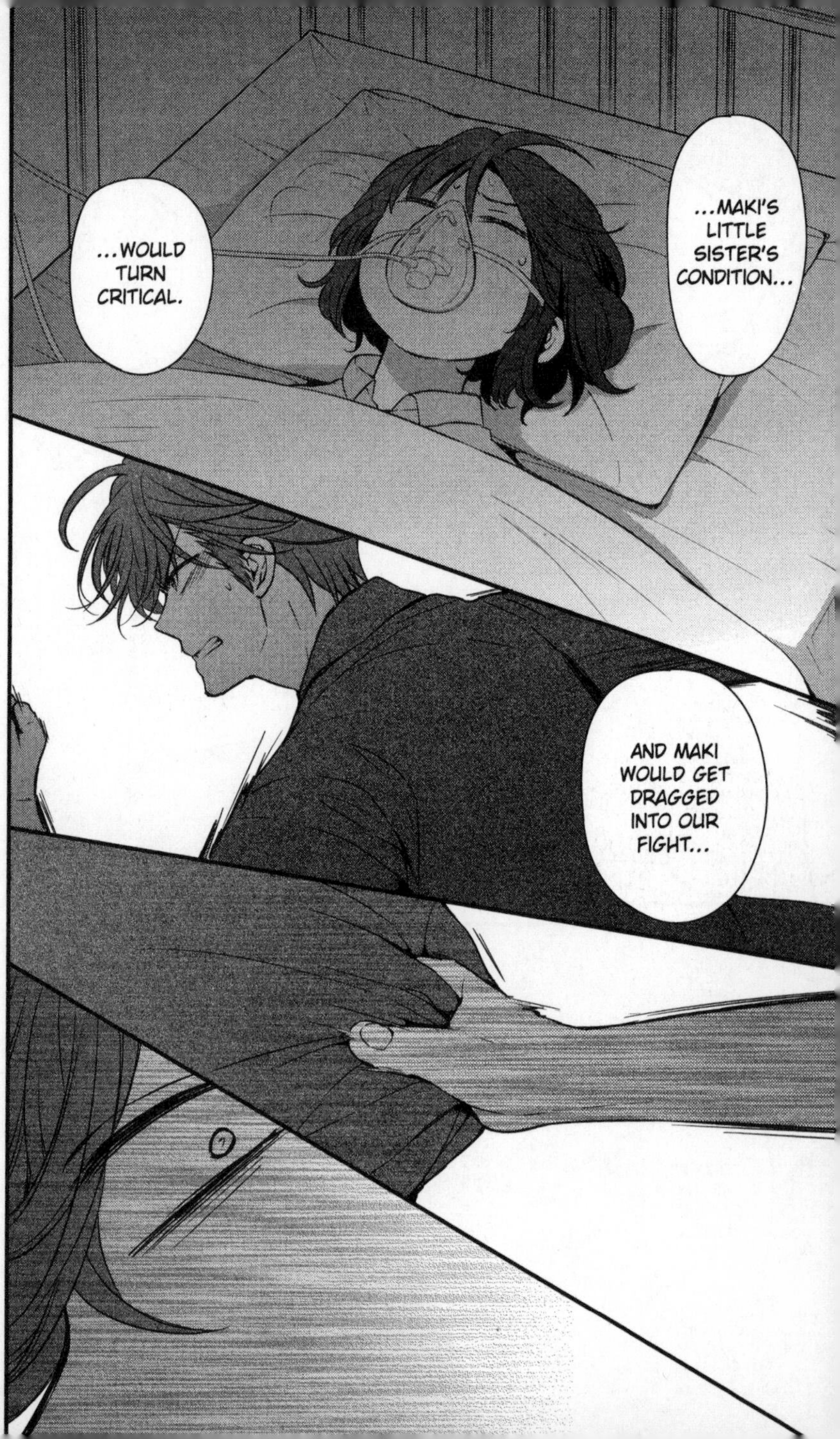
...MAKI'S LITTLE SISTER'S CONDITION...
...WOULD TURN CRITICAL.
AND MAKI WOULD GET DRAGGED INTO OUR FIGHT...

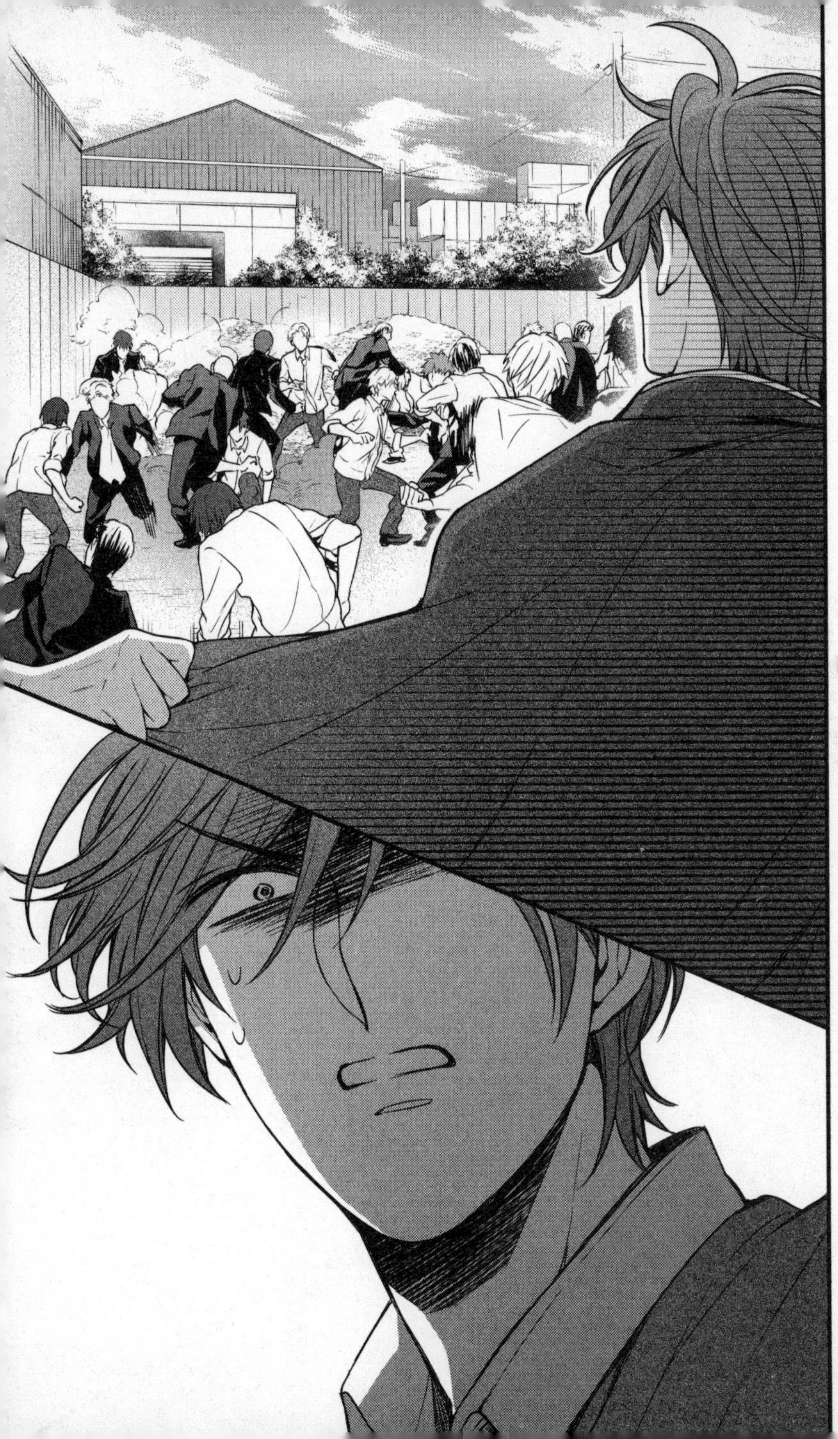

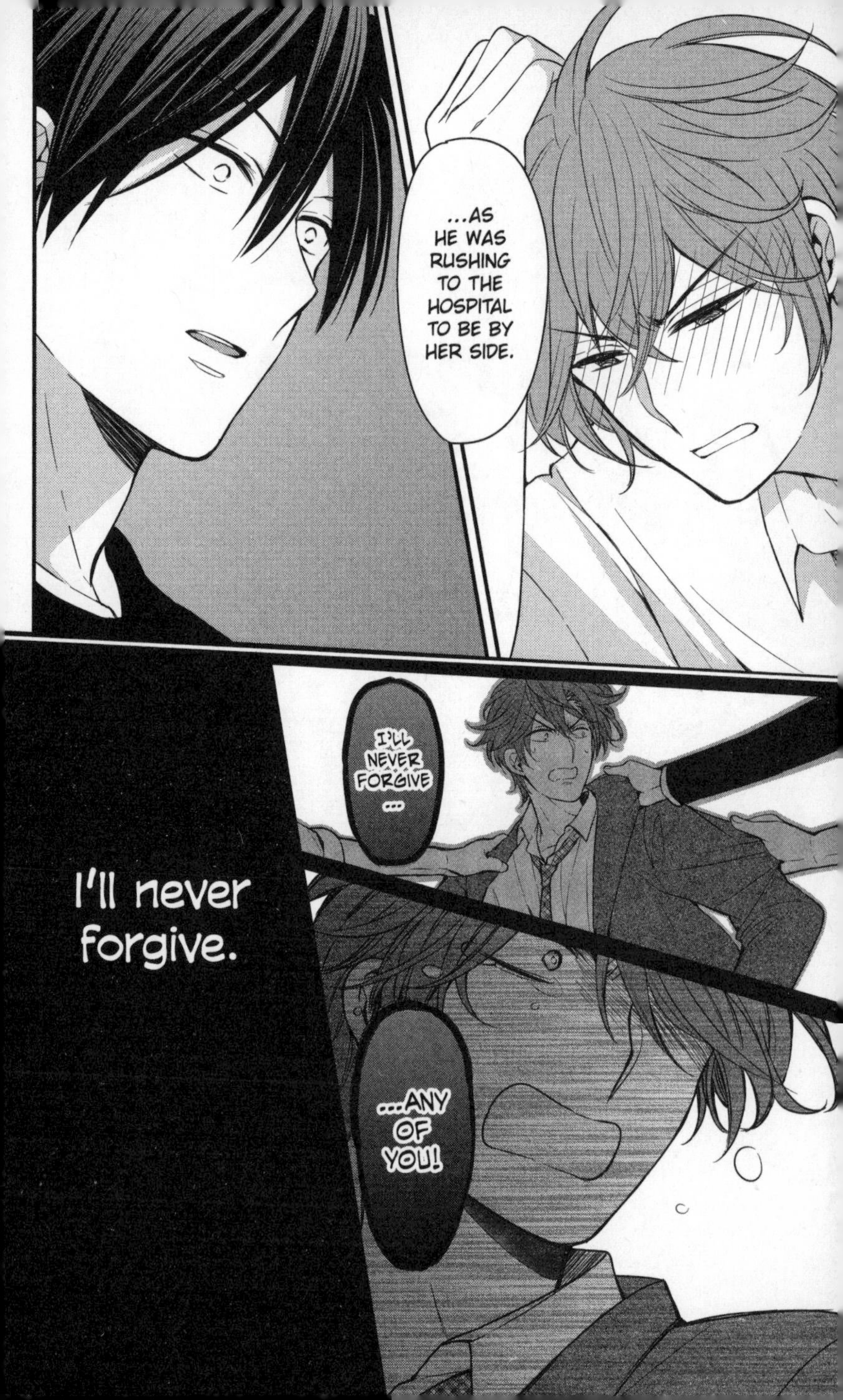
...AS HE WAS RUSHING TO THE HOSPITAL TO BE BY HER SIDE.
I'LL NEVER FORGIVE...
I'll never forgive.
...ANY OF YOU!

BONUS MANGA

Okegawa's College Debut

TO A NEW LIFE

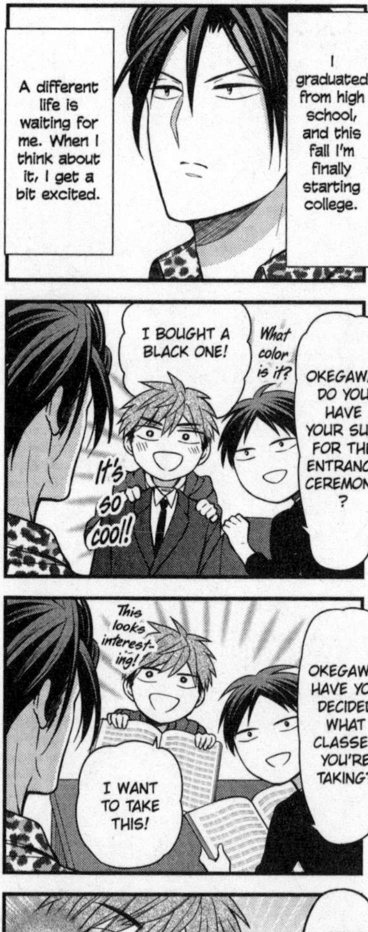
I graduated from high school, and this fall I'm finally starting college.
A different life is waiting for me. When I think about it, I get a bit excited.
OKEGAWA, DO YOU HAVE YOUR SUIT FOR THE ENTRANCE CEREMONY?
What color is it?
I BOUGHT A BLACK ONE!
It's so cool!
OKEGAWA, HAVE YOU DECIDED WHAT CLASSES YOU'RE TAKING?
This looks interesting!
I WANT TO TAKE THIS!
WE'RE IN THE SAME CLASS.
ISN'T THAT EXCITING?!
I'm not excited at all...

A CLEAR PURPOSE

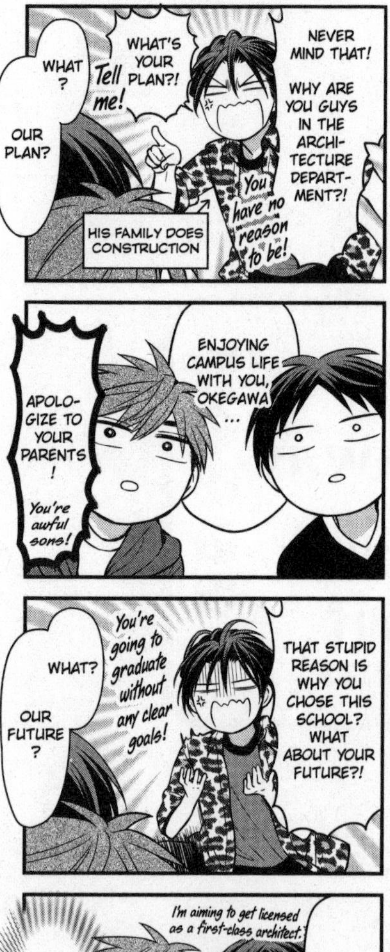
NEVER MIND THAT!
WHY ARE YOU GUYS IN THE ARCHITECTURE DEPARTMENT?!
You have no reason to be!
WHAT'S YOUR PLAN?!
Tell me!
HIS FAMILY DOES CONSTRUCTION
WHAT?
OUR PLAN?
ENJOYING CAMPUS LIFE WITH YOU, OKEGAWA...
APOLOGIZE TO YOUR PARENTS!
You're awful sons!
THAT STUPID REASON IS WHY YOU CHOSE THIS SCHOOL? WHAT ABOUT YOUR FUTURE?!
You're going to graduate without any clear goals!
WHAT?
OUR FUTURE?
I'm aiming to get licensed as a first-class architect.
I'M GOING TO WORK AT YOUR BROTHER'S COMPANY.
I'M GOING TO WORK AT ONE OF YOUR FATHER'S SUBSIDIARY COMPANIES.
Working on site looks like fun.
Why is that the only thing you're specific about?!
Stop it!

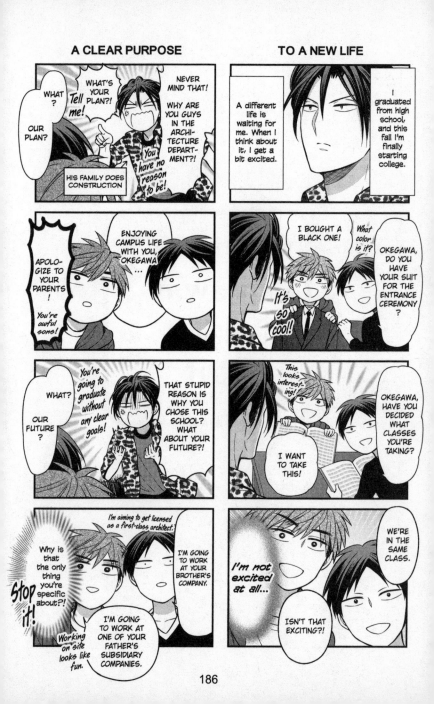

KAWAUCHI, THE BRAIN

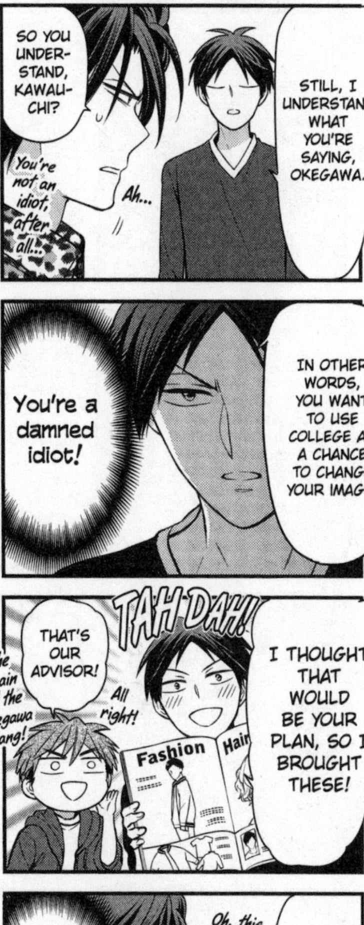
STILL, I UNDERSTAND WHAT YOU'RE SAYING, OKEGAWA.
SO YOU UNDERSTAND, KAWAUCHI?
Ah...
You're not an idiot, after all...
IN OTHER WORDS, YOU WANT TO USE COLLEGE AS A CHANCE TO CHANGE YOUR IMAGE!
You're a damned idiot!
I THOUGHT THAT WOULD BE YOUR PLAN, SO I BROUGHT THESE!
TAH DAH!
Hair
Fashion
All right!
THAT'S OUR ADVISOR!
The brain of the Okegawa Gang!
I'LL LEND IT TO YOU ONCE I'M DONE READING IT.
Oh, this might be good.
So it's for you!

KAWAUCHI, THE READERS ALLY

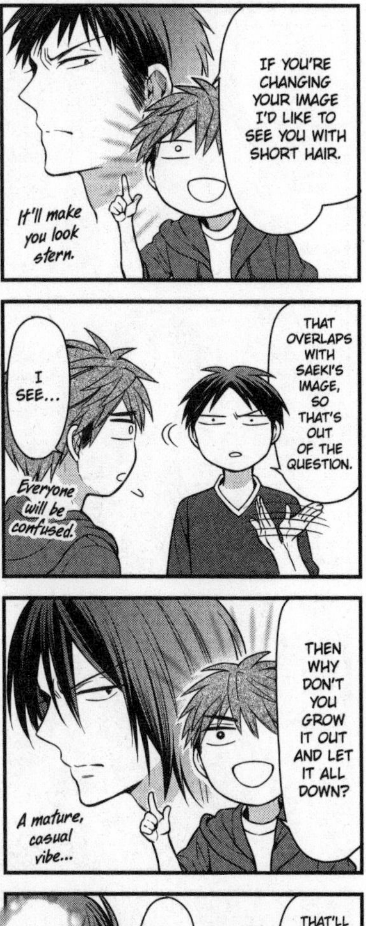
IF YOU'RE CHANGING YOUR IMAGE I'D LIKE TO SEE YOU WITH SHORT HAIR.
It'll make you look stern.
THAT OVERLAPS WITH SAEKI'S IMAGE, SO THAT'S OUT OF THE QUESTION.
I SEE...
Everyone will be confused.
THEN WHY DON'T YOU GROW IT OUT AND LET IT ALL DOWN?
A mature, casual vibe...
THAT'LL OVERLAP WITH NOGAMI AT KIYAMA HIGH, SO THAT'S OUT OF THE QUESTION TOO.
Everyone will be confused.
I SEE...
Who is "everyone"?

IF YOU LOOK CLOSELY

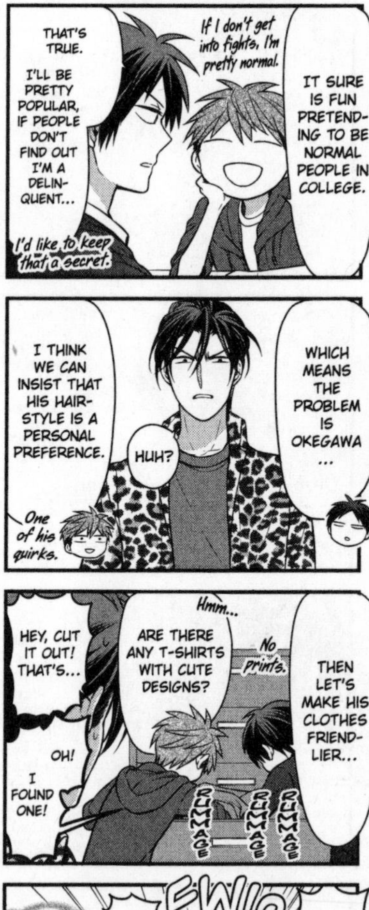
IT SURE IS FUN PRETENDING TO BE NORMAL PEOPLE IN COLLEGE.
If I don't get into fights, I'm pretty normal.
THAT'S TRUE. I'LL BE PRETTY POPULAR, IF PEOPLE DON'T FIND OUT I'M A DELINQUENT...
I'd like to keep that a secret.
WHICH MEANS THE PROBLEM IS OKEGAWA...
I THINK WE CAN INSIST THAT HIS HAIRSTYLE IS A PERSONAL PREFERENCE.
HUH?
One of his quirks.
Hmm...
No prints.
THEN LET'S MAKE HIS CLOTHES FRIENDLIER...
ARE THERE ANY T-SHIRTS WITH CUTE DESIGNS?
HEY, CUT IT OUT! THAT'S...
OH! I FOUND ONE!
RUMMAGE
RUMMAGE
RUMMAGE
FWIP
IT'S CUTE!
...
MANLY PATH
It's not cute at all...
...
What is this?

I RENTED SOME VIDEOS

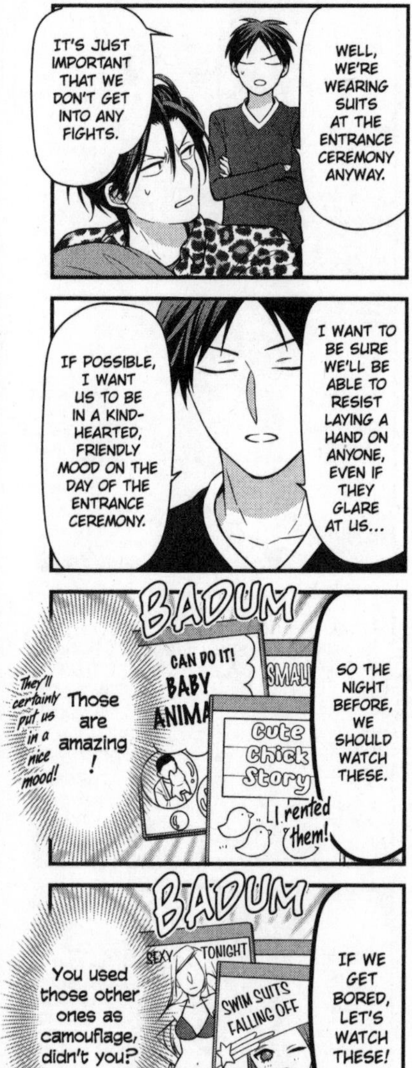
WELL, WE'RE WEARING SUITS AT THE ENTRANCE CEREMONY ANYWAY.
IT'S JUST IMPORTANT THAT WE DON'T GET INTO ANY FIGHTS.
I WANT TO BE SURE WE'LL BE ABLE TO RESIST LAYING A HAND ON ANYONE, EVEN IF THEY GLARE AT US...
IF POSSIBLE, I WANT US TO BE IN A KIND-HEARTED, FRIENDLY MOOD ON THE DAY OF THE ENTRANCE CEREMONY.
SO THE NIGHT BEFORE, WE SHOULD WATCH THESE.
BADUM
SMALL
CAN DO IT! BABY ANIMA
Cute Chick Story
I rented them!
Those are amazing!
They'll certainly put us in a nice mood!
IF WE GET BORED, LET'S WATCH THESE!
BADUM
TONIGHT
SEXY
SWIM SUITS FALLING OFF
You used those other ones as camouflage, didn't you?
HID THEM ON THE WAY TO THE REGISTER

GOOD AT SWITCHING GEARS

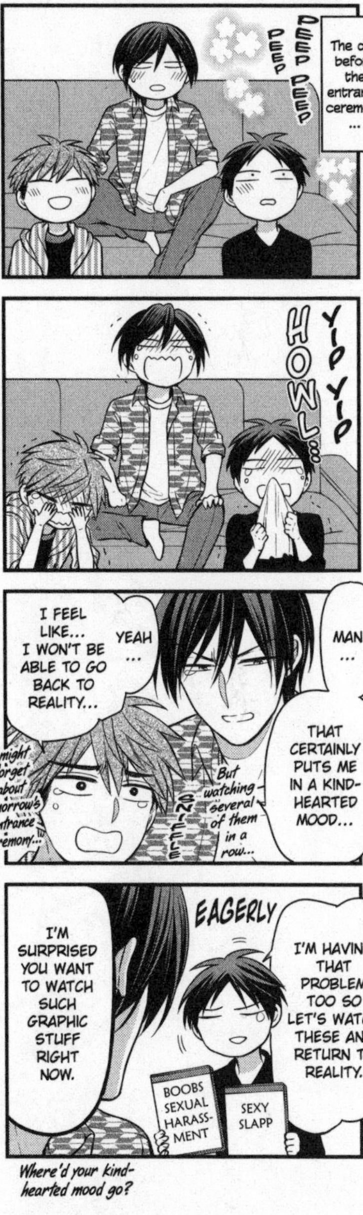
The day before the entrance ceremony...
PEEP PEEP
PEEP PEEP
HOWL...
YIP YIP YIP
MAN ...
YEAH ...
I FEEL LIKE... I WON'T BE ABLE TO GO BACK TO REALITY...
THAT CERTAINLY PUTS ME IN A KIND-HEARTED MOOD...
But watching several of them in a row...
SNIFFLE
I might forget about tomorrow's entrance ceremony...
EAGERLY
I'M HAVING THAT PROBLEM TOO SO LET'S WATCH THESE AND RETURN TO REALITY.
I'M SURPRISED YOU WANT TO WATCH SUCH GRAPHIC STUFF RIGHT NOW.
SEXY SLAPP
BOOBS SEXUAL HARASS-MENT

Where'd your kind-hearted mood go?

STARTING TOMORROW WE'RE NORMAL PEOPLE

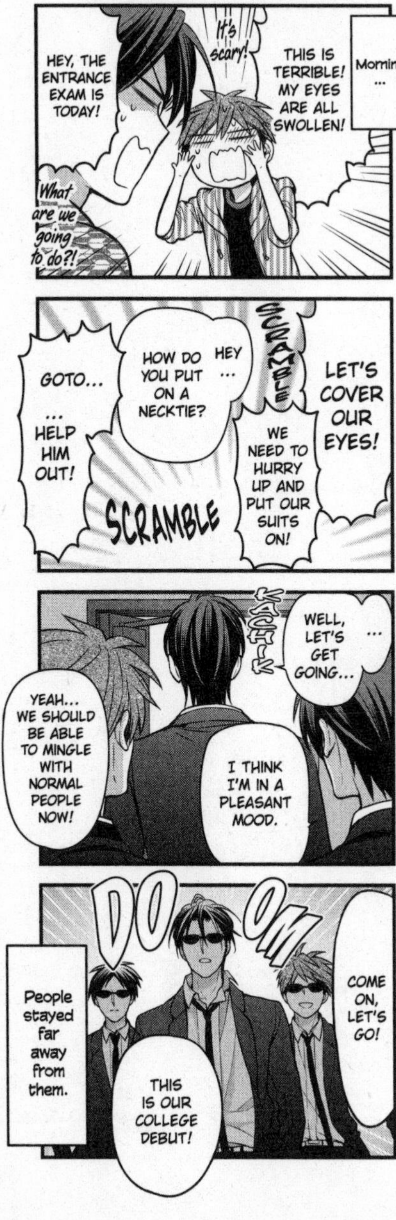
Morning ...
THIS IS TERRIBLE! MY EYES ARE ALL SWOLLEN!
It's scary!
HEY, THE ENTRANCE EXAM IS TODAY!
What are we going to do?!
LET'S COVER OUR EYES!
SCRAMBLE
HEY ...
HOW DO YOU PUT ON A NECKTIE?
WE NEED TO HURRY UP AND PUT OUR SUITS ON!
GOTO... ... HELP HIM OUT!
SCRAMBLE
...
WELL, LET'S GET GOING...
KACHIK
YEAH... WE SHOULD BE ABLE TO MINGLE WITH NORMAL PEOPLE NOW!
I THINK I'M IN A PLEASANT MOOD.
DOOM
COME ON, LET'S GO!
People stayed far away from them.
THIS IS OUR COLLEGE DEBUT!

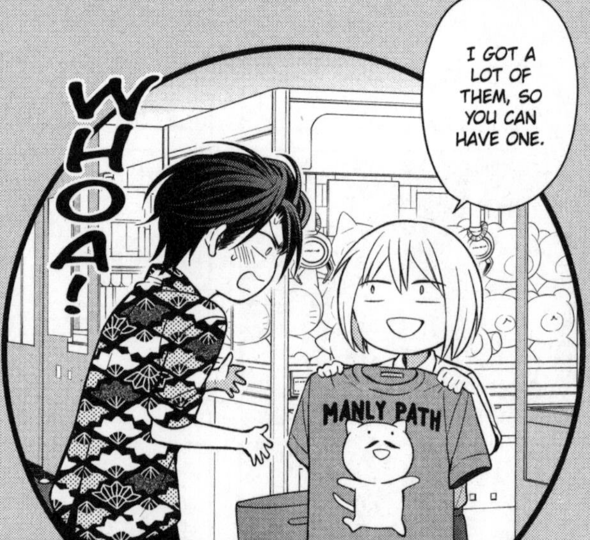
I GOT A LOT OF THEM, SO YOU CAN HAVE ONE.
WHOA!
MANLY PATH
ARC
MAFUYU WON THE T-SHIRT AT THE ARCADE

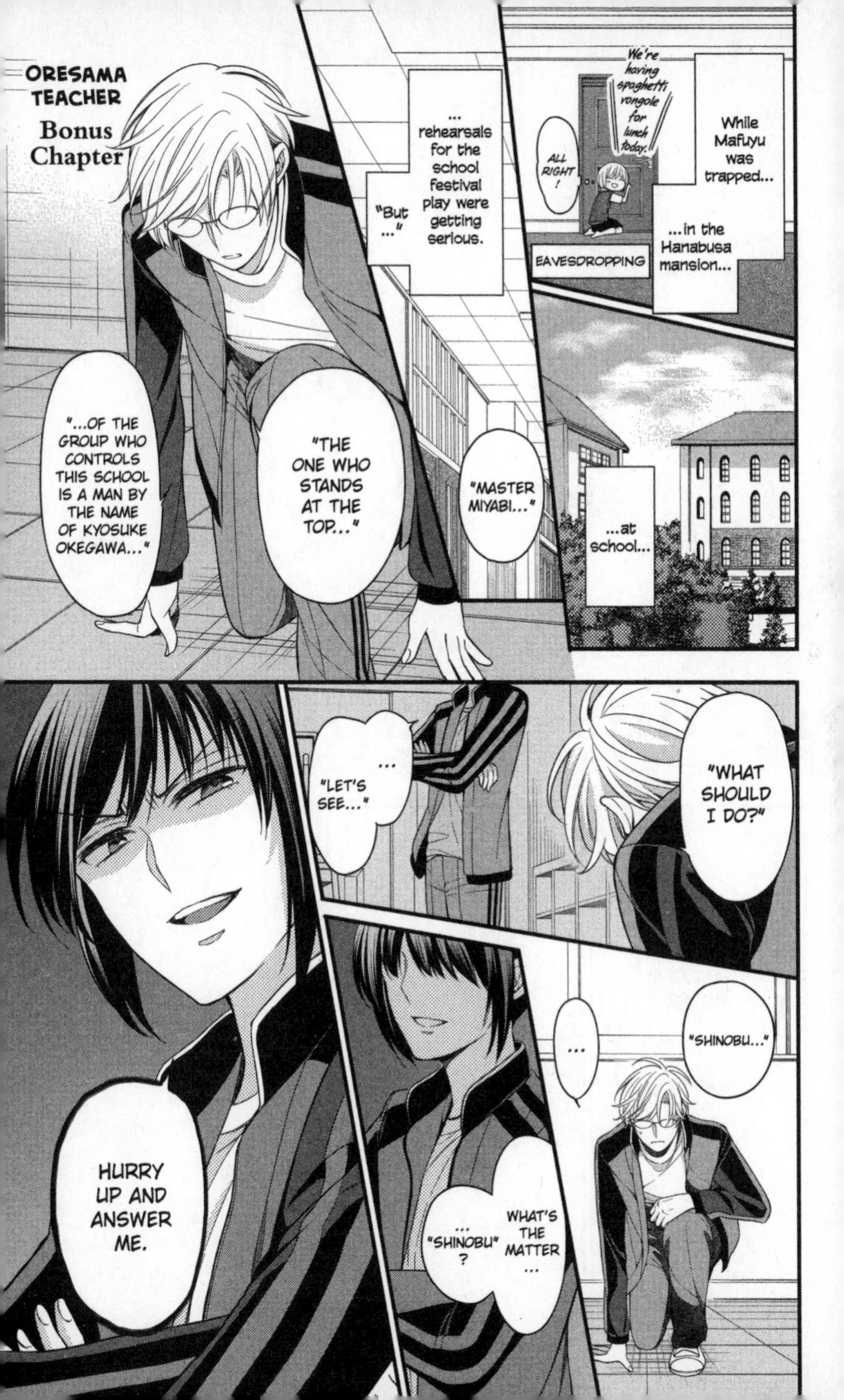
While Mafuyu was trapped...
...in the Hanabusa mansion...
We're having spaghetti vongole for lunch today.
ALL RIGHT!
EAVESDROPPING
...at school...
...rehearsals for the school festival play were getting serious.
"But..."
"MASTER MIYABI..."
"THE ONE WHO STANDS AT THE TOP..."
"...OF THE GROUP WHO CONTROLS THIS SCHOOL IS A MAN BY THE NAME OF KYOSUKE OKEGAWA..."
ORESAMA TEACHER
Bonus Chapter
"WHAT SHOULD I DO?"
...
"LET'S SEE..."
"SHINOBU..."
...
WHAT'S THE MATTER...
..."SHINOBU"?
HURRY UP AND ANSWER ME.

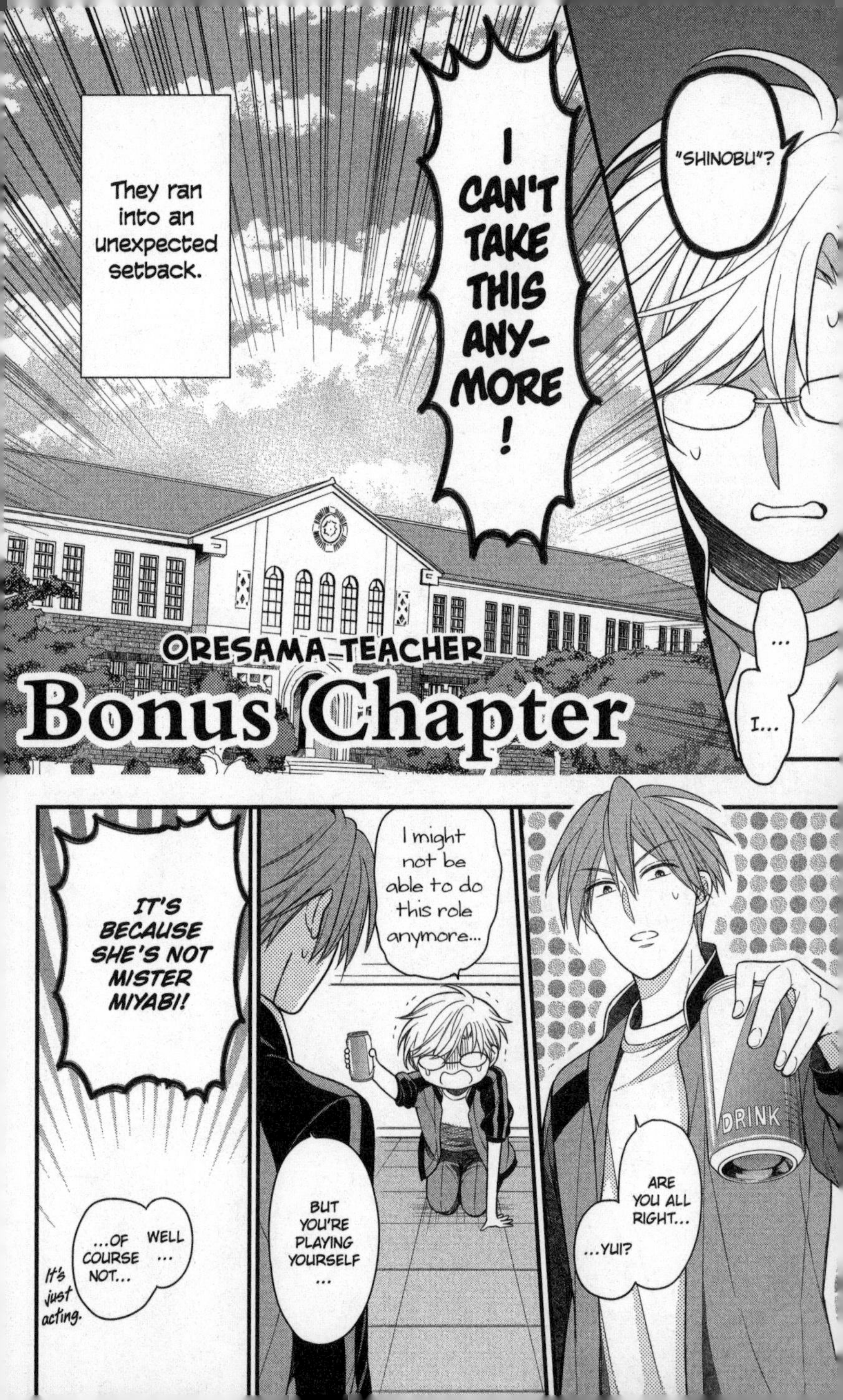

"SHINOBU"?
...
I...
I CAN'T TAKE THIS ANY-MORE!
They ran into an unexpected setback.
ORESAMA TEACHER
Bonus Chapter
ARE YOU ALL RIGHT...
...YUI?
DRINK
I might not be able to do this role anymore...
BUT YOU'RE PLAYING YOURSELF...
IT'S BECAUSE SHE'S NOT MISTER MIYABI!
WELL...
...OF COURSE NOT...
It's just acting.

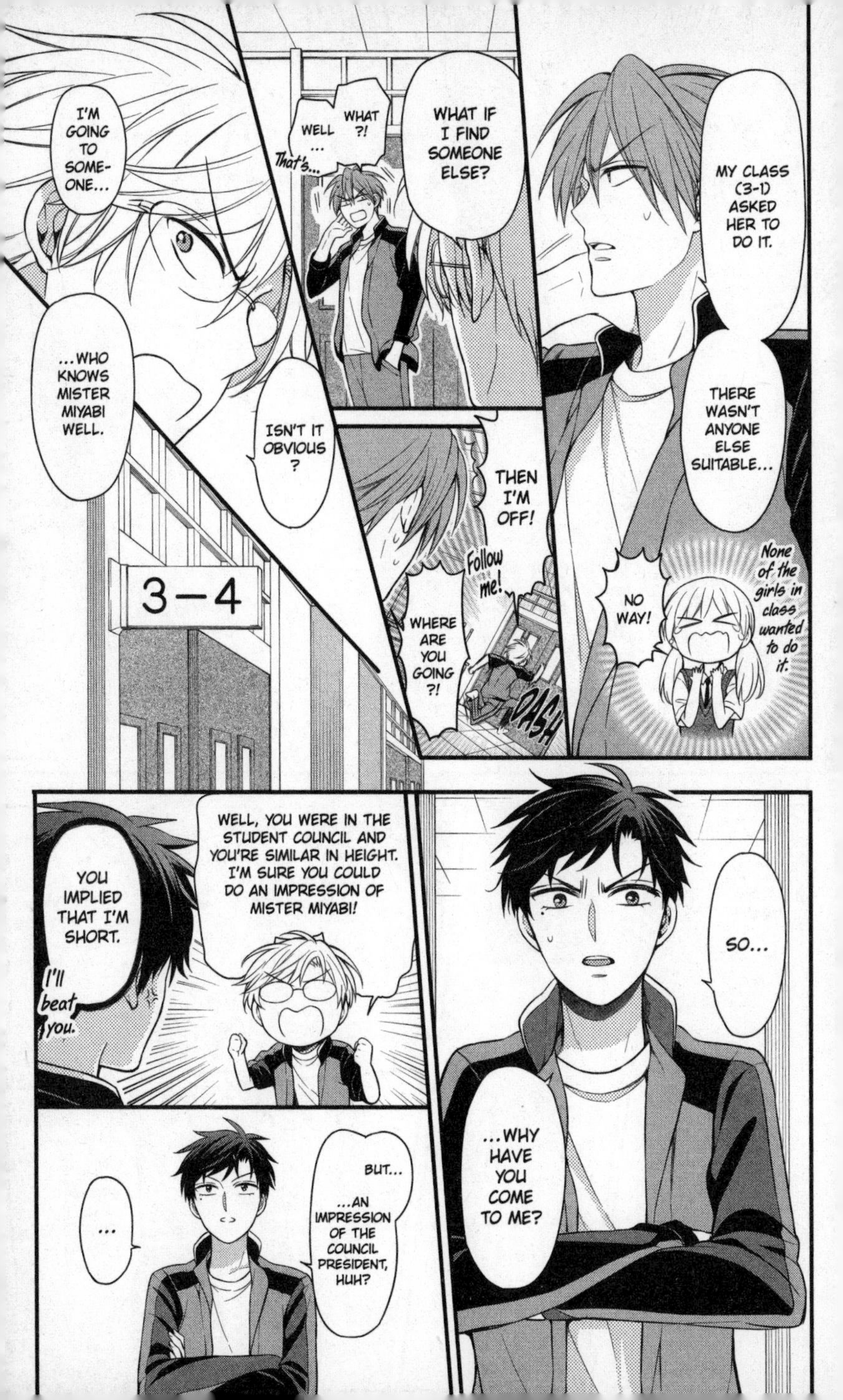
MY CLASS (3-1) ASKED HER TO DO IT.
THERE WASN'T ANYONE ELSE SUITABLE...
None of the girls in class wanted to do it.
NO WAY!
WHAT IF I FIND SOMEONE ELSE?
WHAT ?!
WELL ... That's...
THEN I'M OFF!
Follow me!
WHERE ARE YOU GOING ?!
DASH
ISN'T IT OBVIOUS ?
I'M GOING TO SOME-ONE...
...WHO KNOWS MISTER MIYABI WELL.
3-4
SO...
...WHY HAVE YOU COME TO ME?
WELL, YOU WERE IN THE STUDENT COUNCIL AND YOU'RE SIMILAR IN HEIGHT. I'M SURE YOU COULD DO AN IMPRESSION OF MISTER MIYABI!
YOU IMPLIED THAT I'M SHORT.
I'll beat you.
BUT... ...AN IMPRESSION OF THE COUNCIL PRESIDENT, HUH?
...

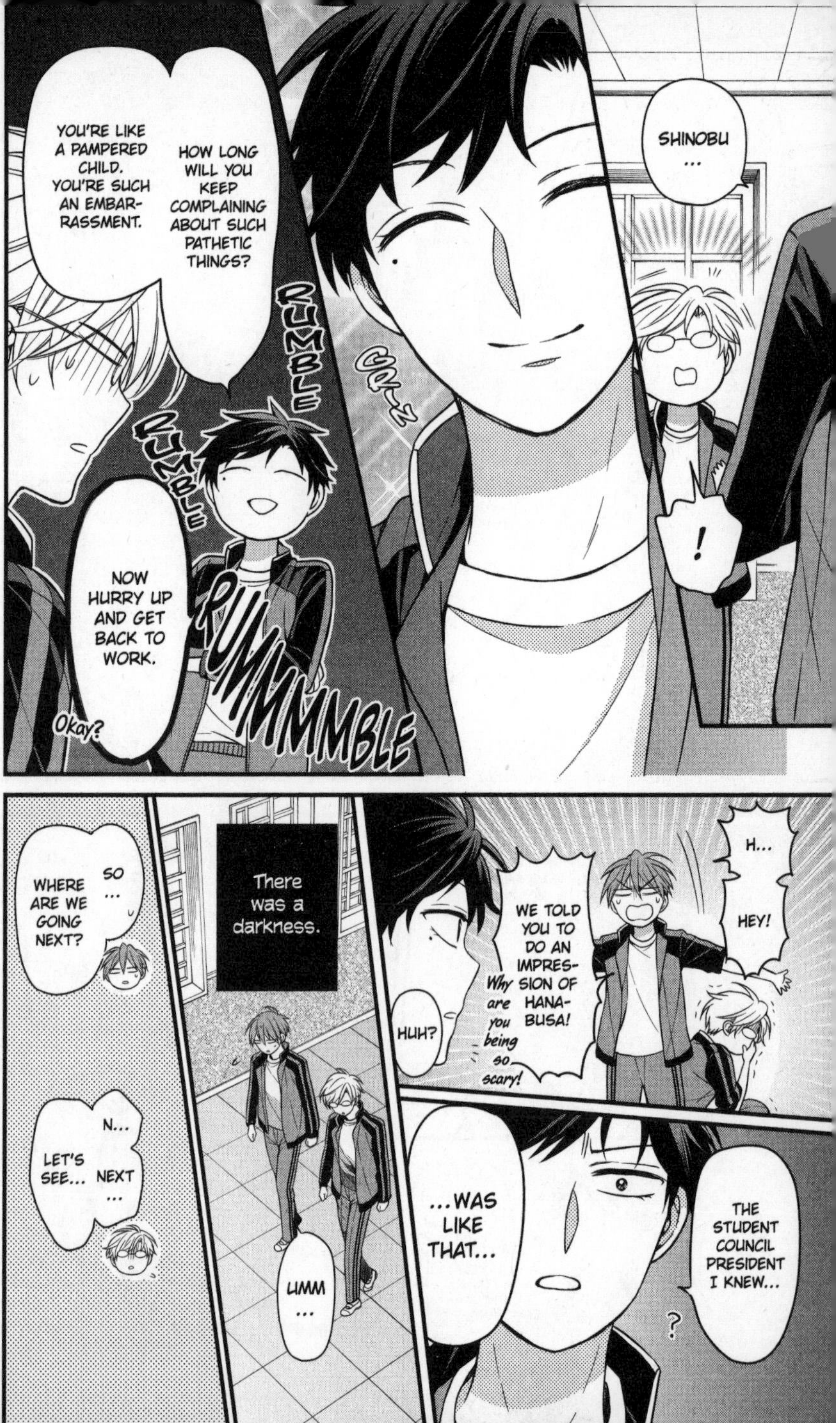
SHINOBU ...
!
GRI-N
HOW LONG WILL YOU KEEP COMPLAINING ABOUT SUCH PATHETIC THINGS?
YOU'RE LIKE A PAMPERED CHILD. YOU'RE SUCH AN EMBAR-RASSMENT.
RUMBLE
RUMBLE
NOW HURRY UP AND GET BACK TO WORK.
Okay?
RUMMMMMBLE
H... HEY!
WE TOLD YOU TO DO AN IMPRES-SION OF HANA-BUSA!
Why are you being so scary!
HUH?
THE STUDENT COUNCIL PRESIDENT I KNEW...
?
...WAS LIKE THAT...
There was a darkness.
UMM ...
SO ...
WHERE ARE WE GOING NEXT?
N...
LET'S SEE... NEXT ...

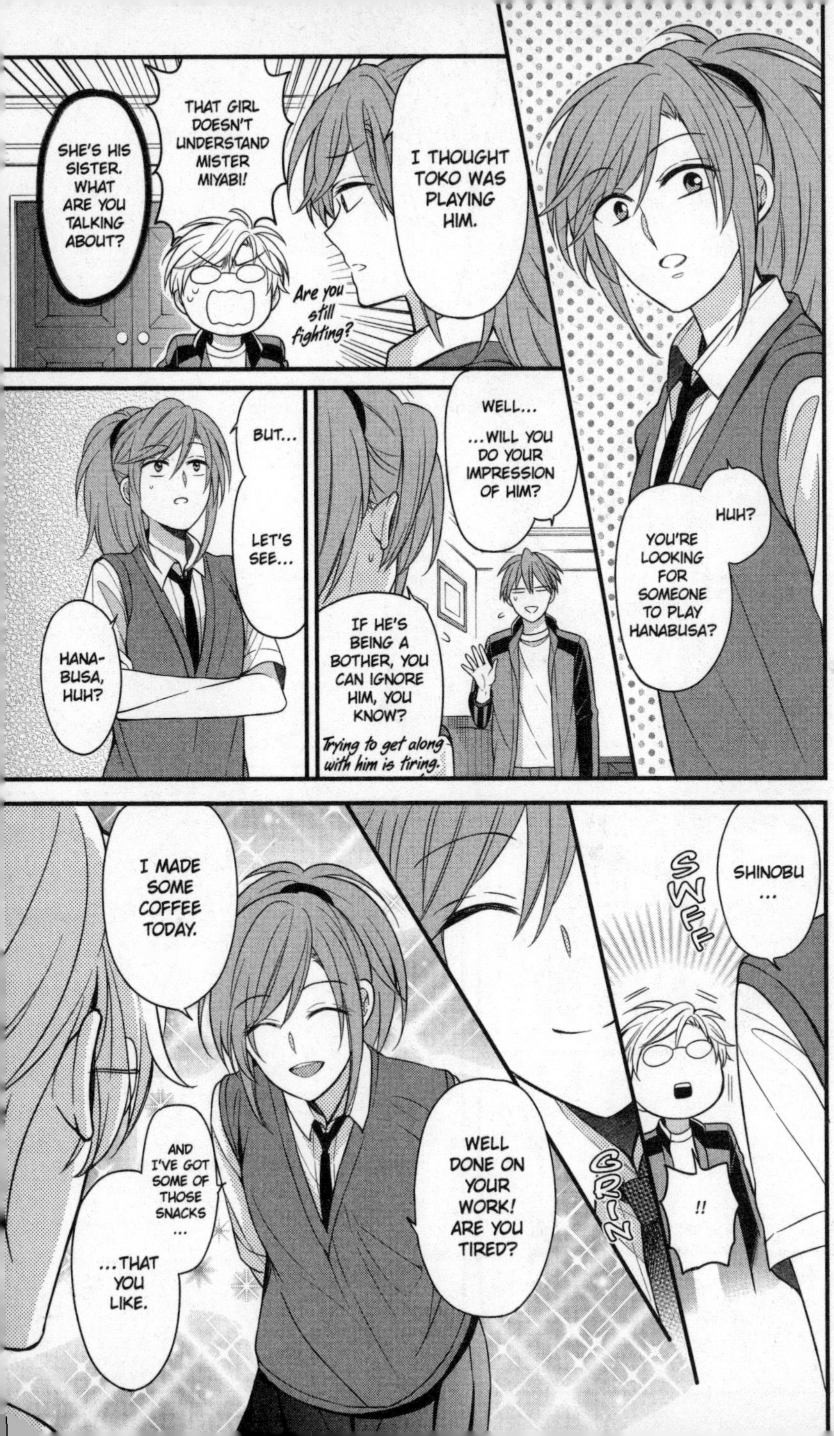
HUH?
YOU'RE LOOKING FOR SOMEONE TO PLAY HANABUSA?
I THOUGHT TOKO WAS PLAYING HIM.
Are you still fighting?
THAT GIRL DOESN'T UNDERSTAND MISTER MIYABI!
SHE'S HIS SISTER. WHAT ARE YOU TALKING ABOUT?
WELL... ...WILL YOU DO YOUR IMPRESSION OF HIM?
IF HE'S BEING A BOTHER, YOU CAN IGNORE HIM, YOU KNOW?
Trying to get along with him is tiring.
BUT...
LET'S SEE...
HANA-BUSA, HUH?
SHINOBU ...
SWEE
!!
GRIN
WELL DONE ON YOUR WORK! ARE YOU TIRED?
I MADE SOME COFFEE TODAY.
AND I'VE GOT SOME OF THOSE SNACKS ...
...THAT YOU LIKE.

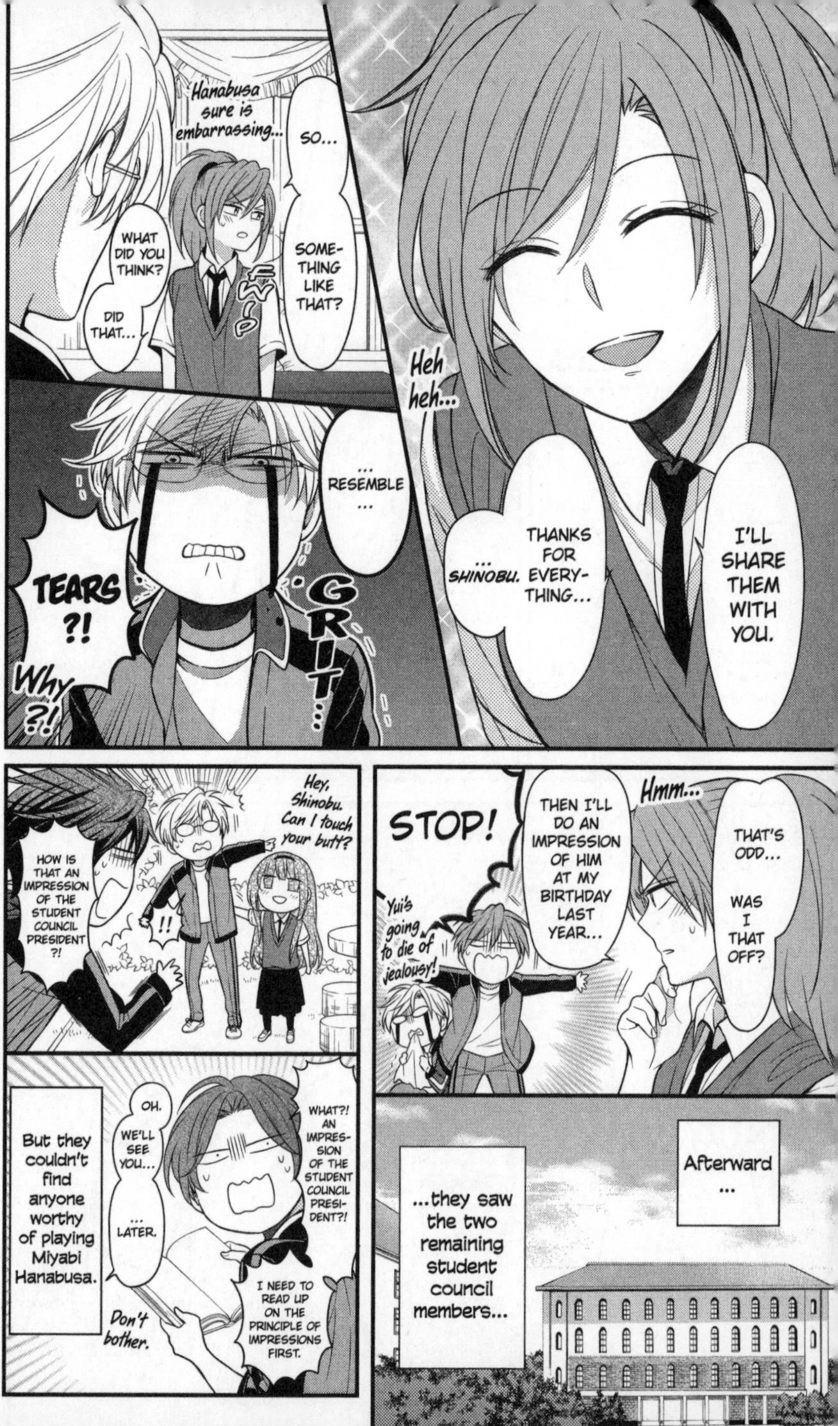
Heh heh...
I'LL SHARE THEM WITH YOU.
THANKS FOR EVERY-THING...
...SHINOBU.
Hanabusa sure is embarrassing...
SO...
SOME-THING LIKE THAT?
FWIP
WHAT DID YOU THINK?
DID THAT...
...RESEMBLE...
GRIT...
TEARS?!
Why?!
Hmm...
THAT'S ODD...
WAS I THAT OFF?
THEN I'LL DO AN IMPRESSION OF HIM AT MY BIRTHDAY LAST YEAR...
STOP!
Yui's going to die of jealousy!
Hey, Shinobu. Can I touch your butt?
!!
HOW IS THAT AN IMPRESSION OF THE STUDENT COUNCIL PRESIDENT?!
Afterward...
...they saw the two remaining student council members...
WHAT?! AN IMPRES-SION OF THE STUDENT COUNCIL PRESI-DENT?!
OH.
WE'LL SEE YOU...
...LATER.
I NEED TO READ UP ON THE PRINCIPLE OF IMPRESSIONS FIRST.
Don't bother.
But they couldn't find anyone worthy of playing Miyabi Hanabusa.

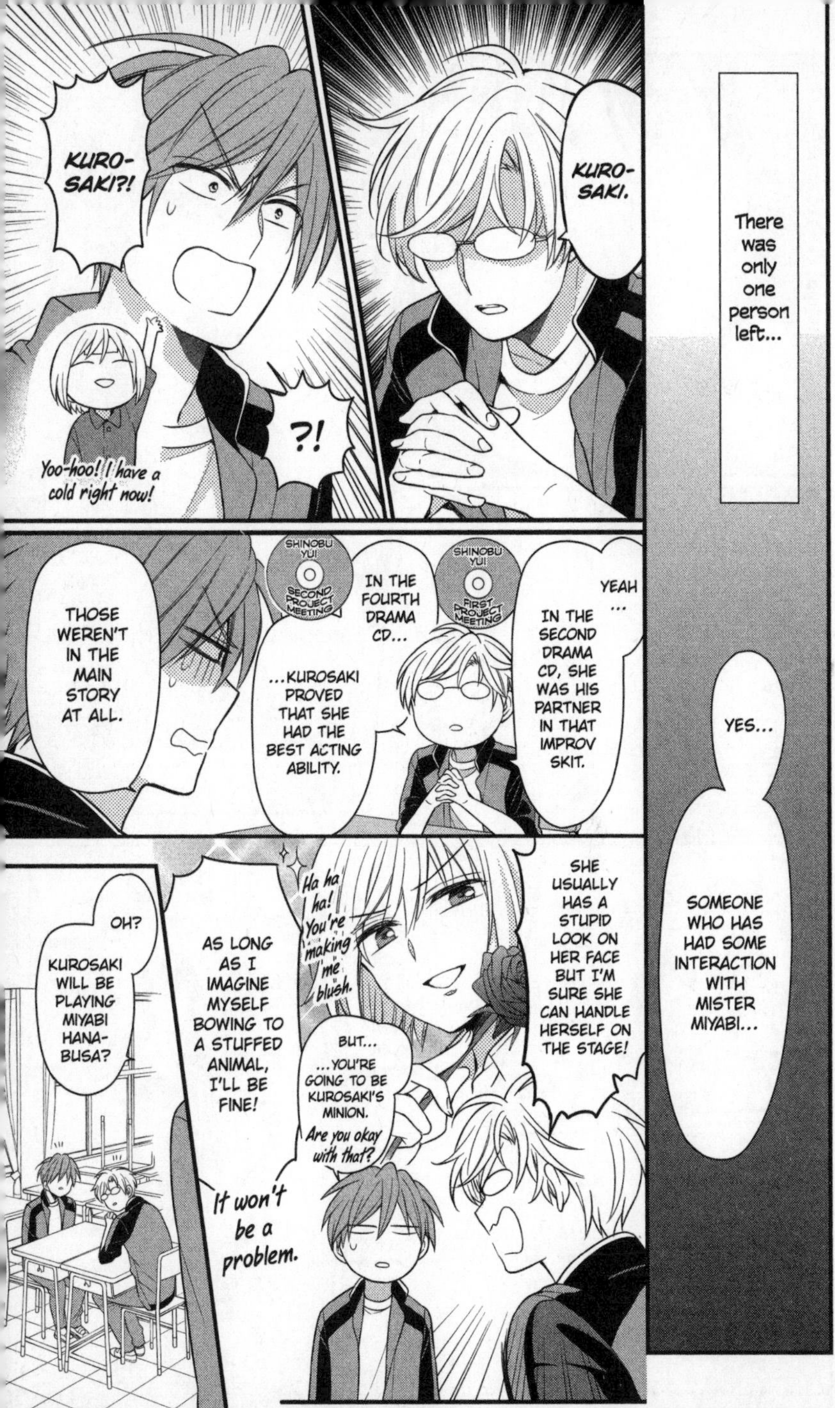
There was only one person left...
YES...
SOMEONE WHO HAS HAD SOME INTERACTION WITH MISTER MIYABI...
KURO-SAKI.
KURO-SAKI?!
?!
Yoo-hoo! I have a cold right now!
YEAH...
IN THE SECOND DRAMA CD, SHE WAS HIS PARTNER IN THAT IMPROV SKIT.
SHINOBU YU! FIRST PROJECT MEETING
IN THE FOURTH DRAMA CD...
...KUROSAKI PROVED THAT SHE HAD THE BEST ACTING ABILITY.
SHINOBU YU! SECOND PROJECT MEETING
THOSE WEREN'T IN THE MAIN STORY AT ALL.
SHE USUALLY HAS A STUPID LOOK ON HER FACE BUT I'M SURE SHE CAN HANDLE HERSELF ON THE STAGE!
Ha ha ha! You're making me blush.
AS LONG AS I IMAGINE MYSELF BOWING TO A STUFFED ANIMAL, I'LL BE FINE!
OH?
KUROSAKI WILL BE PLAYING MIYABI HANA-BUSA?
BUT...
...YOU'RE GOING TO BE KUROSAKI'S MINION.
Are you okay with that?
It won't be a problem.

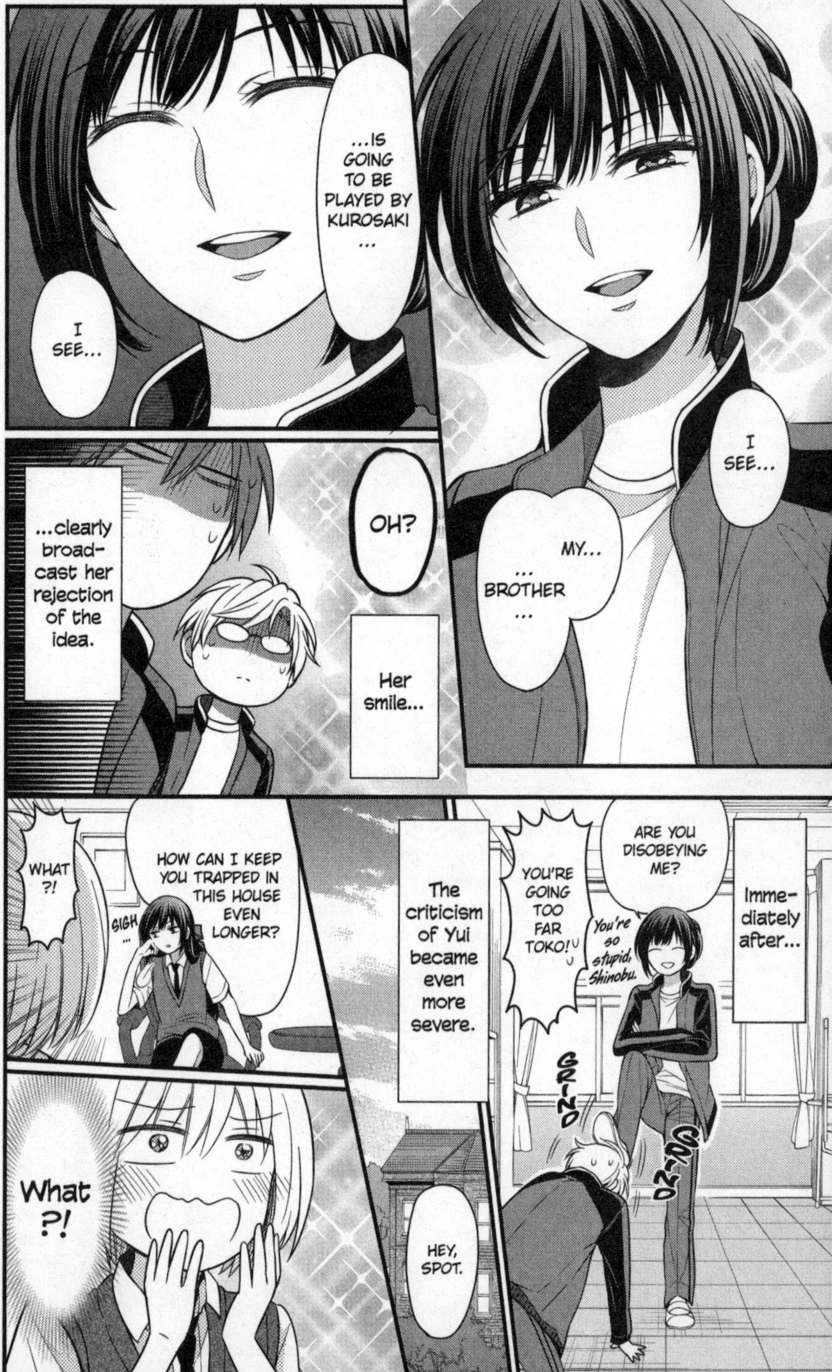
I SEE...
MY...
... BROTHER ...
...IS GOING TO BE PLAYED BY KUROSAKI ...
I SEE...
OH?
Her smile...
...clearly broad-cast her rejection of the idea.
Immediately after...
ARE YOU DISOBEYING ME?
You're so stupid, Shinobu.
YOU'RE GOING TOO FAR TOKO!
GRIND
GRIND
The criticism of Yui became even more severe.
HEY, SPOT.
HOW CAN I KEEP YOU TRAPPED IN THIS HOUSE EVEN LONGER?
SIGH ...
WHAT ?!
What ?!

Izumi Tsubaki began drawing manga in her first year of high school. She was soon selected to be in the top ten of *Hana to Yume's* HMC (*Hana to Yume* Mangaka Course), and subsequently won *Hana to Yume's* Big Challenge contest. Her debut title, *Chijimete Distance* (Shrink the Distance), ran in 2002 in *Hana to Yume* magazine, issue 17. Her other works include *The Magic Touch* (*Oyayubi kara Romance*) and *Oresama Teacher*, which she is currently working on.

ORESAMA TEACHER
Vol. 26
Shojo Beat Edition

STORY AND ART BY
Izumi Tsubaki

English Translation & Adaptation/JN Productions
Touch-up Art & Lettering/Eric Erbes
Design/Yukiko Whitley
Editor/Pancha Diaz

ORESAMA TEACHER by Izumi Tsubaki © Izumi Tsubaki 2018
All rights reserved. First published in Japan in 2018 by HAKUSENSHA, Inc., Tokyo.
English language translation rights arranged with HAKUSENSHA, Inc., Tokyo.

The stories, characters and incidents mentioned in this publication are
entirely fictional.

Printed in the U.S.A.

Published by VIZ Media, LLC
P.O. Box 77010
San Francisco, CA 94107

10 9 8 7 6 5 4 3 2 1
First printing, July 2019

viz.com   shojobeat.com